The Transformation of American Catholicism

The Transformation of
American Catholicism

*The Pittsburgh Laity and
the Second Vatican Council, 1950–1972*

Timothy Kelly

*University of Notre Dame Press
Notre Dame, Indiana*

Published in the United States of America

Library of Congress Cataloging-in-Publication Data

Kelly, Timothy I., 1960–
The transformation of American Catholicism : the Pittsburgh laity and
the Second Vatican Council, 1950–1972 / Timothy I. Kelly.
p.   cm.
Includes bibliographical references and index.
ISBN-13: 978-0-268-03319-4 (cloth : alk. paper)
ISBN-10: 0-268-03319-6 (cloth : alk. paper)
1. Catholic Church. Diocese of Pittsburgh (Pa.)—History.   2. Laity—Catholic
church.   3. Pittsburgh Region (Pa.)—Church history.   4. Vatican Council
(2nd : 1962–1965)   5. Catholic Church—United States—History.   I. Title.
BX1417.P5K45   2008
282'.748809045—dc22

Contents

Preface

Vatican II was not simply part of the ebb and flow of the church's tide as one age follows another. It was more like the sea rising to a new level and breaking through the rocks and cliffs of the shoreline, forming a larger sea with a new configuration, changing the topography. We have not yet been able to chart this sea or fully understand it.

—THE MOST REVEREND KENNETH E. UNTENER (1988)

IN THE AUTUMN OF FOUR YEARS BETWEEN 1962 AND 1965 ROMAN Catholic bishops from all over the world gathered in Rome for the Second Vatican Council. The decisions they made during those sessions proved so powerful that Catholics continue to see it as the primary historical divide of the past century. Yet we do not fully comprehend its impact, especially as it relates to the laymen and laywomen who constitute the vast majority of the Catholic Church. This book seeks to address that shortcoming at least in part by exploring the dramatic way in which the Catholic laity transformed their religious beliefs and practices in the decades leading to and following the Second Vatican Council. It focuses on Catholics in one diocese, Pittsburgh, in order to facilitate the depth of study necessary to understand such a thoroughgoing transformation. This diocese is a particularly advantageous subject. Its leaders in the 1950s and 1960s played significant roles in the national ecclesiastical and cultural scene, and attempted to manifest in Pittsburgh their powerful visions of how the Church ought to be. As a result, Pittsburgh maintained a national stature in these decades that it did not enjoy in the years before or since. At the same time, Pittsburgh was not so aberrant in those years as to make its story unique. One can read the Pittsburgh story without worrying that other American dioceses had completely different experiences.

I began this study more than a decade ago as an attempt to understand the impact that the Second Vatican Council had on American lay Catholics. I knew from my own experiences that a great divide existed within the laity between those who grew up before Vatican II and those, like myself, who came of age in the post-Conciliar Church. Older Catholics shared a set of references and behaviors that were alien to me. I could observe the gap readily and knew that those who discussed the divide, as many often did, attributed them to the Second Vatican Council. They relayed stories of liturgical and social change that emanated down the Catholic hierarchy from the bishops to ordinary lay Catholics. But no historian had yet produced a study of the social experience of the Second Vatican Council. It seemed to be an important and approachable topic for a dissertation. Though I was a young graduate student of social history immersed in the study of grassroots American social movements, I did not see the great change in lay Catholic experiences as the product of popular action so much as a response to reforms imposed from above. I knew that these hierarchically instituted changes had many implications for ordinary Catholics, and that they spurred lay men and women to set out in directions that Church officials did not anticipate, but throughout my research I continued to see the transformation as starting with the hierarchy and moving to the laity. The American laity in particular seemed quite content with the existing Church, which flourished among the increasingly affluent American Catholic community. Lay Catholics filled the churches in record numbers for Sunday Masses, sent their sons and daughters to seminaries and convents, and crowded Catholic schools beyond their capacities. The great questions about Vatican II, it seemed, revolved around the various ways in which Church officials and the laity interpreted and implemented the changes that emanated from the Council. My dissertation reflected this perspective.

There were many reasons to adopt this interpretation, as so many people identified the Council as a critical turning point in Catholic history. Everyone in the 1960s seemed to note the Council's significance. The American mass media especially trumpeted its importance for society. *Newsweek* magazine quoted German theologian Hans Küng as stating that the Church had "initiated a new epoch in Christianity." *Life* magazine told readers that the just concluded Council was "the most impressive religious event this century has yet seen." The *New York Times* editorialized that the Council was "beyond question the most important held by the Roman Catholic Church since the Council of Trent four centuries ago," and predicted that the Vatican II reforms would "profoundly affect Catholics for generations or centuries to come."[1]

The academics who addressed the Council shortly after its conclusion dropped their habitual restraint to echo the popular view of Vatican II's importance. Stanley I. Stuber and Claud D. Nelson, two American Protestant theologians, wrote that the Council "changed both the external face of the Roman Catholic Church and its internal spirit." Douglas J. Roche wrote that the Second Vatican Council started a "revolution" within the Church "fermenting as much in the grass roots as in the intellectuals' studies." *National Catholic Reporter* publisher Donald J. Thorman wondered if "revolution" was "a word adequate to the task of describing what is happening to Catholicism today," which, in the words of David J. O'Brien, was the opening of "a new era in Christian history." John Tracy Ellis even compared the Council to the upheavals initiated by Martin Luther in the sixteenth century, and Sidney Ahlstrom, probably the most influential historian of American religion, agreed.[2]

Even after the initial glow of the Council passed, and with the benefit of decades of reflection, academics still considered Vatican II to be profoundly significant.[3] Bishop Kenneth E. Untener of Saginaw, Michigan, summed up the theological opinions when he stated that "What happened at Vatican II might be compared to the great plates shifting beneath the earth" because its effects were "monumental."[4] Historians concurred with theologians' conclusions. Martin E. Marty maintained that post–Vatican II Catholicism "was infinitely more diverse in appearance than what had gone before." James Hennesey wrote that the Second Vatican Council brought about "dissent, change, and diversity at the highest levels of the church" which represented a "staggering reality for American Catholics used to believing the church never changed." Jay Dolan argued that the post–Vatican II American Catholic religion was a "new Catholicism," very different from the old Catholicism shaped at the sixteenth-century Council of Trent.[5]

Sociologists read empirical data in the same way. Andrew Greeley examined survey data on Catholics over the twenty years since the Council's end and concluded that Vatican II accomplished an "enormous transformation." Twenty years later, Greeley concluded that Vatican II had started a Catholic revolution. Others agreed. Jim Castelli and Joseph Gremillion considered Vatican II to be a "dramatic event in the history of the Catholic church" which "changed the way the Catholic church thinks about itself and the way its members think about their church." George Gallup, Jr., also writing with Jim Castelli, called the Second Vatican Council "the dominant fact in twentieth-century Catholicism," and argued that American Catholics "came of age religiously" because of it.[6] There seemed little reason to doubt that the world's Catholic bishops had begun a major transformation when they arrived in 1962 for the Council's opening session.

But my continued research pointed toward a new direction. The more I studied American lay Catholics in the 1950s the more I realized that even if they had not called for or deliberated at the Second Vatican Council, they had initiated a transformation of their religious practices which anticipated and propelled the Council reforms in the U.S. context. The lay experience of Catholicism did change dramatically in the 1960s, but this transformation began earlier, before the Council, and continued throughout the next decade. The Council did not represent a shock to a complacent laity so much as a reform necessary to keep pace with the laity's changing religious and broader social and cultural sensibilities. Other scholars studying the 1950s began publishing works that confirmed the significance of this pre–Vatican II decade, even if they did not always note the scope and popularity of the shift the laity had undertaken.[7]

But the popular discussion of Vatican II did not note these new findings. Instead, it focused on a debate over whether the Second Vatican Council's changes were for good or for ill. The American laity today seem disaffected with the institutional Church, even to the point of crisis, and some observers put Vatican II at the center of this disenchantment. They argue that overzealous reformers misunderstood the Council changes and forced the laity to abandon cherished and efficacious practices that bound them to the Church.[8] The lay disaffection from the institution can be traced, in these critics' eyes, to the unwarranted wholesale changes that Church officials sanctioned in the 1960s and 1970s. Those more content with the reforms see the cause of the recent lay disaffection to be the failure to embrace fully the Council's implications, especially regarding women's roles within the Church. Both place Vatican II, and the tensions over its interpretation and implementation, at the heart of the current crisis.[9]

This book seeks to resolve this debate by pushing our attention back to the decade preceding the Council, and then examining the laity in the 1960s in light of the great changes that they undertook before the Council even met. Though the Second Vatican Council remains central to the story of American lay Catholics in the twentieth century, close scrutiny of ordinary Catholic men and women in the 1950s suggests that the Council did not so much presage as give direction to a religiosity already undergoing profound change. Joseph Chinnici's recent synthetic interpretation of American Catholics at prayer establishes persuasively that the Pittsburgh laity shared in a broad-ranging national movement to transform Catholicism.[10] The Council did not cause the laity to change their religious practices and understandings, in this interpretation. That change had begun already. Rather, the Council was central to lay efforts to formulate a new Catholicism to replace the one that they had already begun to reject.

The transformation is not so evident in the public documents of the Pittsburgh Church, which did not acknowledge that such a shift was under way. But it can be seen by comparing evidence of actual lay behavior against the Church officials' assertions of how they ought to act throughout the 1950s. This comparison reveals a growing gap between normative and actual religious practices, and suggests strongly that the American laity had begun to reject the model of Catholicism that they had once embraced. Part One of the book explores both the prescriptions Church officials issued and evidence of lay behavior during the decade preceding the Second Vatican Council. It examines the "public discourse" of Catholicism—the ways in which Catholics spoke to each other publicly about their Church in the diocesan newspaper and organization newsletters. Bishops and priests spoke prominently in this discussion, but they did not crowd out the laity completely. These sources and others provide sufficient evidence to see the laity acting in light of the powerful clerical voices.

Though I focus on the diocesan level primarily, I also examine evidence from three representative parishes within the diocese in order to understand more clearly how lay women, men, and children acted during the period. Differences between parishes were reflected in the laity's experiences, so the study explores a suburban parish, an urban parish, and an ethnic parish.

The second part of the book provides a brief overview of the Second Vatican Council itself and of developments in Pittsburgh during the years that the Council met. It highlights those developments in Rome that held particular importance for American lay Catholics and examines Pittsburgh Catholics acting during the years that the Council met—years when these Catholics began to understand more fully the scope of the transformation under way in the local and international Church. It follows the Pittsburgh Liturgical Commission as it struggled during the Council years to understand Council developments and implement reforms consistent with these changes. Here we see diocesan officials acting in a formal capacity to implement the changes still under debate in Rome. For the first time, though, lay Catholics participated in this official effort to prescribe normative liturgical practices.

Part Three examines the laity during and immediately after the Council. The Council clearly reshaped the lay experience of Catholicism dramatically, even as it trailed the changing lay sensibilities of the 1950s. At a minimum, Vatican II gave official sanction to the direction in which the laity had pointed the Church. But it did far more. The Second Vatican Council invited clergy and laity to reimagine self-consciously their Church in light of the modern world. It joined all segments of the Church in the common endeavor to redefine themselves as Catholics and citizens of the world. In doing so it sanctioned a process still under way for Catholics more than four decades after the last official session ended. That so many have seen the Council as the start of this process is reasonable given the enormous boost that the Council provided to the process begun in the previous decade. The Council merits all the attention and much of the credit it received, as it provided both venue and direction for nothing less than the transformation of the Church. But the laity had begun their transformation before the Council met and would have changed the Church significantly had Pope John XXIII never called the bishops to Rome.

Pittsburgh Catholics moved self-consciously to reimagine their Church in light of what they were coming to see more fully as a new era in American Catholic religiosity. Part of this new perspective for area Catholics was a recognition on the part of local Church officials that the laity had valuable insights worth discerning. For the first time in Pittsburgh, therefore, diocesan officials sought to understand lay opinions and behaviors rather than simply prescribe for them how they ought to think and behave. These efforts sometimes took the form of social surveys, democratic arenas that solicited lay positions, and less formal study of the laity. The results of some of these studies and deliberations survive and provide a treasure trove for historians seeking to better understand the laity at this pivotal moment. The evidence reveals the strong lay desire in the late 1960s for greater authority in a more democratic Church.

This book allows us to see lay Catholics in an American diocese as they lived through the Council period. It places those experiences in the context of 1950s Catholicism, and it reveals a people who sought to refashion their religion in the midst of great social and cultural dynamism.

Acknowledgments

I WROTE THIS STUDY IN THREE PHASES AND OWE MANY THANKS TO a range of people in each of them. It began as a dissertation at Carnegie Mellon University, where a concentration of extraordinary social historians had joined to form an exhilarating environment for successive cohorts of graduate students. Peter Stearns, Mike Weber, Anne Rose, Joe Trotter, Kate Lynch, and especially John and Judy Modell pushed and guided me to examine the past in ways I had not considered. Though none of them focused on American Catholics in their work, they encouraged my interests and supported my efforts to approach the study from a social history perspective. John Modell especially deserves special thanks for the influence he had on the project and on my work generally. His infectious enthusiasm and unflagging intellectual energy made even the slightest progress seem monumental. He was the consummate dissertation director, whose gentle prodding and generous example made the difficult work enjoyable.

A number of others were also instrumental in my work at this phase. Fr. Edward McSweeney, then the archivist at the Historical Archives of the Diocese of Pittsburgh, proved to be a welcoming and generous host. He gave wide access to materials under his control and offered regular support and interest in the project. Jackie McElligott, the Diocesan Archives secretary, proved a wonderful conversationalist on the long afternoons spent at the archives. Fr. Carl Hoegerl of the Redemptorist Provincial Archives, Baltimore Province, opened his holdings for two separate visits to the Brooklyn holdings. Fr. Eric Hoog, C.Ss.R. from Saint Philomena graciously afforded free access to the parish records, as did Fr. Kenneth White at Saint Thomas More parish and Fr. John Jendzura of Immaculate Heart of Mary parish. The staffs at the Archives of Industrial Society at the University of Pittsburgh and the Pennsylvania Room of the Carnegie Library of Pittsburgh were very helpful. The Institute for the Advanced Study of Religion at the University of Chicago very generously awarded me a dissertation fellowship as part of their Congregational History Project. I want to thank James W. Lewis and James P. Wind especially for this.

The second phase of this study took place during a long stretch of time after I had finished the dissertation. I explored areas that I knew merited more research and analysis in my efforts to expand the study. My greatest joy during this time was the time spent collaborating on short pieces with my brother Joseph Kelly, a literary critic at the College of Charleston, whose disciplinary influence can be seen most powerfully in the major revisions of the earliest parts of the work. We coauthored three articles in these years that melded the social history and new historicist literary critical approaches to studying the past. Two of those studies further developed research on American Catholics and helped to improve the book you hold in your hand. I absolve Joe from any blame for the less than refined way I have incorporated literary critical methods in this work. My enthusiasm for the approach exceeds my skill in its use.

The Center for Religion and American Culture at Indiana University–Purdue University Indianapolis sponsored a conference in October 1992 at which I first presented material on Holy Name Society's outdoor eucharistic rally. R. Stephen Warner provided perceptive and supportive commentary that helped to guide my further work in this area.

Peter Stearns deserves special mention here as well. He very graciously published some of my further work in the *Journal of Social History* during these years, and in so doing sustained my hopes that this was a reasonable pursuit. He has consistently supported my efforts to develop new approaches, was instrumental in my finding the academic employment that made continued work possible, and proved especially supportive in my efforts to enter the third phase of this work. Long after he owed any obligation to a former student, he continued to extend himself on my behalf.

Despite the support that various folks offered in the years after I completed the dissertation, it began to look as though I might never complete the book project. A fifteen-month stint as a college administrator killed the project's momentum at a critical phase, and my return to teaching at Saint Vincent College demanded so much time in the classroom that I began to despair of completing such a large project. But the study entered its third phase when, in what appeared to me to be divine intervention, R. Scott Appleby and the Cushwa Center for the Study of American Catholicism at the University of Notre Dame offered a full-year fellowship to complete the revisions. They took what must have looked like quite a gamble on this fellow from a small Benedictine liberal arts college in rural western Pennsylvania. Once they invested their resources in my project, I promptly spent too much of that time doing further research, and stretched the year into almost three before finally completing the manuscript. Every historian should experience at least once the kind of stimulating, supportive, and energizing program that Scott Appleby, Barbara Lockwood, John Haas, and Christopher Shannon at the Cushwa Center put together for its Catholicism in Twentieth-Century America project. Dozens of distinguished scholars from all over the country, talented graduate students doing innovative research, and accomplished intellectuals from various nonacademic arenas shared two extended working sessions and an extraordinary final conference during a two-year period. Patrick Allitt led the working group on public Catholicism that provided very useful feedback on two chapters of this study. The discussions proved very useful for me, and I want to thank Richard Fox, John McCreevy, Bruce Nelson, David O'Brien, Ellen Skerrett, Margaret O'Brien Steinfels, James Fischer, Steve Rosswurm, Mary Wingerd, Colleen Doody, Kristine LaLonde, Andrew Moore and Mark Santow for the engaging and challenging seminar sessions. I particularly benefited from the formal comments that Peter Steinfels and John McGreevy provided on my presentation at culminating conference. Perhaps most helpful and certainly most enjoyable were the extended conversations that I shared with Joseph Chinici, O.F.M. and Steve Rosswurm during the periodic gatherings. Our early morning breakfasts fostered new friendships and affirmed that collegiality flourishes in the academy. Joe Chinici's thorough work on Catholics at prayer stands as a model worthy of the highest praise and emulation.

Barbara Hanrahan at the University of Notre Dame Press has been supportive and responsive throughout the process of publishing this book, even through a period of great change at the press. Margo Sherman and Rebecca DeBoer skillfully guided the manuscript to final publication and made this final stage of my project very enjoyable. Two anonymous readers whom the press provided gave generous assessments of the manuscript and wise suggestions for revision, and I want to thank them for their efforts.

A number of people at Saint Vincent College were instrumental in this third phase of work as well. My department chair, the Rev. Rene Kollar, O.S.B., helped persuade the college Provost, Br. Norman Hipps, O.S.B., that this project merited granting to an untenured faculty member a full year of leave to work with the Cushwa Fellowship Program. Fr. Rene and Br. Norman supported my efforts in numerous other ways as well and deserve to be recognized for their forbearance. The Faculty Development Committee awarded three summer grants to support the research and writing. Fr. Chrysostom Schlimm, O.S.B., John Benyo, Denise Hegeman, and Jack Macy graciously allowed me to monopolize the microfilm reader and hardly complained at all when I moved much of their mid-twentieth-century American Catholic history collection to my office.

A small but energetic community of scholars from a range of disciplines at Saint Vincent's has persuaded me that one can teach four classes each semester and still maintain active research interests. I especially appreciate the atmosphere that Thad Coreno, George Leiner, Dennis McDaniel, Marie Frank, John Smetanka, Ron Tranquila, Alice Kaylor, and Rene Kollar have created.

Though my parents and their friends never lived in Pittsburgh, this work derived to a great extent from my appreciation for the Church that they worked so hard to create in other parts of the United States. As a child I saw the effort that Bill and Mary Lou Kelly, Ann and Will Storz, Bill and Mary Good, and a host of their contemporaries put into helping this new, emerging understanding of Catholicism transform society. They gathered on weekends and vacations to discuss, debate, and plan the momentous changes under way and how they might best serve the social good. By a fortuitous coincidence, two of those contemporaries re-entered my life through the Cushwa Center's auspices. Peggy Steinfels served as one of the Public Catholicism working-group mentors, and her husband, Peter, joined the group both informally and then as official commentator at the closing conference.

Finally, I owe my greatest debt to my wife, Kim, and our three children, Caitlin, Erin, and Eamon. I have worked on this project throughout our children's entire lives. I spilled their baby formula on early dissertation drafts and later competed with them for time on our home computer. We together embarked on what felt like an endless tour of Catholic grade school gymnasiums — the seemingly sacred spaces where we participated in the celebrated rites of parochial school basketball tournaments. Both Caitlin and Erin are now off at college and old enough to feel obligated actually to read this study. They no doubt wish that I had worked more quickly. Eamon might reasonably cite his youth as reason to keep his gaze firmly on more engaging subjects like baseball, but this project has been his lifelong companion. Kim has endured for too long my intermittent immersion in this work, and is graceful enough not to explain the importance of meeting reasonable goals in a timely fashion. I complete this work as we enjoy our twenty-sixth year together, and look forward to many more. She remains an extraordinarily talented individual whose efforts to balance home and work will, I hope, become lighter at this moment. Her love and support have made this extended project possible, and I cannot adequately express my debts to her.

PART ONE

The Pre-Conciliar Church

CHAPTER ONE

Pittsburgh Catholics and
the Materialist Crisis

The Renaissance has been a bold program, but it was conceived without any deep involvement of neighborhood people. It has been a repeat of past history. The highways, airport, factory sites needed by industry have been produced, but the neighborhoods have been little improved.

—JAMES CUNNINGHAM

We are living in an age of almost total indifference to spiritual things and to things pertaining to faith and morals. The vast majority of people do not bother themselves about God, about sin or about eternity. They are only concerned about their material and physical well-being, with pleasure and enjoyment, licit or illicit, of the things of this life.

—ARCHBISHOP JOSEPH E. RITTER (1957)

PITTSBURGH CONTEXT

The city of Pittsburgh lies in the Appalachian Plateau, to the west of the northern reaches of the Appalachian Mountains. Geologists tell us that the Appalachian Mountains formed about 200–300 million years ago when North America collided with Africa, and the force of this continental crash pushed skyward what had until then been low-lying sedimentary rocks. These ranges' once mighty peaks have since eroded considerably, leaving modest mountains by geological standards, but significant delineators for cultural, political, and social development. To the mountains' east lies fertile farmland close enough to the Atlantic coast that European settlers flooded into the region in the seventeenth and eighteenth centuries.[1] The continental collision that produced the mountains also compacted carbon deposits east of those mountains into the dense anthracite coal that fueled the very early industrial revolution in America. West of the Appalachian ranges the story is quite different. It's a region cut through with rivers and ravines formed by warped sedimentary rock run through with beds of the softer bituminous coal. One section of those beds, called the Pittsburgh Seam, proved to be one of the richest mineral resources in the world. This abundant coal fueled Pittsburgh's rise during the nineteenth century, and shaped—perhaps defined—the social, cultural, and political development of the region well into the twentieth. Limited by dramatic slopes, rocky soil, and poor access to eastern markets, farmers in western Pennsylvania never prospered so well as their counterparts to the east. The Pittsburgh economy took off primarily with the iron, steel, and glass industries' boom in the nineteenth century.[2] One of the principal ways in which the physical geography shaped the region's culture, therefore, was by facilitating and encouraging large-scale industrial development. The Pittsburgh Seam almost ensured that the city built on top of it would become the quintessential American industrial metropolis. The Church that rose in that environment inevitably grew in light of the economic, social, and demographic strictures that industrialism imposed.

Industrialization's most salient shaping influence on Pittsburgh Catholicism may have been the powerful magnet it created to draw European immigrants to the area. The immigrants who flooded the region in the nineteenth and early twentieth centuries brought their Catholicism with them. The diocese came of age during waves of immigration from Eastern and Southern Europe and had to accommodate a range of relatively distinct Catholic traditions. Though they varied in many particulars, these immigrant Catholics brought a heavily devotional sensibility to the region which flavored Catholic practices until the middle of the twentieth century. At the same time, Catholics confronted industrial exploitation on a massive scale and supported the development of strong voices for Catholic social justice. As Kenneth Heineman so persuasively argues in *A Catholic New Deal,* Pittsburgh Catholics articulated a clear alternative to the laissez-faire capitalism that area industrialists favored.[3]

The topography shaped the region in other profound ways as well. Three major rivers divide Pittsburgh into distinct areas, and within each area the dramatic slopes and deep hollows further carve the city into distinct geographic units. The hills often prove too steep for car and pedestrian traffic, so residents have constructed numerous "inclines" and staircases to reach homes, and bridges to connect neighborhoods on adjacent peaks.[4] At various times local governments have attempted to alter the topography to facilitate travel and commerce, sometimes flattening hills and other times filling hollows. This topographical setting has shaped the experiences of the area's residents in powerful ways, and no less the Church's experiences.

The physical geography allowed — even forced — a social separation that other cities and regions had to establish artificially. Where other major cities often rely on major avenues, thoroughfares, railroad lines, and parks to provide boundaries between neighborhoods, Pittsburgh has abundant natural divides. The struggle for Pittsburghers has less been one of establishing boundaries than of bridging them. Frederick Law Olmsted made just this point when he observed that no city "of equal size in America or perhaps the world, is compelled to adapt its growth to such difficult complications of high ridges, deep valleys and precipitous slopes as Pittsburgh."[5] Between 1923 and 1931 alone, Allegheny County constructed 99 bridges to facilitate traffic over rivers and hollows in an effort to conquer the topographic difficulties that divided the city and the region. A 2006 effort to count bridges put the total at 446 for the city proper and hundreds more in Allegheny County.[6]

What did this mean for the city and region residents? The physical geography fostered an exaggerated localism that could have led to ethnic, racial, religious, and economic segregation on a larger scale than in other cities with more permeable topographical boundaries. John Bodnar, Roger Simon, and Michael Weber suggest that this may have happened in Pittsburgh in their study of Pittsburgh's Italians, Poles, and African Americans. They argue that some relatively homogenous European ethnic neighborhoods persisted as late as the 1960s, decades after white ethnic groups in cities like Detroit and Chicago integrated fully.[7] Racial segregation certainly existed, and still exists, in the city, and it does rely on natural boundaries to a degree. But the city's most heavily segregated African-American neighborhoods do not always straddle hollows or rivers, and often fall in areas bounded by mere socially constructed borders.[8]

Despite the strong potential for ethnic segregation that the natural topography could have facilitated, the opposite seems to have occurred. People certainly felt the physical and social constraints that the rivers and hills imposed, but they lived in heterogeneous neighborhoods filled with a variety of ethnic and religious groups all trapped together in island neighborhoods. Those same natural boundaries that made it difficult for residents of contiguous neighborhoods to interact, forced residents within each separate neighborhood to devise mechanisms for living in the small world imposed upon them. The result for Catholics throughout much of the twentieth century, therefore, was a prolif-

eration of churches within single neighborhoods. Catholics established powerful social boundaries because geographical boundaries forced them to live with
each other and also with Protestants and Jews. Italian, Polish, and Slovak parishes
flourished cheek by jowl within the boundaries of the mostly Irish and German
territorial parishes. Protestant churches and Jewish synagogues dotted the same
landscape, leading observers to call Pittsburgh the city of churches. Pittsburgh
Catholics mastered the skill of negotiating a multitude of social boundaries
within a constrained physical space. For example, the city's "Strip District" neighborhood, which occupies the flat stretches east of downtown along the southern
banks of the Allegheny River, contained separate parishes for Germans, Irish, Slovaks, and Poles. Just up Penn Avenue was the Italian parish, located a few blocks
from the territorial (though mostly German) church.

The same situation exists in communities outside the city as within. The
physical landscape resulted in many crowded mill towns and coal mining patches
in which residents lived as close together as in the large urban neighborhoods in
the city proper. Here too Catholics of different ethnic backgrounds worshiped
in separate facilities located within easy walking distance of each other. In the
small town of Homestead, for example, where workers battled Andrew Carnegie's and Henry Clay Frick's Pinkerton guards in 1892, area residents attended
one of a number of churches. The town lay low along the Monongahela River on
its northern boundary, with the Carnegie (later United States) Steel works on
its eastern edge, and the rapidly rising slopes of Munhall and Lincoln Place
on its south. Homestead contained sixteen Protestant houses of worship, a Jewish synagogue, and four Catholic churches. The town's Irish and German Catholics worshiped at the territorial Saint Mary Magdelene Church, the Slovaks attended Saint Ann's, Lithuanians went to Saints Peter and Paul, and Poles filled
Saint Anthony's.

For years the rivers and the coal-rich hills around them spurred the industrial development that nourished the city and transformed the landscape. So
long as proximity to coal figured heavily in making industry efficient, the Pittsburgh economy flourished. Thousands of farmers and immigrants poured into
the area during the latter half of the nineteenth century to work in the expanding steel mills, coal mines, and glass works. The city quickly gained and held
tenaciously on to its reputation as America's most industrial city.

This economic prosperity ruined the environment. No other American city,
historian Roy Lubove noted, was so frequently compared to hell. Everything was
"shaped by a relentless economic discipline" that rendered the city an economic
rather than a civic entity. "The desecration of a superb natural environment—
one of America's most spectacular in its combination of water-breaks, topography,

and verdure—was total."[9] And the combination of industrial dominance and environmental desolation persisted through the 1940s. One Pittsburgh resident recalled coming to the city for the first time as a child in the early 1950s:

> A gray-black cloud hung over Pittsburgh, and the only color I can remember was the orange-red brimstone of some furnaces. The billowing grime coming from the smokestacks smelled like sulfur. Torrents of raw gunk flowed out huge pipes right into the industrial sewers we now call rivers.
>
> Cars drove with their lights on in the middle of the day.
>
> What passed for houses were crow-barred right next to each other—haven't these people heard of lawns, I wondered—onto hillsides that sustained the kind of scraggly brush that can't be killed by acid rain. Money didn't grow on trees. Neither did leaves, it seemed. . . . The place had made a deal with the devil. Dirt means dollars, folks used to say.[10]

But the 1950s saw an extraordinary transformation. "Pittsburgh Welcomes You!" exclaimed a 1950s pamphlet intended to draw tourists and conventioneers into the city turned around. "We want you and your organization to see this new Pittsburgh, to witness the incredible changes that have taken place, and are taking place, in this historic 'Gateway to the West.'"[11] Private corporations and the city government cooperated to change the city and its image from that of an environmental wasteland to the country's best hometown.

Many of the city's residents and boosters believed it had successfully made the transition from "economic entity" to "economic entity with a conscience" by 1953, when the *Pittsburgh Sun-Telegraph* devoted a November Sunday edition to extolling the city's virtues and accomplishments. Pittsburgh was by this time "the most dynamic and progressive city in the United States, where the slums of yesterday are being transformed into the factories, skyscrapers and cultural centers of tomorrow."[12] It had accomplished a great redevelopment and renaissance that proved that "great urban centers can be revitalized and maintain their leadership in Twentieth Century civilization."[13] Pittsburgh remained the nation's "industrial giant, the citadel of the capitalist free enterprise system." The system's success made Pittsburgh the eighth-largest metropolitan area in the country, and the seventh-largest employer of workers.[14] It continued to draw economic sustenance from heavy industry, but it also nourished five colleges and universities, forty-four research laboratories, two hundred cultural enterprises, and more public pools per capita than any other city in the country.[15]

The city's efforts to eliminate its terrible smoke problem began during World War II and finally succeeded in the early 1950s. Pittsburgh industry and residents reduced the city's "heavy" smoke 98.7 percent and its "moderate" smoke 85.8 percent between 1946 and 1954.[16] The city's remarkable renaissance set a tone of great possibilities for its residents—or at least for those who prospered from the changes and breathed the cleaner air. And few could help but notice that these changes resulted from the unprecedented cooperation of the city's old-guard Protestant economic and social elite and its Catholic political leaders.[17]

In addition to its remarkable postwar renaissance, the city of Pittsburgh claimed more residents in 1950 than in any other year in its history—676,806. Never before or since had as many people crowded around and between the banks of the Monongahela, Allegheny, and Ohio rivers. But despite such boasts by boosters, the total population stood within 7,000 people of where it had been twenty years previously. In this sense 1950 more resembled than differed from the twenty preceding years. The city population stood in 1950 at the end of a relatively long plateau, poised on the edge of a steep slope over which more than a third of its population, over a quarter of a million people, would fall, jump, or get pushed.[18]

Like most American cities, Pittsburgh supported numerous religious institutions. Pittsburghers maintained a great number of churches throughout the 1950s, 1960s, and 1970s, though their numbers declined even faster than people left the city. In 1940 Pittsburghers maintained 635 churches in 45 separate denominations. The vast majority of the churches were Protestant, and the largest Protestant denominations, in descending order of size as measured by number of churches, were the Baptist, Methodist, Presbyterian, Evangelical Lutheran, United Presbyterian, and Episcopal churches. Pittsburghers belonged to 29 other Protestant denominations as well. The city's residents also supported 34 Jewish congregations. Fifty-two churches aligned with no denomination.[19] Pittsburghers in 1940 supported one church per 1,058 people.

By 1951 the ratio had declined to one church per 1,163 people, as the city's population rose very slightly and the number of churches fell to 582 in 38 denominations. The decline hit every Protestant denomination as well as the Jewish congregations, which fell from 34 in 1940 to 29 in 1951.[20] In 1960 Pittsburgh had one church per 1,238 residents.[21]

The Roman Catholic share of churches in the city rose throughout the period even though Catholics built no new churches. Catholics accounted for 14 percent of the city's churches in 1940, 15 percent in 1951, and 18 percent in 1960. In each period Roman Catholicism represented the largest denomination in the city.

The Catholic Church organizes itself into dioceses, and the Pittsburgh diocese encompasses six counties of western Pennsylvania. In these six counties, the Catholic population both increased by itself and as a percentage of the total population. The 666,826 Catholics who lived in the six counties constituted 32 percent of the diocese's total population in 1940, and the 912,959 who lived there in 1980 represented 42 percent of all residents.[22] While the rate of Catholic population growth declined in the 1950s, the Church probably continued to grow until at least the middle of the 1970s.[23]

But the growing Catholic population between 1940 and 1960 attended a rapidly diminishing number of parishes, which dramatically increased the average parish size. The average Catholic parish in 1940 served 1,488 parishioners, the 1951 parish served 2,001 parishioners, and the 1960 parish contained 2,901 Catholics. The average parish size topped 3,000 Catholics by 1975, before declining slightly in 1980 to 2,844.

The religion these Catholics practiced facilitated and even encouraged the development of large parishes, and the hierarchy's emphases over the past few decades also encouraged such growth. Church officials in the 1950s fostered a devotional faith that emphasized deference to superiors and large community activities. Bishops and priests worked to enlarge and maintain those physical manifestations of their faith, such as churches and schools, which might enable Catholicism to survive and grow in the decades to come.

MANY CATHOLICS IN THE EARLY TWENTY-FIRST CENTURY LOOK BACK on the 1950s as a period of social cohesiveness, family stability, economic expansion, and political consensus in which American Catholics understood and observed clearly defined and widely shared modes of behavior. These were the good old days when Catholics knew who they were and embraced a cultural construct that rendered them distinct from other Americans and enabled them to flourish in their personal and public lives. Even if the cultural strictures chafed a bit, the Catholic community stood united in behavior and belief, largely content and generally optimistic.[24]

American Catholics in the 1950s seem not to have seen themselves in this light. Despite the victory in World War II and the years of unprecedented economic prosperity stretching out before them, Pittsburgh Catholics could hardly have mistaken that they lived in a period of social and cultural crisis. The signs were everywhere, and if the laity could not see them on their own, Pope Pius XII, American bishops, local pastors, the diocesan newspaper, organization newsletters, and parish bulletins pointed them out regularly. Though the nature of the crisis was multifarious and diffuse, and required regular attention and interpretation, one could sense it everywhere, in all areas of the world, the nation, the

TABLE 1.1   Diocese of Pittsburgh Statistical Trends, 1940–1980

	1940	*1951*	*1960*	*1965*	*1970*	*1975*	*1980*
Churches/parishes	448	416	303	315	321	320	321
Priests	782	1,030	789	860	911	969	957
Catholic population	666,826 (32%)	832,745 (39%)	879,255 (38%)	916,214 NA	924,893 (40%)	962,412 NA	912,959 (42%)
Total population	2,100,842	2,147,891	2,319,834	NA	2,295,715	NA	2,167,138

Sources: The Official Catholic Directory, 1940, 1951, 1960, 1965, 1970, 1975, 1980; Bureau of the Census, Population, 1940, 1950, 1960, 1970, 1980.

neighborhood, and even the home. The surviving historical evidence indicates that Catholics believed that dangers lurked everywhere. They touched every level of Catholic lives, from the broadly economic and political to the most intimately personal, and they seemed to circle around an all-pervasive and insidious "materialism," an ideology that often denied the supernatural and always subordinated it to the physical. On top of this materialism, elements within American society seemed to target the faith itself and almost demanded that Catholics close ranks for their own protection.

This chapter lays out the crisis discourse that engulfed Pittsburgh's Catholics in the years leading up to the Second Vatican Council. The discourse consists of the public discussion Catholics held about their religion, themselves, and the world through the light of their religion, as this discussion has survived in the written records of the period: the diocesan newspaper (the *Pittsburgh Catholic*), newsletters, parish bulletins, and various other texts that these sources directed the laity to read.[25] As one might expect, the hierarchical voice speaks louder than the laity's in the records, and so much of the discourse reflects what the hierarchy thought and did.

Though the public discourse of Catholicism in pre–Vatican Council II Pittsburgh does not coincide exactly with lay behavior and belief (as future chapters will make clear), it did set a context for lay experiences and influenced lay behavior powerfully. Chapters 2, 3, and 4 lay out the prescription Church officials devised to overcome each aspect of the crisis identified in this chapter, and examine lay behavior relative to these prescriptions. By reading the discourse carefully and supplementing this with other sources, one can discern a great deal about the laity's behaviors and beliefs during the period. These chapters explore the successes and failures of the hierarchy's prescription for conquering the materialist crisis, and in the process explore the ways in which Catholic laymen and laywomen transformed their religious sensibility and actions in the 1950s and 1960s.[26]

MATERIALISM AND ANTI-CATHOLICISM

Catholic theologians, social commentators, and prelates believed that materialism so thoroughly infused Western culture that humans could hardly escape its corrosive force. In the terms of the Catholic discourse, "materialism" was a way of viewing human experience that denied the primacy of each individual's spiritual dimension.[27] In its most pernicious form materialism consciously denied the existence of the supernatural realm. In its more benign yet still troubling manifestations it simply made the physical so dazzling as to cause people to lose sight of their spiritual dimension.

Communism

The clearest, most menacing materialist crisis to threaten American Catholics—and the entire world—was Communism. Communism both emphatically asserted the primacy of the physical, material world and denied the very existence of the spiritual. In the words of Pius XII, it was the "inimical doctrine which seeks only the things of the earth and scorns the things of heaven."[28] To Catholic eyes, the entire Communist ideology understood humans solely as material beings whose greatest end could be measured only through an assessment of their relation to the means of producing material goods.

Concerns about Communism in its international and domestic forms worried many Pennsylvanians—Protestants, Jews, and Catholics alike—a great deal in the early 1950s. It is no surprise, then, that Pittsburgh's Catholics shared these concerns. But Catholic Church officials held their position with such fervor and for such specific reasons that Catholic anti-Communism might reasonably be seen as distinct from the general American disdain.[29] The Catholic discourse on Communism certainly pulled no punches, such as in the Holy Name Society warning to its members that "the modern Diocletians are on the march and their goal is destruction."[30] Similarly, the *Pittsburgh Catholic* regularly conveyed concerns about Communism to readers. Editor John Collins warned that Communists worked "feverishly" to transform the world and American society to a materialist ideology while Americans went along "too placidly about our pleasures and routine concerns." Communism was a "veritable tide of evil, ruthless and cunning beyond anything the world has seen heretofore."[31] Collins covered the threat in his weekly editorials, gave front-page coverage to the plight of priests and nuns behind the Iron Curtain, and supported labor columnist Fr. Charles Owen Rice and his regular attacks on Communists in the labor movement.[32] Even so, Collins remained reluctant to participate in what he considered to be dangerous and mean-spirited attacks on individuals.[33]

Collins's successors clearly intensified the paper's emphasis on the Communist threat throughout the decade and into the 1960s. For example, while Collins worried that the Red-baiting Louis Budenz crossed the line in his fanatical anti-Communism, Bishop Dearden's *Pittsburgh Catholic* ran his syndicated column each week on its editorial page. Other rabid anti-Communist columnists joined the diocesan weekly as well, including local cleric Richard Ginder.[34]

Capitalism and the Commercialization of Society

Communism's most touted alternative, capitalism, carried its own materialist baggage. It sought to commodify and commercialize almost everything, from the food and shelter people needed to sustain themselves to the celebration of Christian holidays. Like Communism, capitalism elevated the material world over the spiritual and left little room for God's intentions in the social structure. It caused American Catholics to desert their "Christian standards of conduct and [adapt them]selves to the methods of the pagan materialists." America had become "all too concerned with its material well-being, and has grown unconcerned, to a deplorable state, about its spiritual well being." Just as the Roman empire crumbled under external pressures and internal collapse, so too America faced the twin threats of "barbarism on the outside, refined materialism and moral decay within."[35]

The crisis discourse focused intensely on capitalism's evils, and greed led the list. Capitalism allowed, almost demanded, that the rich exploit the poor— a behavior clearly denounced in the discourse. The *Pittsburgh Catholic* ran a series of articles that focused on "the abuses found in the wake of a system of human endeavor unique in the history of mankind, namely, modern Industrialism, based upon the capitalistic system of finance." John Collins decried capitalism's lessons that "it is all right to take advantage of their neighbors, to charge unfair prices, to hoard and to gouge, without regard for the rights and necessities of others."

Church officials felt comfortable criticizing Communism, but Communists did not set the wages and working conditions in Pittsburgh's mills. They did not wield the official powers of government to support the greedy capitalists. What did the Church have to say about the real barriers to dignified life in southwestern Pennsylvania? In fact, critiques of capitalism often came up when Catholics criticized Communism (with the Christian social system proposed as a middle ground). If our society were more justly ordered, Catholic social thinkers and prelates argued, Communists would have no leverage at all. The *Pittsburgh Catholic* gave front-page coverage to a bishop's claim in 1950 that "the time has come when it is necessary to reject both opposing false social systems, crass materialism with its revolutionary violence, and blind, selfish liberalism with its studied ignoring of the place and plight of the great majority of men." Pope Pius XII deemed priests who failed to confront capitalism to be as cowardly as those too afraid to criticize Communism, because capitalism failed to use production "to the advantage of the whole of society and as a means of support to the defense of liberty and the dignity of the human person." John Collins liked the critique so much that he made it the lead story on page 1 two weeks in a row.[36]

Concerns about capitalism's shortcomings were not new to Pittsburghers in the 1950s. The region's working class had long been peopled with Catholics who battled with capitalists in some of the most widely reported and bloodiest labor disputes in the nation's history. Fr. James Cox led a march of unemployed men to Washington, D.C., from the Saint Patrick parish grounds in Pittsburgh's Strip District during Herbert Hoover's presidency, and worker priests Fathers Carl Hensler and Charles Owen Rice spoke out for workers and unionism regularly through the 1930s and 1940s. In fact, Father Rice had a regular radio program and a weekly column in the *Pittsburgh Catholic* devoted to union work and critiques of capitalist exploitation.[37]

In the crisis discourse, capitalism also begat commercialism. Americans, it seemed, mediated everything through the market—through commercial transactions. This included the obvious realms of wages and goods, but it also extended to areas not so clearly embedded in the market. The discourse contested commercialism over a wide range of ground in the 1950s, including, it seems, the very arena of commerce itself. For example, though many Catholic voices had long decried the commercialization of popular culture—movies, television, magazines, comics—a panel of Catholic commentators at Loyola University in Los Angeles unanimously agreed that Walt Disney was the exception. He stood out as a principled and "beneficent" contributor to movie and television "art." He had somehow escaped crude market impulses to produce creatures "subtle in their parodies on human strength and weakness; rich in their fragrant spray of good philosophies and sound morals." Disney represented the true ideal in the cultural marketplace: he proved that one need not sink to pure commercialism in the cultural arena. William Mooring, Hollywood's syndicated columnist to Catholic newspapers, agreed. But a few short weeks after his visit to the newly opened "Disneyland" he conveyed his disappointment. Commercialism, it seems, had corrupted even the last true artist left in Hollywood. Mooring called it "a fiasco the like of which I cannot recall in 30 years of show life."

> To me it felt like a giant cash register, clicking and clanging, as creatures of Disney magic came tumbling down from their lofty places in my daydreams to peddle and perish their charms with the aggressiveness of so many curbside barkers. . . . Now in the mammoth supermarket Walt calls "Disneyland," they come down to us instead; into our world of crass materialism to charm; to be touched by and to "touch" us for a quarter or four bits a time![38]

Even Mickey Mouse, it seemed, had gone commercial.

The discourse reserved its greatest commercial concerns for the ways the market undermined those very days Americans set aside explicitly to turn away from their material existence, to reflect upon, worship, and otherwise honor God. Increasingly over time, Americans in general and Catholics in particular turned the Sabbath into a "bargain shopping day." Church officials urged all Catholics to support the "Keep Sunday Sacred" drive in their efforts to wrest control from commerce. Worse still were capitalism's corrupting influences on the most sacred moments in the Catholic calendar. Christmas itself had devolved into concerted efforts to make "a commercial success of the Christmas season."[39]

Sensuality, Indecency, and Licentiousness

If Pittsburgh's Catholics worried a great deal about the larger economic ideologies that ordered society, they also feared the mesmerizing spell of the sensual. In the words of one Pittsburgh priest, "The terrible scourge of sensuality, heightened in our day, lashes the imaginations and bodies of Christian men and women." Pius XII put it only slightly more mildly when he observed publicly that "the thirst for pleasure is increasing in a disquietening manner."[40]

The sensual in the crisis discourse referred to those things from which people derived extraordinary bodily pleasure. It included the overconsumption of food and attachment to luxury, both of which weakened the primacy of spiritual attention and signaled a disregard for reason in the face of people's physical desires. In the words of Fr. Hugh Wilt, O.S.B., "If our ideas are concerned with ourselves, our wants and our fears . . . then we are limited by them and must ever remain small and fearful little men."[41]

Though no contributor to the Catholic discourse dwelled for long on the specific dangers that a full stomach or ostentatious dress and home furnishings might pose, many provided a steady argument for the necessity of moderation, self-abnegation, and the need to subordinate individuality for the community. Catholics worried here about passions ruling behavior, about individuals calling attention to themselves, about people being unable to transcend their animal impulses. All of these had to be restrained. Any behavior that let loose the bonds of personal restraint made individuals more susceptible to the materialist lure. In the words of one Catholic writer, "People in general are easily tempted to spend their money by the offering of goods, pleasures, and entertainment catering to the low human passions."[42]

Most of all, though, Catholic concerns about sensuality concentrated on sex. Sex outside of marriage, whether between teenagers, among divorced adults, for widows, or in extramarital affairs aroused reams of warnings, while particularly satisfying sex within marriage seemed only slightly less likely to block one's entrance to heaven. The sensual world exerted great power over Catholic males, who might seek on dates to satisfy their "selfish, sinful desires," or let the bonds of restraint fall away at disreputable office Christmas parties, or even become distracted from the true purpose of coital intimacy within the marriage relationship.[43] But cautions about sex were aimed mainly at females, who learned of their great prowess in the realm of sensuality and the need to control that power. In women's hands, it seemed, lay the fate of the virtue necessary to individual salvation and social harmony.

And if the actual participation in sexual liaisons could damn one for eternity, anything that might engender thoughts of such couplings was dangerous too. Indecency in literature, movies, and, as the decade proceeded, in musical productions and recordings proved worrisome. As Bishop John Dearden opined upon his appointment as new head of the U.S. Bishops' Committee for Decent Literature, "Publishers have created in youth a state of mind toward sex matters."[44]

Education and Science

The Catholic concern about public schools had by the 1950s become a concern about the materialist ideology they sought to impart. If Catholics in the nineteenth century worried about the vigorous Protestant attempts to proselytize children in the public schools, by the middle of the twentieth century Catholics clearly feared that public schools had abandoned religion altogether. Unlike their public counterparts, Catholic schools recognized each student's material and spiritual character, and employed curricula and teaching methods that reflected this. Public schools too often fell under the materialist spell of John Dewey's progressivism and put children's souls at risk. Cardinal James McIntyre, archbishop of Los Angeles, asserted that these progressives

> have labored diligently to ignore the fact of God's existence as well as the antecedent, consequent and transcendent righteousness evident in the natural law. We cannot expect our youth to survive without help if they will overcome the nefarious, subtle and insistent attempts to impose upon them and the curricula of their schools, dangerous teaching—entirely separated from God.

Even at Dewey's death in 1952 John Collins ruminated that "it will probably be a long time before the public schools recover from the pernicious effects of the Dewey thinking."[45] Catholic parents who wished to expose their children to this danger required special dispensations from their pastors, who had to answer to the bishop for granting them.

Colleges too proved dangerous places for Catholics. John Collins was appalled to discover in 1952 that only 95 percent of college graduates believed in God. Four percent responded in a *Catholic Digest* poll that they did not believe in God, and another 1 percent did not know whether or not God existed. He concluded that "apparently the fields of higher education and technical training in this country have been affected by some unsound thinking."[46] What caused this dangerous development? New York's Cardinal Spellman told those gathered in Saint Paul's Cathedral (Pittsburgh) for Duquesne University's seventy-fifth anniversary that colleges and universities had "rejected the original program and hierarchy of studies instituted by their founders." He continued that

> where theology once reigned in queenly splendor, there are only deserted chairs and discredited professors. Where philosophy once held out to students the sure and stable norms of right reason, there now is only the dreary denial of reason and the contemptuous dismissal of the fact of the existence of absolute truth.[47]

Concomitant with the decline of religion in public schools came the rise of science in the curriculum and in society more generally. Catholics could not easily reconcile their insistence on the spiritual dimension of humans in our culture with a discipline that insisted upon empirical verification for reality—especially one that defined "natural" laws in unorthodox ways. Solutions to the world's problems would come from Christ, not from science. The crisis discourse was certain on this point. The *Holy Name Newsletter* explained it clearly:

> Men in the market place are eager and waiting for the truth. They are tired of cold wars, political babble and empty promises. They are seeking for ways and means to build a nobler way of life. This can be achieved not by men of science but by men of the Eucharist.

Pius XII agreed, and warned Catholics not to believe too much in the manmade world in which "science alone can solve all mankind's problems."[48]

News of the Soviet space satellite Sputnik introduced a special tension in the Catholic insistence that Americans should shun science in favor of religion. But Catholic educators and cultural commentators refused to forsake their emphasis on religion over science.

Transforming Women's Roles

If materialism stood as the greatest threat to American Catholics in the 1950s, and religious virtue as the best defense, then the loss of virtue's traditional guardian proved a terrifying development. Women—wives and mothers especially, but school-age girls and single women as well—nurtured and passed virtue on to their husbands and children in Catholic homes throughout the nation and the Pittsburgh region. They were the heart of the Catholic devotional life, the soul of the family, and the hands of the parish. Should women ever shed their natural virtue or their commitment to the work of the Church, the materialists could hardly lose.

And women too were at risk in the materialist attack—doubly so. On the one hand, they had been "degraded and torn apart by the purveyors of filth in print, in picture magazines, in the movies and on the radio."[49] So they faced the sensualists' onslaught and the potential dissolution of the female ideal. On the other hand, the market called to them with powerful voices to join the paid workforce and expand their consumer power. The prospect of women entering America's offices and factories, leaving the haven for the heartless world, terribly unsettled the hierarchy. The Church could hardly expect to weather that storm. And that is why, when women began to join the workforce in greater and greater numbers throughout the decade, a panic set in that reverberated through-out the Catholic literature and brought about the decline of the devotional practices so central to Catholic identity for generations. The transformation of women's behaviors was probably the largest single force that came to bear on the pre–Vatican II Church, and was possibly the agent that most changed Ameri-can Catholicism in the latter twentieth century.

Direct Threats to Catholicism

Coupled with the threats that derived from and connected to materialism in American culture were those dimensions of the culture that Catholics under-stood to be specifically hostile to their faith and community. The perception of a general Protestant effort to convert Catholics or simply to undermine Catho-lic adherence to the true faith stood out most. This sometimes took the form of overt evangelizing, such as when the Rev. Billy Graham rolled into town, but most often came in the personal struggles of Catholics entering marital relation-ships with Protestants or others and the tensions over what religious tradition the family should follow.

Catholics expressed regular concern about overt attempts to steal the faith-ful or attack the Church directly, though the more subtle threats also generated fears for the Church's survival. Perhaps the best examples of direct threats came from evangelizing Protestants who seemed to target Catholics directly. The Billy Graham Crusade that came through Pittsburgh in 1952 to evangelize the city, rep-resented just such a moment. The evangelist had a wide range of resources at his disposal put up by local Protestants, including a massive advertising campaign that encompassed billboards, radio promotions, television spots, and plenty of space in the local papers. Downtown churches opened their doors to Graham, as did the Hunt Armory in Shadyside (literally across the street from one of the diocese's largest Catholic churches and typically home to the auxiliary bishops), and even Forbes Field. But by the end of the four-week stay Graham had accu-mulated only 5,693 conversions, enough fewer than John Collins had initially feared that he breathed a sigh of relief.[50]

Collins was not so sanguine when the *Christian Herald,* "a Protestant monthly of New York City," released results of its survey assessing conversions in the United States. The survey reported that 4,144,366 Catholics had converted to one Protestant denomination or another in the past ten years. Collins was incredu-lous. "If four million became Protestants in the past ten years . . . that would mean that some 17,000 of them are in Pittsburgh—more than the adult membership of two or three of the largest congregations here. It's just not credible." A similar *Christian Herald* survey conducted five years later reported an almost 7–1 ratio of conversions to Protestantism over conversions to Catholicism. This time the National Catholic Welfare Conference Bureau of Information conducted its own poll in rebuttal, and found the ratio to be 24–1 in favor of conversions to Catholicism.[51]

If Graham came through temporarily on his national evangelical tour, other groups offered a more permanent threat to the Church. The *Pittsburgh Catholic* kept vigilant watch for signs of anti-Catholic bigotry in the diocese and throughout the nation, and reported threats to its readers. Catholics learned, for example, when the forty-three congregations of the Monongahela Presbytery of the United Presbyterian Church worried publicly about the "trend toward the kind of religious monopoly which the Church of Rome covets for itself." The *Pittsburgh Catholic* alerted readers when the Pennsylvania Supreme Court overturned a lower court ruling and granted a charter of incorporation to Conversion Center, Inc., a Philadelphia-area group that aimed "aggressively, militantly" to proselyte Roman Catholics in their efforts to "foster, promote and encourage understanding and good will among members of all religious faiths." The paper also told readers about the Jehovah's Witnesses' efforts to construct a "Freedom Hall" in a wealthy Pittsburgh neighborhood. This proved troubling because, as Fr. Richard Ginder later explained, the Jehovah's Witnesses were strongly anti-Catholic and they "just show up at the front door every once in a while with their curious books and pamphlets."[52]

Most threatening of all, however, was the organization called Protestants and Other Americans United for Separation of Church and State (POAU). This national group with a sporadically active Pittsburgh chapter aimed much of its effort at curbing Catholic influences on public policies, especially the perceived (and real) Catholic attempts to garner public support for parochial education. The ninth national POAU conference in Los Angeles, for example,

> denounced a Fordham University "land grab" in New York: payment of state funds for maintaining Vermont state wards in parochial school; granting of a TV license by the Federal Communications Commission to Loyola University of New Orleans, and the naming of St. Joseph Church, Philadelphia, as a U.S. historic shrine.

Some prominent Pittsburgh Protestant ministers played high-profile roles in the national POAU, and they kept an intermittently high profile in the region.[53]

TAKEN IN THEIR ENTIRETY, THE THREATS OF MATERIALISM AND anti-Catholicism combined to frighten Catholics about the prospects for the faith and the faithful as they moved into the second half of the twentieth century. The central theme, especially in the early years of the decade, was that Catholics confronted a grave crisis that demanded a concerted response. Though the crisis seemed to touch almost every aspect of Catholic life, and in doing so appeared very diffuse at times, it stemmed from a common root: a concern about the rising power of materialism to overwhelm society's collective religiosity and each individual's essential spiritual dimension. But the crisis discourse did prescribe a response to the perils which promised to protect the Catholic community and ensure its survival far into the future. Chapters 2, 3, and 4 explore the prescribed response to the crisis in an effort to understand the vast range of behavioral instructions the laity received in the years leading up to the Second Vatican Council.

Historians face greater difficulty discerning how the laity actually behaved, and what they actually believed, in the years before the Second Vatican Council. Church records rarely address these concerns directly. Church officials had a relatively clear sense of how a good Catholic ought to behave, and saw little need to explore the ways the laity departed from these normative prescriptions. Even so, chapters 2, 3, and 4 address actual lay behavior during the years leading up to the Second Vatican Council using the evidence that does survive. After the Council, when even Church officials assented to the conception of the Church as the "people of God," lay actions and beliefs received greater attention. Part 3 addresses the changed official prescriptions and lay behavior in the wake of Vatican II.

CHAPTER TWO

Anti-Communism and the Decline
of Catholic Devotionalism

THE SOLUTION TO THE MATERIALIST CRISIS THAT SO WORRIED Pittsburgh's Catholics proved just as pervasive and complex as the problem itself. The crisis discourse urged Pittsburgh Catholics to fight materialism with three primary strategies, though these were not presented as a coherent three-pronged program. The first and most heavily emphasized strategy was a continued (and intensified) emphasis on the spiritual dimension of everyday life. Catholics had been accomplishing this through devotional exercises for generations, and the discourse recommended continued participation in these existing rituals. Secondly, Catholics were to combat the hostile culture by maintaining a parallel one that mirrored the larger American scene in all but its immoral dimensions. They were to perpetuate a separate Catholic social and cultural experience—a Catholic ghetto—that they inherited from their parents and grandparents. It was to be a private world in the public sphere, apart from the broader American social and cultural scene. Finally, they were to create a socially just society based upon the principles of Catholic social teaching. These strategies intertwined throughout the 1950s in ways that make their separate analyses a bit artificial. But I have chosen that route so as to make them clearer and so that we can better see the ascendancy of one over another as Catholics approached and then worked through the Second Vatican Council. The weight that each solution carried varied across the decade depending upon who edited the diocesan paper and who served as bishop. The decade saw three bishops and three *Pittsburgh Catholic* editors, and while none of the six explicitly dissented from the three-part prescription, they did differ in their support for each.

Bishop Hugh Boyle led the diocese at the decade's outset, and John Collins edited the lay-owned diocesan newspaper. Both men supported devotions strongly, backed Catholic social and cultural separatism intensely, and pushed social justice fervently. Bishop John Dearden succeeded Bishop Boyle, bought the paper, and replaced John Collins with John Ward. The new tandem embraced devotionalism and Catholic separatism wholeheartedly, but offered only tepid support for social justice. John Wright followed Dearden to the Pittsburgh See in 1959 and brought with him from Worcester, Massachusetts, his own editor for the *Pittsburgh Catholic*. John Deedy and Bishop Wright embraced social justice with even more enthusiasm than had Boyle and Collins, supported Catholic devotionalism, but sought to mitigate Catholic separatism by pushing Catholics to participate fully in the broader American culture. By the decade's end, even the talented John Wright could not have upheld the Catholic separatism had he chosen to do so, and his efforts to maintain a fervent devotionalism did not succeed. Whether he succeeded in defining the Church through its social justice mission constitutes the story of the 1960s and 1970s and, to a significant extent, continues today.

This chapter addresses the first and, for the early 1950s in Pittsburgh, the dominant of the three strategies: devotionalism.

THE DEVOTIONAL BATTLE AGAINST COMMUNISM

Catholics did not limit their battle against Communism to the devotional arena, nor did they frame all of their devotional activities as anti-Communist endeavors. Catholic politicians led anti-Communist campaigns aimed at purging leftists from public life—and even from residency within the city and nation. Italian-American leader and county judge Michael Musmanno spearheaded a series of public attacks on Pittsburgh residents whom he deemed too sympathetic to Communist causes. He sought to have them fired from their jobs, deported from the country, or jailed for their public support of civil liberties for Communists. He also sought to boost his political ambitions with these public attacks. Catholic labor priests and union organizers worked hard within factories, mills, and other workplaces to limit the clout of Communist labor organizers, and within unions to oust Communists from positions of power. In fact, Fr. Charles Owen Rice, Pittsburgh's most famous labor priest, focused more attention throughout the 1950s on battling against Communism within unions than he did on fighting for unions against management. And the Catholic press throughout Pennsylvania attacked Communism at home and abroad earlier and more vociferously than the secular and Protestant press during the decade. The Catholic press often addressed specific domestic and international political developments directly, and put their criticisms of Communism in apocalyptic terms.[1] Catholic working men and women could identify readily the specific unions that Church officials recommended they should join, and often the specific candidates for union offices they should support (or reject). There is no doubt that the broader public discourse on Communism contained a strong Catholic voice regarding political and economic issues. But while the Catholic discourse on Communism encompassed more than devotionalism, it focused heavily and strategically upon devising and maintaining a devotional response to the Communist materialist threat.

Similarly, Catholic devotionalism meant more than the best means to combat Marxist materialists. But Church officials understood Communism to pose the most direct organized materialist threat to Catholics in the 1950s, so much of the intense Catholic spiritual emphasis in Pittsburgh can rightly be seen as a response to the Red menace. The peculiar intensity with which the hierarchy pushed devotions in the 1950s derived substantially from the crisis mentality that Communism fueled so powerfully. After all, with what better means than a devotional communion with the supernatural could American Catholics battle an ideology that insisted on the primacy of the material world?

However, devotionalism did not arise generally, arrive in Pittsburgh specifically, or exist entirely to battle Communism. Devotional Catholicism represented a particular mode of religious expression that began in America well before Catholics raised concerns about Marxism and likely would have persisted through the 1950s to some degree, and in some form, had there been no Communist threat. The devotional ethos had shaped American Catholicism for generations by 1950, and it conveyed much beyond a battle against Communism as well. It was a fine cure for all of the materialist dangers swirling about the crisis discourse in the 1950s. This section examines devotional practices as a response to Communism, but it also explores other critical dimensions of the devotional ethos that shaped Catholics' experiences and understanding of their world.

The antimaterialist dimensions of Pittsburgh's devotional practices can best be seen in large public devotions targeted specifically at Communism. Pope Pius XII declared 1950 to be a Holy Year and then promptly linked it to the battle against Communism when he issued an encyclical letter calling for a crusade of prayer to combat "those on the other side" who worked "so hard to destroy the very basis of the Catholic religion and Christian culture."[2]

Six months later, in September 1950, the Pittsburgh Holy Name Society hosted an overflow crowd of 115,000 men at Forbes Field in a public eucharistic rally aimed at least in part at Communism. The long history of such public displays in Pittsburgh conditioned rally organizers and other Church officials to insist that it had no public meaning other than a simple outpouring of religious devotion, but the context clearly conveyed a powerful political message.

The Holy Name Society had been parading through Pittsburgh off and on since 1910. These marches often drew tens of thousands of marchers and sometimes sparked counterdemonstrations of tens of thousands of Protestants. Bishops had canceled parades some years because of the tensions that the marches fanned between Catholics and Protestants. Diocesan and Holy Name officials consistently denied that the parades meant anything more than Catholic devotional commitment to Jesus and moral rectitude, but the context for the events clearly suggested that they carried powerful social meanings for the larger community far beyond love for the Lord. These processions dramatically asserted the Catholic presence in the Pittsburgh region at a time when nativist fears in the area and across the nation rose to dominate the political agenda. The fact that bishops scheduled or canceled processions in light of their likely reception in the city, and that tens of thousands of Protestants marched in response to some of the Catholic parades, makes the Catholic insistence that the processions had no political or social meaning seem either hopelessly naive or astutely calculated.

Similarly, when the diocese began to hold major eucharistic rallies in the city's two major sports arenas, Pitt Stadium and Forbes Field, organizers insisted that they had no larger political significance. But these rallies, held in 1930, 1936, and 1941, all came at critical moments in the region's or nation's history. The first came at the outset of the Great Depression, which posed severe economic danger to lay Catholics. The 1936 rally took place in the midst of the continuing depression and in the wake, literally, of the great flood that washed over the city of Pittsburgh. The flood killed or injured more than 3,000 Pittsburghers and rendered homeless 135,000 additional residents—more than a fifth of the city's population.[3] The 1941 rally preceded Pearl Harbor by a mere two months, and called Catholic men together in the face of growing anxiety about developments in Europe.

Just as with earlier rallies, the 1950 event came at a critical political moment for the civil society. Not only did it crown the papally designated Holy Year (aimed in part at Communism), but it also took place at the outset of U.S. involvement in the Korean War—a hot war fought against Communist North Korea and, eventually, China as well. And local pastors had already primed parishioners to dedicate their private devotions to the battle against Communism. The Rev. Robert J. McBride, diocesan director of the Sodality of Our Lady, told Catholics to think of rosary recitation as a competing ideology to Communism.[4]

He explained that "to the Communists the workers' chains are a sign of failure and defeat. For the Catholic, the sodalist, the rosary-chain is a weapon of life—bringing combat and victory." A bit later he pushed private rosary recitation more urgently, as he exhorted parishioners to stop putting off daily recitation. Was fifteen minutes each day too much to ask for peace? "Or are you so taken with the 'live dangerously' philosophy of life that you will enjoy hurrying for shelter when the A-bombs and H-bombs begin raining down from the sky?" Only prayer and sacrifice could beat the Communists. Yet in September, with the prayer and shooting war a fearful reality, thousands of men poured into and around Forbes Field for what the *Pittsburgh Catholic* judiciously called "a religious observance, pure and simple, a public profession of faith."[5]

Catholic officials had so mastered the carefully nuanced public pronouncements regarding large-scale public devotions since 1910 that they almost reflexively denied any political significance for the 1950 event. Protestants should understand the event "not as a protest against anyone or anything; not as a challenge or defiance; not as a 'show of strength.'"[6] It was an exercise in piety, nothing more. Diocesan officials played up its devotional character, and the rally did convey powerful devotional values.

Historian Jay Dolan described a devotional ethos that developed in the middle of the nineteenth century and reached its apogee in the decades after World War I as a religious sensibility that rested on respect for clerical authority, a strong emphasis on the prevalence of sin, an affinity for formal ritual, and a belief in the miraculous.[7] The rally included each characteristic.

The eucharistic rally began officially at 7:30 in the evening, but men poured into the stadium when the gates opened an hour earlier. By 7:00 they filled the stands completely, and those who followed spilled out onto the field itself. Because of transportation congestion, men kept arriving and entering the field even after the ceremonies began. Soon men so filled even the field that latecomers stood outside of the stadium, some on the hills of Schenley Park behind the outfield walls. The *Pittsburgh Catholic* estimated that forty thousand men filled the stadium seats, another twenty-five thousand crowded onto the field, and fully fifty thousand more surrounded the stadium. In anticipation of liturgical splendor (and a fire marshal's nightmare) each man held in his hand a candle, waiting for the signal to light it.[8]

The rally contained a great deal of formal ritual, including prayers, processions, hymns, and a benediction. The Rev. Vincent J. Rieland opened the rally at 7:30 by leading the men through Pope Pius XII's Holy Year Prayer. The Very Rev. Henry C. Graham, national director of the Holy Name Society, followed with a fully participated rosary recitation (concluding with the Fatima petition), and then everyone sang "O Mary, My Mother."[9]

The great procession then entered the stadium, with hierarchy members in plain view. Participants surely understood the centrality of Church authority on this night. Pastors, monsignori, an abbot, two archabbots, and, finally, three bishops (with two attendant chaplains each) had special roles and places of honor at the evening events—fully eighteen steps above the laity on the field. Pittsburgh bishop Boyle lay dying in Mercy Hospital, but Coadjutor Bishop John Dearden spoke briefly, joined the group in singing the "Star Spangled Banner," and then read a cable from the Vatican Secretariat of State. Bishop Mulloy gave a sermon that emphasized the Holy Eucharist's power to transform men and urged them to receive Communion frequently—though not that night.[10]

Then came the evening's high point. Solid ranks of three thousand altar boys entered the stadium through the left field gate. The *Pittsburgh Catholic* described the scene as follows:

> By the hundreds they [altar boys] marched in, white surplices over cassocks of red or black, a corps of policewomen directing them. Then a double file of uniformed police and firemen, their Holy Name Society banner at their head. They were the escort for the black automobile in which the priest carrying the Blessed Sacrament had come from St. Paul's Cathedral.

When the car reached the outfield gate, all the men lit their candles, organizers doused the stadium lights, and

> a carpet of candle flames spread over the field . . . banks of light covered the slopes of the stands . . . a soft glow bathed the altar and its great red reredos . . . the points of light stretched out into the adjoining park where the overflow crowds were gathered . . . A broad stream of gentle flames came rippling through the space before the altar as an additional array of altar boys, candles burning in their hands, followed the automobile into the field. The scene was awe-inspiring.[11]

Bishop Dearden then performed the benediction before the hushed crowd and led the procession out of the stadium. In all, the rally lasted until almost 10:00 at night, still later for those who had traveled any distance to come.

If organizers insisted that people should read nothing into the rally but a public profession of faith, some observers did see more. The evening also helped atone for the many sins that individuals and society had committed. Father McBride understood it to be "just as much a public act of penance, especially on the part of those who could not be seated in the stands." Further, "we are not going to be successful in our endeavors to attain peace in this world merely by getting all worked up over the threat of Communism. We must turn completely and unashamedly to Christ."[12]

Only men participated in the 1950 eucharistic rally, save for the policewomen who marshaled the altar boys into Forbes Field. Women did not typically partake in public devotions that brought them outside of church grounds. Men dominated public devotional displays in the Pittsburgh diocese, and wives and mothers did not expose themselves to the potential dangers public immersion entailed. But this was only technically true in the 1950s, as two public devotions, also aimed in part at the materialist Communist threat demonstrate.

Pittsburgh Catholics typically divided themselves by gender for devotional practices, with rare exceptions. Only one explicitly anti-Communist public devotion in the Pittsburgh diocese specifically called women to participate. Mount Mercy College sponsored an annual Mary's Day devotional exercise on its campus for female and male students attending Mount Mercy, Duquesne University, Carnegie Institute of Technology, Pennsylvania College for Women, and the University of Pittsburgh. The devotions began in 1949 and extended into the 1950s. Organizers consciously scheduled the event on May 1 to counter Communist May Day celebrations throughout the world. In this they resembled other efforts across America to take May first from the Communists. These evening public devotions, like the 1950 Holy Name Society rally, consisted of formal sermons, candle-lit processions, and benedictions.[13]

The public devotion differed from the all-male devotions in some critical respects, however. First, both men and women participated together. This was rare. Second, though the devotion was public in that it took place out of doors, it occurred entirely on the Mount Mercy College campus. It began in Antonian Hall, near the college entrance on Fifth Avenue, and proceeded up the driveway to the field on the upper section of campus, a distance of about two or three hundred yards. The benediction took place in the field near Saint Joseph's Hall. Finally, the Mary's Day activities involved college women and men, a group that included very few, if any, married women. All of the women identified specifically in *Pittsburgh Catholic* accounts of the events were single.

If the Mount Mercy College Mary's Day public devotions did not call married women out of their homes, a 1951 eucharistic rally did. But it took place in the Saint Vincent College stadium, home field of the all-male Catholic college's football team, surrounded by the campus and the archabbey's extensive cornfields.[14]

Organizers planned the Marian eucharistic rally to provide a forum for women both to affirm their belief in the miraculous and to combat Communism. Women could assert their belief in miracles at the rally by honoring Pius XII's recent proclamation of the Dogma of the Assumption—a phenomenon that no materialist could abide. Catholic women could do their part to battle Communism by praying for peace: asking God to intervene to convert Russia. Organizers therefore scheduled a rosary recitation, a sermon, and a benediction. Unlike the Holy Name Society rally and the Mount Mercy College Mary's Day events, the Marian eucharistic rally took place during daylight hours, under a baking August sun. There would be no candles for the women at the Marian eucharistic rally, and they would be home in time to put the kids to bed. The *Pittsburgh Catholic* predicted that six thousand women would attend, and expressed great surprise when more than fifteen thousand actually showed up.[15]

Each of these large-scale public devotional events bore witness to the broader society that Catholics rejected materialism in all its forms, and especially its Communist manifestation. Concern for the world's "things" might dominate the secular culture, but Catholics would still assert God's reign in heaven and on earth. However, the events also reminded Catholic participants that they lived in a spiritual as well as a material world, and that they must work steadily to maintain their connection with the spiritual dimension. This reminder took other, less dramatic forms in the Catholic devotional culture as well.

Catholics labored in parish and diocesan organizations to build and maintain their firm commitment to a spiritual dimension to their lives, to assert through regular and practiced behaviors their belief in the primacy of the spiritual realm. Parishes and the diocese structured devotional activities primarily through gender-segregated organizations such as the Holy Name Society for males and a host of women's organizations linked in the Diocesan Council of Catholic Women for females. A brief examination of each of these traditions sheds a great deal of light on the devotional ethos that characterized the Catholic religious sensibility in the early 1950s.

The Male Devotional Experience

The Holy Name Society dominated male devotional experiences in Pittsburgh during the early 1950s. Not only did it organize the large-scale public rituals that drew so much attention to the Church, but it shaped male religiosity on the parish level as well. No exploration of male devotional culture in Pittsburgh could continue for even a short while without confronting the Holy Name Society and its powerful presence. This resulted from the organization's thorough infusion throughout the diocese. In 1956 the Pittsburgh Diocese Holy Name Society claimed that 93 percent of its 334 parishes and missions housed canonically instituted societies. Of these, 269 had charters and 41 missions shared their "mother" parishes' charters. The Pittsburgh police and fire departments also had charters, as did the Auberle Home for Boys in McKeesport, and Duquesne University. The diocesan organization considered fully 90 percent of the existing units to be "active," by which it meant that they held meetings and supported committees.[16] By 1959 the official membership count stood at 75,000 in 300 parishes.[17]

The Holy Name Society served a variety of roles for Catholic men, including as a focus of male social activity. It sponsored smokers, dinners, trips to ball games and the like. But it existed to foster a particular kind of religious practice, to mold male behaviors to conform to a standard set out explicitly in the society's official pledge. This pledge conveys the powerfully devotional nature of the society, and sheds light on the nature of male devotional life in postwar America. The pledge began

> Blessed be God.
> Blessed be His Holy Name.
> Blessed be Jesus Christ true God and true Man.
> Blessed be the Name of Jesus.

The society existed foremost to honor and respect the name "Jesus Christ," and Holy Name officials encouraged their members to do so. The diocese published and distributed to each parish chapter a monthly newsletter, and many issues contained explicit instructions, or not so subtle stories, designed to foster a respect for the second commandment. The *Newsletter*'s editors urged their readers to show respect for Jesus and his name in a variety of ways.

A 1954 issue carried the story of a star high school fullback who ruined his team's chances of winning a particularly crucial football game when officials ejected him for swearing. A 1957 story told of a Holy Name member who picked up golf and within weeks began to win local tournaments. He explained that he learned that golfers cursed when they missed putts, so he had to putt perfectly to remain true to his Holy Name pledge. Another issue urged members to bow their heads when they heard Jesus' name as "a partial means of reparation for the widespread misuse and dishonoring of the holy name."[18]

Christ's divinity justified honoring his name, and Holy Name members asserted that divinity in the next part of the pledge:

> I believe O Jesus
> That Thou Art the Christ
> The Son of the living God.

That divinity demanded more than mere respect for Christ's name, it called for persistent public acts of faith.

> I promise to give good example
> By the regular practice
> Of my faith.

Church officials urged Holy Name members to take part regularly in group devotions that not only drew the participant closer to God, but also modeled virtue for others in the community. The most common devotions in which Holy Name men participated were lay retreats, prayerful meditation before the Holy Eucharist, rallies that gathered hundreds—and sometimes thousands—of Catholic men together, and special Holy Week activities. During the 1950s the Holy Name director and retreat house directors pushed retreats as the most significant act a Holy Name member might perform. Retreats held no official liturgical function, emphasized personal, introspective reflection, and segregated participants by age and gender. They functioned especially well in the devotional context, as they emphasized personal prayer and piety.

Retreats took place primarily during the summer months at seminaries, colleges, and monasteries within a few hours driving distance of Pittsburgh. Retreat centers sponsored retreats for extended weekends, short weekends, daylong sessions during the week, or even four-hour evening sessions. Participants normally attended a Mass and informal talks by retreat masters in monastic chapels, participated in devotional exercises, and had free time in their rooms for reading, thinking, and praying on their own. Larger sessions often gathered the group together for a photograph at the end of the retreat, turning the private devotion into a public act as the photos turned up in newsletters and on parish bulletin boards. Typically the members gathered for a specific retreat came from organizations that existed already, such as parish or deanery Holy Name societies. Organizations sponsored specific weekends to encourage participation, though not all men attending retreats at those houses on those weekends necessarily belonged to the organizations.

Pittsburgh's bishop Hugh Boyle promoted retreats as a means to combat the materialism swirling about American culture in the twentieth century. He relayed that he welcomed the retreat movement because Americans

> are concerned with things more than we have ever been concerned with them before, and the supernatural ends and purposes of mankind we find are often completely lost sight of because our time is occupied by a group of things that belong to this world, whose end and purpose is in the sphere of material and transitory things.[19]

John Collins, writing in 1952, emphasized that

> a retreat is an extraordinary effort to strengthen oneself against the temptations and the "customs" and the "trends" that are debasing society; that these evil influences are frighteningly powerful is shown by the number of "good Catholics" identified with public and private corruption. They are being carried along in the tide of pagan selfishness and recklessness that are part of the materialism of the day.
>
> A retreat is the using of proven, supernatural means to recover self-mastery and a right conscience in the midst of these evil conditions.[20]

And retreats emphasized the evil conditions that surrounded participants as they lived their everyday lives. For example, one prayer that men on retreat at Saint Vincent College recited during their retreats contained the following statements:

> We are now resolved to expiate each and every deplorable outrage committed against Thee; we are determined to make amends for the manifold offenses against Christian modesty, in unbecoming dress and behavior; for all the foul seductions laid to ensnare the feet of the innocent; for the frequent violation of Sundays and Holy days; and the shocking blasphemies uttered against Thee, and Thy Saints. We wish also to make amends for the insults, to which Thy Vicar on earth and Thy priests are subjected; for the profanation by conscious neglect, and for terrible acts of sacrilege of the very Sacrament of Thy Divine Love; and lastly for the public crimes of nations, who resist the rights and the teaching authority of the Church which Thou has founded.[21]

In addition to retreats, and often during retreats, the Holy Name Society also encouraged members to participate in eucharistic adoration. Participants in eucharistic adoration entered a church and knelt before the tabernacle that held hosts transformed into Christ's body during the rite of transubstantiation. Participants typically remained in this pose for a half hour or an hour, when others took their place. The devotion continued for twenty-four hours each day, and typically stretched for forty total hours. In order to facilitate this type of adoration, the priests sometimes placed a transformed host in a special implement, called a monstrance, which enabled those present to see the host. Often this exercise would be done at a side altar so that other activities could take place at the main altar. Some groups, such as the Holy Name Society, printed materials for formal prayer during adoration. Catholic officials expected that the time Catholics spent in close physical proximity to Christ's body, especially when combined with prayerful communication, would make participants more receptive to grace. This divinely given grace could not but help a Catholic to live out his or her faith more fully.

The *Holy Name Newsletter* often called on members to partake more often in eucharistic adoration and praised parishes or societies that supported programs. Eucharistic adoration seemed to follow a pattern of much support in and around important religious holidays, and then decreased participation during other times, especially the summer.

Catholics tied eucharistic adoration closely with eucharistic rallies, miniature and more localized versions of the large 1950 eucharistic rally held in Forbes Field. The North Side parishes held an annual "Holy Name Rally" in June in which the members gathered early on a Sunday afternoon, marched from one church through the North Side to a large meeting site, and then held their ceremony. In 1956 they met at the Church of the Nativity, proceeded down Franklin Road to Perrysville Avenue and then to the Byzantine Seminary Greek Rite of Saints Cyril and Methodius, where Fr. Edward Joyce led more than one thousand men in saying the rosary and the Very Rev. Monsignor Thomas J. Quigley gave a sermon. The parishes dedicated that year's rally "To God, the Father of Us All."[22]

Participation in rallies, marches, retreats, and eucharistic adoration constituted a good portion of male Catholic devotional life. The hierarchy also emphasized a particularly intense period of devotional behavior during Holy Week, the annual celebration of Christ's last week on earth before his crucifixion and resurrection. It began with Palm Sunday and lasted until Easter Sunday, though Holy Thursday and Good Friday drew the bulk of the devotion.[23]

On Holy Thursday members gathered at their local parish for a Mass commemorating the first Mass. Following this a Eucharist remained in exposition for forty hours (signifying the forty hours that Christ lay in the tomb between his death and resurrection). Holy Name officials encouraged members to come and kneel in adoration for at least some part of the forty hours, and during the 1950s revived a sixteenth-century tradition called a "seven-church walk." Members gathered in their own church and then walked to six other local churches to pay respect to the Eucharist on Thursday evening. To its parish affiliates the Holy Name Society sold pamphlets containing prayers to say at each different church. Finding seven churches within walking distance was not always easy in Pittsburgh, so the *Newsletter* suggested visiting fewer churches or using buses and cars.[24]

The Holy Name Society sold Holy Thursday vigil posters and Good Friday cards each year to guide members in their devotional exercises and remind businesses to close on Friday. The *Newsletter* urged members to buy these cards and often published order forms for them.[25]

The Holy Name Society encouraged men to say the rosary at virtually all of these devotions. Various parish societies offered specially made rosaries as gifts for some member's accomplishments. Saint Clare's HNS in Clairton, for instance, gave Charles Vines a silver rosary in honor of his being the oldest known living Holy Name member in the Pittsburgh diocese. Saint Peter's on the north side offered two Vercelli rosaries as prizes to students who won their annual essay contest on Blessed John Vercelli, the Holy Name Society founder, in 1959. Not only did the Holy Name Society encourage rosary recitation during community events, it sponsored a "radio rosary" every evening over station WCAE for many years. Father Lackner urged HNS leaders to say rosaries as one of nine steps to invigorate their parish society, and especially encouraged the leaders to emphasize rosaries for the dead of the parish.[26]

Devotions generally fostered deferential behavior toward ecclesiastical and civil authority, and the Holy Name Society reified this with explicit pledges to honor and obey powerful members of society. Holy Name members supplemented their strong devotional activities with what some have termed the "cult of the Papacy,"[27] though members extended this cult somewhat more widely to include bishops and priests. The Holy Name pledge made this stance clear and unwavering.

> I proclaim my love
> For the Vicar of Christ on Earth.

And later,

> I pledge my support
> To all lawful authority
> Both civil and religious.

The Holy Name Society strongly urged its members to pay heed to the pope's wishes. It also demanded fealty to the local bishop and, by extension, to priests. The HNS took a back seat to no group in supporting and deferring to Church officials.

The *Holy Name Newsletter* is replete with reminders to its readers to honor and obey the pope, the bishop, and priests (primarily pastors). It carried stories and photos of members receiving papal blessings and exhorted readers to aspire to the great faith that was possible only under the Church's leadership "as expressed in her teachings, her Papal directives and the leadership of her Hierarchy."[28] The society suggested that each parish take as its theme for 1958 "The Holy Father and the Holy Name Man," and focus each month on the modern popes' writings, especially those of Pius XII (1939–58). The parishes might address such topics as "The Pope and Education," "The Pope and the Modern Businessman," "The Papal Viewpoint on Sports," "The Pope and Television," "The Papacy and the Liturgy," and "Pope Pius XII and the Mystical Body."[29] Father Lackner recommended that, in these days when major developments were happening daily, the Holy Name man must be aware of what the pope had to say about the world—and he said quite a bit. Lackner urged parishes and deaneries to form committees to convey this to parishioners in order that they might "comment intelligently" on the world.[30]

Perhaps because the diocesan society interacted more regularly with the local bishop, the *Newsletter* urged obedience and praise for him more regularly than for the pope. It encouraged members always to seek to do that which the bishop requested, to make the bishop's priorities Holy Name priorities, and to celebrate the bishop's triumphs and milestones.[31]

The *Newsletter* reserved the most frequent entreaties for deference and obedience for the parish pastors, though, as they were the people on whom the parish societies depended for regular instructions and encouragement. If the editors stressed honoring bishops and the pope, they insisted on obeying the pastor.

Often the priests asked for fuller participation in the devotional exercises the Holy Name Society sponsored or supported. But they also asked that members act in a "clean and upright" manner. The Holy Name pledge specified that

> In honor of His Divine Name
> I pledge myself against perjury
> Blasphemy, profanity and obscene speech.

Holy Name officials interpreted this to mean that members should both behave themselves and support the Legion of Decency's efforts. (See chapter 3 for a discussion of the Legion of Decency in Pittsburgh.)

The Holy Name Society was nothing if not patriotic, and so each member professed that

I pledge my loyalty
To the flag of my country
And to the God given principles
Of freedom and justice and happiness
For which it stands.

The Society's officials encouraged members to manifest their love of country and its principles through support for officeholders and through an untiring campaign against Communism at home and abroad.

The Pledge ended,

I dedicate my manhood
To the Honor of the Sacred Name of Jesus
And beg that He will keep me faithful
To these pledges
Until Death.

The Female Devotional Experience

The male-only Holy Name Society was clearly the best-organized and most fully funded lay organization in the Pittsburgh diocese, but women more than men constituted the backbone of devotionalism in the parishes. While Pittsburgh's Catholic men joined the Holy Name Society, Catholic women served in a number of smaller societies that diocesan officials repeatedly attempted to unify under the title Diocesan Council of Catholic Women. Women belonged predominantly to parish organizations such as Rosary and Altar societies and Christian Mothers, but after 1920 American bishops attempted to shape women's experiences and efforts through a national organization called the National Council of Catholic Women (NCCW).[32]

Bishop Dearden reorganized the Pittsburgh DCCW in 1953 and combined an emphasis on popular devotions with support of "Catholic Action," a more public campaign to transform society along Catholic ideals. The new structure incorporated deanery officers and committees and parish councils.[33]

Though Catholic women belonged to separate organizations from their husbands, fathers, and brothers, women's groups emphasized many of the same kinds of devotional practices that male organizations stressed and encouraged the same deference to the pope, bishops, and priests. The Holy Name Society and the Diocesan Council of Catholic Women sometimes organized participation in the same rituals, and the DCCW newsletter on occasion carried messages from HNS spiritual director the Rev. Paul Lackner. The DCCW emphasized a more private or family devotion, however, which encouraged private rosary recitation and parish-based eucharistic adoration, but which discouraged the kinds of large-scale public displays of faith, such as marches and rallies, in which men partook.

Mary Jo Weaver argues that the American bishops founded the National Council of Catholic Women to organize American Catholic women better to work on programs or campaigns that the bishops supported. Given this beginning, Weaver maintains,

> NCCW has consistently reflected the American Catholic experience, espousing causes dear to the hearts of the American hierarchy: their strong opposition to communism and feminism and their support of Radio Free Europe and the Hatch amendment against abortion follow the lead of the bishops exactly.[34]

The Pittsburgh affiliate followed this model very closely. A 1956 issue of the monthly publication *News* maintained that Bishop Dearden brought the Pittsburgh DCCW into existence in order to unite "YOU in your organization to millions of other women throughout the world in doing the work of the Church under the direction of the Hierarchy."[35]

A 1958 issue of the Pittsburgh diocese's monthly newsletter described the process of promoting the cause of Christ in the world as follows:

> The council chain through which programs pass is from National to Diocesan to Deanery to Parish. Reports of accomplishments of these programs pass in reverse—from Parish to Deanery to Diocesan to National. Parish units are the strongest links in the chain because it is in the parishes that the work is done. . . . the success or failure of the NCCW depends upon how effectively the parochial units do the work.[36]

Not surprisingly, therefore, the Pittsburgh Diocesan Council of Catholic Women manifested the same respect for the hierarchy that the Holy Name Society expressed. The DCCW encouraged women to acknowledge each bishop's personal milestones and triumphs. A 1960 issue told members that their officers "will strive to help you put into action the desires of your Bishop for you and your group."[37]

The council's treatment of bishops mirrored closely the Holy Name Society's messages to its members, though the DCCW stressed doing the bishop's will more than did the Holy Name Society. No doubt because the DCCW operated as a group affiliated to the National Council of Catholic Women, which in turn came from the National Catholic Welfare Conference (an organization of American bishops), the DCCW asked member organizations to follow their bishop's desires. The Holy Name Society existed apart from any episcopal structure and sought to follow primarily the pastor's directives. The DCCW's "orders" came from either the NCWC or the Pittsburgh bishop directly, and bypassed the pastor entirely. This led to an interesting, though still deferential, relationship with the pastor.

But the DCCW did not see pastors as intrinsically supportive of their activities, perhaps because pastors had little faith in women's abilities to undertake the more daunting tasks that the DCCW attempted or because the pastors did not directly control or guide the groups. The November 1959 issue told women interested in getting their fellow female parishioners active in parish life to handle the pastor gently.

> Under no circumstances, approach any pastor with the eleven or so projects with the DCCW at one time. If he does not know the setup of the Council on a national, diocesan, deanery, and parish level, he certainly would judge this task impossible. Take a little bit at a time, do it well, and other things can be added as time goes on, and as success is enjoyed.

The issue explained that a "pastor may fear that once the women get started, he may lose all semblance of authority to guide the destinies of his parish."[38]

The DCCW flourished in the 1950s with Bishop Dearden's strong support. In 1956 the Pittsburgh diocese affiliated 252 organizations within the federation, and by June 1957 the Pittsburgh Diocesan Council of Catholic Women boasted of 100 percent membership, by which it meant that each women's organization in each parish affiliated with the DCCW.[39]

The DCCW urged members of the revitalized DCCW to partake in devotional exercises. The Pittsburgh DCCW *News* encouraged members to partake in eucharistic adoration, retreats, and Marian devotions, especially rosaries, though their clear responsibilities raising children and maintaining households discouraged participation in activities outside the home. Women more easily and readily said rosaries than attended retreats and eucharistic adorations, though they did participate to some extent in the latter two activities.

Though the Diocesan Council of Catholic Women encouraged eucharistic adoration and retreats, these devotional practices proved difficult for women. Each demanded that the woman leave the household. A convention speaker in 1959 insisted that "if a woman REALLY wishes to make a retreat, some plan can usually be made for the handling of her usual chores," but the DCCW never presented women with such a plan. The DCCW also supported a Marian devotion in which women could participate in part while at home. At times the Marian devotion carried over into devotions that men reserved for the Trinity. For example, Catholic men attended retreats to open themselves to God and so that God might act on them in some way. The DCCW urged women to attend retreats in part because "the Blessed Mother of God seeks your company."[40] The Holy Name Society asked Catholic men to partake in the Marian devotion too, but the DCCW pushed this more frequently and emphatically for women.

The diocesan moderator, the Rev. William P. Weirauch, told the 1954 convention that the dedication of that year to Mary provided a "single motive for all the actions and endeavors of the women of the diocese" and accounted "above all for the success of this organization during the past year." He suggested further that such a devotion to Mary might offer "to a distressed world a message of hope, a plan for unity and harmony in the affairs of mankind."[41]

Women manifested their devotion to Mary by communicating with her regularly in prayer, by emulating her life, and by visiting shrines in her honor. The DCCW also sought other ways to honor her. It most commonly suggested the recitation of the Hail Mary prayer, often in the context of the rosary, as the best way to honor Mary or to accomplish something else through entreaties to Mary. Many Hail Mary recitations sought to honor or in some way aid the pope and the local bishop. The *News* encouraged members to offer rosaries for vocations in appreciation of the bishop's interest in the DCCW, and to offer directly to the bishop gifts of Hail Marys said in unison at the end of women's meetings— something known as "spiritual bouquets." The *News* asked members to report to the DCCW offices the number of rosaries and spiritual bouquets offered to the bishop so that they might be tallied and presented together.[42]

The reorganized DCCW began a practice of offering these accumulated rosaries and Hail Marys to the bishop at the annual convention and at Christmastime. In 1954 the council announced that "the women of the 270 affiliates of the Pittsburgh Diocesan Council of Catholic Women are reciting rosaries, which will number many, many thousands of this intention: 'THAT GOD WILL BLESS OUR DIOCESE WITH MORE VOCATIONS.'" The announcement continued that the DCCW offered this to Bishop Dearden. The following year the DCCW organized the gift sufficiently well to announce that women had actually recited 20,197 rosaries. The total rosaries offered climbed to 24,855 in 1956 and then to 37,051 in 1957 before the convention book stopped reporting actual rosaries recited. The DCCW presented Bishop Dearden with a 1955 Christmas gift of 248,943 Hail Marys said in unison, and offered 325,000 the following Christmas.[43]

OF ALL THE MATERIALIST THREATS THAT AMERICAN CATHOLICS confronted in the early 1950s Communism loomed largest. Church officials therefore turned their most powerful weapon, the very devotional ethos that had characterized lay religious sensibility since the nineteenth century, against the Red menace. In large-scale public displays of devotional homage to Christ and the Church itself, the hierarchy sought to marshal the Catholic army into battle against materialist Communism. But devotionalism had long meant more than that, and it constituted the longest standing and most widely adhered-to means for Catholics to combat the dangers that materialism presented. American Catholics used their devotional ethos to understand the world and seek to leverage some control over their lives. They understood their families, neighborhoods, and world through a devotional mindset and acted accordingly. No wonder then that Church officials sought to turn this powerful sensibility into a weapon to use against Communism, the greatest materialist threat that they perceived on the world horizon.

The Decline of Devotional Catholicism

Church officials continued throughout the 1950s to emphasize the hierarchically constituted world, the necessity of segregating by gender, the importance of divine intervention in temporal matters, and the immeasurable value of retreating from the sinful world even as they aimed these at the Communist threat. But the laity, who seemed so enthusiastic about this effort in the early 1950s, clearly began to reject the devotional strategy by the decade's end. Chapter 2 traces the lay rejection of devotionalism in the 1950s and proposes an explanation for why the laity found the devotional response unappealing in the years leading to the Second Vatican Council.

Bishop Dearden pushed the laity hard to embrace devotions more fully and to marshal them against the Communist materialist threat. The laity seemed to respond well at first, especially with their enthusiastic participation in the great outdoor public rituals in the early 1950s. But the laity's positive response rapidly gave way to indifference, or even rejection. If diocesan officials saw devotions as the best route to battling Communist materialism in the 1950s, the laity did not long share either the hierarchy's concern for the threat or their confidence in the strategy to combat it.

Catholic men swarmed to the Holy Name Society's 1950 eucharistic rally in Forbes Field, filling the stadium and then surrounding it as fully 115,000 converged on Pittsburgh's Oakland neighborhood. This massive support affirmed the lay commitment to the diocese's emphasis on devotions and public rituals. And though Hugh Boyle served as bishop during the 1950 event, he lay dying in the hospital when the men gathered. The rally really reflected John Dearden's emergence as Pittsburgh's Catholic leader. He fully expected the next eucharistic rally, held in the same place in conjunction with the 1955 Holy Name Society's national convention, at least to replicate if not exceed the 1950 success. After all, thousands of Catholic men from cities like Cleveland, Boston, New York, and even San Antonio would converge that October weekend for a convention that included the eucharistic rally, a major parade down Fifth Avenue, and conference sessions on a host of issues critical to the society's continued success. Event organizers worried about how to accommodate crowds even larger than those that had come to the 1950 event.

Taken out of the context of past public rituals in Pittsburgh, the 1955 events did seem grand. What Pittsburgher could not have been impressed with the two 1955 events? Even had they not actually seen the rally and parade in person or on television, or heard the radio broadcast, the daily papers provided front-page coverage. The *Pittsburgh Post-Gazette* headlines reported 50,000 men present at the Forbes Field eucharistic rally, and the *Pittsburgh Press* predicted on Saturday that 135,000 men would march in Sunday's parade. The rituals provided good copy, as well as opportunities for impressive photographs. Thirty-five thousand candles lit Forbes Field on Friday night. Sixty thousand men marched along Fifth Avenue two days later, including 1,500 New York City policemen and 700 firemen. Five thousand marchers came from Cleveland for the parade (with 500 police and firemen), 1,500 from Philadelphia (50 priests), 500 from Boston, and at least 300 from Louisville, Kentucky.[44]

Nearly sixty floats and thirty bands representing parishes and deaneries throughout the Pittsburgh diocese and beyond rolled down Fifth Avenue. The *Pittsburgh Catholic* called the events the "mightiest religious spectacle in the history of Pittsburgh and one of the greatest ever witnessed anywhere." The Rev. Harry C. Graham, Holy Name Society national director for twenty years, claimed that the 1955 Pittsburgh rally and parade were bigger and better than the 1951 rituals in Detroit, the 1947 events in Boston, and the 1936 convention in New York City.[45]

Moreover, the *Holy Name Newsletter* reported that the rally transformed those who attended. It imparted grace, which engendered a spirit of moderation, comportment, and awe that stayed with the participants through at least the trip home and possibly long enough to empower them to take up the crusade.

> Now it was all over, but you felt something inside you that possibly you had never felt before. Tears had been streaming down the cheeks of not hundreds but thousands of good strong stalwart Catholic men assembled there that night. Without the question being asked, dozens of Pittsburgh policemen volunteered the statement that this was the most orderly crowd they had ever seen at Forbes Field. The street car conductors and the bus operators echoed the same thought. Swiftly, carefully, you were returned to your parish and to your homes. Before you fell asleep you said to yourself "this, I shall remember, this, I shall not forget." And the benefit you received was a special grace given to you that night by almighty God for having participated in this Eucharistic Rally.[46]

The 1955 rally did succeed on many levels, and viewed by itself could reasonably be seen as further lay affirmation of the devotional ethos. But understood in the context of previous rallies, the 1955 events testified more to Catholic devotionalism's decline than to its continued rise. For though thousands turned out, the event did not measure up to similar public rituals held within the past decade, and fell far short of published expectations. Despite Father Graham's observation that the Pittsburgh rituals were the biggest in Holy Name history, the 1947 Boston eucharistic rally saw 15,000 more men crowd into Braves Field than had packed Pittsburgh's Forbes Field. Pittsburgh's 1955 parade had 60 floats and 30 bands, but Boston's had 75 floats and 106 bands. While 60,000 men marched in Pittsburgh's parade, 130,000 marched in Boston. And 100,000 spectators lined Pittsburgh's parade route while 3.5 million stood to see the Boston parade.[47]

Much of Boston's greater turnout might be attributed to the city's larger size, but prior public rituals in Pittsburgh also outshone the 1955 events. Eucharistic rallies in previous years drew significantly more men to Pittsburgh's Forbes Field and the University of Pittsburgh Stadium. Roughly 75,000 men came to a Forbes Field rally in 1930; 90,000 packed Pitt Stadium in 1936; and 80,000 jammed in and around Forbes Field in 1941. Most impressively, 115,000 engulfed Forbes Field just five years before the 1955 eucharistic rally—fully 80,000 more than the 1955 crowd.[48] (See fig. 2.1.)

FIGURE 2.1 Attendance at Pittsburgh Eucharistic Rallies

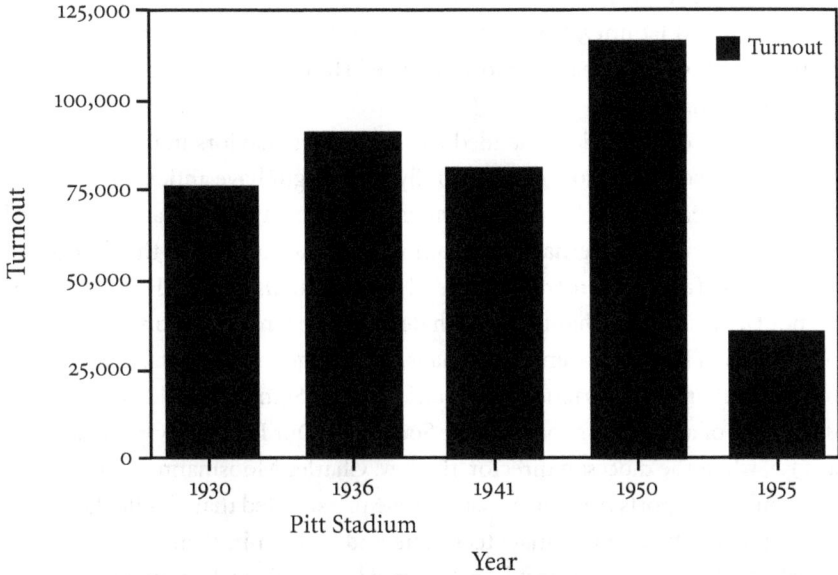

Source: Pittsburgh Catholic.

The 1955 turnout not only paled in comparison to previous rituals, but must have disappointed 1955 organizers as well. The Holy Name Society had ordered 80,000 candles for the eucharistic rally but could distribute fewer than half of these. The *Pittsburgh Catholic* boasted just days before the rally that 100,000 men would crowd in and around Forbes Field on Friday night, a projection that likely exaggerated the turnout by nearly 200 percent. The *Pittsburgh Catholic* also claimed that Sunday's parade would include 125,000 Holy Name men, while the actual numbers constituted just under half of that projection. The *Pittsburgh Press* told its readers that 135,000 marchers would participate in the parade.[49]

The numbers that had so recently and consistently testified to growing success in the Catholic devotional struggle with materialism turned suddenly wrong. Catholics no longer embraced the eucharistic rally to the same degree as they had in the past. And it appeared that the laity had cooled to other public rituals as well. The Christian Mothers, the Catholic Daughters of America, and the Sodalities of Washington County hosted a "Family Hour of Prayer" at Canonsburg Stadium in August 1955. The two-hour service included a "living rosary," formed by 150 women out on the field, four priests' talks, and the blessing of a relic from the newly canonized Saint Pius X. Organizers announced that

10,000 women would turn out for the event, but only 5,000 actually came.[50] Just four years earlier, when Catholic women hosted a Marian eucharistic rally in Westmoreland County, the turnout was double that which organizers anticipated. In 1955 only half of those expected showed up. The numbers disappointed again.

Had diocesan officials attended closely to lay behaviors in the years since the wildly successful 1950 eucharistic rally, they might have anticipated the 1955 decline. Evidence of the lay disengagement from devotional behaviors surfaced in a number of areas. Perhaps most ominous for supporters of the devotional prescription (and demonstrated so clearly by the August Family Hour of Prayer turnout), the lay disenchantment with devotions extended to women as well as men. Women had long been devotionalism's strongest supporters, and any sign of female alienation portended difficulties ahead. Signs abounded in the most devotional of all women's societies, the Sodality of Our Lady. They began as early as 1952, when the diocesan director, the Rev. Charles Moosmann, started relaying troubling reports from area pastors. One priest noted that his efforts to generate spirituality among female teenagers and women in their twenties in his parish had become "an almost hopeless case today." They demonstrated no interest in spiritual or moral uplift, and when he attempted to get them to participate in spiritual programs,

> they refuse to cooperate. The only time you can get Catholics, young or old, to turn out in large numbers and to show some half-hearted interest, is when the societies run a dance at some public hall, or hold a general Communion, with an elaborate breakfast in the hall below the church, while Masses are going on upstairs.

Moosmann commented that "no sodality should be allowed to deteriorate into a mere social club." Sodalities should sponsor only a few social events, and if the girls and young women do not come to the spiritual meetings, then stop inviting them. "Better a small sodality of zealous members, than a long list of names at every reception or so-called reorganization, every year or two!"[51]

Perhaps in an effort to offset the decline in sodality devotional participation, the Reverend Moosmann attempted to regenerate interest in a program that had proved very successful just a few years earlier. At that time, five thousand sodalists from eighty-five parishes participated in a week of devotional exercises centered on four Pittsburgh churches strategically located throughout the city. These predominantly working women began the week with a Sunday evening kick-off session, then rose early each morning to attend daily Mass and receive Communion before heading off to work. Each evening they ate dinner in town and then went to the evening missions. They completed the week with a Sunday evening consecration to the Blessed Virgin. At the last session, participants pledged to avoid mixed marriages and to refrain from intercourse before they married. Each woman presented her registration card at every devotional function that she attended so that officials could certify her presence. By the week's end, hundreds presented cards testifying that they had attended every activity, and thousands made each evening session. "If others have done it— why can't we to-day?" Moosmann asked. He encouraged sodalists to organize a similar event in their upcoming meeting and to hold it during October, a month already focused heavily on devotions. No one did. That such a program focused on working women reflected the Church's discomfort with women in the workplace—a perspective mirrored in the specific pledges program organizers asked women to take. That such a program no longer appealed to working women in 1952 reveals a great deal about women's changed attitudes.

Women's interest in devotional exercises seemed only to slacken over time. The pastor of a large and successful parish with six crowded Sunday Masses reported a troubling decline in attendance at devotional activities. He lamented that "by actual count hardly 40 to 50 persons come to our evening devotions." Moreover, "not even sodalists will attend on the evening especially assigned to them. What is wrong? What more beautiful opportunity to think of God and His Blessed Mother between Sundays! Not even Benediction with the Most Blessed Sacrament, with which the devotions end, will induce Catholics to come more regularly." The lack of interest baffled pastors. Why did women, who only recently appeared eager to attend devotions, stop coming? The Reverend Moosmann asked the question again the following year: "Why are churches crowded for five or six Masses on Sundays and hardly half-filled for the special devotions, sermons and Stations of the Cross ...?"[52] Had women's changed social roles made them less receptive to the devotional messages?

Even a special devotional campaign that Bishop Dearden initiated himself, with extensive media coverage and widespread clergy support, could not generate sustained lay participation. The program began successfully enough, and seemed at the outset to provide only affirmation for the devotional prescription that Bishop Dearden so resolutely advanced. Dearden determined in February 1955 that each parish in the diocese would begin a perpetual adoration program on Ash Wednesday. But unlike previous programs, which ran for a defined period of time and aimed at a short-term goal, this program would go on forever.

Dearden worked out all the details for the program and announced them in the newly acquired *Pittsburgh Catholic* before he even notified pastors. The Holy Name Society and the Diocesan Council of Catholic Women were to promote the campaign through the newly formed HNS "Our Lady of Fatima Committee for Daily Eucharistic Adoration." Pastors had the responsibility to make sure that the laity in each parish established bulletin boards on which they kept the adoration schedule. Parish adoration committees distributed devotional literature to all those attending and made sure to record all special intentions. Bishop Dearden promised great benefits to the diocese if parishioners participated, and pointed to one parish where perpetual adoration produced greater Mass attendance and increased Communion reception. The Pittsburgh program aimed for three outcomes: true and lasting world peace, increased vocations to the priesthood and religious life, and the conversion of sinners. The *Pittsburgh Catholic* urged all area Catholics to participate, if only to show God that America was better than Communist nations, where antipathy for Christ could be understood. Though the program began on Ash Wednesday, all promotional materials emphasized that "the Daily Eucharistic Adoration will be a continuing one that will be carried on every day of the year."[53]

The laity responded enthusiastically at first. More than 80 percent of diocesan parishes sent representatives to the deanery-level organizational meetings at which participants made plans to implement the bishop's wishes. The turnout for the planning sessions led Father Lackner to predict a high attendance at adoration. Organizers distributed 150,000 adoration leaflets explaining the program, 100,000 religious cards to give to each worshiper, and 75,000 petition leaflets on which participants could write individual petitions. The *Pittsburgh Catholic* reported after Ash Wednesday that "thousands of men, women and children thronged their churches to combine the traditional Ash Wednesday rites with the inauguration of the new program of devotions designed to pay perpetual homage to their Eucharistic King." The *Pittsburgh Catholic*'s spot check of parishes in different parts of the diocese generated reports from pastors that attendance was "satisfactory," "better than expected," or even "excellent." It reported that people often stayed beyond their half-hour time slot, and that mothers with young children brought them along for the adoration. Father Lackner reported that

> The response has exceeded our highest expectations. The reports of the turnouts everywhere on Ash Wednesday are truly amazing, and most edifying. With such a fine start, I am confident that the attendance figures will continue to be high all during Lent, and that after Easter, the Daily Eucharis-

tic Adoration program will have become a glorious tradition throughout the year in the Diocese of Pittsburgh.[54]

Father Lackner had every reason to be optimistic, as the Holy Name Society and the Diocesan Council of Catholic Women had made adoration a top priority. The DCCW newsletter featured a front-page exhortation for women to participate in "Daily Eucharistic Adoration," and urged its members to visit church at least every other week to pray before Christ's body. It promised great blessings for all participating parishes and individuals. The *Holy Name Newsletter* similarly highlighted the program and urged members to use it as a foundation for bringing Christ into all areas of their lives.[55]

Pastors generally supported the daily adoration program initially, just as instructed. Immaculate Heart of Mary's bulletin told parishioners that Bishop Dearden asked each of them to give a half hour each week to a daily adoration program that would begin on Ash Wednesday and "continue every day of the year." Because Immaculate Heart of Mary parish had no DCCW society, the parish Holy Name Society promoted the devotion. Similarly, the newly formed suburban Saint Thomas More parish bulletin announced the program and asked parishioners to commit in writing to a time slot by the following Wednesday (Ash Wednesday). By contrast, the urban territorial St. Philomena parish bulletin made no mention of the program at all.[56]

In every exhortation to participate, in each presentation of the adoration in the diocesan paper and society newsletters, as well as from the pulpit, Church officials stressed that this adoration would go year-round. It was truly perpetual and represented a new era in Catholic devotional life. In May the DCCW *News* enjoined members to "never, never cease to beseech the Living Presence of God for world peace, for religious vocations and for the conversion of sinners."[57]

But two weeks into Lent, in the midst of what Father Lackner had termed "truly amazing" turnouts, Immaculate Heart of Mary parishioners had not committed themselves. A second announcement called upon "every decent parishioner" to sign up for a half-hour time slot and extended the possible intentions beyond Bishop Dearden's three to include

> temperance, world peace, conversion of Russia, deceased members of the family, to be blessed with children, vocations, control of temper, recovery of health, Poor souls, business problems, safe return of those in service, guidance in life, good marriages, for the fallen away, purity, peace in the family, bringing up of children, morality among youth, employment, happy death, etc.

On the Sunday following Easter the bulletin told parishioners who had enrolled but had stopped coming that they must persist in their devotion "or give reason why they do not wish to continue" to the Our Lady of Fatima Committee "by phone or letter." In December the *Holy Name Newsletter* noted a slackened attendance at the adoration in parishes overall and announced that the HNS Our Lady of Fatima Daily Adoration Committee would soon initiate a new campaign to increase devotions.[58]

By June even the DCCW *News* reported that while adorations had yielded an "increase" in religious vocations, parishes ran the risk of lapsing in their adoration practices. It warned members to be "untiring and ceaseless" in their efforts. Mention of eucharistic adoration became less and less frequent in the *News* over the course of the next year, and it more often than not came in a trio of "spiritual" activities that the DCCW encouraged: the Mass, adoration, and retreats. By January 1956 the *Pittsburgh Catholic* as much as admitted the program's failure by reintroducing it as though for the first time. Though the announcement referred to the 1956 program as an enhancement of the existing adoration activities, and framed the new exhortation as a call for an increase in the current participation level, it also noted that "in some instances, interest waned with the passing of time." Despite the repeated explanations that the adoration would continue year-round, the *Pittsburgh Catholic* suggested that in other instances, confusion about its intended duration caused problems. It reported that some lay men and women "were of the opinion that the program was instituted only for the Lenten season." No matter; with the bishop's new letter to priests instructing them to "offer their people every possible encouragement" to participate, the parishes would surely see increased participation and the diocese would just as surely receive untold blessings.[59]

Again the program met fleeting success. Saint Thomas More parishioners encountered mention of the program only among a list of eight recommended Lenten exercises, sandwiched between Sunday afternoon sermons by a Redemptorist preacher from Saint Philomena's and the family rosary. The DCCW exhorted women to "encourage the members of families and neighbors to keep the *Daily Eucharistic Adoration* devotion alive." The following February the *News* asked members to revitalize the devotion quickly, before Lent began, so that women in their parishes would not think that it was for Lent only. But women did not respond, and the Archconfraternity of Christian Mothers then joined the DCCW in an effort to get women to participate during Lent itself. While admitting that in some parishes "the request has not been answered as well as it might have been," the organization noted in its *Pittsburgh Catholic* column that the "faithful" had responded well in many parishes. Why not emulate the successful parishes? After all,

> while the Eucharistic visits were not meant to be a Lenten exercise, the penitential season is a good time to start or begin again. If faithfulness to the half-hour visits is practiced during Lent, there will be no difficulty in carrying out the practice throughout the year. In this way we will benefit, as well as the family, the parish and all those who come within the circle of our influence.[60]

Continued lay indifference stifled all attempts to revive the practice, and organizers found themselves without a strategy to revive the devotional program. By October 1957 Father Lackner admitted that "at this day, [adoration] does not enjoy the same vitality in all parishes that it had when it was inaugurated." The HNS Eucharistic Committee had resorted to "laying plans to reinvigorate the program in the parishes."[61] But if the committee ever devised such plans, it never revealed them to the larger community. Despite the bishop's imprimatur, a massive media campaign, and exhortations from parish priests, parishioners did not heed the call. The daily eucharistic adoration program died within a year and a half of its birth, after seventeen months of illness. A 1959 attempt to resurrect the program failed miserably as well, as the Pittsburgh laity demonstrated no interest in daily adoration.[62]

Of the three parishes upon which this study focuses, Saint Philomena's in Squirrel Hill took least notice of Bishop Dearden's daily adoration campaign. A number of possible reasons explain this. The Redemptorists who ran the parish operated with a degree of autonomy that few other parishes in the diocese shared. The order owned the property on which Saint Philomena school and rectory stood (the school contained the church), which made it one of the few pieces of Catholic real estate in the diocese that the bishop did not own himself. Saint Philomena's pastors rotated through the parish with such regularity that they had little investment in pleasing the local bishop. Their significant relationships, lasting friendships, and fundamental loyalties lay within the Redemptorist order, not with the Pittsburgh ordinary. But the most likely reason the parish took little note of the bishop's adoration campaign was that the parish already maintained a heavy devotional schedule, including weekly Sunday afternoon adoration. The Redemptorists made their mark in missions, in the work of regenerating parish interest and commitment to the Church, and in postwar America this meant breathing life into parish devotional culture. The Redemptorists at

Saint Philomena were likely the most sympathetic of all parish priests to the renewed energy Bishop Dearden wanted to infuse into parish devotional practices.

At first blush, then, Saint Philomena's lack of interest in Bishop Dearden's devotional plans seems to derive less from a decline in devotional fervor within the parish than to a fervor directed in other devotional manifestations. But upon closer examination, even Saint Philomena parish provides strong evidence for a decline in Catholic devotional practices. For a decline could be seen even within Saint Philomena's signature devotional practice, the perpetual novena to Our Lady of Perpetual Help.

For twenty years following 1930 Catholic women and men flocked to Saint Philomena Church in Pittsburgh's east end to participate in the novena to Our Lady of Perpetual Help. In doing so, they joined with thousands of other Catholics across America performing devotions to perhaps the most popular religious icon of the twentieth century. Though the priests at Saint Philomena had long encouraged parishioners to support the devotion, it grew to great popularity when the pastor, Father Meighan, began the perpetual weekly novena in 1930. From that point on, Catholics could attend any series of nine consecutive Wednesday services, which included a sermon, public prayers and hymns, blessing of the sick, benediction, and then veneration of the painting at the Communion rail. They attended in greater and greater numbers as time passed. Eventually, the ritual proved so popular that Father Meighan had to schedule five separate meeting times each Wednesday to accommodate the pressing demand. He encouraged other parishes to begin devotions to Our Lady of Perpetual Help as well, both to relieve the pressure on his parish and to spread the veneration even wider. By 1939 forty-four parishes and convents in the Pittsburgh diocese offered weekly novenas of their own. Still the crowds came to Saint Philomena's every Wednesday, so that each session averaged 340 participants, exceeding the small church's seating capacity. On some special occasions, such as the 1933 Immaculate Conception novena, 4,000 Catholics crowded in and around the church for nine consecutive weeks.[63]

But in 1950 the crowds began to thin. In fact, their numbers declined so rapidly that by the end of the decade the once popular devotion drew only 40 percent of the 1950 attendance. Attendance at the perpetual novena to Our Lady of Perpetual Help had undergone fluctuations before, but these changes resulted from readily identifiable short-term causes.[64] The 1950s decline began a long slide in participation from which the devotion never recovered. The Redemptorist priests who ran the parish continued to emphasize the devotion fervently throughout the decade, so that parishioners and others could have perceived no lessening of official sanction and encouragement for the practice. The parish introduced no alternative devotion in the period to draw potential participants away from the novena to Our Lady of Perpetual Help. The parish population fluctuated a bit through the decade but remained relatively stable and could not explain the steep decline in attendance.

Diocesan officials had grown accustomed in the early 1950s to pointing to the numbers of Catholics who participated in devotional exercises, especially the large-scale public rituals, as proof that the Church could overcome the materialist crisis. But now the numbers turned against them. The laity simply did not support the devotional prescription as before. Though one might expect the change to have troubled the clergy, they seem not to have noticed. In fact, in their public statements they simply continued to assert what had once been true: that the laity affirmed religion's primacy with their increasing participation in devotional activities. Despite the lay trend away from certain devotions, Church officials continued to hail the "increasing" participation as proof of the Church's strength to meet the materialist challenge.

To be sure, the laity had not yet disengaged from all devotional activities, and in fact continued to increase their participation in at least one highly visible and readily quantified activity almost up until the Second Vatican Council began meeting. Throughout the 1950s, more and more men left their homes and families to attend overnight or extended weekend retreats at Catholic monasteries and colleges. In doing so they continued a trend that had begun early in the century, accelerated in the years following World War II, and peaked in the early 1960s. Church officials could, and did, point to these numbers as evidence for the success of the devotional strategy. (See fig. 2.2.)

But after fifty years of steadily increasing their participation in retreats, Pittsburgh laymen came to abandon even retreats in the early 1960s. Not even the establishment of parish retreat clubs, the expansion of facilities at Saint Paul's retreat house in Pittsburgh, and powerful episcopal voices in support could keep men attending in the same high numbers throughout the 1960s as they had in the late 1950s. In fact, attendance plummeted right through the 1960s until it reached less than half of the decade's opening participation level. That attendance peaked at Saint Vincent College before the Second Vatican Council's opening session and at Saint Paul's Retreat House the same year that Vatican II began suggests that laymen had begun to reject this form of devotional behavior independent of Council developments.

The data for women's participation is less clear than for men, and it suggests that women abandoned retreats earlier and more dramatically than did men. According to the *Pittsburgh Catholic*, nearly 80 percent fewer women attended retreats in 1955 than had participated just four years earlier.[65]

FIGURE 2.2   Laymen's Retreat Totals

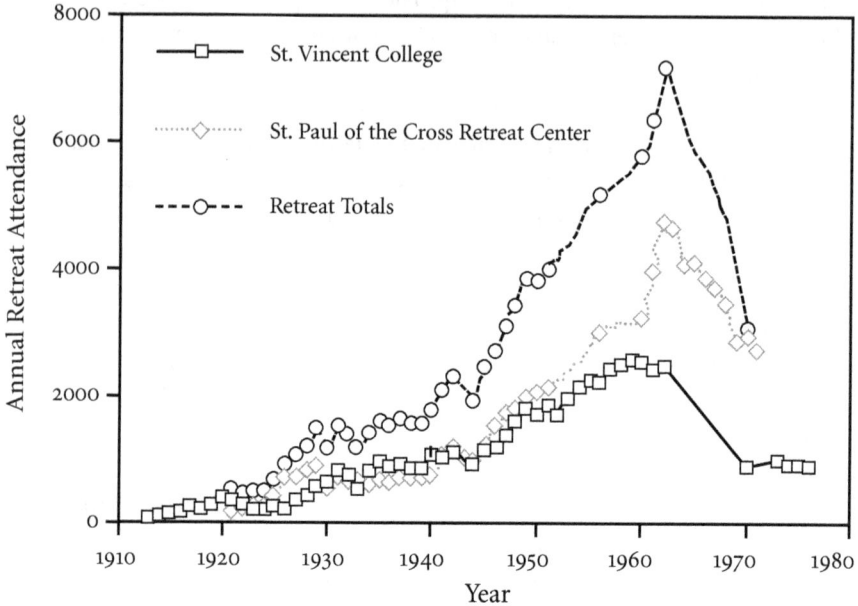

Sources: *Pittsburgh Catholic,* Saint Vincent Archabbey Archives, Saint Paul Archives.

CAUSES OF DECLINE

Though evidence suggests strongly that laymen and laywomen participated less and less in devotional activities in the years leading up to the Second Vatican Council, it does not so clearly explain the reasons for the decline. In part this results from the persistent emphasis in the public discourse, which remained heavily prescriptive throughout the period, on continuing devotional practices. The public discourse admitted of no debate about devotionalism's efficacy, and recognized no trend away from full and enthusiastic participation. The *Pittsburgh Catholic* and the men's and women's organizations' newsletters never consciously addressed the decline, let alone sought to explain it. Rather they continued to recommend devotions as a hierarchically supported means to battle the materialist crisis and to bring individuals to greater holiness. Furthermore, Catholic devotional decline did not result from any opportunity shortage. The structures of devotional Catholicism outlasted lay interest. Parishes continued to offer novenas, missions, and forty-hours devotions even as fewer and fewer parishioners participated, and diocesan officials continued to push private devotions throughout the period.

The most fruitful explanations for the decline come from examining lay lives, and especially changes in their lives, in light of the messages that devotional practices reinforced. In other words, Catholics who came to reject devotional practices made a choice to do so. That choice derived from their perception that the devotions no longer served them in satisfying ways. By understanding the messages that devotions conveyed to participants, we can better understand why Catholics increasingly rejected them.

Weakening Foundations of the Devotional Ethos

Recall Jay Dolan's explication of a devotional ethos that developed in the middle of the nineteenth century and reached its apogee in the decades after World War I. He described a religious sensibility that rested on respect for clerical authority, a strong emphasis on the prevalence of sin, an affinity for formal ritual, and a belief in the miraculous.[66] Inherited devotional practices not only flourished in such a culture, but depended and insisted upon it. As these messages no longer resonated among lay Catholics, the devotional faith that they fostered and which depended upon them declined. Developments in the 1950s touched profoundly on at least two of these areas, and weakened lay attachment to the devotional foundation that Dolan described.

The Decline of Deference

Church officials framed devotional practices, and particularly the large-scale devotional rituals, as a Catholic response to materialist Communism. Thus lay Catholics who took the discourse seriously understood their participation to be a clerically sanctioned resistance to Communist influences on American society and culture. So long as the Communist menace came from outside the United States, or from marginal or unempowered sources within the nation, Catholics could simultaneously and comfortably exercise anti-Communism and deference to "authority." Church authority and civil authority both supported challenges to Communism, and Catholic devotional culture affirmed these deferential manifestations of the anti-Communist impulse.

Once the anti-Communist movement called Catholics to challenge authority, however, even if those challenges concentrated on civil authority, it ran counter to the devotional ethos' emphasis on deference. Catholics could not readily reconcile the attacks on the U.S. president with their deferential devotional practices. Thus *Pittsburgh Catholic* editor John Collins could both praise official anti-Communist efforts that the FBI and the Justice Department undertook and decry Joseph McCarthy's attacks on the State Department. Collins opposed McCarthy not only because he attacked "innocent" and vulnerable citizens, but because he operated outside accepted structures of authority. One can detect this in Collins's early rebuke of McCarthy: "If [McCarthy] has proofs of what he alleges, he should present proofs to the proper authorities so that, by constitutional procedures, the guilty may be punished."[67] The reckless attacks in the press simply weakened the authority that the civil government held in society. Similarly, Catholics who sang the national anthem at eucharistic rallies and prayed for ailing civil officials (as Holy Name members did for President Eisenhower in 1955) had to integrate these signs of civil deference with the vicious attacks on civil officials that they read in Fr. Richard Ginder's and Luis Budenz's newspaper columns.

Ironically, when Catholic officials so closely linked devotional participation with attacks on authority, even civil authority, they weakened the very ethos they sought to marshal on their behalf.

The Declining Need for Miracles

The devotional ethos included a strong belief in miracles, not only in the repository of Church tradition, but in the everyday lives of ordinary Catholics who struggled with problems in the nineteenth and twentieth centuries. Catholics who participated in devotions clearly did so with specific, often material, ends in mind. They prayed to find marriage partners, to heal illness, to escape financial pressures, to keep their loved ones safe from harm, and to discern their vocations in life. They sought through devotional practices to gain supernatural intervention to master their temporal conditions. So long as Catholics could not exercise autonomy and control over their temporal lives, they sought help from Mary, other saints, and God.

Once Catholics found alternate routes to temporal stability, they no longer responded to the miraculous aspect of devotional religion as powerfully as they had previously. Critical scientific developments (particularly in medicine) and economic growth during the 1950s eroded devotionalism's power to attract lay Catholics. By the middle of the 1950s, many Catholics believed that they had achieved a level of control over their own lives that diminished their need to seek assistance from elsewhere.

One of devotionalism's greatest appeals was its ability to transcend scientific limits and the natural order in the service of ordinary people. This was most evident when Catholics confronted terrible illnesses that physicians (representatives of science) pronounced themselves unable to cure. Devotional literature abounded with testimony from Catholics who found their participation efficacious. A story from a Saint Philomena parishioner, published in the Our Lady of Perpetual Help newsletter, mirrors dozens of other stories published each year. The Saint Philomena parishioner wrote in to relate that "my child became dangerously ill" shortly after the parishioner began her first novena to Our Lady of Perpetual Help. The story continued, "I received word that the child was dying and could not live. The doctors all agreed on this verdict." The parishioner "immediately thought of O.M.P.H. [Our Mother of Perpetual Help]. I came to the church—and prayed at her shrine—asking her to save my child. Today my child is at home and fully recovered contrary to all expectations."[68]

In still another story from Saint Philomena's parish, a young boy fell while climbing a fence and punctured his intestines. Physicians determined that the injury had become so infected as to prevent intervention. They closed up the wound and told the boy's parents that he would almost surely die. Many parishioners then devoted their just-begun nine-day Feast of Our Lady of Perpetual Help to the boy's recovery. Soon after the feast's conclusion, doctors recognized a change in the boy's condition which allowed them to operate and save his life.[69]

In the second case recounted above the problem was a dangerous infection that doctors could not treat effectively. In this instance it cleared up without medical intervention, though in others the infections did not. People died or faced long periods of debilitation as infections ravaged their bodies. The development and widespread use of antibiotics in the middle of the twentieth century alleviated a range of health threats that once terrified Americans. This advance alone provided greater security for American Catholics.

But the most powerful medical scare in the middle of the twentieth century continued into the 1950s. Poliomyelitis, better known simply as polio, struck children and young adults in epidemic waves that left thousands of victims in its wake. Though many died outright, others became disabled, dependent upon leg braces and wheelchairs. They not only suffered themselves, but also served as visible reminders of the danger that threatened the nation's children. Successive outbreaks in 1950 and 1952 helped to fuel a massive federally supported initiative to devise a cure or vaccination. Roughly 100 million Americans contributed to a March of Dimes campaign to raise money to find a cure. Then Dr. Jonas Salk announced in 1953 that he had developed a vaccination in his University of Pittsburgh laboratory (located just blocks away from Saint Paul's Cathedral). He mounted a successful national inoculation program by 1954–55. Historian James Paterson describes the national response when Salk announced in April 1955 that the vaccine proved effective: "It was one of the most exciting days of the decade. People honked their horns, rang bells, fired off salutes, dropped work, closed schools, and thanked God for deliverance."[70] Medical science had produced one of its greatest triumphs in modern history and alleviated millions of Americans' fears.

General increases in wealth also contributed to Catholic distancing from the miraculous. As Catholics achieved a modicum of financial security their need for supernatural intervention to stave off oppressive debt or to achieve physical comfort diminished.

Many factors contributed to American Catholics' climb to financial security. The general national prosperity following World War II created employment opportunities nonexistent just a few years before. The GI Bill played a major role in affording veterans opportunities to share in that boom through education and housing subsidies, and unions successfully raised workers' incomes throughout the period. Both real weekly wages and family income sky-rocketed between 1950 and 1960. Economic historians refer to the twenty-five years following World War II as the "longest and most successful period of expansion in American history." And unlike that of the 1990s, this expansion narrowed the distance between the rich and poor workers. The disparity in wages between high- and low-paid workers fell at the end of World War II and stayed relatively low throughout the postwar era.[71]

The situation in Pittsburgh mirrored that of the nation at large. Pittsburgh's working class generally improved its financial situation from the end of World War II through 1960. Ethnic working-class Pittsburghers, for example, saw greater upward social mobility between 1945 and 1960 than in any period since 1900.[72]

The greatest economic change throughout the period was the rise in women's participation in the paid workforce, and especially married women's participation (which accounts for the continued rise in family income even after real weekly wages declined). Because devotional Catholicism depended so much on women's participation, it suffered disproportionately from this development. Pittsburgh women appear to have followed the national trend toward working outside the home during the same years that devotionalism declined in the diocese. In 1940, 78,022 (28 percent) of the 275,190 women who lived in the city of Pittsburgh worked outside of their homes for pay. The figure may have fluctuated in the 1940s, as women's participation did nationally. If so, Pittsburgh women would have entered the workforce during the war and then exited as men returned. The census reports the 1950 level of female work outside the home to be roughly the same as that of 1940. But Pittsburgh women increasingly worked through the 1950s until by 1960, 34 percent held jobs outside their homes. The rate climbed again through the 1960s until 38 percent of the 213,543 women in Pittsburgh held paying jobs.[73]

Married women especially formed the backbone of Catholic devotional life, and some data on married women's work patterns exists. Variations in the way the census reported information across these decades make clear statements about Pittsburgh married women's work patterns between 1940 and 1960 impossible, though we can discern some facts. Female city residents who fell into the age bracket 35–44 years old (those most likely already to have married and not yet become widows) increased their paid labor force participation rate from 27 percent to 39 percent between 1940 and 1960.[74]

Pittsburgh women, and particularly those of marriage age, clearly worked outside their homes for pay in greater and greater numbers after World War II than before, with the most dramatic increases occurring in the same years that lay participation in devotions throughout the diocese declined so significantly.

Pittsburgh Catholics may have become less attached to formal ritual and less fearful of the consequences of sin in the 1950s, developments that clearly occurred by the 1970s. Though declining participation in devotional rituals could have resulted from disenchantment with ritual generally, Catholics attended Mass more regularly during the decade than in any other period for which good data exists. This suggests that the laity did not reject ritual per se, but simply preferred some types over others. Similarly, concern about sin and its consequences, which so pervaded the devotional discourse, had to share ground with an emphasis on the positive consequences of living virtuously.

Family Life and Suburbanization

In addition to those factors that touched directly on the four characteristics of the Catholic devotional ethos that Jay Dolan identified, other changes affected devotionalism's lure for Pittsburgh Catholics. Catholics structured devotional activities toward individual adults, and typically segregated them by gender. High marriage rates, the baby boom, and suburbanization made this structure both less feasible and less desirable for Catholics.

Catholics organized much of their devotional experiences as male- or female-only activities. The large-scale eucharistic rallies held in Pittsburgh sports arenas included only men, while only women attended the Marian eucharistic rally in the Saint Vincent College football stadium. The retreat movement carefully segregated men from women, as did almost every other organized devotional activity.

Even the radio rosary program prohibited mixed gender groups. By the 1950s Catholics could tune in to at least one rosary recitation session each night on the radio. WCAE broadcast sessions six nights each week, while the seventh varied across time among a few other stations. The typical program consisted of a guest leader, almost always a priest, and a group of adult respondents who taped the show on the day of the broadcast. Consistent with the Church's practice of segregating many of its functions, and nearly all of its devotional activities, by gender, no respondent group included men and women. Church officials explained that mixed groups contained such a variety of voice ranges that they would not carry well on the radio, though this position was more asserted than demonstrated.

But social developments in the 1950s made such an organization difficult for Catholics. The baby boom had a great impact on any activity that called women away from their families. Mothers found it increasingly difficult as their families grew to leave the house or apartment without children in tow. Even when devotion organizers invited women to bring their children, the nature of devotional experiences did not lend itself well to children's dispositions. The perpetual adoration campaign, for example, did not specifically exclude children or even mixed groups of males and females from participating. An early report on the devotion's success even applauded mothers who brought their young children along for the hour or half-hour session spent in silent mediation before the exposed Eucharist. But Catholic mothers recognized the difficulty that such an activity presented. Few infants or toddlers, let alone young school-age children, readily managed the self-discipline involved in attending Mass. Silent adoration required children to exercise extraordinary self-control, and few mothers welcomed the prospect of keeping order while concentrating on their meditation.

More significantly, the suburban social ideal did not favor separating families for social activities. Instead, it encouraged family-centered ventures that drew together rather than separated mothers, fathers, and children. Margaret Marsh suggests that such an ideal emerged in the early decades of the twentieth century in which men and women shared more leisure time together, and men took on greater family responsibilities. This new social ideal, which Marsh calls "masculine domesticity," encouraged men to play larger roles in child rearing, to spend less time with male friends, and to take on "limited domestic duties." Other evidence supports this merging of family and suburban ideals. William Dobriner reported after his review of all available quantitative studies of 1940s and 1950s suburban migration that Americans moved primarily for family reasons—they thought the suburbs were better for children, and they chose their place of residence around their children's needs.[75]

Marsh is not alone in suggesting that the suburbs raised the family's role at the expense of the street, neighborhood, or other social sphere found in urban living. Sam Bass Warner made a similar argument in his influential *The Private*

City and *Streetcar Suburbs* decades earlier, and others have explored this claim for suburbanization in the 1950s and 1960s. Even academics who seek to downplay the differences between urban and suburban social experience suggest that a more family-centered social life existed in the suburbs than in central cities.[76] Perhaps most significantly, John Modell concluded from his examination of ward-level data in four American cities that the suburbs differed from the inner cities in family patterns more in the period after World War II than in the decades from which Marsh derived her understanding of the distinctive suburban social ideal. In other words, Modell's work suggests that Marsh's distinctions between urban and suburban ideals likely would be more pronounced in the 1950s than in the 1920s.[77]

Other historians highlight this transformation in lifestyle as Americans moved to the suburbs as well, and suggest that the concentration on family pushed people away from commitments to participation in larger social networks. S. D. Clark concluded from his study of Canadian suburbs that the "evidence was overwhelming of a general social apathy among the [suburban] population, of an unwillingness to become in any way involved in forms of organized activity demanding time, effort, and money." This perceived reluctance to engage in outside activities led those studying Protestant suburbanites to focus their work on whether or not the suburbs fostered secularization.[78]

Though the ideal first developed early in the century, it was rooted in the architectural designs, housing plans, commuting patterns, and social organization of the suburbs. Catholic men and women would have lived this ideal as they moved to the suburbs, which they did in greater and greater numbers in the aftermath of World War II.

By the middle of the 1950s, Americans had already begun to move to the suburbs at the rapid rate that would push the suburban population above both the central-city and rural populations by the end of the next decade. The suburban population grew more than four times faster than the central-city population in America during the 1950s, so that 13 million more Americans moved to the suburbs than to the central cities in the decade. Suburban population growth constituted 76 percent of metropolitan-area growth in the 1950s. This trend was even more pronounced in manufacturing belt cities, such as Pittsburgh, where the suburban population expanded while the central-city population actually declined. Between 1950 and 1960 the city of Pittsburgh had a net loss of 72,474 people, or 11 percent of its population, while the area outside the city grew by 22 percent. The suburbs in Allegheny County alone saw an even more significant increase of roughly 40 percent.[79] While it is impossible to determine precisely what percentage of suburbanites Catholics constituted, there is no evidence that Catholics remained disproportionately in the city.

FIGURE 2.3   Pittsburgh Urban and Suburban Parish School Population

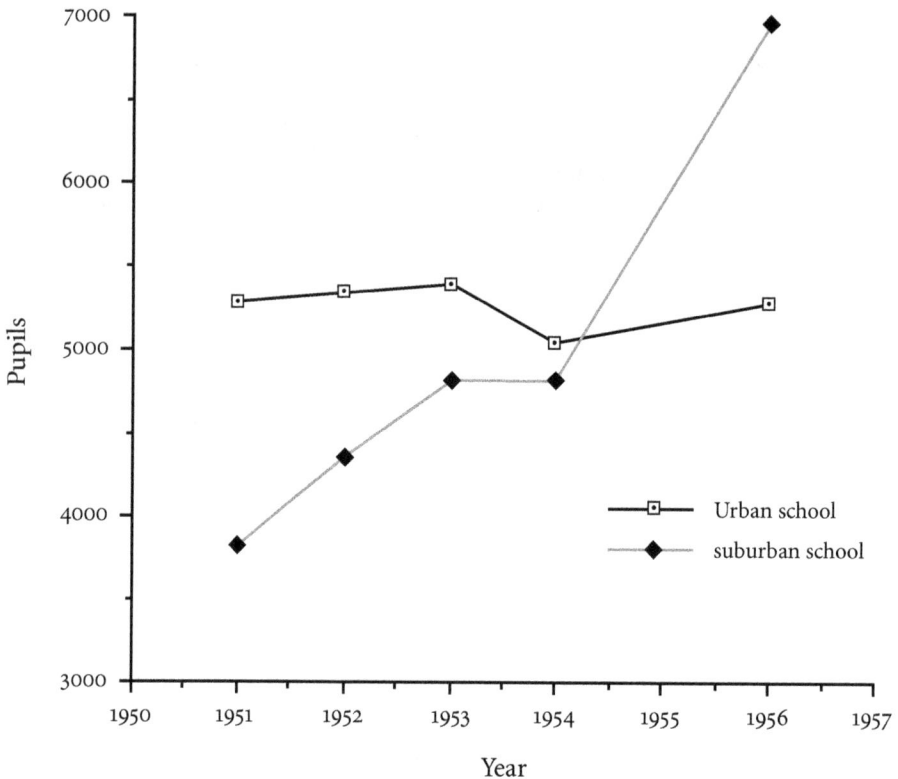

The numbers of Catholics who lived within suburban and urban parish boundaries are difficult to discern, but some data are available that might shed light on the suburbanization of Pittsburgh Catholics. A comparison of the number of pupils attending Catholic schools in two sets of parishes, one urban and the other suburban, reflects this suburban trend. The total student population in a sample of ten urban parishes and ten suburban parishes illustrates the dramatic growth of suburban schools at a time when urban schools grew more marginally. The urban school sample contained almost 1,500 more students than the suburban school sample in 1951, but by 1956 suburban schools taught almost 1,500 more students than their urban counterparts. Though we must remain cautious about making conclusions about the overall Catholic population from school data, the suburban school population growth suggests a significant expansion of the suburban Catholic parish population.[80] (See fig. 2.3.)

Suburban growth clearly posed problems for any social activity premised on gender segregation, and Catholic devotional life proved no exception. Catholics who embraced the suburban social ideal built around family activities found devotions that called them away from their wives, husbands, and children increasingly unappealing.

THE CATHOLIC ATTACKS ON CIVIL AUTHORITY, THE DECLINING NEED for divine intervention to exercise control in the temporal world, the increase in women working outside the home, and rapid suburbanization all contributed to the decline in devotional participation. Social experiences in the 1950s increasingly alienated Catholics from the devotional ethos that had resonated so profoundly for decades, and presaged a changing religious sensibility. The social experiences also strained Catholic social and cultural separatism, and helped to transform Catholic experiences there as well.

CHAPTER THREE

Catholic Separatism and
the Opening of the Catholic Ghetto

IF CHURCH OFFICIALS PRESCRIBED DEVOTIONALISM TO COMBAT
Communism and affirm society's spiritual dimension, they also instructed
Catholics to create a social and cultural world relatively safe from the forces in
American culture that denied the spiritual realm. Catholics were to build and
sustain a cultural ghetto that clearly separated them from others. Walls separating Catholics and Protestants on specifically religious matters stood most rigidly,
but the limits to interaction existed in a broad range of areas.

The ghetto was not a geographical locale in which only Catholics lived
and interacted, but rather a cultural and social space in which Catholics could
operate apart from their fellow citizens or in ways that distinguished them from
their neighbors. Charles Morris suggests in his recent history of American Catholics that Church officials sought to establish, and largely succeeded in creating,
a "state within a state," an environment in which Catholics could "carry out
almost every activity of life—education, health care, marriage and social life,
union membership, retirement and old age care—within a distinctly Catholic
environment."[1] Many separate Catholic cultural practices were unique but not
countercultural. They protected Catholics from the implications of full immersion but did not fundamentally challenge or condemn American culture.[2] Catholics could inhabit this space safe from contamination and still operate in the public culture. Catholics first constructed the ghetto walls in the nineteenth century
when American culture was more overtly hostile to the faith, but maintained
the barriers through the twentieth at great economic and social cost. By 1950
Pittsburgh Catholics operated not only distinct worship sites and practices, but
an entire school system for many of its children and an elaborate set of social

and cultural rules for all which prescribed strong cultural insularity. Church officials worked hard to maintain these rules, and the Catholic discourse consisted in large part of their regular interpretation and reiteration.[3]

Catholic separatism emphatically prohibited overt attempts to bridge denominational differences and extended beyond into the "secular" world as well. Though the ban on interfaith discussions did not officially extend to nonreligious matters, Catholics constructed a world that sought to minimize such contact. Catholics maintained an extensive array of organizations for the laity, for example, that served primarily to affirm the members' Catholic identity with little other basis for existence. Catholic teachers might belong to the Catholic Audio Visual Educators organization to keep up to date on the latest A/V pedagogical techniques, though no discussion in the Catholic discourse revealed a uniquely "Catholic" take on audiovisual education. Similarly, Catholic physicians might join the Saint Luke's Guild for Catholic Doctors, and Catholic nurses might belong to the Catholic Nurses Association, though these organizations identified no distinctly Catholic health care perspective.[4] Catholic students at non-Catholic institutions could join either the University Catholic Club or the National Federation of Catholic College Students, or both. Catholic students at Catholic colleges might join the latter organization. Though these organizations urged participation in liturgical functions, they served primarily as an avenue for social interaction. Catholic women who worked outside of the home could join the Catholic Business and Professional Women's Association, a group that met occasionally to provide networking opportunities and to assist programs that the Diocesan Council of Catholic Women sponsored.

Even when Catholics interacted with non-Catholics in endeavors the Catholic discourse sometimes created an artificial separation that allowed parishioners to see a separate Catholic world. For example, for a number of years in the 1950s the *Pittsburgh Catholic* published the National Catholic Welfare Council's All-Catholic All-American football team roster composed of standout players from Catholic colleges and universities. No all-Catholic league or conference existed from which to choose the players, and non-Catholic players could make the team. So even when the football lives that the players, coaches, and fans experienced did not exist within the Catholic cultural ghetto, the discourse could manufacture its appearance. Similarly, when the Pittsburgh Pirates finally found themselves in a pennant race unusually late in the season (mid-June), the *Pittsburgh Catholic* ran a feature story on the team's eight Catholic players and one Catholic coach.[5]

In Pittsburgh, the Catholic cultural ghetto shaped almost every aspect of Catholic lives, though nowhere more clearly than in the areas of worship, education, and marriage.

Worship

Predictably enough, church officials worried about and warned most often against any interfaith efforts between Catholics and Protestants because they might lead to a compromise of Catholic doctrine. Protestants might hold interfaith meetings aimed at Christian unity, but Church officials forbade Catholics to attend. After all, in the words of *Pittsburgh Catholic* editor John Collins, "The Catholic Church has the full revelation of Christian truth, which can be the only basis for real unity, and therefore has no reason for entering into 'discussions' in search of unity."[6] When a lay Catholic suggested that the Anglican Church seemed pretty "close to the Catholic Church," Father Brennan warned readers that "where truth is concerned, there is not a matter of 'closeness,' not a matter of 'near' truth, or a 'little' error. There is only truth or error." Anglicans taught error, especially when they denied the "authority and infallibility of the Holy Father."[7]

Similarly, diocesan officials banned any attendance at a non-Catholic worship activity. The *Pittsburgh Catholic* told readers that "all active, direct and intentional assistance in the distinctive religious functions of non-Catholics is grievously sinful and forbidden." Further, "all passive presence with non-Catholics at their religious functions is also, in general, forbidden, on account of the danger of perversion, scandal, and even the eternal profession of a false worship."[8]

The hierarchy's chief concern regarding non-Catholic worship focused on Protestant services, for these could be familiar enough to undermine the laity's resistance to the potentially pernicious practices. Under no circumstances were Catholics to participate in Protestant services, even if refusing to do so caused personal sacrifice. The *Pittsburgh Catholic*'s lead editorial on June 18, 1959, for example, praised a group of Catholic private school students in Maine who lost the privilege of receiving their diplomas because they refused to attend the academy's "Protestant baccalaureate services." The editors argued that the students "merit special admiration in contrast with the occasional tawdry young socialites who bend their knees at any altar and conform with any code in order to be 'accepted' by snob schools."[9]

Education

The most visible sign of the Catholic cultural ghetto was the elaborate school system that Pittsburgh Catholics supported to ensure that curricular and extra-curricular programs acknowledged each child's spiritual and material dimensions. Fr. Richard Ginder explained that students in public schools might learn to "read and write and figure," but they were "never taught Who made them and why. They never learn about Jesus and Mary."[10] Parents could ensure that their children learned both the material and the spiritual by enrolling them in Catholic schools from first grade through graduate or professional study, though the system's strength lay in the elementary school years. Catholic pastors had been establishing grade schools within their parishes ever since the U.S. bishops had encouraged each to do so in the nineteenth century. Pastors of new parishes often built school buildings before churches, and held Masses in the basement, the gym, or the auditorium while parishioners labored to raise enough funds to complete parish physical plants.

Pittsburgh diocesan statutes required Catholic parents to send their children to Catholic elementary schools in no uncertain terms:

> It is [the parents'] duty to see to it that their children attend Catholic elementary schools, except in those places where no Catholic school is found, or where, for grave reasons approved by the Ordinary in individual cases, it is not possible to send their children to a Catholic school.[11]

The *Pittsburgh Catholic* regularly reminded parents of their obligations under diocesan law and, for greater emphasis, sometimes recounted the code of canon law as well. Code 1374 stated that

> Catholic children must not attend non-Catholic, neutral or mixed schools, that is, such as are also open to non-Catholics. It is for the Bishop of the place alone to decide, according to the instructions of the Apostolic See, in what circumstances and with what precautions attendance at such schools may be tolerated, without danger of perversion to the pupils.

Lest anyone wonder what this meant in real terms, the diocesan paper explained that "parents and guardians who willfully fail in their obligations cannot be considered properly disposed for the reception of the Sacraments." They therefore had the duty and responsibility, "at the peril of their souls," to send their children to Catholic school.[12]

Nor should parents understand these diocesan statutes and canon law codes to be merely arbitrary rules that the hierarchy concocted to support the parochial school system. Fr. Daniel Brennan explained to readers of his Question Box column that the parents' duty "arises from the natural and divine laws." Parents must rear children "in accord with the purposes of creation—that we may know, love and serve God."[13]

Catholic education did not stop at grade school, and Pittsburgh Catholics supported more than twenty Catholic high schools throughout the diocese in the 1950s. The *Pittsburgh Catholic* reminded readers that diocesan statute no. 119 required parents to send their children to Catholic high schools. The statute stated that "where such institutions are available to their children, parents may not in safe conscience fail to enroll their children in those schools, unless they have obtained in advance the approval of their pastor." Those parents who disregarded this rule were "stubborn and even stupid."[14] The reasoning behind the statute mirrored that for elementary education.

Similarly, Church officials required parents of college-bound students to send their children to Catholic colleges or universities. Statute 119 extended to higher education as well. But Church officials did not rely on the statute alone to compel enrollment in Catholic institutions. They reminded parents regularly to enroll their children in Catholic colleges, as when Cardinal Samuel Stritch admonished that "parents should not exaggerate their liberty in choosing institutions for the education of their children. The real liberty is to choose Catholic institutions and only in exceptional circumstances to permit their children to attend other colleges and universities." The Reverend McDowell concurred, and noted that the high number of Catholics in Pittsburgh's secular colleges and universities "should provoke a great deal of concern on the part of parents and students alike." Why the concern? Jesuit Avery Dulles warned that a Catholic student in a secular institution would "find himself in possession of much better arguments against his religion than in its favor." Worse yet, "a day may come when he wakes up to discover that he no longer has the Faith at all." Duquesne University president the Very Rev. Vernon F. Gallagher, C.S.Sp., suggested that parents risked their eternal salvation when they sent their children to secular institutions. After all, "Catholic parents shall stand before God, responsible and answerable for the education of the children they brought into the world." But parents risked even more than their own souls when they allowed their children to attend secular institutions. According to one American bishop, this practice weakened efforts to combat the crisis of "the prevalence of religious errors, widespread religious indifference, the repudiation of the moral law on the part of millions as witnessed by the prevalence of divorce and remarriage, and by the advocacy and practice of contraception."[15]

If public education in general posed a great risk to Catholic students when it neglected their spiritual dimension, secular science education in particular proved most dangerous because it demanded empirical verification to legitimate knowledge and promised material solutions to social ills. Extreme scientism could be seen as a subset of materialism. And yet Catholics could not oppose science generally without sacrificing their children's opportunities to succeed in and to understand more fully the world God created. This tension resulted in a Catholic ambivalence toward science that caused teachers and students to walk a kind of tightrope. Catholics schools taught science but privileged the arts.

The arts, and especially the fine arts, had always been central to Catholic education, according to Pittsburgh's superintendent of diocesan schools: "It has only been here in the United States during the time when utilitarian and material values became prominent that the cultural values developed through the Fine Arts were set aside." The solution was an "education which emphasizes the development and direction of the whole man," with a special emphasis on his emotional, imaginative, and aesthetic powers.[16]

The containment of science education extended especially to colleges and universities. For as the *Pittsburgh Catholic* editors asserted in 1956,

> At a time when our nation calls for more intellectual leadership — more scientists, more scholars in every field of endeavor — it is heartening to note the response being made by our Catholic schools of higher education ... [which produce students who] have an understanding of their religion which is on a par with their development in secular subjects. ... No mere "intellectuals," these. And as "educated Catholics" they are the world's best hope for dispelling the clouds of secularism and materialism which threaten to engulf it.[17]

For, they later wrote, it would be "better to have no scientists at all than scientists without a sense of morality."[18]

Catholics celebrated religion's triumph over science regularly, especially in the rich devotional literature that contained story after story of prayer healing patients whom doctors claimed could never recover. Religion trumped science in other areas as well, as in the story of Frederick Anthony Rossini. The son of Carnegie Tech's chemistry department chairman, Frederick excelled at school. He finished first in his graduating class from the diocese's most prestigious high school, won a National Merit scholarship, and gained admission to the heavily science- and engineering-oriented California Institute of Technology in Pasadena, California. He had been for a short while the *Pittsburgh Catholic*'s poster child for Catholic achievement in the sciences both because of his already significant achievements and the bright scientific future that lay before him. But he was also heavily involved in Catholic organizations such as the Holy Name Society, the Saint John Vianney Society, and the Saint Paul Altar Society. Shortly before heading off to Cal Tech, Frederick decided instead to join the Jesuit Novitiate of Saint Isaac Jogues in Wernersville, Pennsylvania. He chose religion over science and affirmed the primacy of the spiritual over the material. The *Pittsburgh Catholic* trumpeted his decision with the headline: "NO. 1 STUDENT QUITS SCIENCE TO BE JESUIT.[19]

Marriage

Marriage proved a crucial ground on which to wage the struggle against materialism. It was, after all, inextricably linked to the powerful sensual realm, and, despite the elaborate formal institutional apparatus Catholics created and supported, the family remained society's fundamental and most powerful socializing institution. The hierarchy, parishes, and schools might overcome lukewarm family support for the Catholic ideal, but they stood little chance against parental hostility. Church officials needed husbands, wives, and parents to support its cultural and social norms if it had any hope of surviving the materialist crisis. Church officials therefore insisted upon strict rules governing the marital enterprise, and they took strong measures to enforce them. Above all, Catholics were to marry within the fold.

Interfaith relationships posed the most dangerous threat to Catholic efforts to maintain cultural separation because they brought Catholics into the most intimate personal contact with "outsiders," and because they put at risk the future children's religion. Church officials regularly and vociferously discouraged Catholics from marrying non-Catholics. Jesuit sociologist John L. Thomas warned that mixed marriages caused religious indifference and resulted from a newly developed "individualism" in which people exercised their newly assumed "right" to choose their own mates. The National Catholic Welfare Conference's Monsignor DeBlanc asserted that "mixed marriages might eventually destroy Christ's own Church in various communities, because no one can be half-Catholic."[20]

Worse yet were mixed marriages undertaken outside of Church purview. The hierarchy maintained stiff and unyielding opposition to these exogamous marriages, and called upon Catholics to shun their relatives and friends who chose this path. Fr. Daniel Brennan quoted diocesan statute 91, which stated:

> Catholics are forbidden to take part in, or attend, weddings of divorced persons, or weddings before a civil magistrate or a non-Catholic minister when one of the parties is a Catholic. Catholics are forbidden to attend receptions or showers in connection with such weddings because of the scandal involved.[21]

No Catholic was to attend or in any other way sanction a wedding between a Catholic and a non-Catholic which did not take place within a Catholic church.

But what of former Catholics who married non-Catholics outside of the Catholic Church? These weddings between two non-Catholics would seem not to fall under the sanction listed in the diocesan statute. Could friends and relatives attend their weddings or give gifts to them? Here again, the answer was no. To do so would constitute a "sin of scandal." Though Father Brennan acknowledged that this seemed uncharitable, he insisted that condoning these "evil acts" would only make the transgressors "more firmly rooted in the moral wrong doing." The act of shunning friends and relatives in this case was the true "charity."[22]

Church officials understood any union between a practicing Catholic and a lapsed, nonpracticing, or indifferent Catholic—let alone a non-Catholic— to open marriage and child rearing to great risk. The discourse admitted no exceptions. This raised difficulties when celebrities, about whose lives ordinary Catholics knew a great deal, seemed to transgress the rules in their marital endeavors. How could the Church insist upon one set of universal rules and at the same time seemingly sanction unions that broke the norms? Local and national celebrities therefore saw their marriages analyzed and judged openly in the crisis discourse.

Ralph Kiner's experience is illustrative. Kiner played outfield for the Pittsburgh Pirates and, for many years, stood as the sole reminder to disappointed fans that the city actually fielded a major league team. The Pirates defined ineptness in all facets of the game for years and proved the most potent cure for any slumping opponent. The team could not field, hit, or pitch. Yet they had Ralph Kiner. The congenial right-handed left fielder pounded towering fly balls that frequently landed safely over Forbes Field's left field wall in what came to be called "Kiner's Korner." He did this with such regularity that he perennially stood among the National League's best power hitters, and even won the home run title a number of times. He was the city's one major league superstar, Pittsburgh's sole reason to claim any dignity in the baseball world. And he was Catholic. In fact, he regularly attended Mass at All Soul's Church in his Alhambra, California, home during the off-season—a fact that the *Pittsburgh Catholic* touted in its sports pages.

But in 1951 he fell in love with a Protestant woman, and they married in a Protestant church. How could Ralph Kiner break the Church ban on such weddings, Catholics wondered? How could the *Pittsburgh Catholic* reconcile its insistence on this marriage rule and remain silent when one of the city's most popular and well-known Catholics disregarded it? Readers wanted to know, and they wrote to the paper for an explanation. Editor John Collins provided the answer. Yes, the *Pittsburgh Catholic* had reported on at least three occasions that Ralph Kiner was Catholic, and it did so in good faith. Kiner himself told sportswriter Sebastian Isabella as much explicitly in 1949 and in 1950. But it turns out that Kiner was not Catholic. He only claimed to be Catholic because he attended Catholic services regularly and exclusively and preferred the Catholic faith over all others. But he had never been officially baptized. He was therefore free to marry outside the Church, and local Catholics could hope that his disposition toward the faith might some day lead him and his bride into the fold.[23]

The final act of shunning came with death. All baptized held a right to a Christian burial unless they forfeited that right under the laws of the Church. Catholics who married outside of the Church fell into this category and could be denied burial as "a punishment for deliberate wrongdoings, and as preventative for others who might think of violating God's laws." Even Catholics in mixed marriages that the Church recognized could not be buried next to their non-Catholic spouse unless parish cemeteries established special "mixed marriage sections." But even then, the Chancery had to give permission after determining that the mixed couple had satisfied five specific criteria.[24]

MODESTY AND RESTRAINT: THE BATTLE AGAINST SENSUALITY, INDECENCY, AND LICENSE

One area in which Catholics differed more in degree than kind from the broader culture was in their efforts to restrain impulsive sensual behavior. No religious body urged licentious or impulsive behavior, but none sought greater self-denial than Catholics, nor did others root their value in hierarchical interpretations of natural law. The crisis discourse prescribed modesty, restraint, humility, and containment to overcome sensuality and license. Catholics could best constrain their impulses and desires by carefully subjugating their individual aspirations to communal norms. The Catholic path to transcendence over the materialism of physical satisfactions and individuality traveled through the cultural areas of diet, dress, and personal expression.

Above all, Catholics were to recall that they were part of a larger enterprise that took precedence over individual needs and aspirations, and which required that one seek to blend in rather than stand out. The *Holy Name Newsletter* told readers, for example, that a "Catholic Man is one who is not an individual star, but one who works with the team, who knows the value of teamwork, who cooperates with all other Catholic men in the work of the Church."[25] Msgr. Irving A. DeBlanc, director of NCWC's Family Life Bureau, instructed Catholics to live at "the lower level of [their] status, not the highest degree in it."[26]

The values of modesty and humility could be seen in a variety of forums but perhaps nowhere as clearly as in liturgical choirs. Church organists and choirmasters spent much of the 1950s trying to suppress individuality among the boys who sang at Mass. This was in part because official rubrics discouraged individualism. Pittsburgh diocesan music regulations, for example, forbade musical compositions for "solo," as well as any solo singing (save for incidental phrases). The rule applied at weddings and funerals as well. But the strictures against individualism extended beyond the egregious solo singing to the more subtle forms of subverting group norms. The *Pittsburgh Catholic* church organists' column contained regular and emphatic advice to suppress individuality. The diocese liked boy choirs because they were "more or less an impersonal group, for, being vested, all alike, and all practically of a size, no single chorister appears more prominent or conspicuous than do the others, either in procession or in the choir stalls." Choir directors were to make the choirs sound as uniform as they appeared. "Every boy must come in at exactly the same instant on a lead, and release the last note of a phrase with the utmost caution." Should any boy's individual voice be discerned apart from the group, he was to be replaced with a more compliant boy from a younger grade. The model for the boys' choirs was the Benedictine Fathers of Solesmes, who restored traditional chant to the liturgy in part by keeping their "voices in a subdued tone, thus eliminating all harsh individualities."[27]

If boys acted out or sang too distinctly in order to draw attention to themselves in the choir, girls and women could do so by their mere presence. No female could participate under any circumstances. It was better to have no choir than to have females singing before the parish.

The choir was clearly an exaggerated, intensified crucible of self-abnegation. But the stricture for humility and self-restraint applied to all areas of personal expression. The best way to deflect attention from oneself was to live moderately and discreetly, to practice humility and modesty.

The clearest campaign for modesty targeted female sartorial practices and in this focus overlapped a great deal with concerns about sexuality. But the stricture for modesty aimed more broadly than at sexuality, which I will address later in the chapter. Drum majorettes, beauty contestants, and prom-goers offended the prohibition against immodesty the most, and they most often found themselves to be the targets of a campaign aimed at shaping modes of dress. Dressing modestly typically meant wearing more rather than less clothing.

The official campaign for modesty began in Pittsburgh at the decade's outset with concern about the "majorettes" who accompanied high school bands and performed at athletic events, in parades, and in other public venues. Rather than negotiate over dress and dance routines, the diocese simply banned all majorettes from elementary and high schools within the diocese—a decision that affected only four or five schools. But six times as many schools sponsored cheerleaders, whose uniforms stretched (or perhaps shrank) modesty's boundaries. The diocese disbanded all female cheerleading squads as well, save for those performing at female sporting events that were closed to the public.

If majorettes and cheerleaders offended rules against modesty in dress, what of Catholics who attended formal dances? Should they cover up more? The student council at Saint Justin's High School thought so, and so appealed to area department stores to provide a broader range of prom dress styles that were "both modest and stylish."[28] The department stores responded that they each stocked modest dresses, and some suggested that girls tell the "buyer" when they arrived that they wished to see only the modest styles. The Confraternity of Christian Mothers joined the campaign by distributing their leaflet entitled "Modern Yet Modest" to various Catholic women's groups.[29] Two female students from different schools formed a "Modesty and Dress Committee" in 1955 with the intention of demonstrating "the responsibility of youth in social affairs." The girls did not espouse any particular set of rules but wanted to emphasize the "positive." After all, they argued, "We young people don't need to follow fashion blindly. We can be discriminating."[30]

Soon even participants in annual May Crowning devotions came under scrutiny. The Rev. Charles Moosmann, diocesan director of the Sodality of Our Lady, wondered why parishes chose a schoolgirl to crown when only statues of Mary should wear the honor, and why these living queens needed attendants wearing dresses of each color of the rainbow. "There [was] no harm in having the dresses alike, provided they are simple and, above all, very modest."[31]

Throughout the 1950s and 1960s the Diocesan Council of Catholic Women told women that their behaviors might cause males to sin, and so demanded conservative public behavior and dress. The *News* relayed that

> many a Catholic girl who is pure as the snow in the skies has been a source of serious temptation and sin to boys and men because of the way she dressed and has not even realized it. Callous-minded women often quote: "to the pure, all things are pure." That is not true.

The *News* further stated that women who think summer means a vacation from clothes will cause men to sin "no matter how pure the hearts of the men may desire to be." The following issue quoted a Pittsburgh priest who argued that "Catholic women must not only set standards in modesty of dress, but live up to them themselves, especially at public gatherings."[32]

Lest anyone mistakenly understand the campaign for modesty in dress to apply only to females and the laity, Pope Pius XII made clear that the hierarchy too was to follow more modest practices. He ordered modifications in the garb that cardinals wore because "the peculiar conditions of our times call for a more sober tenor of life by all, especially the clergy." The cardinals, of course, wore too much rather than too little. Starting in December 1952 cardinals were to trim their trains by half, from twelve feet to a mere six, make new garments out of wool rather than silk (they could keep the silk they already owned) and eliminate the train that formed part of the purple cassock. Before the new regulations took effect a cardinal's costume typically consumed twenty-six yards of material, enough to outfit a legion of drum majorettes.[33]

Worries about modesty in dress spread infrequently to what boys wore in public. John Collins applauded the actions administrators at Dormont High School took when they discovered that four boys had come to class in short pants. The school authorities were right to take strong disciplinary measures in this case because they must "uphold right standards of taste and conduct." But, Collins reminded readers, Dormont High School encourages female exhibitionism when it sends majorettes out publicly with the school band to go "through their burlesque-house prancing and contortions."[34]

The campaign for modest dress persisted throughout the 1950s and into the next decade. Even Pope John XXIII weighed in for modest fashions, lest style become a "proximate occasion to sin."[35]

Modesty and restraint applied not only to dress but to dietary habits as well. Catholics were supposed to practice abstemiousness throughout the year in their diets, especially on Fridays when they could not eat meat. But during Lent the spirit of restraint took a giant leap forward. In general terms, the hierarchy required the laity to make special sacrifices during Lent in preparation for Easter and in memory of Christ's period of asceticism in the desert. John Collins gave Lent a more contemporary meaning in 1952 when he reminded Catholics that

> Lent should mean that we are about to prepare ourselves, spiritually, to meet the world crisis, the domestic crisis, and the crisis that comes so often in our daily life. For Lent—with its prayer, penance, self-denial, alms-giving, meditation—is the prescription which the Church in her wisdom and experience knows will heal our ills.[36]

The spirit of self-sacrifice for the greater good permeated the Lenten season.

But the specific forms this sacrifice took derived from canon law (with some latitude for local bishops' interpretations) and help point up the complexity of maintaining the Catholic cultural ghetto. Lenten regulations called for "fasting" and "abstinence," which referred to distinct behaviors. Fasting required one to eat less than one normally would, and abstinence prohibited the consumption of a particular food—meat—altogether. Rather than let each Catholic determine the specific forms these general sacrifices should take, the Church laid out definite rules to follow. The bishop explained these in a formal letter to parishioners that the *Pittsburgh Catholic* published on its front page as Lent neared, and then in abbreviated versions on interior pages throughout the period leading up to Easter.

The requirements did not apply to all equally, so Catholics first had to discern which category they fell into. For example, the laws of abstinence (no meat) applied to all Catholics seven years old or older, except for those who worked "at hard labor" and their immediate family members. These people could eat meat once on each day of abstinence, except for Fridays, Ash Wednesday, and Holy Saturday until noon. But to compensate for eating meat on days of abstinence, they were to "perform some voluntary works of self-denial." The laws of fasting (eating less overall) applied to those between the ages of twenty-one and fifty-nine, save for those "who suffer from ill health, or who would be unable without great hardship to perform their regular duties if they fasted."[37]

Once Catholics understood their place in the rubric, they needed to know which days they were required to do what. They were to abstain from meat on all Lenten Wednesdays (save for the Wednesday of Holy Week itself), Fridays, Ember Saturday, and Holy Saturday (until noon). They had to fast (eat less food) each Lenten weekday but could eat meat at their principal meal (save for those days already designated as days of abstinence).

Finally, Catholics needed to understand exactly how to apply fasting and abstinence. Abstinence was easiest, as it required one to forgo any meat or meat-based soup. Fasting proved more complex. Catholics could eat one full meal each day, either at noon or in the evening, which included meat (except for on days of abstinence). They could have a light breakfast (a beverage and a moderate portion of bread) and another meal that did not "exceed in quantity one-fourth of the principal meal." Neither the light breakfast nor lunch could include meat, even on nonabstinence days.

Perhaps recognizing the confusion that these rules might cause, or simply desiring a more uniform approach, Bishop Dearden exercised his special faculties provided for under canon law and changed the regulations in 1952. The *Pittsburgh Catholic* understood the overall intent of the changes to mean that Catholics could claim fewer exemptions. The reforms specifically removed the working-man's exemption from the abstinence requirement and introduced the further nuances of "complete" and "partial" abstinence. "Complete" abstinence meant simply what "abstinence" had meant the year before, and "partial" abstinence allowed one meal of meat (or meat-based soup or gravy), or what "fasting" had meant the previous year. Ember Wednesdays and Saturdays became partial abstinence days. Fasting remained the same. Lenten Wednesdays, save for Ash Wednesday, became simply days of fasting. The two non-main meals on days of fasting were now to equal less than a full meal combined. Those in ill health or whose work might be affected by fasting could ignore the rules.[38]

Perhaps recognizing the puzzlement that might result, Dearden recommended that those confused in any way by the rules on fast and abstinence should consult a parish priest or confessor. The *Pittsburgh Catholic* attempted to make the rules more comprehensible in 1955 when it began publishing a matrix of Lenten regulations. Catholics could clip the matrix and attach it to their refrigerators or cabinet doors for quick and easy consultation.[39] (See table 3.1.)

How serious were these dietary regulations? Fr. Richard Ginder told Pittsburghers in 1957 that they would not be Catholics if they did not believe that God would "send a man to hell for eating a steak on Friday."[40]

Sexuality

The battle against sensuality focused a great deal on limiting Catholic sexual encounters to marital partners. Virginity was the "most beautiful way to Heaven,"

TABLE 3.1   Lenten Guide for Fast and Abstinence

	If You Are . . .	
	Between 21 and 59 Years of Age	Between 7 and 21 Or over 59
And the Day is . . .	You may eat	You may eat
Ash Wednesday (Feb. 23) Friday in Lent Ember Friday Holy Saturday Forenoon	One full meal NO MEAT	Customary meals NO MEAT
Monday, Tuesday, Wednesday, Thursday, Saturday in Lent	One full meal Meat at full meal	Customary meals Meat at all times
Ember Wednesday Or Saturday	One full meal Meat at full meal	Customary meals Meat at main meal

but married couples could achieve salvation despite their sexual activity. Even here the passions sexual stimulation could unleash were to be constrained by the true purpose of coital intimacy—procreation. Catholics were to have no sex before or outside of marriage, and they were not to become too aroused during the marital relations.[41] It is useful to point out that Catholics were not unique in the proscriptions against pre- and extramarital sexual activity, though they seemed to place greater emphasis than many other Christians on the denial of pleasure between married partners.

Catholic rules on sexual behavior were quite clear. No one was to engage in physical behavior that aroused pleasure in the sexual organs save for married couples. In the words of one guide to Catholic marriage, "Christian philosophy maintains that man is endowed with sexual capacity for the reproduction of the race, and, hence, sexual activity is limited to marriage partners."[42] Another specified that "the sex appeal of mind and heart urges man and woman to intimate companionship, which may be shared lawfully in wedlock only."[43] If a man entered the marital state having already engaged in sexual behaviors, he brought trouble to the relationship. He "has yielded to selfishness, he has put the physical above the spiritual, and he has perhaps destroyed the possibility of ever attaining true love."[44]

If Catholic officials insisted that no one practice sexual intimacy before he or she married, they also understood that the strictures against premarital sex were harder to remember in the backseat of a car than in the church pew. Moralists therefore developed a series of recommendations to help Catholics avoid the temptations that could lead to sinful behavior. Perhaps the most obvious was to avoid the backseat of a car altogether. One Catholic etiquette guide recommended that boys and girls on dates make plans for specific activities in advance: "It is more fun and less moral risk to go dancing, see a show, or play cards than it is to drive aimlessly about the countryside or lounge in a tavern."[45]

In order to avoid occasions of sin, Catholic experts on courtship and marriage—most often ordained clergy who had vowed to disdain both—urged young Catholics not to date steadily. Those in steady dating relationships found themselves more at risk of violating the taboo on sexual relations. In the words of one high school principal, "There is a definite danger of restraint being lifted and serious sin resulting."[46] They might find themselves, for example, alone in the car together, facing the dangers other than those posed by high speeds. After all,

> not all fatal wrecks take place while speeding along in an open convertible. In fact, at least the beginnings of many crashes occur while the convertible is standing still somewhere off the highway. In his mad hurry to enjoy the forbidden fruits of married life many a young person has discovered, to his regret, that he has wrecked his life just as surely, or rather, more surely, than would have been the case had he headed into a dangerous curve at too great a speed.

Even the dean of the School of Sacred Theology at the Catholic University of America weighed in against steady dating because it put couples "in an occasion of sin."[47]

Once Catholics made it to marriage, however, the rules for avoiding intimacy changed somewhat. Catholics were now encouraged to engage in intercourse for the purpose of conceiving children. Procreation remained the primary purpose for getting married, and Catholic couples were to welcome conception with every sexual encounter. Or almost every encounter. Catholic couples could practice a form of birth control that did not violate natural law—so long as they did not do so too regularly. Theologians and prelates did permit married couples to practice the "natural" form of birth control known as the rhythm method. But Pope Pius XII reminded Catholic wives in 1951 that they were not to rely upon it too regularly, lest it unfairly restrict husbands from their conjugal rights. Sex might have the added benefit of nurturing a couple's affection for each other and strengthening their marriage, but this was a secondary benefit. Intimacy was not about pleasure, about the satisfaction of physical or sensual desires, but for reproduction. The Pittsburgh diocese even required each couple preparing for marriage to swear under oath that they understood marriage's primary purpose to be "the procreation and education of children."[48]

The gravest danger to the rules for marital sex came from effective birth control, which severed the otherwise inherent connection between intercourse and procreation. If one could successfully separate sex from reproduction, the act would become primarily a sensual, not a procreative, act. Therefore, advocates of "unnatural" birth control came under intense attack in official Catholic circles, especially as researchers (relying on the materialist "science") developed an effective birth control pill and as Protestant denominations lifted their ban on its use. The *Pittsburgh Catholic* regularly constructed arguments against birth control and sought to undermine the arguments made on its behalf. Overpopulation was not a genuine concern, there was no international food shortage, the poor would not be served by having fewer children. Gandhi was a great man because, "like a rock, he stood firm against the advocates of 'birth control.'" Birth control practices robbed Americans of their "inner religious strength" and destroyed "man's tie-up with God," as well as his dignity. The practice of birth control would cause America to "degenerate into the sad land of license to defy God and His Commandments."[49]

Fighting Indecency

Battling sensuality might have proved difficult because much of the sensual behavior was intensely private. It took place behind closed bedroom (and car) doors, away from public view. One could not easily assess the success of any campaign to stamp out petting on dates, or to curtail excessive pleasure among married couples. But one could certainly see the cultural manifestations of the sensual impulse. They were all over the movie screens, television sets, magazines, books, and comics of the era. The Pittsburgh hierarchy regularly sought to recruit the laity into the twin movements to stamp out indecency in print and other media. No Catholic in the Pittsburgh region in the 1950s could have missed the high-profile roles of the Legion of Decency and the National Organization for Decent Literature.

The U.S. Catholic bishops formed the Legion of Decency in November 1933 because they believed that the movie industry largely ignored a code established to guide voluntary censorship of films in 1930.[50] In the bishops' eyes, too many dangerous films had been produced in the three years between the code's adoption and the bishops' November meeting to expect Hollywood to honor the code absent significant pressure. The bishops appointed Archbishop John McNicholas of Cincinnati to head their committee on motion pictures, and bishops John Cantwell of Los Angeles, John Knoll of Fort Wayne, and Pittsburgh's Hugh Boyle to lead the Legion of Decency. The Legion designed and implemented a three-pronged strategy to clean up the movies. They created a pressure group, they initiated boycotts of immoral films, and they supported voluntary compliance with the 1930 code.[51]

The Legion of Decency especially played a high-profile role in Pittsburgh, in large part because Bishop Boyle and his successor, John Dearden, both required every parishioner to recite the Legion's pledge at Mass on the second Sunday of every December. In reciting the pledge, parishioners publicly committed themselves to avoid immoral movies and to support the Legion's efforts. The pledge's text was quite short and to the point:

In the name of the Father and of the Son and of the Holy Ghost. Amen.

I condemn indecent and immoral motion pictures and those which glorify crime or criminals. I promise to unite with all who protest against them.

I acknowledge my obligation to form a right conscience about pictures that are dangerous to my moral life.

As a member of the Legion of Decency, I pledge myself to see only good pictures. I promise, further, to stay away altogether from places of amusement which show pictures that can be an occasion of sin.[52]

The *Pittsburgh Catholic* urged readers to take their pledge seriously, and this committed the paper, parishioners, and other organizations to quite a job of policing. Every parishioner vowed to "form a right conscience about movies that are dangerous to my moral life," which suggested that each should decide personally which movies to avoid. But how could one do this without actually viewing movies, and violating the rest of the pledge? The answer seemed simple enough. The Legion decided which movies to avoid, the *Pittsburgh Catholic* published the ratings, and moviegoers consulted the paper. Catholics who misplaced their paper—or did not subscribe—called various offices, such as the Holy Name Society, that might keep the rating list at hand. (The Holy Name Society established a twenty-four-hour-a-day Legion of Decency ratings hotline in 1957 to field such calls, thereby accommodating all Catholics who developed urgent ratings questions in the middle of the night.)[53] Forming a right conscience became as simple as doing what one was told.

So long as the Legion could rate each movie (in each of its versions), and so long as Catholics recognized the Legion's authority as the final word on films (and no other contradictory authority), the structure worked fine. Furthermore, if enough Catholics avoided bad films, movie houses could not profitably show them. By exerting powerful economic pressure, Catholics could safeguard the morals of others in the community as well. They could remove the appeals to the sensual from everyone's moviegoing experience and reduce everyone's occasions of sin. If movies were especially bad, the Pennsylvania Board of Censors could prohibit public viewings—something the *Pittsburgh Catholic* embraced wholeheartedly.

The economic pressure did not always work, however. Theaters did show objectionable movies, and Catholics had to exert special efforts to locate and point them out to readers. This was the case when the Cameraphone Theater in Pittsburgh's East End showed *Mom and Dad* in 1953, for example. The Legion rated the film "C—condemned," but the theater manager took it anyway. Legion of Decency director the Rev. Paul Lackner (who also directed the diocesan Holy Name Society), visited the manager and pointed out the problem. This was not appropriate material for an "entertainment motion picture theater," because it ignored completely "essential and supernatural values." Would he not discontinue the showing "as a matter of public interest"? He would if it were up to him, it turned out, but his contract with his bookers forbade this course of action. His hands were tied. The *Pittsburgh Catholic* then informed readers that they were "expected to avoid this film."[54]

A similar situation occurred when thirteen local drive-in theaters showed the condemned film *The French Line*. This proved especially troubling because, as few readers needed to be reminded, viewing such movies in the privacy of cars created whole new occasions for sin. Worse still, three local papers, which purported to favor "morality and decency," agreed to run ads for the movie.[55]

A comparable, though lower-profile, organization to the Legion of Decency worked with published materials. The National Organization for Decent Literature (NODL) sought to persuade or pressure publishers and retailers not to allow indecent literature into the public sphere. The task was much more difficult for literature than for movies, of course, because no organization could evaluate all published books, magazines, newspapers, and comics and produce a rating quickly enough to guide would-be readers. Catholics could consult the Index of

Forbidden Books, but that was incomplete and difficult to find, and in any case did not focus on popular literature. (Unlike the Legion of Decency's movie ratings, the *Pittsburgh Catholic* never published the Index, and never mentioned how one might locate a copy.) If readers wished to read only literature about the religion, they could read books given a "Nihil Obstat" and an "Imprimatur," seals of approval that certified that the book contained nothing objectionable and was free of doctrinal error.[56]

Pittsburghers relied upon a local book censor to review books on religion, and had Fr. Richard Ginder, conservative columnist for the *Pittsburgh Catholic* and *Our Sunday Visitor* to perform this task in the middle years of the decade. He advised Bishop Dearden on whether to award a Nihil Obstat. But three months into his term he had screened only one book, which prompted one observer to note that his "job to date has not proved to be overly burdensome."[57]

Though the National Organization for Decent Literature came to be in 1938 under Fort Wayne's Bishop John F. Noll (who also helped lead the Legion of Decency), the National Council of Catholic Men spearheaded the national campaign against indecent literature and housed the NODL headquarters in its Washington, D.C., office. But the U.S. bishops took greater control of the organization in 1955 when it moved the NODL to Chicago and named the director of the Chicago Archdiocesan Council of Catholic Women (a priest) as executive secretary. Bishop Dearden had taken over as episcopal leader of the campaign in 1954, and he worked hard to make the NODL a larger presence in American Catholic lives.[58]

Locally, Bishop Dearden had appended commitments to avoid indecent literature to the annual Legion of Decency pledge as early as 1951, and he supported Holy Name Society campaigns against indecent literature. These campaigns usually consisted of annual surveys of local retailers to see who stocked indecent reading materials, and then committee visits to the offending store managers to persuade them to stop. Sometimes Catholics made special efforts to combat indecent literature, such as when the diocesan Holy Name Society joined with Judge Henry X. O'Brien's Civic Committee on Decent Literature and Assistant Police Superintendent Lawrence Maloney's private campaign against smut to rid stores of offending materials in 1954. Shortly after Bishop Dearden became episcopal chairman of the Bishop's Committee on Decent Literature, the Holy Name Society printed 500,000 copies of cards with the Legion of Decency pledge on one side and the NODL code on the other. The code condemned publications that: "Present Sex in an offensive or objectionable manner. Feature crime. Portray illicit love. Contain blasphemous, profane and obscene speech. Advertise the vulgar and the lewd."[59]

The Diocesan Council of Catholic Women shared the Holy Name Society's concern for obscene literature and indecent movies and television, and it urged women to monitor vigilantly their children's and communities' reading and viewing materials as a means of implementing Catholic Action. The DCCW encouraged women to regulate their children's exposure and to report offending newsstands to the local Holy Name Society representative in charge of censorship.[60]

In addition to attempts to stop people from reading indecent literature and to stop retailers from selling materials, the decent literature campaign encouraged publishers to adopt voluntary self-policing actions and local, state, and federal agencies to censor publication and distribution as well. For example, the *Pittsburgh Catholic* lauded the comic industry's decision to form the Comic Magazine Association of America with a Catholic, Judge Charles F. Murphy, as its head. His task was to lead the industry's efforts to adopt and adhere to a code that banned all comics "offensive to public taste."[61]

FIGHTING CHANGING GENDER ROLES WITH TRADITION

In the 1950s crisis discourse, women both embodied the spiritual virtue at the Catholic ghetto's heart and held much of the responsibility for maintaining the complex code that ordered Catholic lives. The discourse contained an ironic contradiction concerning women. It presumed that women were by their nature more given to spirituality and at the same time more fragile in the face of the materialist onslaught. They were essentially religious, more virtuous, yet also more prone to corruption. Consequently, women had to follow externally imposed strict codes of conduct to preserve their natural dispositions.

Sr. M. Aurelia, director of the diocesan school system's Social Science Department, explained it this way. A Catholic girl was a child of God due to her baptism into the faith, "not a mere human being governed by emotions and desires." If other girls were more inclined to these sensual tendencies, she had transcended them. This meant that her behavior "must be governed by a wholesome discrimination in the type of pleasure she selects, the movies she sees, the kind of broadcasts she listens to, the type of literature she reads, and even the kind of clothes she wears." If girls could only focus on their souls' relationship with God, then they would see "that true happiness comes from within and does not depend upon material things."[62] They would themselves be safe from the materialism that threatened society and be true to their natural propensity.

Any movement that women made away from the spiritual ideal and toward the materialist danger became a dual threat in the crisis. It both degraded the

core of the community and sapped one of its most powerful agents of enforcement. The crisis discourse therefore took great care to prescribe acceptable behaviors and to warn against both individual infractions and popular trends away
from the ideal. The extensive literature on women's dress and sexual behavior
clearly aimed to curtail material lures. But the most powerful gender message focused on what the hierarchy considered the greatest threat to women's essential
religious nature, the phenomenon that put women most at risk. Above all, the
crisis discourse decried women's working outside the home, enmeshed in the
materialist market, prey to the to the exploitative and luring powers of commercial capitalist society. Women differed from men in their essential natures,
according to the 1950s Catholic discourse, and this difference meant that they
should not expose themselves to the same corrupting pressures that men faced.

Msgr. Irving DeBlanc, NCWC Family Life Bureau director, stated the matter
clearly and succinctly when he noted the "serious, sacred fact that God has made
man and woman radically different along every line." God created women and
men deliberately as they were to accommodate their natural roles. "Woman's vocation is to be a physical or spiritual mother." In order to fulfill this role women
"must have certain physical, intellectual, emotional qualities which differ from
those of men." How did women differ from men specifically? Women were weaker
than men because they did not have to work for a living. "She will tire easily
because she, unlike man, is not made for hard work." Women cannot participate
in the same strenuous games as men. As a result, women sometimes become jeal-
ous of men and try to imitate them: "Women dress like men, smoke like men, assume mannish habits, play strenuous games." Rather than do this, women should
simply recognize that their greatest physical attribute is "gentleness."[63]

Gentleness did not suit women for the rough and tumble of the steel mills or
the sensual corruption and seductions of office work. Rather, their physical, natural dispositions suggested another career: "Admitting her comparative weakness,
she is ideally fitted for taking care of the home. Housework, cooking, sewing,
gardening are all suited to her ability." Though these tasks did not require great
strength, in Monsignor DeBlanc's eyes, they did require that women be in sound
physical condition—especially when combined with the stresses of bearing and
rearing "four or six or seven" children. Therefore women should not diet exces-
sively, stay up late at night, or practice "extreme smoking habits." In contrast,
men's strength predisposed them to different roles: "Man's vocation in the world
is to rule. To him belongs authority more than to woman—first, as master of the
home and then, of society." Pope Pius XII further underscored DeBlanc's position
when he argued that women's spiritual qualities, their physical structure, and their
rich sentiments combined to make motherhood women's primary function.[64]

If women's natural attributes disposed them to housework and mother-hood, they did not always come by these vocations "naturally." Girls required training in these areas to succeed, and Church officials knew it. Monsignor De-Blanc recounted that many nuns "looked away in grief when their recent gradu-ates, about to marry, thanked them for all they had done." The nuns knew that they had inadequately prepared these young women for marriage and house-work, and wished that they could have offered at least one formal course in "family living." The schools would catch up some day, but so many had gradu-ated already without adequate training and faced lives of loneliness at home.[65] Not every Catholic high school lacked such a course. Female students at Saint Peter's on the North Side met twice weekly with Sr. M. Peter Nolasco to develop the right skills and attitude for homemaking. Sister Peter explained that "we want the girls to be mindful that homemaking is the most wonderful career for a lay woman. We want them to look forward to the homes they will create— always modeled on the Home at Nazareth." The Nazareth home model as taught at Saint Peter's included good personal grooming, clothing matching, smart shopping, general sewing techniques, and drapery making. Saint Peter's sopho-mores competed for "Best Groomed Girl of the Week," which, Sister Peter em-phasized, was not a beauty contest.[66]

Grooming also mattered to the students at Saint Benedict Academy, West View. They compiled and then published a booklet of rules to guide teenage girls toward the Catholic ideal, and good grooming made it on their list. Saint Bene-dict students divided their ideal into four realms: home life, parish life, school life, and public life. Catholic girls treated their family members with kindness, respect, and consideration, and kept the family troubles private. They went to Mass at least weekly, where they showed up on time and received Communion in modest and attractive attire. They took an interest in the parish youth activi-ties. At school, the girls remained courteous, friendly, attentive, industrious, stu-dious, and punctual. They met criticism, even undeserved criticism, with an even temper and maturity. They displayed their pride in their alma mater by their loyalty and school spirit. Finally, the ideal Catholic teenage girl was always "well-groomed, neat, and modest in appearance," refrained from public discourte-sies, showed a good example when in the company of small children and non-Catholics, and remained trustworthy and sincere. Having compiled the ideal, the Saint Benedict students discovered that they had "created a prototype of the greatest woman who ever lived—Our Blessed Mother."[67]

The best way to achieve this ideal was to attend an all-girls' Catholic school, where a female student would not encounter teachers who "try to teach her to behave like a man." Instead, she would find only teachers who recognize that she is "mentally and emotionally unlike the boys," who dislike competing against girls in school because "they certainly are not keen on losing intellectually to the girls."[68]

In addition to laying down boundaries and providing explicit instruction to ensure a match between women's natural proclivities and their adult vocations, the Church honored models for women to emulate. The *Pittsburgh Catholic* did this informally through brief focus pieces on DCCW officers and other local women who embodied true Catholic womanhood. But the Church did this more formally by choosing annually one American woman to be the Catholic "Mother of the Year," and then highlighting her life for other Catholic women to emulate.

The Catholic discourse on gender not only prescribed the female Catholic standard and held up models for all to emulate, but it also identified those behaviors that threatened the ideal and warned women against them. Working outside the home posed the gravest danger, and the crisis discourse attacked this activity relentlessly.

The *Pittsburgh Catholic* reported that married women working outside the home represented the "most blatant disregard of papal teaching about women on the present American scene."[69] Alexandra Hill, writing the *Pittsburgh Catholic* women's column, put it even more directly:

> There is something miserable and mean about a married woman's working. Husbands who allow their wives to work ought to crawl quietly into the first available hole. And wives who insist upon working over the objections (passive or active) of their husbands ought to be soundly spanked—verbally!

Women did not understand, Hill argued, or did not "want to understand, that they are expected to live on their husband's income." Work removed women from the home, where they belonged. After all, "a woman should be a sanctuary where a man can come and rest at the end of a day. This just doesn't work out if the woman drags home at the same time as hubby and just about twice as tired as he is."[70]

The cause of this problem was not difficult to identify. Regis College's sociology department head explained that women often work simply because our materialist, "gadget-saturated society" induces them to do so.[71] The materialism that so permeated the market had penetrated the family and drew women out of their homes in order to make their homes more pleasant. Ms. Hill claimed that materialism made women too focused on possessions. Women should "do without the new rug (Oh, horror!) if husband can't afford it."[72] Pope Pius XII blamed both Communism and capitalism for drawing women out of their homes and destroying their dignity. He emphasized that

> to restore as far as possible the honor of woman's and mother's place in the home: that is the watchword one hears now from many quarters like a cry of alarm, as if the world were awakening, terrified by the fruits of material and scientific progress of which it before was so proud.[73]

If the alarm bells warning of women's loss of dignity and the home's collapse did not suffice to keep women at home, the crisis discourse raised the possibility of risks to women themselves. Monsignor DeBlanc warned that a working woman could not be certain "that her new work is not creating sterility" and jeopardizing her chance at motherhood. With no children, a woman would "suffer from social isolation and loss of purpose more than any other group except perhaps the old."[74]

The proscriptions against immersion in the broader culture and economy aimed at women constituted an intensified assertion of the Catholic separatist prescription. Catholic women needed a heavier dose of the separation prescription, in Church officials' eyes, because they were most vulnerable to the materialist corruption that threatened all of society. But no Catholic, no matter how well his natural disposition suited him or how well trained and sophisticated, stood immune to the materialist virus. Therefore all Catholics were to live in the Catholic cultural and social ghetto.

THE CULTURAL GHETTO'S DECLINE

Despite the hierarchy's unwavering insistence that area Catholics sustain the cultural ghetto, their changed social experiences transformed the cultural and social ghetto no less than it did the devotional culture. By the end of the 1950s, Catholics no longer lived in a separate social and cultural world, insulated from the materialist dangers against which Church officials continued to warn. Much of the change resulted from the laity's conscious rejection of that world, their interest in moving away from the values upon which that model rested. For, as Anthony Padovano recently reflected,

> We built with pride and prejudice: proud of the structures, prejudiced against all who were not Catholic. We thought we were building out of

strength rather than fear, but, indeed, fear was everywhere. One false step and we might not recover. What if we died before we got to confession? What if we fell in love with someone who was not Catholic? What if we left the ministry? What if our marriages did not last?[75]

The fear called out for relief, and many Catholics sought to build a culture less unnerving and condemnatory. Catholics married outside the faith in greater and greater numbers as the decade progressed and rejected the strictures on movies and literature.

The changes did not always result from larger social forces or even direct challenges to the ghetto structure, however, but came often from Catholic attempts to act in just the ways the Catholic separatist culture dictated. Ironically, the ghetto's demise derived in part from its success. Because the cultural strictures contained internal contradictions, widespread adherence led inevitably to collapse. Catholics responded so enthusiastically in some areas to diocesan officials' prescriptions that they strained the very foundation designed to support the separate Catholic culture. Catholic parents who sought to send their children to Catholic schools often found no spaces available to them—or encountered a space-rationing system that took little account of religiosity. The institutional infrastructure necessary to support Catholic separatism could not support the burgeoning Catholic population and began to collapse under its own weight.

Church officials did not seem to recognize this problem but instead cheered the growth in Catholic numbers that seemed to confirm their strategy. They relied on quantitative measures to chart Catholic successes regularly throughout the 1950s. Increases in the Catholic population made the point better than anything, particularly when those increases came at a higher rate than that of the general population, and especially when they exceeded the Protestant growth rate. The Catholic population in the Pittsburgh region did this so regularly throughout the 1950s that Church officials saw little reason to question the strategies that they prescribed to ensure the Church's future health and success. Why challenge efforts to sustain the Catholic cultural ghetto when Church membership expanded so dramatically within its confines? Surely these increases testified to the efficacy of the insular Church.

The *Pittsburgh Catholic* celebrated the growth enthusiastically throughout the decade. The paper reported new records in the diocese's population each year in the 1950s and characterized the long-term trend as "spectacular" in 1950. The 1950 rise was "the largest increase ever achieved in one year by the Church in this country," and the rate in the Pittsburgh diocese that year exceeded the general population increase by ten times. The numbers in the city of Pittsburgh were even more astounding. While the city's population increased by only 0.3 percent between 1940 and 1950, the Catholic population increased fully 14.9 percent. Whereas Pittsburgh's Catholics constituted only 36 percent of the city's 1940 population, they grew to 43 percent by 1950. Moreover, this growth represented no concentrating of Catholics within the city limits, as the Catholic suburban population exploded with even greater force. The Allegheny County population outside of Pittsburgh increased by 12 percent overall, while its Catholic population expanded by 22 percent.[76] The trend continued right through the decade, and in doing so affirmed that the Church had embarked on the right course. Moreover, the Catholic growth in Pittsburgh mirrored the national and even world scene. The *Pittsburgh Catholic* regularly conveyed reports of the Catholic population expansion in America and over the globe, and roundly criticized studies that challenged the success story.

The more Catholics the better. Though Church officials rarely explained exactly why this was true, those who attended to the public discourse readily understood. The increasing numbers, especially relative to the slower increase for Protestants, testified to the Catholic success in winning over the culture. A heavily Catholic society could best meet the materialist crisis.

One could see the results in the impact that the expanding Catholic population had in a range of areas. The population increases pushed other Catholic numbers up as well, so that by 1952 the *Pittsburgh Catholic* reported record numbers of patients in Catholic hospitals and record circulation for Catholic newspapers and magazines.[77] The separate Catholic world continued to expand dramatically. Victory over materialism could not be far away.

Education and the Limits of the Catholic Ghetto

In many ways the Catholic parochial school system marked both the triumph and the demise of the Catholic cultural ghetto. All the emphasis that Church officials placed upon attending parochial schools, when combined with the baby boom that accompanied and followed World War II, resulted in burgeoning enrollments throughout the diocese. The great upsurge in Catholic school enrollments crowned all arguments extolling Catholic education. Catholic parents testified with their children's enrollments that Catholic schools best served the Church and community, and the *Pittsburgh Catholic* trumpeted their decision with pride and a sense of victory.

The diocesan paper announced record Catholic school enrollments multiple times each year throughout the 1950s. The enrollments expanded so regularly,

FIGURE 3.1   Total Catholic School Enrollment, Pittsburgh Diocese, 1950–1960

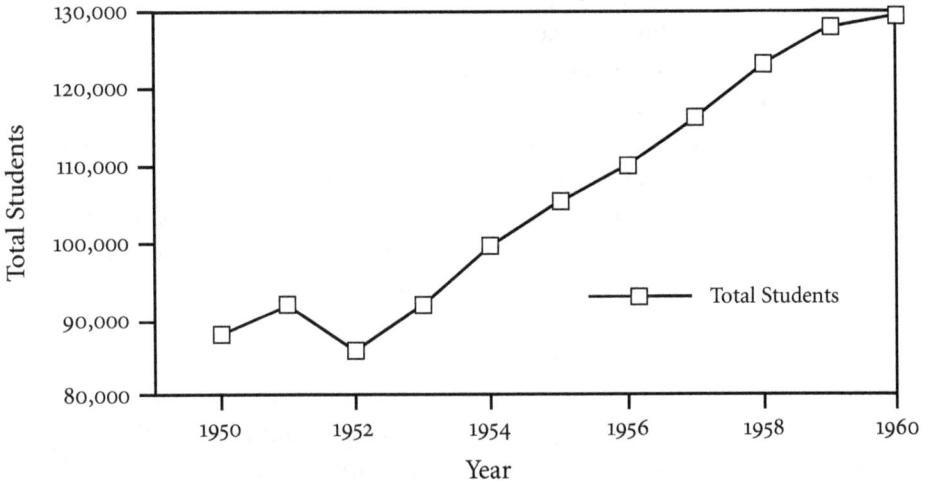

Source: Catholic Schools Annual Reports.

in fact, that they increased substantially even within individual school years. Announcements of attendance at a typical school year's close exceeded those proclaimed in January, which surpassed those from the school year's opening in September, which trumped predictions made for the coming year the previous summer. Catholic parents appeared to take their obligations to send their children to parochial grade schools and Catholic high schools seriously. The expanding enrollments suggested as much.[78] (See fig. 3.1.)

Enrollment patterns were not uniform throughout the diocese, however, as proximity to the city of Pittsburgh itself seemed to dictate the likelihood that a Catholic student would attend a Catholic school. The *Pittsburgh Catholic* reported that fully 90 percent of all Catholic school-age children within the city limits attended parochial schools, but that 60 percent in the surrounding towns within Allegheny County did the same. Outside of Allegheny County, only 34 percent of Catholic schoolchildren attended Catholic schools.[79]

The baby boom caused enrollments to expand. Increases came first among the youngest elementary grades and then reached the high schools—and only later hit Catholic colleges and universities.[80] At first the Catholic school system accommodated the enrollment boom readily, but then it strained under what historian Timothy Walch termed a "crisis of success."[81] A 1952 article in the *Pittsburgh Catholic* boasted that "the Church in the United States is more than keeping pace educationally with the marked increase in Catholic population that has taken place since the close of World War II." But just a few paragraphs later it relayed concerns that "the scope of the task still facing Catholic education is enormous" because "almost 300,000 more Catholic children will be starting their education in 1959 at age 7 than entered schools last fall."[82]

The increases in enrollments strained the diocese and individual parishes in unforeseen ways. When diocesan officials insisted that Catholic parents send their children to parochial schools, few anticipated the problem this would cause. For despite their best efforts, local parishes and the larger diocese could not accommodate the demand that diocesan regulations in combination with the baby boom created. In order to meet the demand, the diocese embarked upon what the *Pittsburgh Catholic* termed "the greatest building program in history, involving new grade schools and new high schools, as well as additions and improvements to present facilities."[83] But even these efforts could not keep pace with the expanding Catholic population. The greatest crunch came at the high school level, where school administrators literally turned away students who had just completed eight years in Catholic schools and expected to continue with four more.

The Pittsburgh diocese simply could not accommodate all of its children. The diocese included 246 elementary schools (first through eighth grade) in 1951, but only 53 high schools. Even a frantic building program in the 1950s that sought to produce regional high schools to meet the growing Catholic suburban population could not keep pace. At their peak in 1958 and 1959, Catholic high schools educated only 58 percent of the students who graduated from Catholic grade school. This represented an improvement over the previous six years, but it still left more than four out of every ten Catholic elementary school graduates out of Catholic high schools. Even more troubling, the actual number of Catholic elementary school graduates who did not go to Catholic high schools increased dramatically. In 1952, 3,512 Catholic school eighth-graders did not attend a Catholic high school, and the number grew by 58 percent in 1960 to 5,993.[84] (See fig. 3.2.)

Some parents of eighth-graders no doubt chose to send their children to public or other private schools, but a great number had no option. The Catholic high schools simply could not accept all who wished to attend. By the middle of the 1950s Catholics recognized that they had little hope of serving even their elementary school students. In 1956 discussion of the problem in Pittsburgh's daily papers forced Superintendent of Pittsburgh Catholic Schools the Rev. John B. McDowell to address the issue directly. The press reported on a recommendation to abandon Catholic education in grades one through four in order to serve all who sought Catholic schools in the later years. McDowell agreed with the di-

FIGURE 3.2   Number of Eighth-Graders Not Enrolled in Ninth Grade, 1950–1960

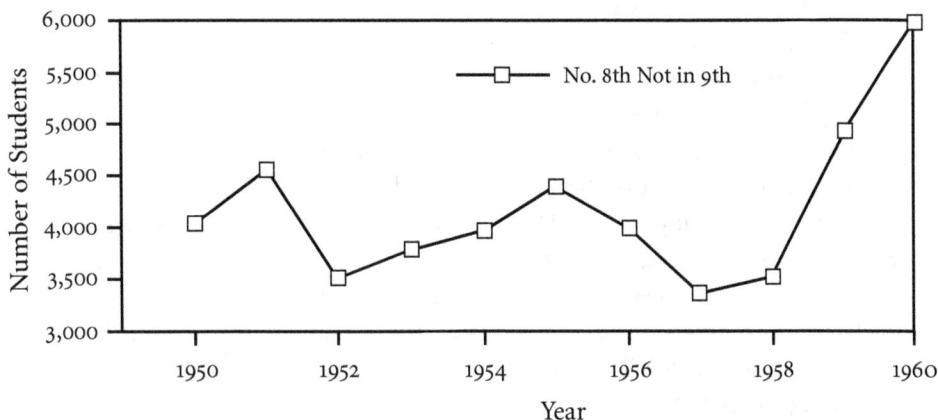

Source: Catholic Schools Annual Reports.

agnosis but not with the prescribed solution. Yes, Catholic schools could not serve all Catholic children. In fact, the schools educated fewer than half of all Catholic children across the nation. Parishes and dioceses had expanded dramatically in recent years to address this concern, but they could not expand quickly enough.

The solution, in McDowell's eyes (and therefore in Dearden's too, no doubt), was the one that many Catholics had advocated for years. If Catholics could not financially support their schools, the state should do so. After all, the Catholic schools educated 25 percent of all Pennsylvania students. European nations succeeded with this model. But this solution provided little consolation for families closed out of the very schools the bishop demanded they attend. And McDowell himself asserted later in the year that "the place for Catholic children is in the Catholic school." In the short term, McDowell concluded, "we . . . should cautiously and prudently expand."[85] But the cautious and prudent expansion did not solve the problem, especially at the high school level.

Given the strained circumstances, diocesan officials working with high school administrators determined to ration the limited secondary resources based upon academic merit. The best students gained access to the schools, and the rest entered a waiting list that the schools maintained through the four-year curriculum. When a high school student did not meet a threshold of academic success, that student lost his or her spot in the school in favor of a student on the waiting list. That this could happen surprised parents and drew coverage in the daily press. Parents did not expect the Church to dismiss students because of a school shortage. McDowell explained that when students so struggled academically, either the programs did not meet their "needs and abilities" or they were not working sufficiently hard. In either case, the abundance of students on waiting lists meant that the schools did not need to expend the effort to reach the floundering students. These children, in McDowell's words, "waste[d] the investment of the people of the diocese." Catholic high schools, he stated, could not "afford to be baby-sitters." The injunction to attend Catholic schools applied only to "deserving" students in this model, and would continue to do so as long as the demand exceeded supply. Though it remained the bishop's and McDowell's ambition "to have every Catholic boy and girl in a Catholic high school—as soon as possible," the likelihood of that ever coming to be became increasingly remote.[86]

In one of the Catholic cultural ghetto's great and irreconcilable ironies, the Church's success in persuading parents that they must send their children to Catholic schools undermined the separate Catholic world it meant to uphold. What were parents who believed the rhetoric about the necessity of the integrated religious and academic education supposed to do when they could not get their children into the only schools that diocesan officials claimed could achieve that aim? A vital component of the Catholic cultural ghetto remained closed to them, and they had to operate in the more fully public sphere.

Even more troubling, did the bishop's decision to ration high school resources based upon performance in academic courses mean that the Church had adopted the same measure of deservedness that secular institutions employed? What were parents to think when Catholic high schools expelled their children because they could not master mathematics or literature? If even Catholic schools measured student success, ultimately, on how well they solved mathematical equations or composed their essays, why go to a Catholic school at all? If Church officials agreed that math, science, and literature mattered most in the end, why would parents not send their children to the school that best taught these subjects, regardless of its Catholic nature?

The issue became even more critical after 1958, as diocesan officials could no longer reasonably harbor the ambition to provide a Catholic education to every student. After 1958 Catholic high schools reached a shrinking percentage of elementary school graduates. Though the decline leveled off in 1964, Catholic high schools by that time taught fewer than half of those students who graduated from eighth grade. (See fig. 3.3.) Similarly, the number of eighth-grade students who did not go on to Catholic high schools grew steadily in the late 1950s before leveling off at around 6,000 in the early 1960s. Catholic high schools made

FIGURE 3.3   Ninth-Grade Enrollment Compared with Eighth-Grade Enrollment, 1950–1965

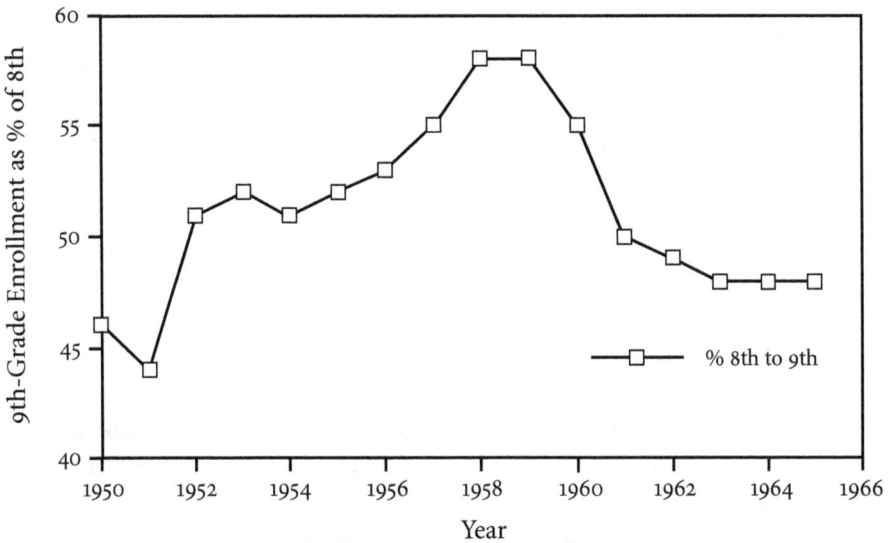

Source: Catholic Schools Annual Reports.

no progress in reducing the number of elementary school students they could not serve.

No matter how ardently Church officials argued in the public discourse about the necessity for Catholic parents to send their children to Catholic schools, this became increasingly impossible. Even parents who wanted to do so could not. The numbers, which looked so positive upon first glance and in the regular front-page articles published in the diocesan newspaper, undermined the separate Catholic world. The Catholic population grew too large to fit within its walls.

Lay confidence in the value of the distinctive Catholic education experience suffered from another development in the 1950s which proved nearly as powerful as the demographic forces that undermined the Catholic cultural ghetto. The Catholic school claim to educational supremacy over public education in the 1950s derived from its strong emphasis on the humanities and liberal arts and its unique ability to infuse the entire curriculum with a Christian perspective. Catholic schools and colleges surpassed other institutions not because they taught science more, but because they kept science in perspective. They understood and communicated science's limits.

But Americans had little interest in affirming science's limits once the Soviet Union launched the Sputnik rocket into space. The dangers that a more advanced scientific community in the Soviet Union posed to the United States sparked a massive public campaign to boost science education at every level. In the words of one Catholic commentator, Americans had entered the "era of missile-madness."[87] Catholic educators gained little cultural power at this moment when they stressed the limits their schools placed on the science mania. But Catholics continued to resist the pressure to beef up science education, and Church officials praised this strategy. The *Pittsburgh Catholic* warned in a 1957 editorial that the recent public school emphasis on science, math, engineering, and teacher education posed "a danger even greater, perhaps, than that by which we are now threatened through lack of such brilliant minds. They cannot be turned out on a production-line basis. True scholarship and true research can thrive only in an atmosphere of Truth, and Truth is God. Better to have no scientists at all than scientists without a sense of morality."[88] Worcester bishop, and future head of the Pittsburgh diocese, John J. Wright agreed. Sputnik proved only that the Soviet Union had a great deal of "know how" education, not that it had any real wisdom. Better that our schools continue with the "'know why' disciplines," such as music, languages, history, poetry, literature, philosophy, and religion. Americans risked further dehumanization if they abandoned these in their frenzied embrace of science.[89]

Pittsburgh Catholic School Superintendent Msgr. John McDowell warned against mimicking the Soviet educational model. Their heavy emphasis on math and science worked for a state that acknowledged only the physical side of humans, as it helped students to "best achieve a control of the material environment." But Catholic education recognized the whole individual: "Only after the harmonious development of all his abilities, natural and supernatural, are we justified in making man into something else—the priest, doctor, lawyer, scientist, artist—but first the man!" Early specialization should arouse fears in all humans, as it would create grave dangers to society. "The growth of man's mind is a danger only if it over-shadows the growth of his conscience, his moral principles—his spirit." The real failure of public education lay not in its inattention to science and math, but in its "lack of a spiritual concept of man and a recognition of his spiritual needs."[90]

Catholic schools labored hard to keep each student's spiritual side in sight. University of Notre Dame professor Vincent E. Smith lectured eight hundred diocesan teachers on Catholic education in a scientific age in 1958. Do not sacrifice the liberal arts in the interests of a "scientific speed-up," Smith warned, for this would ignore the total needs of the child.[91] Even Duquesne University, the diocese's largest Catholic institution of higher education and the only one that offered graduate degrees (other than theology), chose to meet the challenge Sputnik presented with "prudence rather than panic." The university chose not to alter its curriculum in Sputnik's wake, as its president emphasized in 1958 that "no major realignment of objectives is planned."[92]

How did the laity respond to the Catholic resistance to increased science emphasis? Did Catholic parents join Church officials in their repudiation of the national movement toward a greater emphasis on science, or did they reject this model? The evidence is mixed on the answer to these questions. Whatever Catholics' feelings may have been, their response to Sputnik caused no major exodus from Catholic elementary and high schools. Overall enrollment plateaued between 1959 and 1963, and high school enrollments increased dramatically (aided by the opening of still more regional Catholic high schools). Sputnik itself seemed to cause no disillusionment with Catholic education.

However, evidence of new lay disenchantment with Catholic schools exists in two sets of data. The first is the decline in the percentage of Catholic children enrolled in first grade after 1959. But even here the evidence is mixed. Figure 3.4 compares the Catholic first-grade enrollments in each year with the number of infant baptisms seven years prior in an effort to discern Catholic parents' decisions to enroll their children in Catholic schools. The percentage fluctuates between 1949 and 1965, spiking at around 70 percent in 1954 and 1959 before beginning a slow descent through the early 1960s. The timing of the decline might reflect a desire on parents' parts to send their children to schools that more enthusiastically embraced science, but the erratic patterns prior to 1959 cast doubt on this conclusion. The downward movement had occurred at least twice before and therefore suggested no departure from previous patterns.[93] Nevertheless, one should not ignore that a lower percentage of baptized Catholics enrolled in Catholic schools for first grade over time after 1959.

Similarly, a comparison of the enrollment patterns across a class cohort's years of elementary and secondary education reveals that, over time across the 1950s, Catholic students persisted less in Catholic schools as they moved toward graduation. Catholic schools lost increasingly higher numbers of students as they journeyed through the grades. Figure 3.5 compares entering cohorts from 1951–52, 1954–55, 1957–58, and 1960–61. For each cohort, the retention rate decreases across the grade levels.[94] The data suggest that parents who chose to enroll their children in Catholic schools in first grade became increasingly disenchanted with Catholic education over time. Again, this pattern did not result

FIGURE 3.4   First-Grade Enrollment as Percent of Infant Baptisms Seven Years Prior, Pittsburgh Diocese, 1949–1965

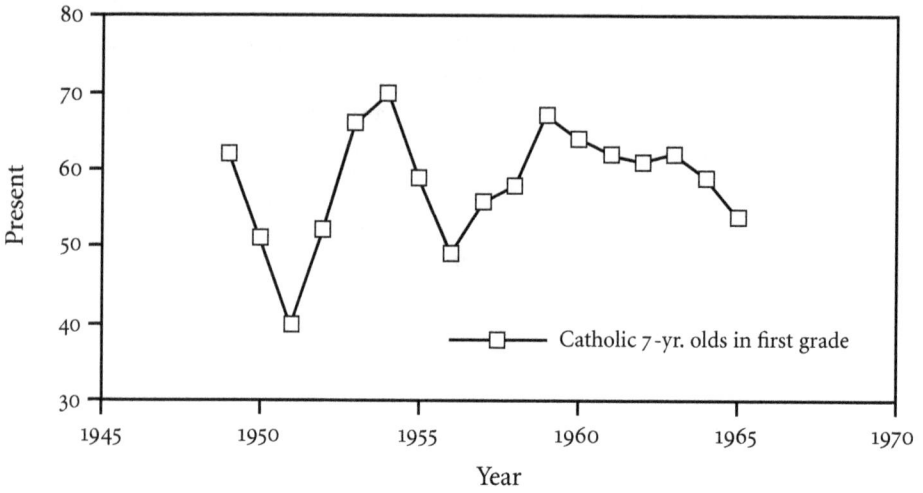

Source: Catholic Schools Annual Reports.

FIGURE 3.5   Catholic School Enrollment as Percentage of First Grade, Pittsburgh Diocese

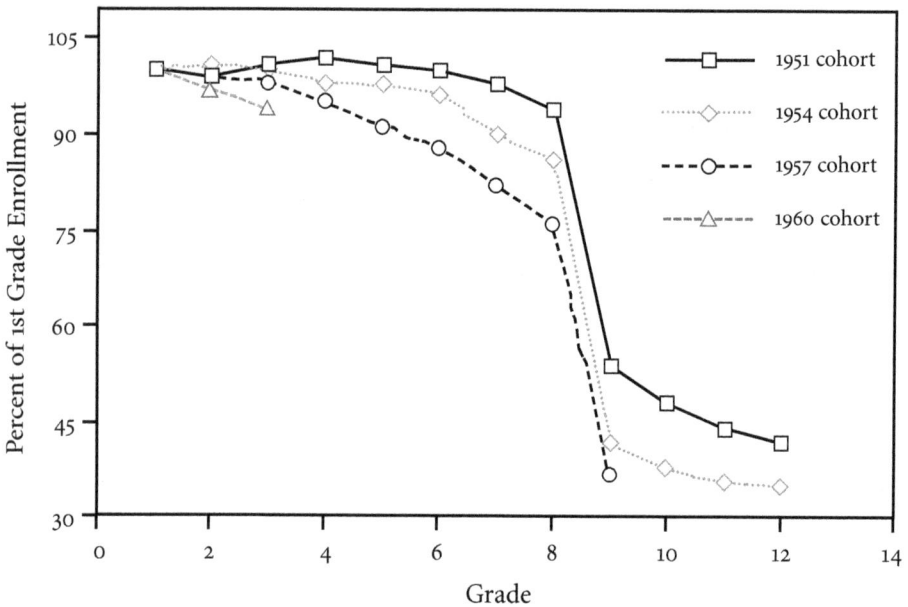

Source: Catholic Schools Annual Reports.

from Sputnik, but it does reflect the Catholic cultural ghetto's weakening power during the 1950s. Catholic parents felt the lure of the Catholic school less and less throughout the decade.

Though education's biggest challenge to the Catholic cultural ghetto clearly came at the elementary and secondary levels, Catholic college graduates also weakened the separate Catholic culture. The challenge here came not from an inability to accommodate students in Catholic institutions, but rather from an inability to incorporate a highly educated Catholic laity into parishes. Catholic college graduates for the most part enthusiastically embraced the Church but found little meaningful role in the existing parish structure. Monsignor DeBlanc reported the question Catholic college graduates so often asked: "Why does the Church insist that we get a Catholic college education, but when we get back into our parishes, all we are asked to do is usher?" Donald McDonald reported the story of one Catholic who emerged from his Catholic college education ready to serve his church and parish. He "knocked on his pastor's door to announce that he was ready to do battle for the Church, the hierarchy, Catholic Action, etc. 'You know my first assignment?' he asked. 'I was given the job of carrying the banner in the monthly Holy Name Society Communion.'"[95]

The college graduate challenge to the Catholic separatist culture derived to a great degree from the failure of the ghetto to accommodate a population that sought, initially at least, to remain within its walls. For the most part, graduates did not come home from college rejecting the Church. Almost the opposite took place. They returned from college eager to play significant roles in the Church they embraced but found little opportunity for them in the model parish priests clung to through most of the 1950s.

The one area open to Catholic college graduates reflected the transforming cultural ghetto. The vast increase in demand for Catholic elementary and secondary schools rapidly overwhelmed a system that depended primarily upon priests, brothers, and sisters to teach. Catholic schools needed teachers, and by the middle of the 1950s administrators acknowledged that no campaign to increase vocations could possibly produce enough clergy and religious to staff the schools. The schools needed lay teachers, and for elementary schools in the 1950s this meant female teachers. The diocese recognized this need publicly as early as 1954, and established a special scholarship program in 1955 for high school seniors who intended to become teachers in Catholic schools.[96] When the shortage reached more acute levels in 1957, the superintendent for Catholic schools pleaded for qualified lay teachers to meet the emergency need for forty-five teachers. Msgr. John McDowell opined that certainly there are many housewives who have all their children in school and some who have their children through school who could help us in this emergency. I am certain that there are any number of housewives who have no family responsibilities and are qualified teachers but have given little thought to returning to the field because they are not in financial need. We are appealing to these people to give a hand in our schools.[97]

Catholic schools needed lay teachers, and the laity met the call. But the increasing percentage of lay teachers throughout the postwar period transformed Catholic schools. The financial implications alone brought great change. The laity could not work for the same wages as sisters, brothers, and priests because they had to support themselves and their families. This obligation to pay a higher (though still quite modest) wage forced Catholic parishes to make still further economic demands upon their parishioners.

Lay teachers also changed the atmosphere of Catholic schools. Clergy and religious no longer interposed themselves between the student and the culture in all areas, but increasingly came to be relegated to the "purely" religious education within the Catholic school. Students still by and large learned their catechism from nuns, brothers, and priests, but they took their math, English, science, and social studies classes from lay teachers. These teachers did not embody the same visible manifestation of the hierarchy's mediating presence as did sisters, priests, and brothers.

Intermarriage

The contradiction that undermined Catholic separatism in education resulted, at least in part, from the baby boom. Catholic schools simply could not keep up with the expanding Catholic population, and so Catholics could not attend the schools designed to maintain the ghetto. The Catholic baby boom derived, to a considerable degree, from the trend toward early marriage and child bearing— two issues connected intimately to the discourse on sensuality. Here too, young Catholics embraced the prescriptions the discourse contained. In fact, they so enthusiastically entered marriages that Church officials began to worry about whether such unions could last. By the middle of the 1950s, Church officials actually discouraged young people from marrying, though they did not endorse sexual activity for unmarried partners. (See fig. 3.6.)

Put in simple terms, the discourse urged young Catholics to refrain from sexual activity, or more precisely, to contain sexual activity within marriage. Catholics more readily assented to the latter proposition in the immediate post-

FIGURE 3.6   Pittsburgh Diocese Catholic Marriage Rate, 1935–1975

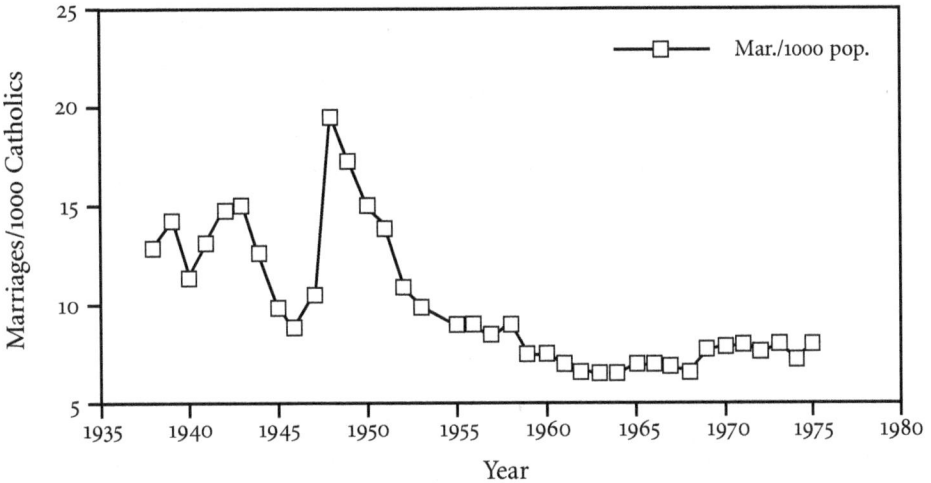

Source: Catholic Directory.

war years, as they married at a remarkable rate through 1949—perhaps compensating for the downward trend World War II created. But in 1950 the Catholic marriage rate in the Pittsburgh diocese began a decline that would not level off until the early 1960s. When it did finally flatten, it stood at a point lower even than that during the Depression's last years, and it suggested that Catholics became ambivalent about the institution. Had Catholics come to reject married life in the very decade noted for domesticity?[98]

One might reach this conclusion from reading the Catholic discourse on marriage. For in the 1950s, Catholic commentators worried publicly about the impact that early marriage and parenthood had on Catholics. They worried especially about the brief postwar rise in the national divorce rate and the potential return to the high numbers of the late 1940s. Even as the divorce rate declined through the 1950s, Catholic commentators continued to rail against anything that might lead to increases.[99]

The concern about potential divorce and unhappy marriages led Church officials to discourage young Catholics from marrying. The concerns emerged in the latter part of the decade, well after the marriage rate decline got under way. The *Pittsburgh Catholic* editors observed in 1956 that "far too many Catholic couples are woefully unprepared for marriage," and reported an unidentified survey in which 69 percent of Catholic men and 82 percent of Catholic women agreed.[100] Monsignor DeBlanc relayed the results of another study that concluded that "most unhappy marriages result from couples who marry under the age of 20," and that age alone definitely affects happiness in marriage.[101]

One solution that Church officials offered to the problem was to encourage Catholic couples considering marriage to attend training sessions that either prepared them for married life or dissuaded them from entering the institution. Local pastors most often handled the preparation, but various other programs also emerged. The Saint Gerard Guild offered some preparation, as did the Cana Conference and Duquesne University through broadcasts over its radio station. The NCWC published a guide entitled "Toward Happiness and Holiness in Marriage."

Others suggested that young Catholics simply not marry. Fr. Francis J. Connell, C.Ss.R., dean of the School of Sacred Theology at Catholic University, favored this strategy. He recommended to young men that they wait until they reached age twenty-five and to young women that they wait until their twenty-third birthday before marrying. Furthermore, young Catholics should not go steady unless there was "a possibility of marriage." Connell urged young couples to recognize that marriage existed to better society, not to make them happy personally. The *Pittsburgh Catholic* published his conclusions and advice on page 1.[102]

Lay Catholics in Pittsburgh appear to have taken the ambivalence in the Catholic discourse on marriage seriously, as they slowed their rate of marriage throughout the decade. Church officials also urged laymen and laywomen to marry inside the faith, a strategy the laity at first adopted and then rejected in the 1950s. Figure 3.7 shows a decline in the percentage of mixed marriages from the close of World War II until 1954. But in 1955 the percentage of Catholics who married a non-Catholic in a Church-sanctioned union began a twenty-year climb. When Catholics married outside the faith least—when they maintained the cultural ghetto walls best—in 1951, 1952, and 1954, fully 81 percent of all marriages within the Church paired Catholics with Catholics. This fell to 63 percent by 1975, after a decline that started dramatically in the mid 1950s.[103] Thus, the Pittsburgh laity began to reject one of the cultural ghetto's strongest pillars in direct contradiction to the unequivocal instructions in the Catholic prescriptive literature. This departure reflected a conscious decision to reject one of Catholic separatism's central tenets.

The Irony of Success in the Battle Against Sensuality, Indecency, and License

The battle against the materialist carnal and corporal impulses proved so daunting that Catholics readily joined forces with others to achieve victory. In endorsing these interfaith efforts to achieve Catholic cultural ideals, Church officials further undermined the distinctive "Catholic" take on these cultural phenom-

FIGURE 3.7   Mixed Marriages as a Percent of All Catholic Marriages, Pittsburgh Diocese, 1943–1975

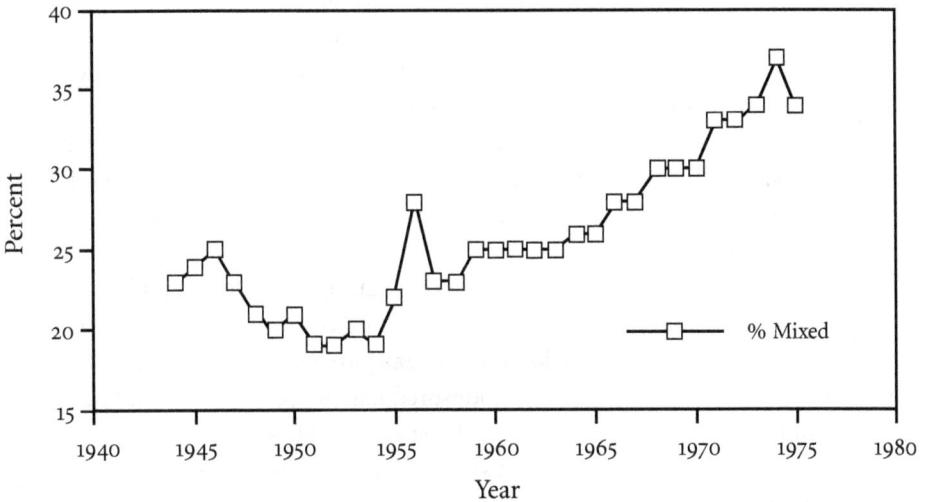

Source: Catholic Directory.

ena. The National Committee of Catholic Charities urged delegates to its 1956 convention to "seek ways of meeting with non-Catholics in trying to solve problems of general community interest."[104] The lay experience with non-Catholics further undermined the cultural ghetto and moved Catholics outward.

A good example of such a program was the "Keep Sunday Sacred" campaign that Dearden assigned to the Holy Name Society and the Diocesan Council of Catholic Women. Though the *Pittsburgh Catholic* presented the effort as a Catholic endeavor, it also reported that it expected "non-sectarian civic and patriotic groups, merchants, business associations and labor unions" to join the drive. After all, similar campaigns in a variety of cities joined Catholics with others to recognize the Sabbath. In Indianapolis, Methodist and Episcopal bishops joined with Catholics. The American Federation of Labor urged its Des Moines members not to shop unnecessarily on Sundays and put up billboards to that effect in Denver. In what appears surprising from a religious (if not a labor) perspective, the Hebrew Butchers' union in New York opposed legislation allowing kosher butcher shops to open on Sunday.[105] Ecumenical cooperation strengthened the campaign to protect the most important time Catholics set aside each week to gather and affirm their exclusive community, but it also pulled Catholics out of the social and cultural ghetto.

Similarly, the "Put Christ in Christmas" campaign forced Catholics to interact with like-minded Protestants, and even the state. Moreover, the movement sought to persuade merchants, many of whom were not Catholic, to stop reinforcing the commercialization of Christmas with their emphasis on Santa Claus rather than Christ. The early (and very modest) successes came in cooperation with merchants' organizations that pledged support for the principle of a lessened commercial focus on Christmas—or at least a commercial emphasis that included religious themes. Christmas cards provide a good example. The American Greeting Card Association reported in 1957 that card companies had finally begun selling religiously themed Christmas cards in large numbers. This development resulted from a ten-year campaign by Catholic and Protestant leaders to spur card companies to produce such cards. Card companies recognized the commercial value these cards held as Americans purchased them in increasing numbers. Other commercial groups sponsored nativity scenes to remind consumers of the "true" reason for their holiday spending. These re-creations of the scene at Christ's birth in a Bethlehem stable typically included statues of shepherds, Joseph, Mary, the infant Jesus, three wise men, and a variety of animals. The *Pittsburgh Catholic* noted and celebrated the trend in 1956, when it ran a photographic series on the various displays in the diocese. It particularly praised the Producemen's outdoor nativity scene erected at Saint Stanislaus Church in Pittsburgh's produce warehouse district.[106]

Church officials may have considered the proven commercial viability of religious items at Christmas time to be a victory for Christianity, but it was less clearly a triumph for the Catholic cultural ghetto. Catholics and Protestants alike pushed retailers to adopt religious advertising themes and to sell religious items for Christmas gifts, and Catholic and Protestant consumers mingled as they patronized these stores. Retailers did not appeal only to "Catholic" shoppers, as such campaigns unnecessarily limited profits. Likewise, the interdenominational success in getting municipalities to honor Christmas in explicitly religious terms also weakened the ghetto walls. For example, the city of Pittsburgh's official 1955 nativity scene in Mellon Park resulted from Catholic and Protestant pressures applied to local officials, and drew Catholic and Protestant (and other) visitors to the park.[107]

Literature and Movies

Many pressures led to the decline of the Legion of Decency in Pittsburgh, some external and some internal. Historians who study Catholic efforts to shape the movies explain the Legion of Decency's decline in two ways. They give most attention to developments in Hollywood and Washington, where cultural and political elites battled over the cultural landscape with significant repercussions for people in places like Pittsburgh. In these explanations, movie studios, producers, directors, and screenwriters increasingly challenged the Production Code Administration, which softened its opposition to films that portrayed social ills frankly as a result. This placed the Legion of Decency increasingly at odds with its former ally, and forced the Church hierarchy to wage the movie oversight battle by itself. This intensified when the Catholic Joseph Breen retired from the PCA directorship in 1954 and the Episcopalian Geoff Shurlock replaced him. Similarly, the U.S. Supreme Court rejected prior censorship of films in a number of cases, and weakened state and local censorship boards' abilities to prohibit theaters from showing films.[108]

More relevantly for the Pittsburgh experience, historians suggest that the Legion lost influence with the Catholic laity, who failed to take their moviegoing orders from the Church hierarchy. Exactly how this happened is less clear, though historians seem to suggest that the laity became increasingly concerned about censorship generally.[109] In this explanation, moviegoers drove the decline by emboldening studios to take on more sensitive subjects without fear of box office failure. The motion picture industry cooperated with the Legion so long as studios and theaters feared the economic repercussions of not doing so. As long as the laity followed the hierarchy's instructions to boycott specific movies or studios, the economic disincentive to produce, distribute, and show such movies remained significant. But the studios feared this less and less throughout the 1950s, suggesting that they came to recognize Church officials' limited capacity to control lay behavior.[110]

But many of the problems the Catholic movement to constrain moviemakers encountered came from internal disagreements over which movies violated moral decency. The consensus even among Catholics who sought to curtail immorality dissipated as the decade progressed, and this weakened their authority.

The Catholic campaign against indecent and immoral movies and literature peaked in 1955 before its steady decline in the latter part of the decade. The greatest blow to its continued success was the growing popular understanding of the work as a form of censorship and narrow-mindedness, two critiques that successfully painted the efforts as inconsistent with American ideals and chafed increasingly throughout the decade.[111]

Gregory Black points to the powerful effect that Jesuit theologian John Courtney Murray's influential articles criticizing Catholic censorship practices had on Catholic priests. Murray published his first article in 1956 and the second in 1957.[112] Incidents in Pittsburgh in 1955 fueled concerns about just this issue and lent support to those who feared that the Catholic crusade had crossed the line. The *Pittsburgh Catholic* reported approvingly on the great success of a parish book burning in McKeesport to rid the city of objectionable comics. Holy Trinity parish and school officials urged children to bring their comic books into the school, where a committee gathered and examined the works. The committee returned comics that they considered moral to the children but gathered the rest for a large book burning. In all, the parish set fire to 1,810 comic books that officials considered objectionable, and then pressed the mayor to "do something" to protect further the community's children.[113]

Not all Church officials advocated book burnings, but the Holy Trinity pyrotechnical efforts, and the prominent space provided to the event in the *Pittsburgh Catholic,* sent a clear message to those who worried about Catholic campaigns to shape popular culture. It did not help that the Legion of Decency condemned the movie *Storm Center* one year later for its forthright criticism of book censors. Though the movie did not violate any of the Legion's criteria for decency and morality, the Legion condemned *Storm Center* anyway because the film portrayed censors and book burners in what Legion officials considered a naively nefarious light. The movie starred Bette Davis as a small-town librarian who fought book censorship on the "specious" grounds that even patrons who read Communist books might come to understand better, and more knowingly reject, the materialist philosophy. The Legion claimed that the movie treated "book burning, anti-Communism, [and] civil liberties" in an "oversimplified" manner. The Legion's executive secretary, Fr. Paul J. Hayes, argued that the movie "confuse[d] liberty with unrestricted freedom," and that only those people with a "solid background, sometimes a specialized background," could safely view the movie. William Mooring, Hollywood's Catholic syndicated columnist, worried that the movie portrayed those who wished to censor books as "crooked, narrow, illiterate or fanatical"—rather than as heroic guardians of public morality.[114]

In the years that followed the book burning, Catholics responded more and more defensively to charges of censorship with strong denials of such motives even while they decried any effort to weaken their powers.

As long as Pittsburgh Catholics recognized the Legion's authority to speak for the Church on the moral propriety of movies (and no other authority), the Legion's power in Pittsburgh remained strong. But Catholic efforts to constrain the laity's cultural exposure ran into internal problems of authority as well as external pressures. The case of the movie *Letters from My Windmill* is illustrative. The movie consists of three short stories, two of which feature priests portrayed in humorous and other than devotional light. The Legion of Decency condemned the film because it "contained in the first two episodes a frivolous, disrespectful and grossly comical presentation of religion and religious characters" which would, in the Legion's eyes, lead to "misunderstanding" religious practices. French Catholic authorities shared no such worries, and deemed the movie acceptable. Papers across the country, including the *New York Times,* pointed out the contradiction. Once American Catholics learned that the French hierarchy permitted the French laity to view the movie, they questioned the Legion's ruling. The Legion's supporters, including syndicated columnist William Mooring, backed the Legion's rating on the grounds that American Catholics perceived films differently than did French Catholics. Mooring pointed out that once before, when the movie *God Needs Men* won a Catholic award in Europe, the Legion had deemed the movie objectionable.[115]

The Legion itself seemed to harbor doubts about its authority, as it altered its rating system in 1957 to determine more finely which movies constituted a danger to whom. The existing rating system proved too crude an instrument for the 1950s moviegoing Catholic population, and the new ratings sought to refine assessments by adding classifications for teenagers. The problem, from the Legion's perspective, was that adults attended "B"-rated movies under the assumption that the objections attended primarily to adolescents. Legion Executive Secretary Msgr. Thomas F. Little argued that this more refined system would clarify for adults that they were not to attend any B-rated films. To do so would not only threaten the adult viewer's spiritual life, but would also endanger the "moral behavior patterns which condition public morality." In other words, even if adult viewers knew that attending a B movie posed no threat to their spiritual lives, they were not to view the movie on the grounds that it might hurt the public good. The Legion's position constituted visible backpedaling in an effort to regain its authority with lay Catholics. Legion leaders understood by this time that many Catholics did not share their concern for the dangers that B movies posed to individual viewers. In fact, even Catholic theologians had just weeks before determined that attending a B-rated film did not constitute a mortal sin. The new classification represented a conscious effort to relegitimize the rating system in the eyes of Catholics who thought it to be too cautious and restrictive.[116] (See table 3.2.)

In realigning the rating system, however, the Legion decided not to reevaluate all movies that it had already labeled. The task was simply too daunting. The new rating system pertained only to movies coming out for the first time, and left questions for moviegoing Catholics about previously released films. How many past films in the B category really fit into the new A-3 category?

An even more significant blow to Pittsburgh Catholic efforts to excise indecent and immoral literature and movies came in 1956, when the state legislature

TABLE 3.2   Legion of Decency Movie-Rating System

Legion of Decency Rating	Explanation	Who Is Eligible to View?
A-1	Morally unobjectionable for general patronage	Adults Teenagers Children
A-2	Morally unobjectionable for adults and adolescents	Adults Teenagers
A-3	Morally unobjectionable for adults	Adults
B	Morally objectionable in part for all	Nobody
C	Condemned	Nobody

failed to enact legislation to reconstitute the state Board of Motion Picture Censors. The state had supported such a board ever since 1915, but successful challenges in state courts in the early 1950s rendered the board unconstitutional. Despite Gov. George Leader's warnings that the state would become the "dumping ground for vulgar and indecent films," the legislature declined to pass a bill to reconstitute a board which could pass constitutional muster.[117] Without state support, Church officials worried publicly about society's increased vulnerability to popular culture's depravities. The hierarchy recognized that moral suasion did not suffice, that Catholics would attend such movies unless the state intervened. The Legion alone could not safeguard public morality.

But the largest blow to the Legion of Decency's authority came from television, which rendered all Legion evaluations of existing movies contingent. Because networks and stations edited movies that they aired to make room for commercials and fit them within the rigid time frame that television demanded, the original Legion ratings for movies shown in theaters ceased to guide viewers accurately. Some television versions of condemned movies still contained the objectionable parts, some did not. The Legion decided not even to attempt to rate each television version of movies that it had rated for release in the cinema.

This meant that ordinary Catholics had to determine their own risks and exercise even greater control over their interaction with culture.

The Church had lost its ability to interpose itself successfully between the laity and American movie culture. Pittsburghers needed to look no farther than the Squirrel Hill Theater for proof of this. In February 1958 the district attorney of Philadelphia seized two copies of the film *And God Created Woman* from two Philadelphia theaters. The legal battle over this action worked all the way to the Pennsylvania Supreme Court, which heard arguments twice and deliberated for so long that its decision came long after the film's first run ended. Unlike the theaters in Philadelphia, the Squirrel Hill Theater had been showing the film to large crowds since January and continued doing so through March. The Squirrel Hill Theater was an independent movie house in one of Pittsburgh's wealthier neighborhoods, an area adjacent to the University of Pittsburgh and the Carnegie Institute of Technology. It regularly showed foreign and art films aimed at the city's highbrow residents. But the theater was only two blocks from Saint Philomena Church, where a dozen or so Redemptorist priests and brothers reigned over one of the city's most famous parishes. America's first male saint, John Neuman, once worked as its pastor, and another former pastor, Francis Seelos, was well on his way to the same honor. The Redemptorists traveled from the parish to give rousing missions throughout the region aimed at reviving parishioner participation and the fear of sin's consequences for wayward Catholics. They thundered from the region's pulpits about the eternal dangers wayward Catholics faced should they stray from the path the Church laid out for them. But the Redemptorists were powerless to stop their neighborhood theater from showing one of the few movies that the Legion of Decency condemned in the 1950s. Whether parishioners actually went to see the movie is an open question, though many certainly passed the marquee daily. And the *Pittsburgh Catholic* reminded parishioners for three consecutive weeks that the theater flouted the Legion's guidelines. Seven drive-in theaters picked up the film in June, when the Squirrel Hill Theater began playing another film that the Legion had condemned.[118] The Catholic ability to limit lay exposure to materialist culture had declined to the point that area patrons sustained an extended run of a condemned movie in the heart of one of the diocese's highest-profile parishes.

The Church's success in shaping movie experiences had always depended on its ability to prohibit the production and distribution, rather than the consumption, of movies to which it objected. Church officials therefore supported campaigns to re-establish state censorship boards. Because the Supreme Court had ruled against prior restraint—the censorship of films before anyone showed them in public—the new efforts focused on establishing censorship boards that would seize films after they had been displayed once or twice but before they enjoyed widespread distribution. The *Pittsburgh Catholic* and the Knights of Columbus supported such legislation in 1959. But in so doing Catholic officials felt more constrained by the growing sentiment that censorship in general was wrong. John Ward opened one editorial supporting censorship legislation with a strong statement on the dangers of government censorship in general. "Government censorship is always suspect," he intoned, before insisting that democracy's survival depended on the state's ability to confiscate movies after they had been displayed once in public.[119] Even after the state supreme court struck down Pennsylvania's obscenity laws, Allegheny County's Catholic district attorney vowed that he would not return any of the sixty-five reels of film that his office had seized just weeks before. The films were "not only lewd and obscene but degenerate," he argued in taking his stand. He too called for new laws that would make his actions legal.[120] Just such legislation passed through the Pennsylvania Senate easily but languished and then died in the House. By the end of 1959 Church officials could depend on no state agency to enforce their morality code for movies, and were forced to rely on both movie studios and theater owners to keep indecent films from reaching Catholic audiences. And this seemed less and less likely as Hollywood and movie chains faced stiff competition from foreign film producers and television.

The last line of defense came down to Catholic movie patrons themselves. The Legion's once-great authority had waned considerably by the late 1950s, though Bishop Dearden continued to insist that all Catholics take the annual pledge, with its attendant promise to avoid indecent literature as well. But by 1958 local Church officials recognized the limited appeal that such a pledge held for the laity, who seemed confident in their ability to judge for themselves whether particular films put their souls in danger. In that year, diocesan officials pitched the pledge not as a way for Catholics to rein themselves in, therefore, but rather as a means of saving others who might not be sophisticated or savvy enough to resist the dangers mature films posed. John Ward reminded *Pittsburgh Catholic* readers on the day of the pledge that Christ commanded each Catholic to love his neighbors. "Consequently, he realizes that even though he might consider a certain film no source of spiritual danger for himself, he still will refuse to patronize it because it is dangerous for his neighbor and especially for his neighbor's children."[121] The logic strained credibility and ceased to persuade area Catholics. When John Wright came to head the diocese in 1959 he took a different approach. Of course Hollywood and foreign producers flouted decency. Of course Catholics were to avoid occasions of sin, and therefore should pass on movies that the Legion condemned. But

> no special pledge should be needed to remind us of what we must reject and avoid by virtue of our very dignity as Christians and of our baptismal vows. These compel us to avoid all "occasions of sin," whether these be immoral movies, places of ill-repute or other focal points of degeneracy.[122]

No parishioner in the Pittsburgh diocese stood during Mass that year, or ever after, to take the Legion's pledge.

BY THE END OF THE 1950S, PITTSBURGH CATHOLICS NO LONGER lived within the separate world in which they had entered the decade. Evidence from education, marriage, and cultural experiences strongly point to the lay exit from the separate cultural and social world that Church officials once took such great pains to maintain. Ironically enough, it was the very commitment to maintaining a separate cultural community in the 1950s with distinct behaviors and beliefs which helped spell the Catholic ghetto's doom by the 1960s. As this chapter argues, it was not only the crisis, but also the strategy to combat it that ultimately undid the elaborate separate world that Catholics had created over the course of the previous generations. But if Catholics no longer defined themselves by their separate cultural world, how did they act "Catholic"? The answer lay in the Church's continued and growing support of social justice.

CHAPTER FOUR

Social Justice and Reform

The role of a priest in social reform is, in a sense, secondary to that of the laity, who alone can bring about a reconstruction of the social order.

—MSGR. GEORGE HIGGINS (1955)

Today we need an army of Catholic laity who will carry the mission of the Church into every field of human endeavor. Our society, disunited religiously and starved spiritually, is fertile ground for one or the other of two things—the seed of Materialism or the seed of the revealed religion of Christ.

—THE MOST REV. COLEMAN F. CARROLL, S.T.D.,

AUXILIARY BISHOP OF PITTSBURGH (1955)

IN MANY WAYS, THE CATHOLIC COMMITMENT TO SOCIAL JUSTICE represented a strategy for combating materialism very different from both devotionalism and the attempt to maintain the Catholic cultural and social ghetto. For the two latter approaches called Catholics out of the public realm (at least partially) and into the private sphere. In this way the Church could secure the laity's virtue by eliminating, reducing, or mediating contact with the materialist culture. But the Catholic commitment to social justice called Catholics into the public sphere, albeit to confront and transform American society along Catholic ideals.

Church officials in Pittsburgh prescribed three main social justice campaigns during the 1950s, though the emphasis on each changed during the decade. The first sought to blunt the exploitation that workers and their families experienced in American capitalism. The second aimed to combat the commercialization of all social and cultural interactions, and the third attempted to eradicate racial bias and discrimination.

When Catholics spoke of "social justice" in the early years of the 1950s they aimed their remarks at the economic system that allowed a relative few to prosper at the expense of many and undermined the basic human dignity of Catholic workers and their families. The attempt to transform capitalism, or at least ameliorate its harshest aspects, dominated the Catholic struggle for social justice until mid-decade. John Collins pushed especially strongly for workers' rights and urged Catholics to support non-Communist union efforts to protect workers and their families. Fr. Charles Owen Rice joined in this effort. Bishop Dearden did not fully share their perspective, however, and when he purchased the *Pittsburgh Catholic* and removed Collins from the editor's position, the emphasis on this aspect of social justice declined markedly.

Collins also decried the growing commercialism that had infiltrated all of American social life, and reduced all social interaction and institutions to commercial exchanges. Bishop Dearden too worried about commercialization, and his influence elevated efforts to combat commercialism to a central place in the social justice movement.

Concerns for racial justice came alive in the public discourse when Collins edited the paper, suffered neglect under Dearden's control, and re-emerged when John Wright became Pittsburgh's bishop. By the time the Second Vatican Council first met, the commitment to racial equality overshadowed concerns about labor and capital in the Catholic discussion of social justice. Racial discrimination, a complex of social customs and legal practices that privileged an individual's skin color or other physical features over his or her spiritual identity, constituted a pernicious form of materialism. It clearly emphasized the "accidents" of apparent physical differences over the "essence" of common humanity and membership in the mystical body of Christ. If the Catholic discourse in Pittsburgh condemned capitalists for exploiting the poor, it also denounced whites for exploiting blacks—especially in the American South.

THE BATTLE AGAINST MATERIALISM

The battle against capitalist materialism took two discernible forms in the 1950s. The first pitted the Church against the greed of the "free market" that indifferently discarded the common good and people's welfare in the unbridled pursuit of material wealth. The discourse called upon Catholics to support labor unions and to reject all endeavors that undermined personal security and human dignity, and opened individuals and families to exploitation. The second called all Catholics to combat society's rapid and pervasive commercialization, the process that commodified virtually all of American culture.

Exploitation

In some ways it is difficult to tease out concerns about capitalist exploitation of the poor from concerns about Communism. For Church officials regularly argued that capitalism's flaws opened the doors to Communist infiltration, that the poor could more easily ignore Communist entreaties if only they did not suffer so much under capitalism. If fears of Communist success constituted the entire Catholic concern about capitalism, then one might reasonably conclude that Church officials saw no major problems with the free market. But capitalism posed serious problems in its own right, and the 1950s discourse addressed these too regularly, emphatically, and comprehensively to dismiss them as mere secondary concerns.

Much of the discourse focused on the free market's propensity to create exploitative situations. Capitalism, in this analysis, promoted disparities in wealth and guaranteed that many lived below the minimum standards for human dignity. Someone or something had to intervene to protect the poor from the greedy rich, and the Catholic discourse recommended two main institutions. The first was the labor union, a group of workers who banded together to represent themselves in negotiation with management. In the early years of the 1950s the Catholic discourse in Pittsburgh saw labor and management to be at odds, and it regularly supported labor's efforts to resist management's attempts to exploit workers (and by extension their families). The second was the government, in its local, state, and federal forms, which appeared in the discourse as potentially dispassionate advocates for economic justice.

The bulk of the discourse on materialist capitalism focused on labor–management conflicts in the early 1950s, with the *Pittsburgh Catholic* invariably supporting workers in their efforts to wrest living wages from their employers. In fact, one might reasonably consider the diocesan paper under John Collins's editorship to be a labor paper. Collins carried reports of labor conflicts and interpreted them in light of the two papal encyclicals that so profoundly shaped Catholic understanding of the economic sphere: Leo XIII's 1891 *Rerum Novarum* and Pius XI's 1931 *Quadragesimo Anno*. Each of these encyclicals placed human dignity at the center of any economic system, found Western societies deficient in ensuring that dignity, and supported workers' rights to organize unions as a sound means to achieving those ends. Both saw cooperation between capitalists and workers as the ideal way to achieve what Pius XI called "social justice."[1]

Though many see *Rerum Novarum* as the beginning of official Church support for workers in their efforts to achieve social justice, the Catholic discourse in the 1950s regularly portrayed it as a mere continuation of a long-standing tradition. For example, John Collins called the two encyclicals "a repetition of the cry the Church has always raised against the oppression and exploitation of man," and he pointed out that the modern popes have always denounced "the injustices which made industrial civilization inhuman."[2]

The two social encyclicals have dominated Catholic social thought ever since their publication, and continue to have a shaping influence more than a century after Leo XIII first issued *Rerum Novarum*. The *Pittsburgh Catholic* argued in 1951 that more Catholics read *Rerum Novarum* and *Quadragesimo Anno* than any of the other papal encyclicals, and that the two letters "have had a more profound influence on social and economic life than any similar documents issued in modern times." John Collins observed that *Rerum Novarum* "caused a terrific impact when it was issued."[3] The regular references to the encyclicals in the Catholic discourse testify to the power they held in early 1950s Catholic Pittsburgh, as did the major coverage their two anniversaries received in the *Pittsburgh Catholic*.

Pittsburgh's Bishop Hugh C. Boyle took the two encyclicals very seriously as he guided the diocese through the three decades leading up to the 1950s. In fact, they provided official Church sanctions to sentiments that Boyle developed through critical life experiences, and offered solutions to the economic exploitation that Boyle felt so acutely as he grew up. As much as any Catholic, Boyle was predisposed to welcome the support for the economically disenfranchised that *Rerum Novarum* and *Quadragesimo Anno* offered. A thumbnail sketch of Boyle's early years tells why.

Bishop Boyle started out his life in the kind of working-class family that *Rerum Novarum* sought to bind to the Church. Both parents immigrated to America from Ireland, and they met and married in the coal and iron city of Johnstown, Pennsylvania. Soon after, they moved to Cambria City, a short distance along the Little Conemaugh River from Johnstown. Boyle's father, Charles, labored in the area coal mines, and his mother worked at home bearing and raising their thirteen children—four of whom died in infancy. The Boyle family knew what it meant to do without as they learned firsthand the gnawing pain of hunger and the chill that winter brought. They knew the limits life in the mines and coal patches imposed on families, and they understood the power the Church constituted for miners' families. Accordingly, they sent their eldest child,

Hugh, away from the mines, to Saint Vincent Preparatory School, College, and Seminary.[4]

If Boyle's early family background and childhood experiences did not predispose him to favor labor in its battle with capital, the events of May 31, 1889, cemented his commitment to working people. On that day, after heavy rains, the earthen dam that supported the South Fork Fishing and Hunting Club's recreational lake burst open and sent floodwaters rushing toward Cambria City and Johnstown. The club served the regions' wealthy capitalists, including some of those who owned the mills in Boyle's future diocese of Pittsburgh. At the dam-supported lake these men and their families enjoyed summers of boating, swimming, and fishing far from the grime and soot that their mills spewed out miles to the west. The dam had deteriorated over the years, and developed "leaks" that the Fishing and Hunting Club director acknowledged but did not repair adequately. It was an expensive undertaking. The intense rain that May morning simply overwhelmed the structure, which gave way and sent 20 million tons of water streaming down toward Johnstown.[5]

Boyle's family sat gathered around the table in Cambria City for an early dinner, unsuspecting, as the baby lay sleeping on the couch in the next room. Boyle himself resided at that moment on the Saint Vincent campus, dozens of miles away. The floodwaters struck the town at about 4:20 that afternoon. The water hit the Boyle's small frame home so hard that it tore the dwelling from its foundation and sent it hurtling downstream. The family went with it. Boyle's mother's hair became tangled in the branch of a tree severed from its roots, keeping her afloat for a twenty-mile journey with the raging flood. Rescuers found her washed up on the riverbank, still breathing, and brought her to Saint Francis Hospital in Pittsburgh. She learned there that only one teenage son had escaped with her. Young Hugh's family had become three. Few working people missed the clear and powerful meaning in this event, and Hugh Boyle was not among them. Workers suffered not only from low wages and dangerous working conditions that capitalists established in their mills and mines, but even from their careless pursuit of leisure.

To cement further his identification with working people, Boyle began his first assignment as a young priest in a working-class parish in the shadow of the Westinghouse Air Brake Company (future site of the great labor battle against Communism that Charles Owen Rice fought almost half a century later). Boyle's biographer suggests that Boyle learned here how to pursue the social encyclicals beyond the seminary classroom in the real world of workers' lives. After five years in Wilmerding, Boyle moved quickly through the diocesan administrative offices and a pastorate in Homestead before being tapped to lead the diocese.[6]

Boyle played a critical role in shaping the Catholic discourse on capitalism up to the 1950s, as might be expected in a rigidly hierarchical structure with a single head. But it certainly helped that Boyle saw eye to eye with the editor of the lay-owned *Pittsburgh Catholic* on most religious and social issues. Much of the prescribed solution to the materialist crisis derived from the collaborative efforts of these two men.

The Catholic social ideal called for labor and management to work together, to cooperate in their common endeavor, and to share the wealth they generated in such a way as to guarantee dignity for all. But prominent voices in the local Catholic discourse recognized that this did not describe 1950s Pittsburgh very well. For this place at this moment, Pittsburgh Catholics learned to put their trust in unions and to support them actively. Unions would best safeguard workers in the dangerous market. In fact, the *Pittsburgh Catholic* relayed, "The Catholic trade unionist who is not a good trade unionist is to that extent not a good Catholic." [7] The discourse also denounced any effort to weaken or undermine unions. For, in *Pittsburgh Catholic* editor John Collins's words, "if organized labor in this country is weakened it will undermine the general welfare." Americans had learned from grim experience that "whenever anti-union corporations have had their way in the past they have thrown the economic system out of balance by exploiting the workers and reducing their purchasing power, and the result has inevitably been—depression."[8] The *Pittsburgh Catholic* gave front-page coverage to Grand Rapids' Bishop Francis J. Haas's denunciation of the Taft-Hartley Act as a "tyrannous usurpation by government of a worker's God-given rights."[9] The diocesan paper supported labor in every strike that it covered, and it covered strikes regularly through the decade's early years.[10]

John Collins also carried Fr. Charles Owen Rice's weekly column entitled "The Condition of Labor" in the diocesan paper. No discussion of the 1950s Catholic economic discourse in Pittsburgh—or the nation really—would be complete absent a focus on Rice's role. He stood among the nation's most widely known labor priests in the 1930s and 1940s, and remained active in battles for social justice through the 1990s. In addition to his regular column, he hosted a weekly radio program, and he rubbed shoulders with Pittsburgh's and the nation's greatest labor leaders.

Rice was born in New York but spent much of his childhood in Ireland before coming to Pittsburgh as a boy. Rice's early years in Ireland, the influence of his father and union-organizer uncle, and the political, economic, and social situation in Pittsburgh (where the Scots-Irish Presbyterians dominated) all conditioned Rice to champion working people and the dispossessed. Rice worked publicly to support unionism in Pittsburgh and joined early Congress of Industrial

Organizations (CIO) organizing efforts in the steel industry. In addition to his dedicated union work, Rice joined with fellow Pittsburgh priest Carl Hensler to form the Catholic Radical Alliance (CRA) in 1937. The CRA sought to educate the public on social justice issues, especially on the two labor encyclicals, in order to transform radically the capitalist economic structure. It also established a Catholic Worker House in Pittsburgh, based on the model that Dorothy Day and Peter Maurin provided in New York City. Rice moved into the house in 1940 and resided there into the 1950s.[11]

Rice was especially close with Philip Murray, United Steel Workers leader and John L. Lewis's successor as president of the Congress of Industrial Organizations, Pittsburgh resident, and active Catholic. Together with Hugh Boyle and John Collins (and a handful of others), Rice guided the Catholic discourse on the economy. He adamantly supported unions in their battle for decent wages and safe working conditions, and within the labor movement opposed any influence that Communists might seek or exercise.[12]

The Catholic discourse recommended other shelters from the liberal capitalist market as well. Successful labor unions effectively shielded workers from capitalist greed and wrested a modicum of the wealth workers played such critical roles in generating. But local, state, and the federal government also protected Americans from market exploitation. It controlled rent, regulated utilities, provided public housing, arbitrated labor disputes, and in a host of other ways intervened to provide a minimum standard below which no Pittsburgher need live. These public entities affirmed communal values in the face of powerful market forces that recognized no human considerations above the laws of supply and demand. While government might not be able to reproduce the medieval ideal of the small village populated by individual craftsmen and guilds, it could certainly protect men, women, and children from the worst that industrialization brought. It could affirm each individual's social obligations in the face of the atomizing market tendencies.

Though unions might be the best way for workers to protect themselves in the wage-earning world, the Catholic discourse often welcomed government intervention as well. The federal government in particular could step into labor disputes and ensure that management did not exert its will upon those who labored to produce companies' products and profits. Rice applauded such intervention to prevent a company lockout of workers in a 1952 wage dispute, and pointed out that "the big heresy of 'liberalism' is the personalization of property and the regarding of property rights as equal with human rights." The economy should serve moral ends, it should support people.[13]

Government intervention in labor disputes was no unmitigated blessing. In fact, the long history of state involvement in labor disputes typically worked against workers' interests. One need look no further in Pittsburgh than the steel strike of 1919 and the great Homestead strike of 1892 to confirm this.[14] The New Deal transformed government relations with workers and created a much more favorable connection, but even contemporary government intervention sometimes reminded workers that they could not count on friendly treatment in their efforts to gain economic security. Still, government intervention had the potential to provide critical protection for workers and their families from the greed capitalism promoted and the indifferent market in which it operated.

The capitalist market economy recognized no individual's "right" to minimum standards in housing, medical care, income, or transportation, but society, through its government, did. The Catholic discourse insisted that government entities protect Americans assiduously and took them to task when they fell short. Collins upbraided the Pennsylvania Utilities Commission when it failed to protect consumers adequately, and lambasted the federal defense mobilization agency for freezing wages but not prices in 1951.[15]

The *Pittsburgh Catholic* also supported public housing and rent control because every family, even the poor, deserved decent shelter. The paper quoted one American bishop's statement that "Many of us believe that American citizens, even those who are poor, have a right to decent housing because they are human beings."[16] Rent control was morally justifiable, the paper related, "under conditions of housing shortage."[17] Moreover, as the National Catholic Conference on Family Life pointed out, the scarcity of small homes in 1952 was "a menace to proper family living." When the Pittsburgh Real Estate Board sought to eliminate rent control in the city, John Collins argued that to do so "would be just inviting the exploiters to take over." He highlighted the National Council of Catholic Men's and the National Council of Catholic Women's program to urge Congress to retain rent control, and called it "the last chance for protecting tenants from devastating increases."[18]

When rent control or public housing disappeared, the discourse urged Catholics to join together to mitigate market influences in other ways. This happened, for instance, when the federal government decided to sell public housing in the Hazelwood section of Pittsburgh. The government constructed the Glen-Hazel Heights Defense Housing Project to accommodate workers in local defense industries during World War II. But five years after the war's close, the federal government no longer wanted to maintain the project—in large part because most of the current residents' incomes had come to exceed the maximum allowed for the federally subsidized housing. Instead, the government proposed that residents form a cooperative and purchase their dwellings. Once 67 percent committed to doing so, the plan was to take effect. The Saint Stephen's pastor urged his parishioners, who constituted slightly more than a third of the 1,100 residents, to join the cooperative. Eventually enough did join for the cooperative to take over the project.[19]

In addition to government efforts to guarantee secure housing and access to transportation, the Catholic discourse strongly supported a national health care system that would serve all of the nation's citizens. John Collins endorsed a system in which all Americans paid money into a fund from which doctors would get paid for their services. Against the American Medical Association's charges that this was "socialism," Collins argued that "it would no more be socialism than is our present social security system, with old-age, unemployment and retirement benefits. It would no more be socialism than are our privately managed hospital associations and our life insurance and fire insurance corporations." There was a "social factor" in all of these programs, "since all participants join to ease the burden of those who suffer disaster or loss; and that is exactly what the governmental health insurance plan proposed to do." And even if it was socialized medicine, the pope himself had declared this to be consistent with Catholic principles.[20]

Commercialization

Capitalist materialism manifested itself not only in the greed-fueled exploitation of workers and their families, but also in the commercialization of American culture. Americans, it seemed, had come to experience their culture too extensively through economic exchange, through the market. This commercialization contaminated even America's central religious celebrations and threatened to undermine American Catholicism's spiritual foundation. Catholics might combat this development by taking back their sacred time.

In the normal rhythm of Catholic life, Sunday stood apart as a day to retreat from the market in communal acknowledgment of God's privileged place. Sunday was for Church and family, not for "business" of any kind. Employers had not always recognized this voluntarily, and one of labor's long-standing battles was to eliminate Sunday work requirements. Church officials enjoined Catholics from a wide range of activities on Sunday, and so they looked with alarm at the growing tendency to perform "market" functions on the Sabbath. But by the 1950s this alarm turned increasingly away from the industrial work arena and toward consumer behavior. Sunday belonged to God, not to Horne's or Kaufmann's—regional department stores.

Sunday shopping had become so widespread nationally by 1955, and had grown enough locally, for Pittsburgh Church officials to register their concern. The problem, apparently, lay with chain stores. They opened on Sunday and forced the locally owned stores either to follow suit or go out of business. Bishop Dearden shared his worries with the diocesan Holy Name Society, whose Public Relations Committee determined to solicit the Diocesan Council of Catholic Women's help in starting a campaign to "Keep Sunday Sacred." Pittsburgh campaign leaders designed a poster to display in stores, buses, and trolleys. The posters proclaimed the campaign's themes: "Keep Sunday Sacred. Go to Church. Shop Week Days Only." Public Relations Committee members also penned standard entries for parish bulletins and prepared a fifteen-minute talk for members of the Speakers Bureau. HNS and DCCW officers agreed to attempt to persuade their friends and neighbors to give up Sunday shopping, and the superintendent of Catholic schools in the diocese notified teaching nuns to "clarify" the third commandment to their students.[21] In the battle to preserve the opportunity to gather in worship and fellowship, the two most significant Catholic lay organizations stood firmly with their bishop. In short order they met limited success. James McGonigle, president of the North Side Board of Trade, pledged to push a resolution at the next board of directors meeting condemning "nonessential" Sunday business. If successful there, he offered to instruct his representative to the Allied Board of Trade (composed of fifteen Allegheny County boards of trade) to submit a similar resolution.[22]

The market incursion into sacred time extended beyond the weekly Sabbath and into moments even more sacrosanct. It was one thing to ignore God on Sundays in the pursuit of "nonessential" shopping, but it was quite another to transform the very celebration of Christ's birth into a vast commercial opportunity. Retailers had turned the central figure of the antimaterialist creed into the justification for America's ultimate shopping event. In addition, businesses had come in recent years to "honor" Christ through the creation of dangerous occasions for sin: office parties loosed the sensual restraints that on regular working days threatened business efficiency. Rather than standing as an occasion for profound reflection on society's essential religious dimension, Christmas stood in danger of becoming the nation's pivotal materialist moment. In response, the Catholic discourse urged avid attention to efforts to take Christmas back from retailers and sensuality. The Catholic discourse on commercialism demanded that Catholics reject capitalism's materialist Christmas in favor of the Church's spiritual celebration.

Pittsburghers opened the 1950s in the midst of the Catholic Cultural Center's campaign to help Christ triumph over Santa, and pushed right through the decade with different efforts in the same general endeavor. The Cultural Center saw evidence for the primacy of the commercial Christmas over the religious in Santa's apparent triumph over Christ. Only three out of thirty-two Catholic first-graders in one class accompanied a family member to see Christ in his crib in 1949, but all thirty-two had gone to see Santa. The center warned Catholics that today's Christmas could best be seen in the "extravagant displays in the store-windows" or in the Santa-filled greeting cards. Even the parlors of many homes contained "laughing Santas and snow-bound scenes. Sleighs and reindeers. Elves and tinsel and trimmings. Bells and balls. Tracks and trains. Stars on top of trees, but no Crib beneath the trees." The signs might read "Merry Christmas," but "there is no Mary and no Christ to be seen." Within weeks the Christian Mothers had taken up the cry to "put Christ back into Christmas" by placing 1,300 posters in Pittsburgh streetcars, erecting two big billboards, and mailing out thousands of leaflets across the country which urged recipients to choose Christ over Santa.[23]

Many voices in the discourse raised the cry to put Christ back into Christmas. John Collins observed Pittsburgh's preparations for Christmas in the same year that the Catholic Cultural Center launched its Pittsburgh campaign and saw primarily commercial efforts:

The Santa Claus parades have been held, the elaborate holiday displays have been set up in the department store windows, and the big advertising campaigns have been started; the sole purpose of all this activity is to make a commercial success of the Christmas season. The approach through the children is being used ("tell Santa what you want"); the snob approach is being used ("everybody who is anybody will give our gadgets to their relatives and friends"); but most of all the approach is plain stampede propaganda: you simply must cast aside all prudence and common sense when Christmas nears and buy frantically and recklessly. . . . Christ and His birth are practically forgotten now in what the world of commerce calls its preparation for Christmas: it has become an occasion for indulgence in the most extravagant, vulgar materialism. . . . It is nothing but a pagan, secular materialistic revel that has been brazenly—one might say, blasphemously—substituted for the sacred anniversary of Christ's birth.

The solution, in Collins's eyes, was to take up the true spirit of Advent. Pray, meditate, do penance. Sing no Christmas carols, relive the dark emptiness of the world before Christ's coming so that Christmas would better reflect the great joy that Christ's birth meant for the world.[24]

One could imagine Collins's shock, therefore, when the Saint Paul Catechetical Guild published a fifty-five-page book the following year to advise Catholics on how to promote a Christ-centered Christmas that accepted "the idea that commercialization of Christmas is all right, provided the commercialization is associated with the spiritual significance of the feast." The book called for an elaborate network of volunteers to canvass merchants and media outlets to make the case for putting Christ into Christmas. But the book also contained the positive response one Cincinnati retailer received from its decision to market its goods with Christ-centered window displays. The retailer described designing displays

> based on suggestions from the "Christ in Christmas" committee for 12 of our windows and we hit the jackpot on good will . . . For instance, our corner window titled "The Honored Guest at Christmas" showed a family (dressed in our best ready-to-wear) greeting a young sailor as their Christmas dinner guest. (Table and side-board supplied by the furniture department, of course.) Our sign explained, "Your Christmas dinner is Christ's birthday feast. Fine linen, silver and flowers give glory to God and joy to your family . . ."

Glory to God through ready-to-wear clothes, new furniture, and silverware? Collins was incredulous. Catholics could not consume themselves into heaven, no matter how nicely dressed. Collins gave qualified approval to the program, despite what it revealed about "how the commercialization of Christmas has permeated even Catholic thinking."[25]

A few years later the *Pittsburgh Catholic* urged everyone to take the ten-point "Christmas Pledge." Nine of the ten points committed pledge-takers to emphasize spiritual dimensions of Christmas, and four of those specifically rejected the commercial Christmas trappings. Cooperating Catholics promised not to observe Christmas "merely as a day to give and receive merchandise," to reject "Santa Claus and his reindeer" as Christmas symbols, to send Christmas cards that did not contain only "candy canes, puppy dogs, ribbons and wreaths," and to teach their children that "Santa Claus" was really a nickname for Saint Nicholas.[26]

Pittsburgh Catholic editors supported a 1958 campaign that melded the twin concerns about Sabbath violations and Christmas commercialization. They found nothing wrong with the slogan "Do your Christmas shopping early," but expressed alarm at the enticements to "do your Christmas shopping on Sunday." The editors asked rhetorically, "What could possibly be more incongruous than to prepare for the celebration of the Nativity of the Son of God by sinfully buying and selling on the day set apart by the Commandment of God: 'Keep holy the Sabbath Day.'"[27] Though the editors probably intended to respond with a resounding "nothing" in answer to this question, Catholics might readily have come up with another answer: the Christmas office party.

The Catholic discourse contained regular admonitions to "clean up" the Christmas office party or to avoid it altogether. The celebration of Christ's birth should not, according to the discourse, be an opportunity for drunkenness and sensuality. No Catholic should ever participate in an activity that endangered virtue, and especially not in a function linked to Christmas. New York's auxiliary bishop Joseph F. Flannelly had celebrants at each Saint Patrick's Cathedral Mass on December 10, 1950, warn Catholics to avoid "pre-Christmas" parties that did not reflect the "penitential season preceding the Feast of the Nativity." The likelihood that any office had organized its Christmas party around the "penance" theme seemed slim, so Flannelly had effectively placed all parties off limits. Pittsburgh's mayor David L. Lawrence did not go quite so far in his 1952 urging to all Pittsburghers to avoid "intemperance and other impropriety" at all office Christmas parties, but he did raise the concerns that the Archconfraternity of Christian Mothers had pressed upon him during their December visit.[28]

Catholic women's columnist Mary Tinley Daly saw in the office Christmas party the potential for an event "so devastating that it turns the whole idea of Christmas stale." She favored eliminating current practices but remained realistic about such a development in the near future. Reform efforts probably would not "seep down to real estate and insurance offices, to brokerage firms and the like for years." Daly went on to explain why the movement to stamp out such parties should prevail. Sensuality reigned supreme at these events, and domesticity suffered the consequences.

A quiet little stenographer, who is a whiz at dictation, finds all of a sudden that she is also a whiz at doing the Charleston with the office manager. She calls up her husband, "Been detained at the office, Honey. Fix your own supper. Be home soon as I get these letters done!"

"Atta baby!" The office manager extends his arms. "Now we can really go to town! Say . . ." He makes his own phone call: "Sorry, Sue," back comes the Office Managerial voice. "I have to work late tonight. Of course, I'm at the office. Music? Oh, some goof turned on a radio. If you don't believe me, call back. Yes! The office number!"

Before he and the little steno have half started another Charleston, the phone rings. "Evans, Johnson and Evans," the office manager answers with a wink. "I told you I was here, Sue. Please let me finish my work . . . No, don't wait up."

The situation degenerates further still, drawing all of the employees into charades that threaten their home lives and poison office relationships. By the next business day embarrassment, resentment, and caterers' bills have permeated the workplace. This was Christmas? Short of constraining Christmas celebrations to the church and home, Daly offered another solution to the office party. Why not domesticate the market? Bring wives and husbands to the office parties to tame the wildness. "The little steno has a chance to bring her husband, studying under G.I. The junior sales manager can bring his girl and become friends with Mr. and Mrs. Senior Sales Manager." Rather than allowing the market to corrupt Christmas, perhaps the domestic Christmas should humanize the market.[29]

CAPITALISM'S TWIN DANGERS OF EXPLOITATION AND COMMERCIALISM posed grave materialist threats to Catholics' essential spiritual dimension. They diminished human dignity and exalted the selfish pursuit of material gain in the physical world over the struggle for eternal salvation. Concern about these two dangers dominated the Catholic discourse on social justice through the 1950s. Over time, another concern drew more and more attention, however. Before the 1960s ended, this social justice issue would prove more divisive than any other.

RACE

The Catholic focus on social justice turned increasingly to racial matters as the decade progressed. In retrospect this seemed almost inevitable as the nation turned its attention to the civil rights movement in the South and the violence used to resist it. The situation in Pittsburgh also pushed Catholics to address racial issues, as the growing African-American and declining white populations changed the city's racial composition dramatically. Between 1940 and 1950 the African-American population in Pittsburgh increased by over a third. The 1950s saw an additional increase of 17 percent, followed by twenty years of relative stability.

The growth took on greater significance when coupled with the dramatic decline in the city's white population. Pittsburgh's white population declined by 15 percent between 1950 and 1960, 18 percent over the next decade, and 23 percent in the 1970s. Between 1950 and 1970 the city's African-American population increased by a total of 27 percent while the city's white population declined by 30 percent. Moreover, in light of the abrupt drop in the white population, blacks came to constitute an even higher percentage of the the city's population. African Americans represented 12 percent of Pittsburghers in 1950, 17 percent in 1960,

FIGURE 4.1   Pittsburgh Population by Race, 1950–1980

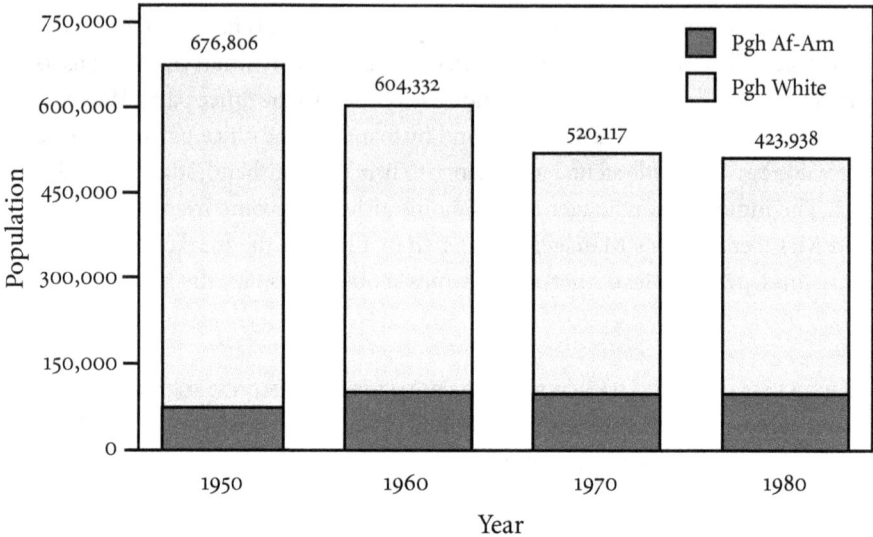

Source: United States Census.

20 percent in 1970, and 24 percent in 1980. Pittsburgh was more black in 1950 than ever before, and white flight to the suburbs and out of the region would raise the proportion of African-American residents higher still in the following decades.[30] (See fig. 4.1.)

Outside of the city the story was quite different. The African-American population outside of Pittsburgh proper increased at a greater rate than did that of whites between 1960 and 1970, when African-Americans increased their numbers by 6.7 percent and whites by only 4.2 percent. But the African-American population was so small to begin with that these figures translated to an increase of only slightly more than 4,000 for blacks and over 73,000 for whites. The city's population consisted of 20 percent African Americans in 1970, while the region's population outside of the city was only 3 percent African American.[31]

The overwhelming majority of Pittsburgh metropolitan area African Americans lived in the city itself, and the overwhelming majority of black city residents lived in highly concentrated segregated ghettos. Pittsburgh's largest and most crowded ghetto was the Hill District, which separated the skyscrapers from the city's cultural center, four miles to the east. Most of Pittsburgh's African Americans, one quarter of the city's entire population, lived in eight wards that covered less than one quarter of the city. The Hill's houses were the worst in the city. Fifty-two percent of all of its dwellings were substandard. If one eliminated public housing from the figures, 6,000 of the 8,500 remaining units (71 percent) fell below the city's minimum standards for housing.[32]

Reporters wrote of sixty-four people sharing a single bathroom in one part of the Hill, of thirty people who shared two outside privies and two outdoor hydrants as their sole source of water—summer and winter—in another.[33] Hill residents were more than two and a half times as likely to die of tuberculosis than Pittsburghers in general.[34] The *Pittsburgh Courier* reported that the city allowed gambling and prostitution to flourish unchecked in the Hill, while "landlords eager to squeeze the last dollar of profit out of their aging properties split houses into small apartments and single rooms" which they let deteriorate without efforts to make any but the most absolutely necessary repairs. Even these apartments were "as scarce as the proverbial hen's tooth."[35] Like many other American cities, Pittsburgh erupted in the aftermath of Martin Luther King's assassination. The mayor's task force appointed to investigate the "disturbances" reported that

> most of the witnesses interviewed by the task force stated that the seeds of discontent in ghetto areas encompass years of frustration born and bred in poverty, poor housing, deteriorated neighborhoods and continued discrimination in Pittsburgh and in the nation's other urban areas.[36]

The Chamber of Commerce boasted in 1970 of the new Civic Arena and its environs. One might attend winter sports events or see stars at night through the retracted roof during open-air summer performances secure in the knowledge that one's car was parked conveniently nearby in the commodious Arena parking lots. Perhaps as important, the chamber reported, Pittsburgh had relocated "some" of the 8,500 Lower Hill residents, who had been living crowded on these 95 acres of the newly converted substandard housing, to public housing (though most crowded even further into the remaining areas open to African Americans in Pittsburgh).[37]

But city efforts to build new housing projects outside of the Hill for its former inhabitants met strong resistance from residents adjacent to the proposed sites and from private developers. Organized efforts to stop such housing often discouraged city council members from pushing the projects eagerly. Opponents to one project in the city's overwhelmingly Catholic Southside neighborhood chartered five buses to ferry two hundred angry people to a council meeting. Thirty people lectured the silent council for ninety minutes on public housing, taxation, Communism, Joseph Stalin, Mayor Lawrence, and other topics.[38]

This was the context in which Pittsburgh's Catholics began their public discussion on race.

A review of *Pittsburgh Catholic* articles on race reflects both the growing centrality of racial justice to Catholic social justice concerns and the changes in editorship that accompanied Bishop Dearden's purchase of the paper and the later arrival of John Wright as Dearden's replacement. The prescription here seemed unequivocal. Americans should establish a society in which racial prejudice and discrimination did not limit opportunity or access to public and private resources.

In the years before Bishop Dearden purchased the paper, *Pittsburgh Catholic* editor John Collins became more and more persuaded that racial prejudice and discrimination constituted serious problems in American society, and that Catholics had to work to create equal opportunities for all. Collins shared his growing concern with readers. At the decade's outset, the *Pittsburgh Catholic* included articles on race in only nine of fifty-two issues, and the number of articles increased only incrementally in each of the next two years.[39] But in 1953 Collins published thirty-one articles on African Americans. While a majority of the articles in each year addressed race in places other than Pittsburgh—especially the South—Collins gradually turned the *Pittsburgh Catholic*'s gaze on the diocese itself. The articles highlighted the African-American presence in the Church through a focus on baptisms in Pittsburgh's Hill District neighborhood and on the total numbers of African-American Catholics. Collins also celebrated the elimination of racial barriers to full participation in Catholic institutional life, such as the elimination of policies prohibiting African Americans from studying in Catholic nursing schools. These articles implicitly endorsed the virtue of an integrated Catholic community. Collins cheered the formation in January 1954 of a Pittsburgh Catholic Interracial Council, and the opportunity to move the Pittsburgh community toward greater integration.

Bishop Dearden purchased the diocesan paper in the fall of 1954, however, and installed a new editor. John Ward shared Dearden's more conservative views and shed the social justice slant that Collins so strongly emphasized. Ward came over from the *Pittsburgh Sun-Telegraph,* a struggling daily with which Collins had occasionally sparred over interpretations of the Catholic position on labor disputes. Ward dropped many of the *Pittsburgh Catholic* contributors, including Fr. Charles Owen Rice, and replaced them with nationally syndicated, largely conservative columnists.

This move effectively ended the focus on race for over a year. Despite the increasing efforts that civil rights workers made throughout the South to end seg-

FIGURE 4.2   Articles on Race Appearing in the *Pittsburgh Catholic,* 1950–1960

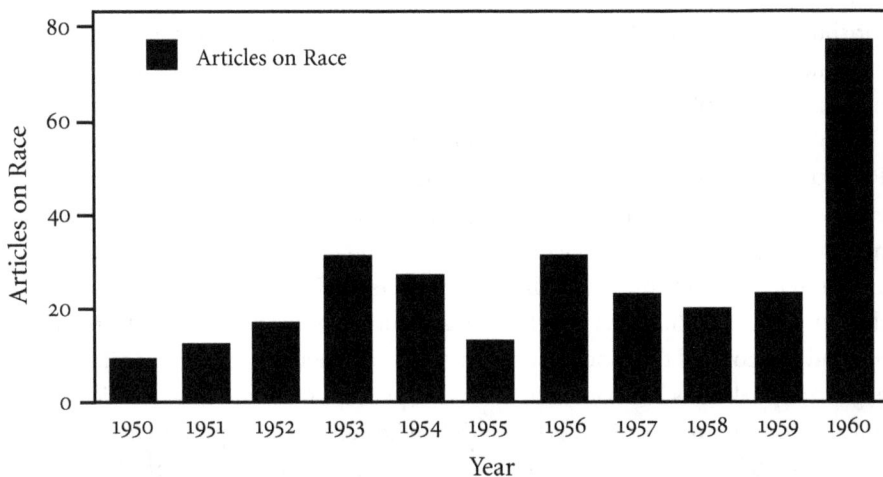

regation and discrimination, and the fledgling efforts that Pittsburgh's Catholic Interracial Council expended to examine race in the diocese itself, Pittsburgh Catholics read less and less about racial justice in their diocesan newspaper. The 1955 totals return to the levels of 1951 and 1952. (See fig. 4.2.)

Not until Catholics themselves became embroiled in some of the most difficult school integration battles in the South did the *Pittsburgh Catholic* again find the issue relevant to its readers. The *Pittsburgh Catholic* focused most heavily on developments in Louisiana, where New Orleans Archbishop Joseph F. Rummel embraced and then retreated from integrating the Catholic school system. In fact, the *Pittsburgh Catholic* published more than twice as many articles on race in Louisiana in 1956 as it did on race in the Pittsburgh diocese.[40] Even though the diocesan paper under John Dearden's more direct supervision looked at racial issues only reluctantly, it never wavered from an integrationist position when it finally focused its gaze. In the words of one 1956 editorial, Catholic "leaders have emphasized and continue to emphasize that all men are members of the Mystical Body of Christ."[41] But even this commitment to racial integration and equality remained abstract for Pittsburgh Catholics. The arguments that the laity encountered in the diocese's official organ addressed theological justifications or Catholics confronting these issues in relatively faraway places. *Pittsburgh*

Catholic readers might reasonably have understood issues of racial justice to concern people in such places as seminaries and the South, but not so much in Pittsburgh itself. Still, the issue existed, and Pittsburgh Catholics could not escape the knowledge that Church officials condemned segregation and discrimination in principle.

John Wright's arrival as Dearden's successor transformed the public face of Pittsburgh Catholicism profoundly. Wright was a dynamo who seemed to be everywhere—both inside the diocese and out—speaking before diocesan and national organizations, writing oft-cited essays and speeches, lending his name and presence to high-profile intellectual projects, invigorating the diocese and the national Church. It was not that Wright outworked Dearden, for Dearden too had invigorated the diocese with his remarkable energy and extraordinary organizational skills. But Dearden offered—perhaps demanded—traditional practices on a grander scale. If Pittsburgh had hosted one large public eucharistic rally in each decade since the 1930s, Dearden wanted two in five years. If each Pittsburgh parish offered special forty-hour devotions once or twice each year, he called for continuous forty-hour devotions in every parish, every day of the year. If every parish in the diocese called the laity to swear publicly once each year to uphold the Legion of Decency's strictures and avoid immoral and indecent movies, Dearden added a pledge to reject indecent literature as well. Dearden affirmed the primacy of devotional practices and the social and cultural ghetto for Pittsburghers in a period of rapid demographic, economic, social, and cultural change. In the face of a dramatically changing world for the laity, Dearden insisted that the laity remain the same, only with more energy. John Wright embraced the new, almost celebrated it. He was clearly a new man for the new era and promised to bring the laity along with him—or perhaps to accompany them on a journey that they had already begun.

To help him on this journey, John Wright brought a key figure with him from Worcester. Bishop Wright's appointment of John Deedy as the *Pittsburgh Catholic* editor in 1959 transformed the Catholic public discourse on race in the diocese. John Ward resigned his position as *Pittsburgh Catholic* editor after Wright's appointment to Pittsburgh. Perhaps he recognized the significant differences between his editorial positions and Wright's public stances. It would have been a very strained marriage had he stayed. Instead, Ward chose to follow Pittsburgh Auxiliary Bishop Coleman Carroll to his new assignment as the first bishop of the new diocese in Miami, Florida, and Ward edited the new diocesan paper there. John Deedy especially forced Pittsburgh's Catholics to confront the reality that racial prejudice and discrimination existed in Pittsburgh too. More unsettling, the editor insisted that local Catholics bore responsibility to work for racial equality.

It would be hard to imagine a more striking contrast to Bishop Dearden than his replacement, John Wright. Where "Iron John" Dearden was known as a man of few words and a quiet yet firm manner, John Wright was perhaps the most eloquent of American bishops and a rising star on the American Catholic cultural scene. Wright was as liberal as Dearden was conservative, as at home in American culture as Dearden was wary of it.[42]

John Wright grew up in Boston, attended public schools, Boston College, Saint John Seminary in Brighton, Massachusetts, and then the North American College in Rome. He was ordained in Rome, and he continued to immerse himself in the world of letters. Wright taught at Boston's seminary before becoming secretary to its archbishop. Pope Pius XII appointed him to be auxiliary bishop of Boston in 1947. Three years later, when Pius XII formed the new diocese of Worcester, Massachusetts, he named Wright to be its first bishop. Wright served in Worcester for a decade before coming to Pittsburgh in 1959. While he was in Worcester, Wright's national star continued to rise. He became the chaplain for some national organizations, such as the Laywomen's Retreat League, served as episcopal moderator of the National Catholic Laymen's Retreat Conference, and supported a greater role for the laity throughout the Church. His support for labor gained recognition in places not accustomed to praising Catholic leaders, such as the *Nation* magazine in a 1962 profile.[43]

Historian David O'Brien describes how Wright served as a champion of reform in Worcester, pushed the Church into greater immersion in American culture, and embraced intellectuals. Wright prohibited his pastors from criticizing Catholic students who attended public schools and the parents who sent them there, and pushed each parish to establish religious education programs for those children. Wright was no populist, in fact O'Brien suggests that Wright's firm adherence to classical culture rendered him an intellectual elitist (he had attended the Boston Latin school, pushed strenuously for classical education throughout his career, and attended lectures on literature and classical civilization while on vacations).[44] He supported the Catholic hierarchical governing structure wholeheartedly.[45] But Wright championed the life of letters and strongly urged Catholics to resist parochialism and embrace the broad and distinguished intellectual heritage that he saw as the Church's true legacy.

Wright was also no stranger to Pittsburgh when Pope Pius XII appointed him to the see. He had visited the diocese officially at least five times during his years at Worcester and had been featured seventeen times in *Pittsburgh*

Catholic articles. The articles, which all focused on Wright's public intellectual activity, conveyed his intellectual dynamism and enthusiasm. Wright was as publicly energetic as any American bishop, with a strong intellectual commitment to social justice and a national reputation.

Wright appointed John Deedy, the editor of his Worcester diocesan paper, to lead the *Pittsburgh Catholic.* The two swiftly reintroduced the emphasis on social justice that Dearden had muted. Like John Collins, John Deedy saw racial prejudice as one of the central moral dilemmas facing American Catholics in the postwar years. Unlike Collins, Deedy decided to address racial issues in Pittsburgh itself. He turned the paper's focus on the growing population of African Americans in the city, on the poverty in which they lived, and on the experiences they had in their attempts to negotiate segregation and discrimination in the diocese. The Catholic discourse on race in the 1950s had always stressed racial equality, the need to treat all humans with dignity and fairness, and the errors of segregation. But Deedy made the discussion present in Pittsburgh Catholics' lives by insisting that Catholic ideals called them to feel certain ways about their neighbors and to act to ameliorate the disadvantages that African Americans experienced.

Deedy accomplished this in two ways. First, he gave broad and regular coverage to the civil rights movement in the American South, especially as it connected to Catholics. This necessarily entailed a continued focus on Louisiana and the painful vacillations that Church officials underwent in their efforts to reconcile a principled commitment to integration with a powerful pragmatic accommodation tradition. In addition, Deedy generated reports on race in Pittsburgh itself. The combination of these two foci, in addition to the new letters to the editor section that he introduced, vastly increased the Catholic discourse on race in the weekly paper. The number of pieces on race in the *Pittsburgh Catholic* more than tripled in Deedy's first full year as editor.

Deedy was emphatic in his commitment to racial equality. In one strongly worded essay, for example, he wrote,

> If one group more than any other is an embarrassment to the Church in America, it is those Catholics who resist or defy the Church's traditional teaching of equality under God. The policy of the Church on racial matters is clear and unmistakable; we are created equal; there is no room for bias.[46]

But what did that mean in the Pittsburgh context? It meant that Pittsburgh Catholics must support passage and enforcement of Pittsburgh's fair housing practices law, that parish Holy Name societies should focus more of their ener-

gies on changing "the un-Christian attitude of a few people on the race problem" rather than on organizing "smokers," and that skilled craft unions should
integrate African Americans into their ranks.[47] It also meant that Pittsburghers
should be aware of the problems that African Americans faced in the diocese.
Consequently, Deedy published articles that explored life in African-American
ghettos and detailed for his largely white readers the difficulties residents of the
Hill District, East Liberty, and Homewood encountered in their lives. He also
weighed in on Pittsburgh's ongoing urban renewal programs, especially when
they eliminated low-income housing with little or no provision made for the
displaced poor.[48]

No Catholic familiar with the public pronouncements emanating from
Church officials and suffusing the Catholic press in Pittsburgh could mistake
the moral imperative in favor of racial equality. The message was clear. Segregation and discrimination harmed African Americans and violated Catholic moral
teaching.

If the *Pittsburgh Catholic* moved fitfully throughout the decade toward embracing racial equality and opposing segregation and other forms of discrimination, the Holy Name Society under the Rev. Paul Lackner's lead moved much
more steadily in the same direction. He used the *Holy Name Newsletter* as a
bully pulpit to push the Catholic men of the diocese to act to bring about racial
equality.

The Reverend Lackner declared the South to be in open revolt against
America over integration of the schools and public institutions in general, and
for "disobedience to the decisions of the Supreme Court." He believed that the
Southern attitudes on race required the transformation of the entire social structure, the "complete way of life." But Lackner did not confine racist attitudes to
the South. He argued that

> segregation is still largely a policy of the thinking of many people and many
> communities in the North. In numerous areas negroes [*sic*] cannot purchase
> homes; in many businesses they are denied access, while in others they have
> no hope of advancement; and to many social groups they find the door shut
> and securely bolted.[49]

Further, many Catholics participated in the "more serious sin" on the "conver-
sational level" where the social pattern was formed. According to Lackner, some
Catholics bitterly opposed blacks, some favored keeping them in their place,
some favored integration in principle, but . . . , and some spoke up to defend

"the Christian viewpoint." Lackner suggested that parish Holy Name societies set up special programs on the subject with "carefully chosen speakers." The programs might address the following issues:

> What is the moral involved in integration?—May I sell my home to a Negro family?—Should my family move away when a Negro family moves into my neighborhood?—If I begin to serve Negroes in my restaurant I will lose all my customers. What's my responsibility?—Are there integrated Catholic schools in the South?—What did the Supreme Court actually say in its recent decision?—What line of strategy is Gov. Faubus following?[50]

Seven months later these questions formed the centerpiece of the diocesan Holy Name Society quarterly meeting at Central Catholic High School, where the Catholic Interracial Council (CIC) presented a panel discussion. HNS executive board member Arthur Sullivan insisted that "no Catholic can be Catholic and deny the teachings of the Church concerning the Mystical Body. Still, we become mental delinquents when the problem becomes a reality—particularly in regards to race." Sullivan insisted that "we must open our minds to the teachings of Christ in an attempt to apply them to modern day problems."[51]

Robert A. Dumas of the Philadelphia Catholic Interracial Council spoke at the quarterly meeting and emphasized that the Catholic Church advised against segregation because the segregationist engaged in activity "that could result in the loss of his soul." He told Holy Name members that

> the church's policy has been clear from the very beginning of the Church. It has not changed one iota, and is implicit in all of her teachings. We are all children of God, and a part of the Mystical Body of Christ. The simple rule for living is to love your neighbor as yourself. This applies whether your neighbor be black or white.

He further insisted that "we as Catholics have a responsibility to speak out against injustice and to work diligently to correct any injustice that adversely affects our brother."[52]

Seven months before the first session of the Second Vatican Council, the official diocesan voice of the Pittsburgh Holy Name Society argued that lay Catholics had to work as hard as humanly possible to consecrate society. The single social issue on which the Holy Name Society defined specific behaviors for its members was race relations. Catholics must integrate, the *Newsletter* stated, or they would lose their souls and bring doom onto society.

SOCIAL JUSTICE AND CATHOLIC ACTION

The growing lay rejection of both devotionalism and Catholic separatism meant that two of the three prescriptions for meeting the materialist crisis promised little success. Without lay support, the two could not reasonably form the foundation for Catholicism's immediate or long-term future. Social justice fared somewhat differently, however, in large part because laywomen and laymen, and even Church officials, expanded the prescription more widely to include a variety of "reforms" that empowered the laity. Though conceived initially as means to better enable the laity to transform the world, many of these reforms remade the lay experience within the Church itself. The reform thread started in the social justice arena, but it moved quickly through almost all aspects of Church life and opened an institution heavily invested in stability and permanence to the value of change more generally. The reforms that the Second Vatican Council wrought certainly accelerated and disseminated change quite rapidly, but the reform impulse had grown quite strong by the time the world's Catholic bishops first met in the autumn of 1962.

The laity did not respond with unambiguous enthusiasm to the social justice prescription, and evidence survives to point to lay ambivalence toward the specific remedies that they encountered in the diocesan paper and organization newsletters. The social justice solution did not take the day easily and in many ways ultimately fell short. But the premise for this solution, that the laity must do the work themselves, did catch on rapidly and spread to other areas. Church officials surely wanted to educate the laity on how they ought to work for social justice, but the hierarchy also understood that the laity would have to be at the center of these efforts. If devotionalism and separatism sought to contain and constrain lay behavior, the impulse to achieve social justice demanded that Church officials empower and then release the laity into the broader society. Catholics heavily enmeshed in social justice efforts necessarily operated with more independence from the clergy than did those avidly practicing devotions. More than either devotionalism or Catholic separatism, social justice inescapably entailed significant lay leadership and empowerment. This impulse did carry the day.

Church officials in Pittsburgh initially sought to move the laity to transform society through a loosely defined program called Catholic Action. Though Catholic Action was a specific program with papal sanction and episcopal support, it is difficult to define precisely for three reasons. First, its most ardent proponents in the early and middle twentieth century took great pains to portray it as a continuation (or restoration) of early Church practices. In their efforts to affirm its orthodoxy, they argued that it was really nothing new. One 1960s proponent of the program claimed that "basically and substantially it was born with the Church and has followed her steps and vicissitudes for twenty centuries."[53] So even as Church officials called the laity to participate in new ways, the hierarchy insisted that the call represented no novel departure from Church tradition.

Second, Catholic Action varied from locale to locale. As a lay movement Catholic Acton clearly had the potential to subvert the Church's hierarchical structure, so Church officials placed great emphasis on clerical prerogative. The bishops and their clergy remained in charge. The laity, in the words of one Catholic Action proponent, "have neither the powers nor the special commission which would enable them to exercise the apostolate as do the clergy." Further, the laity could "never 'share' in the apostolate of the bishops, but only collaborate with it to a greater or lesser degree."[54] Each bishop could therefore define the form that Catholic Action took in his diocese, and the bishops took varying interest in the program. Though Catholic Action held special papal sanction in general, no pope specified a particular course of action for each bishop to implement. Syndicated columnist Donald McDonald explained in 1954 that "Catholic Action takes whatever specific form the hierarchy, or bishops may designate at a given time and place."[55] Some bishops interpreted Catholic Action to mean intensified devotional activities, while some urged the laity to engage in social reform activities. Some resisted it altogether.

Finally, even in a specific location Catholic Action could mean almost anything. Though Catholic Action was often associated with social justice efforts, Father Lackner, spiritual director for the diocese's Holy Name Society, explained that Catholic Action also meant helping out at Mass, raising money for the new church roof, or engaging in social action that aimed at transforming society. It was, in Lackner's words, "any action done according to the principles of the Catholic religion."[56]

In Pittsburgh, both Bishop Hugh Boyle and his successor, John Dearden, called regularly for increased lay activity in general, and for participation in Catholic Action in particular. Bishop Dearden especially attempted to jumpstart lay action by linking area Catholics to national Catholic Action programs. He did this through the Diocesan Council of Catholic Women and the Holy Name Society, which he designated as Catholic Action's official arms in the Pittsburgh Diocese.

John Dearden moved rapidly after Hugh Boyle's death to energize the diocese on a number of fronts, particularly those that combated the materialist crisis. Dearden sought to use Catholic Action both as a catalyst to generate increased lay activity and as a mechanism through which he could coordinate and control those efforts. As director of the Holy Name Society, Fr. Paul Lackner served as Bishop Dearden's point man for Catholic Action in the diocese. Lackner pushed Catholic men not only to continue with the projects that they had done for years, such as receiving the sacraments regularly, participating in membership campaigns, attending retreats, and saying the rosary for the dead, but also to "broaden their views to include a more universal apostolate."[57] They must seek to transform society.

But Dearden and Lackner recognized the potential this program had to revolutionize relations within the Church as well, and attempted to negotiate the delicate balance between spurring the laity to use their power to effect change and keeping them always obedient to ecclesiastical authority. Dearden wanted to awaken the lay giant, but keep it from wandering where it pleased. Lackner explained to HNS members that this broader apostolate did not permit the laity to infringe on "work which belongs exclusively to priests and religious." Nor were the laity to undertake work independent of clerical oversight, as "every Catholic Action group must have a priest-chaplain." Obedience to authority remained key. "Thus Catholic Action is really 'in action' when all the members are doing something in a manner that the leaders of a group have indicated." Furthermore, each Catholic Action group had to have lay leaders, and those leaders had to "bring into realization the orders and direction of the hierarchy, to whom they must always be obedient."[58]

Lackner also understood Catholic Action to be inseparable from the theology of the mystical body of Christ, which stressed both the common connection between the laity and the clergy, and their hierarchical arrangement. As members of a common social organization, the Catholics belonged to certain groups such as the ordained priesthood and the laity, which could be likened to the organs of a body. Each was vital to the body's survival, and each contributed to the constitution of the being. Each member therefore linked with the others in a single body. This notion of commonality served to bond people together in ways that forced them to acknowledge their connections with each other.[59]

Each member of this body did not share equally, however. Theologians understood the body to consist of organs arranged "in due order," and therefore argued that the Church too contained a hierarchical ranking of constituent parts.[60] Christ was the head, and others occupied less significant parts. In the current world, the pope occupied the highest rank and the laity the lowest. Catholic theologians came to argue that this was no simple analogy, but rather that each Catholic represented some unspecified part of Christ's actual body.

A group of theologians in America initiated a "liturgical movement" in the late 1930s which promoted the concept of the mystical body of Christ. It centered around Virgil Michel at Saint John's Abbey and College in Collegeville, Minnesota, and introduced the mystical body to Catholics such as Dorothy Day who sought to ameliorate human suffering and exploitation through social action. Dorothy Day founded the Catholic Worker Movement, its newspaper, and Catholic Worker houses, and stood as a moral exemplar for the wider Catholic American population. Though the Catholic Worker Movement did not spread through mainstream American Catholicism, whose members often criticized it as radical and socialist, it did anticipate later Vatican II changes and informed the wider Catholic understanding of those Council changes. Moreover, Day's associates recalled that she came to appreciate fully this understanding of the mystical body of Christ while on retreat under the direction of Pittsburgh priests John J. Hugo and Louis Farina.[61]

Proponents of efforts to energize such movements as Catholic Action often emphasized the commonality such membership rendered over the hierarchical organization that it also entailed. They sought to infuse the laity with the affirming power that their baptism provided in order to move them to greater action. Catholics reinforced their constituency in Christ's mystical body by physically consuming his body at Mass.

With Catholic Action thus conceived and presented to the Pittsburgh laity, diocesan officials hoped that it would prove to be a useful spark and safe conduit through which to channel the greater lay role for which the hierarchy called. Under Dearden's leadership, Catholic Action in Pittsburgh first sought to increase lay participation in devotional activities. But Catholic Action also became the venue through which social justice advocates sought to implement their ideals.

SOCIAL JUSTICE AND ITS LIMITS

The specific prescriptions that the 1950s discourse advanced did not meet with universal and unmitigated success. Lay Catholics did not unambiguously embrace the Catholic message to relieve exploitation in the capitalist economy, to resist commercialism, and to strive for racial equality. It is important to remember that the search for social justice and the reforms that it inspired transcended these specific prescriptions over time, however, and that the movement for social justice gathered strength and defined lay Catholic experiences to a degree that devotionalism and Catholic separatism were unable to accomplish.

The Catholic struggle to eliminate or at least ameliorate the power of commercialism to control American culture is illustrative of the limits that Catholics encountered in their social justice efforts. The Catholic campaign to sever
commercialism from Christmas did not succeed. In the end, the office Christmas party survived the campaign to stamp it out. Though good data on the
office Christmas party's relative popularity is difficult to find, evidence does exist
that Catholics thought they had ended the practice in Pittsburgh in the early
1950s. John Collins confidently asserted in December 1953, for example, that
"the rowdy, alcoholic 'office party' which for several years was distressingly common just before Christmas has now gone into the discard."[62] Collins's successors at the *Pittsburgh Catholic* reported the following year that "some of the
larger firms" had discontinued office parties altogether, while others had replaced them with opportunities to perform community service. Though the editors credited "secular" causes for the change (too many car accidents involving
drunken revelers and lost productivity at the office), they did suggest that "there
is no doubt that somewhere along the way, the removal of occasions of sin must
have resulted in many spiritual benefits too."[63] The diocesan paper triumphantly
declared that same year that "Christ is returning to Christmas!" The evidence?
The Pittsburgh-based Archconfraternity of Christian Mothers' campaign to restore Christ to Christmas, begun seven years earlier, had spread to Milwaukee,
Chicago, and other places. Local Pittsburgh stores had started putting religious
displays in their store windows (a victory of sorts), and even the Pittsburgh
Chamber of Commerce determined in 1954 to put a "crib scene" in its building.
The paper reported with "great joy" in 1955 that "Pittsburgh has put 'Christ in
Christmas' again."[64] But that same year women's columnist Mary Tinley Daly
predicted that real estate and insurance offices were years away from implementing any of the office party reforms the movement advocated.[65] Pittsburgh remained a commercial society, and even Christian holidays remained commercial events.

The story of the *Pittsburgh Catholic* itself, the medium through which Bishop
Dearden waged his battle against materialism, proved how difficult such efforts
could be in a capitalist society. In order to better achieve his aims, Dearden
wanted the *Pittsburgh Catholic* to become a larger, more sophisticated, and more
widely read paper than it had been when under lay control. Until 1954 the paper
consisted of twelve pages, few photographs, and columns that local writers contributed. About ten thousand people subscribed to the weekly. Dearden wanted
sixteen pages, lots of pictures, nationally syndicated columnists, and increased
circulation. Toward this aim he had John Ward launch a massive diocesanwide

campaign to sell subscriptions to parishioners. Ward's *Pittsburgh Catholic* Circulation Crusade enlisted every child attending Catholic schools to go door to door and solicit subscriptions, and set up opportunities for other Catholic children to participate as well. He divided the diocese into nine divisions and pitted the children against each other in a competition to sign up the most readers. Each child received twenty-five cents for each four-dollar paid subscription, and the child with the most subscriptions received a gold wristwatch or fifty dollars. The child with the second-most subscriptions received twenty-five dollars, and the one with the third-most received fifteen. Division winners received five dollars, second- and third-place finishers received three and two dollars respectively. The paper might preach anticommercialism, but it built its readership by offering Catholic children greater power in the market it condemned.[66]

Twelve-year-old seventh-grader Paul Fitzgerald from Saint Lawrence O'Toole parish in Pittsburgh won the contest by selling thirty-seven of the paper's thirty-five thousand new subscriptions. Two tied for second place, with thirty-four subscriptions each. Paul decided to forgo the wristwatch in favor of the fifty-dollar prize. After all, Christmas was just around the corner.[67]

Despite the dramatic increase in the total number of subscriptions, John Ward determined that only 6 percent of Catholic families subscribed to the paper directly at the end of the 1954 crusade. Diocesan officials soon realized that increased readership was not enough to keep the paper afloat in its new expanded and more expensive format. If the paper was to win the battle against commercialism, it needed more revenue than even forty-five or fifty thousand subscribers provided. In an ironic strategy to bolster its campaign against commercialism, the *Pittsburgh Catholic* devoted significant energies to increasing its appeal to advertisers. The first step was to convince potential advertisers that the numbers of readers that the *Pittsburgh Catholic* touted actually existed. In order to do this, it joined the Audit Bureau of Circulation, an association of advertisers, advertising agencies, and newspaper publishers which measured the circulation of newspapers and periodicals. The paper proudly told readers, and advertisers, that

> by reason of its membership in the Audit Bureau of Circulation, the *Catholic* is able to insure its advertisers and potential advertisers of the integrity of its circulation figures and of its tremendous value to them among the vast Catholic population of the six-county area of the Diocese of Pittsburgh.[68]

The paper then urged readers to consult the ads that retailers, realtors, and others placed in the paper. The very paper that aimed in its editorials and news articles to combat commercialism had joined a national organization in order to court advertisers, the most egregious purveyors of the commercial ethic. The paper had offered to deliver the Catholic consumer to retailers in the effort to fund the battle against consumption. In short order it mimicked the most commercial of all advertising pitches. One front-page news article told area Catholics that "even if you're not in the market for anything, classified ads make interesting reading." It went on to list proudly some of the commercial transactions that the *Pittsburgh Catholic* had generated: "This newspaper has sold everything from meat cleavers to used music, from rides on a merry-go-round to trips to Paris."[69] Commercialism had little to fear from the voice of the Pittsburgh bishop. The Catholic struggle against commercialism in the Pittsburgh region did not end, however, and resurfaced periodically throughout the decades that followed.

Perhaps the most devastating blow to the primacy of the spiritual over the commercial came when a young entrepreneur sought to profit from area Catholics' devotional practices, and in the process elicited a response that undermined the very devotions that Church leaders sought to protect. The story began when a young man in his twenties named Murray Kram determined to start a mail-order religious goods business. Kram founded the "Religious Culture Society" as a for-profit mail solicitation business in 1950. He paged through phone directories from across the country to construct a mailing list of names that sounded Italian or Slavic, and reasoned that these people might be recent immigrants, were likely to be Catholic, and would be relatively unsophisticated in the ways of mail-order solicitations. He then put together a packet to mail to each that consisted of a very inexpensive religious article, such as a cross or medal, attached to the right side of a card. The left side of the card contained a prayer and a note stating that the article was intended to please the recipient. The note asked recipients who were pleased to send twenty-five cents to the Religious Culture Society. Cards sent a bit later asked for fifty cents. The note further asked that the recipient forward the names and addresses of other good Catholics.[70]

Kram ran the business for several months before the Fraud Division of the U.S. Post Office received complaints about the enterprise, and determined that Kram deceived those on the mailing list into thinking that his business was actually a religious organization.[71] The Post Office ordered him to stop the practice, and Kram agreed that any future solicitations would identify Kram as the sole owner of the business and that all proceeds would go to the "sole benefit of an individual." Kram continued his solicitations, and the Fraud Division of the Post Office directed him to change wordings in his solicitations at various points before advising Kram twice that he had not complied with the "spirit" of his agreement. Kram agreed on February 15, 1952, to stop sending the solicitations under the name Religious Culture Society or under any other name.[72]

But Kram established a new business called the Religious Distributing Company, located on Penn Avenue in Wilkinsburg, and continued sending religious articles with solicitations for money, this time for one dollar. The U.S. Attorney's Office indicted Kram in December 1955 and put him on trial the following June. Kram hired Marjorie Matson, a well known civil liberties attorney, to defend him in court.

Matson was a pioneer female attorney who later became president of the Pittsburgh branch of the American Civil Liberties Union, argued three cases before the U.S. Supreme Court, and assisted in the successful National Organization of Women court battle to end gender segregation in newspaper classified advertising. By the time Kram hired her, Matson had already served as the first female assistant district attorney for Allegheny County and as its first female assistant county solicitor as well. She successfully defended herself against charges by the Pennsylvania attorney general in 1951 that she should be fired for Communist sympathies, but by 1955 was in private practice and available for Kram to hire. Given her interests and commitment to civil liberties, Matson's determination to take the case suggests that she saw in Kram's prosecution potential First Amendment concerns.[73] Was this merely a case of commercial fraud, or did the U.S. Postal Service and the U.S. Attorney's Office pay special attention because Kram used religious goods and targeted Catholics?

The religious dimension clearly played a significant role in the prosecution. First Assistant U.S. District Attorney Hubert Teitelbaum argued that Kram set out to deceive those he had solicited into thinking that the religious articles came from a religious organization. Teitelbaum used as evidence packets Kram sent between July 1954 and August 1955. Kram's mailings included the following note:

This Crucifix and chain, which is made in Italy is being sent to you in hope that you find it worth keeping. If so, please insert $1.00 and mail in the enclosed envelope. If you do not wish to keep your crucifix and chain you are under no obligation.

It is being sent to you by an enterprise that is owned and operated for the benefit of Murray Kram.

He sent out at least 1,300,000 packets between July 1, 1954, and June 30, 1955.[74] Teitelbaum argued to jurors that Kram fooled recipients when he used the word *religious* in the company name, copied the format of the literature and religious articles that genuine religious organizations employed in their mailings, and included the phrase "for the benefit of Murray Kram" in the packet. The prosecutors called forty witnesses from all over the country to testify that they thought that Kram's religious articles came from a religious organization, and that they sent Kram one dollar based upon that understanding. Charles Zamaria, from a small mill town east of Pittsburgh, testified that he thought that Kram's solicitation came on behalf of "an individual who was handicapped in some way, or for a veteran or religious organization." Mary Louise Groff testified that she thought Kram's solicitation came from a religious organization. She always responded to such solicitations, "no matter what," because "I'm a Catholic and I always try to help." Mrs. Jennie Colella, a restaurant cook, told jurors, "I work for my money, why should I give it to him [Kram]." She sent the money because she saw the prayer and read no further. Teitelbaum asserted that Kram "took advantage of the finest instincts people have, and made a calculated mockery of religious faith."[75]

But Teitelbaum insisted that the "real crux of the case are the intentions of Murray Kram . . . exactly what was in his mind when he used the mails." The law did not protect religion from mockery, after all, only U.S. citizens from being deceived through the mail into buying goods under false pretenses. Toward this end, Teitelbaum produced the most dramatic witness of the trial. Kram's ex-wife and ex–business partner, Mrs. Bernice Goldman, testified that Kram often received more than the requested one-dollar donation. The implication here was that such respondents must have thought that they were donating money to a religious cause. Why else would someone deliberately overpay a businessman? But Kram's attorney successfully blocked Teitelbaum's attempt to have the former Mrs. Kram reveal the "pet name" that Murray Kram used for the lists of people to whom he sent the solicitations. Presumably it was not flattering to the targets of Kram's solicitations. Perhaps he called them "suckers" or "dupes." The records do not reveal it. Moreover, Mrs. Goldman had divorced Kram two years before the activities for which he was on trial and had no personal knowledge of Kram's work during that period. Teitelbaum provided no evidence that Kram sought to deceive other than the testimony of those who felt deceived once they learned that Kram was not a religious organization.[76]

Kram's attorney, Marjorie Matson, stressed this as she argued that Kram's disclaimer was clear evidence that he was honest and straightforward in the solicitations. She pointed out that some of the witnesses called to testify as to the effect that Kram's solicitation had on them did not even read the enclosed literature. How could they be defrauded by language that they did not encounter? Given the prosecutor's failure to provide direct evidence of Kram's intent, Matson asked Judge Marsh for a directed verdict of acquittal. After all, the packets contained no misrepresentations, and the U.S. attorney had not shown that the operation would deceive a person of ordinary prudence and comprehension. Matson wanted Judge Marsh to dismiss the charges outright.[77]

Marsh denied the motion in November 1956 on the grounds that the law prohibits any scheme "devised with the intention of defrauding," even if the scheme is not effective or deceptive. Prosecutors need only prove that Kram intended to deceive recipients of his mailed solicitations in order to win a conviction, according to Marsh, and he allowed as evidence the format and appearance of the cards even when the specific language was technically accurate. He asserted further that people "imbued with religious, sympathetic or generous impulses" have clouded discernment and must fall under the law's protection.[78] Even if Kram's solicitation did not deceive people of ordinary prudence, it might have fooled religious people. For, in the words of Teitelbaum, "we are here not only to protect the wise or innocent, we are here to protect the gullible, too."[79]

Matson proceeded with her defense. She produced two witnesses who sent in money for religious articles that they had received in solicitations from Kram. One liked the articles so much that she sent for three more.[80] They were not defrauded and they received the same materials as did Teitelbaum's witnesses. Not all recipients believed themselves to be victims of fraud, and so the prosecutor's case could not depend upon the perceptions of Teitelbaum's forty witnesses. Matson turned the case back to Kram's intentions, and argued that his material was clear and accurate. Kram surely sought to make money from his solicitations, but this was a common use of the mails.

Nevertheless, the jury found Kram guilty of ten counts of mail fraud, each of which carried a potential penalty of a $5,000 fine and one year in jail.[81] Kram faced a sentencing hearing for his convictions. Matson pled for leniency, and relayed that a downtown jewelry store had offered Kram a sales job. It seemed that he might depart from the mail-order religious goods business altogether. The assistant U.S. attorney disagreed in his call for a prison sentence. Teitelbaum insisted that Kram "is not the type person who can be rehabilitated through probation." Judge Marsh agreed, as he fined Kram $4,500, sentenced him to three months in prison, and added three years of probation. Marsh did let Kram out on $2,500 bond while he appealed his conviction.[82]

Unchastened by his legal setbacks, Murray Kram then established a new religious trinket business on Penn Avenue in the Garfield section of Pittsburgh. His K&R Religious Sales Company operated in the same manner as had his previous businesses.[83] He may also have worked in a downtown jewelry store, but accounts offer no record of this.

Matson took Kram's case to the Third Circuit Court of Appeals, and this time Kram prevailed. The three-judge panel ruled in September 1957 that the United States had to prove both that Kram intended the mailings to deceive recipients and that he used the mail to carry out his scheme. The judges agreed that Kram used the mails, but ruled that the U.S. attorney had provided no evidence that Kram sought to defraud. In fact, the opposite seemed to be the case. They reasoned that many companies that supply religious articles use some form of the word *religion* in their name, and that the U.S. attorney had offered no evidence that the printed materials were intended to deceive.[84] Murray Kram was free to return to the mail-order religious goods business, which he apparently had already done. And the battle over Catholic material culture was fully under way.

As Murray Kram's case worked its way through the courts, the official Catholic response became increasingly animated. Though Church officials focused most of their criticism on Kram himself, they attacked and dismissed the religious icons as well. In the process they pushed Catholics to consider the crucifixes, rosaries, and medals as something other than religious symbols. Or, they forced Catholics to distinguish between one crucifix and another based not upon their apparent physical characteristics, but instead upon their provenance, or perhaps deliverance. One can sense this through the diocesan press coverage of Kram's case and in developments related to it.

The *Pittsburgh Catholic* warned readers from its earliest stories about Kram that he was a "junk dealer" who sought to dupe the public. Though the vitriol was aimed at Kram, the attacks hit the religious icons just as squarely. In any other context, it would be difficult to imagine a diocesan newspaper characterizing rosaries, crucifixes, and other Catholic icons as religious "junk," "pious trinkets," and "pseudo-religious sucker bait."[85] But the *Pittsburgh Catholic* did just that in its stories on Kram during 1956 and 1957. In fact, these characterizations remind one of the traditional Protestant attacks on Catholic "idol worship." But they came from the official voice of the Catholic bishop of Pittsburgh. When Miami-based Max Kram re-entered the religious goods mail-order business in 1958, after declaring bankruptcy the year before, Bishop John J. Wright of Worcester, Massachusetts, told a radio audience that the miniature statues of the Virgin Mary that Kram mailed out were "sheer junk."[86]

What was an ordinary Catholic to make of this? After all, Murray Kram's crucifixes did not differ in shape or form from those offered by groups more favored by Church officials. What made these icons "junk," and those from the Knights of Columbus sacred? What made the Knights of Columbus medal an object of veneration if Murray Kram's medal was mere "pseudo-religious sucker bait"?

One possible answer might be found in the quality of the icon's manufacturing, and the *Pittsburgh Catholic* noted on a number of occasions that Kram purchased the medals, rosaries, and crucifixes for mere pennies while he asked for up to a full dollar in return. Kram profited handsomely from each icon sold. But most religious organizations that used religious articles to aid their appeals did so to raise money as well. They sought to make more on the donation than they spent on the icon. Church officials endorsed these efforts. And Catholic bookstores also sought a profit from their sales of religious items.

Church officials really asked Catholics to make a pretty sophisticated distinction in the call to reject one set of religious symbols and embrace another whose physical properties were largely identical. The distinction lay in their provenance, or perhaps their use within the moment of exchange. One set came from within the fold and acted as a physical bridge that united Catholics in a common devotion to a shared belief system. When religious orders, confraternities, or missionary societies offered the religious articles in exchange for a donation, the icons affirmed the donor's shared identity with the recipient, and affirmed their mutual attention to a common form of religious expression.[87] The other set of religious icons, those offered by Murray Kram, sought to exploit that religious bond and, in the process, threatened to sever it. When the icons became a mode of market exchange, a means of enriching one member of society in his or her search for wealth, they put devotionalism in the service of commercialism. The icons became primarily, or at least substantially, commercial items rather than religious. As Hubert Teitelbaum stated, they made a "calculated mockery of religious faith."

In their rush to condemn this profit-seeking act, however, Church officials may have undermined the very shared vocabulary that they sought to preserve. For Catholics encouraged to disdain one set of religious icons might not so easily venerate the other—particularly if they appeared identical. And yet remaining silent in the face of this commodification of religious symbols risked acquiescence in a process that might also lead Catholics to disown these powerful facilitators of devotional Catholicism. Commercialism here struck at the very heart of American Catholic devotional practices.

This very tension surfaced in the *Pittsburgh Catholic* once John Wright became bishop of Pittsburgh. The diocesan paper for the first time included a regular "letters to the editor" section, and this issue arose in 1960. The editors started the debate by noting in October that they had received the first of an anticipated flood of Christmas gift catalogues "aimed specifically at Catholics." They went on to call the catalogues, which offered such items as a shoe-shine kit "with the 'St. Christopher emblem stamped in gold inside'" and a Virgin Mary mechanical pencil, "perverse appeals to piety." The items themselves were "pure and absolute rubbish." The editors trusted that readers have "the good taste to heave catalogues like that of the Stemper Co. precisely where they belong—in the waste paper basket."[88]

A number of readers wrote in to challenge the condemnation. One reader asked, "Why condemn a businessman of the commercial world when our religious orders are actually sending the merchandise, expecting a donation in return?"[89] Another posed the question central to the dilemma in which the anti-commercial campaign placed Catholics:

> Where do you draw the line between "junk" and "good" taste, true artistic value, etc.? How can any religious article be called "junk" if used properly— as of no value in itself, but as a reminder to lift our thoughts, hearts and prayer to God, His Blessed Mother, the angels or saints.[90]

Even the religious articles store that sent the offending catalogue wrote in to cry foul. Stemper of Milwaukee addressed a number of the specific articles that the paper had denounced, defending each. The "Mechanical Pencil featuring a full colored figure of the Blessed Virgin" might seem like religious junk to the *Pittsburgh Catholic* when the mail-order company sought to make a profit from it. "But the pious person who purchases one of these will everytime he uses the pencil look at the Blessed Virgin statue and probably say 'Sweet Heart of Mary, be my salvation' (300 days of indulgence each time he says it)." Stemper argued that this held true for each article from whose sale it made a profit. For

> what is true of the above mentioned articles, applies to all the religious articles ridiculed in your article, when bought by an earnest God fearing pious man, woman, or child, and after having them blessed, put them to beneficial use. They truly become just as valuable and beneficial as dipping your finger in the Holy Water font and piously making the sign of the cross. Such "junk," as you call them, could make us more saintly and even be a determining factor in the struggle to save our immortal souls.[91]

One person's "perverse appeal to piety" was another's invitation to eternal salvation. Of course, Murray Kram could have made the same argument.

MURRAY KRAM'S EXPLOITATION OF THE CATHOLIC MATERIALIST impulse helps demonstrate that Church officials did not triumph over commercialism in the 1950s and, in their efforts to do so, may have contributed to the demise of the very devotionalism that they sought to preserve. If lay Catholics did not fully embrace the war against commercialism, how did they respond to the call to social justice?

SOCIAL JUSTICE AND LAY EMPOWERMENT

The social justice and reform impulse gained support and even official sanction in the growing insistence that the laity play a greater role in the Church's mission to sanctify the world. A regular cascade of instructions emanated from Church officials imploring, instructing, and insisting that lay Catholics become more active. Father Lackner urged Holy Name Society members to become more active in their communities, and the *Pittsburgh Catholic* carried messages from various priests, bishops, and even the pope himself urging the laity on to greater and greater efforts. One archbishop told the National Council of Catholic Men that "if all things are to be restored in Christ, the work will have to be done, in the main, by the laity."[92] Toward this aim diocesan officials steered the Holy Name Society toward greater social action. This was, after all, the largest and most potent lay organization. The diocese would follow a similar path with the Diocesan Council of Catholic Women in coming years. In addition, a handful of specific programs and movements provided paths toward this greater lay involvement. Three in particular merit attention in the Pittsburgh diocese, as they laid the groundwork for the lay embrace of a new model for the Church in the twentieth century. The first consisted of a well-organized adult education program aimed directly at better preparing the laity to sanctify the world. The second took a more circuitous route to lay empowerment, as it worked through the reform of the liturgy. The third aimed to use families in an effort to transform the broader society.

Adult Education Institute

Bishop Dearden established an adult education program in 1950 with the explicit aim to "help adult Catholics, young and old, to play a more effective role in the reconstruction of modern society along Christian lines." The program offered a slate of courses by the mid-1950s which ranged from the explicitly political ("Why Catholics Make Good Citizens") to the frankly vocational ("Typing I and II"). The institute's very existence testified to diocesan officials' growing acknowledgment that the laity played increasingly critical roles in society and that the institutional Church had a stake in better preparing them for their tasks. Just as significantly, the program coincided with the laity's expanding role within the Church itself. The laity learned in these sessions the skills and values that better enabled them to transform the Church.[93]

The Adult Education Institute focused on a range of topics and skills for Catholic adults, but it had a social justice cast from its inception. Bishop Dearden appointed as its first director the Rev. Carl P. Hensler, S.T.D., one of the diocese's leading labor priests and a cofounder of the Catholic Radical Alliance. Though his program accommodated a range of interests, Hensler knew the critical importance that education for social justice had to play. Early programs offered courses entitled "Better Living Through Economic Justice," "Labor Problems and Principles," and "Politics, Parties, Pressure Groups."[94] One course entitled "Catholic Doctrine and Practice in Human Relations" asked students to consider that God had given Americans "a mission to prove to a perplexed world that men can be different and still love one another, still seek their happiness together and in peace." The course moved students through a study of official Church doctrine on human dignity and the rights of conscience and then asked them to consider a series of questions, including: "Do you fear or dislike Negroes? Are you anti-Semitic?"[95]

In addition to courses that touched directly on social justice, the institute also regularly taught the skills necessary for Catholics to act successfully within organizations. Courses in parliamentary law, basic English writing, and public speaking prepared Catholics to serve in critical roles in labor unions, on civic committees, and in the broader political arena. Courses in Catholic theology and liturgy helped students to understand the Catholic Church better and to lay the groundwork for the substantial reforms that followed.

It is difficult to evaluate very precisely the Adult Education Institute's impact on the diocese's laity in the years leading to explicit reforms. The program did reach more and more Catholics throughout the 1950s, as evidence from course enrollments reveals. Students took up 696 seats in 1950, 1,100 in 1951, and 1,600 in 1952. Data on subsequent years is more sketchy, though the program appears to have attracted 1,420 students in 1956 and fully 2,000 in 1957. Clearly not all the students sought out courses in social justice, though many did. The most popular courses in the years for which reports on individual class enrollments survive focused on some aspect of psychology. In one year it was the "psychology of adjustment" and in another "general psychology" that drew the most students. But the courses that emphasized social justice and the skills necessary to succeed in organizations attracted healthy numbers.[96] More significantly, the program reflected the shared understanding between the hierarchy and the laity that laymen and laywomen would necessarily play expanded and more central roles in society and in the Church itself.

Social Justice and Reform: The Liturgy

The liturgical movement played the most profound role in sparking and sustaining the reform spirit in the Pittsburgh diocese. It too sought to expand lay roles and to empower the laity to transform the world. The movement's national and international leaders sought through increased lay participation in a reformed ritual to inspire and prepare the laity to move more confidently to change the society in which they lived. Official efforts in Pittsburgh were less confident and sure-footed, but early attempts to renew the liturgy laid the groundwork for the more dramatic changes that followed the Second Vatican Council. More importantly, if the laity had become alienated from the devotional Church and Catholic separatism, liturgical reform animated them intensely. It gave voice to their sentiments for a Church responsive to their needs. The laity wanted an intelligible liturgy that lent meaning to their lives and experiences, and the liturgical movement promised just such a ritual. More powerfully still, it linked the central Catholic ritual explicitly to life outside church walls—to social reform.

As earlier chapters establish, Catholic participation in a range of devotional rituals began to decline in Pittsburgh in the 1950s. This was not true for the central Catholic ritual during this decade. In fact, the liturgy, or the Mass, as Catholics more often referred to it, experienced a boom in the same decade in which novenas and forty-hour devotions lost their appeal. Nationwide, a majority of Catholics reported to pollsters throughout the 1950s that they attended Mass every week, and by 1958 fully 75 percent claimed that they attended the liturgy weekly. Catholics seemed to be concentrating their ritual participation on the Mass.

Many Catholics understood that the Mass they attended linked them through common experience with Catholics who attended the exact same ritual centuries and even millennia before. In their eyes, the Mass remained static, unchanged, an elaborate mystery. And it emphasized lay passivity. The priest was the Mass's central actor, and he performed most of the ritual with his back to the laity, used a language reserved solely for formal Catholic ceremonies, and wore clothing peculiar to clerics when they filled this role. If the Mass modeled the broader society, it told the laity that they should leave critical social roles to experts. But laymen and laywomen could easily draw no parallels to their broader lives, as the Mass seemed very powerfully and self-consciously otherworldly.

Many Catholics sought to change this, to infuse the Mass with the power they understood that it ought to play in lay lives. The most innovative and popular voice pushing for such change in the 1950s was known throughout Europe and America as the liturgical movement. Its American center was a journal published at Saint John's Abbey in Collegeville, Minnesota, called *Orate Fratres* (later *Worship*) and the Liturgy Program at the University of Notre Dame in South Bend, Indiana. Advocates of liturgical renewal sought to reform the Mass in order to improve its ability to draw people to God, to impart God's grace to those who participated in Mass, and to spread that grace throughout society. They advocated greater lay participation in the Mass to make it more meaningful and powerful for lay Catholics, to better achieve these three functions. The movement's most widely identified leader, Virgil Michel, saw the Mass as a potentially powerful means of achieving social justice. He believed the Mass could combat the evils of the industrial world. An admirer later wrote that Michel thought the Mass could

> counteract the destructiveness of individualism by its communal banquet, its transcendence of class barriers in admitting all equally to the celebration, its eucharistic ministry to the sick, its prayers that those in positions of worldly power would act justly, its collections of money and goods for the needy, its biblical injunctions to live in solidarity with the poor, and its warnings against a materialistic lifestyle. But Michel also saw that to accomplish these, the liturgy had to be reformed. It would have to expel clericalism and promote active lay participation, symbolize an authentic community, and inspire service to the world at large.[97]

Movement supporters understood that it could succeed only by transforming the devotional style of lay passivity in the Mass.[98]

If the Mass was to be an instrument to transform society, it had to become more forcefully present in the lives of those who attended. It had to inspire and empower the laity to transform the grace they affirmed in Mass to the outside world. Liturgical reformers therefore advocated using vernacular language in the ritual, incorporating music that resonated with the laity, and in many other ways more fully involving those outside of the Communion rail in the ritual.

The American hierarchy did not support the movement, with a few exceptions, and only gradually moved to incorporate its suggestions. The American bishops seemed more disposed to avoid discussion of the liturgy at all than to deal with these radical reforms. They largely resisted efforts to address the liturgy formally, and refrained from participating in international movements to change the central rituals of the faith. But in November 1957 enough interest existed for the National Catholic Welfare Council (NCWC) to form a committee to study the possibility of establishing a commission on the liturgy. The committee recommended to the NCWC that it establish an Episcopal Committee for the Liturgical Apostolate. The NCWC agreed and appointed five bishops to serve on it—including Bishop Dearden, who had just left Pittsburgh for Detroit.[99] The committee was to act as a conduit between Rome and the American dioceses, to develop uniform practices for the American dioceses for all of the reforms then under way, and to act as liaison with the North American Liturgical Conference.[100]

In 1947 Pope Pius XII encouraged each diocese to establish its own Liturgical Commission, and in 1958 he required each to do so. Very few American dioceses had them, however, so the Episcopal Committee for the Liturgical Apostolate worked principally in the early years to encourage dioceses to establish these liturgical commissions. Though Dearden had actively sought to infuse energy into a host of Pittsburgh's Catholic organizations and conservative movements, and served on the NCWC committee to consider establishing a liturgical committee, he demonstrated little interest in liturgical reform.[101] Dearden made no move to heed the pope's call for diocesan liturgical committees.

Once John Wright replaced Dearden, however, Pittsburgh became a leader in the liturgical movement. Wright embraced the possibilities the liturgical movement promised. He had served on the national Liturgical Conference from his days in Worcester, and he continued his personal commitment to reform in his new diocese. He quickly sent a delegation of Pittsburghers to Notre Dame for "Liturgy Week," and he then established one of the nation's first liturgical commissions.[102]

Wright envisioned the commission as part of a larger structure designed to reinvigorate the liturgy throughout the diocese. The Liturgy Commission stood as one among three new commissions, including also the Sacred Arts Commission (focused primarily on church architecture) and a Sacred Music Commission. But the Liturgy Commission was to stand slightly taller than the other two, even "supervising" and "outlining" for them principles of good participation, though not duplicating their actions.

Wright asked the members to form a commission with five primary tasks, each oriented toward the parishes. Because no such commission had existed previously, pastors did not know how to receive them. Did the commission exercise the bishop's authority? Wright did not intend them to do so—but pastors could not be sure of this. The commission drew resentment over changes in the liturgy away from Bishop Wright at the same time that it satisfied Wright's genuine desire to broaden somewhat the power concentrated so heavily in the bishop's office. The commission's power was purely persuasive, and rested completely on the pastors' belief in the bishop's support for the commission's suggestions and their sympathy for the reforms introduced.

The Liturgical Commission began with a clear determination to improve lay participation in the Mass, but with little understanding of how it might do that and how it might overcome resistance from pastors. An increase in lay participation entailed a significant alteration in a ritual that many clergy and laity valued so highly in part because of its perceived stability over time. Some members felt that they had to convince both the clergy who presided and the laity who attended that change was good, could be achieved, and merited their support. The Liturgical Commission embraced the reform ideal, but moved fitfully and cautiously in its early years.

Commission members recognized immediately that they needed some sense of the ways parishioners practiced the liturgy. Everyone knew the priests' rubrics, or course, but they did not know what the laity did. Did they sing hymns, read missals, say rosaries, and receive Communion? Had any pastors begun to introduce the changes that the successive popes had recommended to improve participation independent of any official diocesan mandates? The commission sent out a questionnaire to every priest in the diocese to get a sense of the level of lay participation, and within a couple of months received over two hundred replies. While it worked out an acceptable questionnaire and waited for responses, the commission also devised a strategy to improve participation. Members assumed that the parishes did not have a great deal of participation and worked on that premise even before tabulating the survey responses.[103]

The commission devised a two-pronged strategy to achieve greater participation. One targeted the clergy, the other the laity. At certain points the two efforts merged, but the strategy contained a keen sensitivity to these groups as separate, to be approached independently and in different manners. At the same time, though, the commission struggled to determine what form this improved participation should take. Should parts of the Mass be conducted in English? If so, which parts? The members' confusion about the new liturgical structure tempered their firm commitment to greater lay participation.

The confusion remained in some form up through the first session of the Second Vatican Council in the fall of 1962. The commission operated under the assumption that translation of Latin into English would improve participation, and focused heavily on this translation. But they were uncertain about what they could permissibly translate, and, once they determined that some parts could be translated, what a permissible translation would be. This fear of doing wrong kept the commission from introducing a diocesan standard for a "participated Mass."

The entire issue of translating parts or all of the Mass into English proved quite animating, as many sought such reform and others resisted. A growing debate raged in the diocese and broke out in the diocesan paper as well. Though it began modestly, the debate grew to become the hottest topic in the newly instituted letters to the editor pages of the *Pittsburgh Catholic*.

The *Pittsburgh Catholic* had begun to cover the vernacular movement under John Collins's editorship, but any mention of English in the Mass disappeared when John Ward took over the paper under Bishop Dearden. Ward's replacement gave the vernacular movement little direct attention in the news sections, but the issue entered the discourse through letters to the editor and through some of the syndicated columnists John Deedy published. William Storey, a member of the Christian Family Movement and chair of the Duquesne University history department, started off the debate over Latin with a letter in the winter of 1960. He suggested that a recent *Pittsburgh Catholic* editorial lamenting the downgrading of Latin and Greek at Oxford and Cambridge universities might be off the mark. These institutions had flourished for centuries because of their "versatility in at once clinging to the essentials of their ancient roots and in adapting themselves to the needs of any given age." Storey then moved to the liturgy. "If even on the academic level, including that of our own seminaries to a larger and larger degree, Latin is being relinquished in favor of living speech, something must be done regarding the language of the Roman liturgy." The continued use of Latin had proved to be the major barrier to more active lay participation, in Storey's perspective. "Let us worship God in a language we know and love."[104] The debate that Storey started with this letter endured to the Second Vatican Council.

Letters poured in from the Pittsburgh diocese and beyond debating the merits of Latin or the vernacular in the Mass. The overwhelming majority of local writers sought an English liturgy, while those from outside the diocese favored Latin. The arguments remained roughly the same throughout the entire debate. The Pittsburgh laity sought a Mass that they could understand, that was intelligible to them. The Latin Mass alienated them at the very moment when Church officials, from the pope down to the local pastor, called them to be more active in the liturgy. They pointed out repeatedly that the Latin Mass came into being because the common man and woman in Rome could not understand the Greek ritual. Latin was the vernacular at its inception. But now the language was dead to almost all Catholics, including those very priests who used it each Sunday in the liturgy. Laymen and laywomen in Pittsburgh spoke English and wanted an English Mass. "Please, please let us pray the Mass in silence or audibly in the vernacular," wrote one woman, because "when we know what we are praying for, we are more ardent in its purpose."[105]

Proponents of the Latin Mass most often pointed to its universality. Every Roman Catholic attended the same Mass, in the same language. One local writer worried, for example, that the vernacular Mass would risk the "potential germination of many new forms of particularism," and he stressed that "universality is one of the marks of the Church."[106] Others wrote of the great joy they experienced when attending Mass in foreign countries, particularly Vatican City, and encountered the familiar Latin intonations. One area resident responded to this argument with the observation that it hardly seemed reasonable for all Catholics to suffer weekly so that one might "wax nostalgic at the dear, familiar sounds, as incomprehensible to him on any point on the globe, as they are in his home parish."[107] Latinists did not dispute that few understood the Latin liturgy, but responded in two general ways. First, they argued that people ought to understand Latin, and any failure to do so resulted from intellectual or cultural shortcomings. One writer, for example, claimed that Pittsburghers did not appreciate the Latin because they were "culturally cold and intellectually lazy."[108] Second, Latinists argued that it did not matter that people could not understand Latin because God did. Only the exterior experience of worship mattered to them, while those who favored the vernacular Mass sought a more meaningful interior experience. This point revealed the crucial link between liturgical reform and social justice. Reformers sought an intellectually authentic experience in the Mass that might transform participants and empower them to go out and transform the world.

The *Pittsburgh Catholic* editors took no stand on Latin, though they did favor increased lay participation. Bishop Wright's love of classical studies and Latin in particular did not dispose him to embrace the vernacular movement, though he supported other aspects of the liturgical movement ardently. The heart-felt disagreement over Latin left the diocesan Liturgical Commission in a difficult position. Evidence of this problem emerged soon after it formed, as members attempted to produce some substantive recommendations for the parishes. In January 1961, two months after the commission formed, members determined that four specific parts of the Mass could be translated into English for parishes. But they were not comfortable with any specific translation, and so decided that they should encourage pastors to use English language-versions of the Gloria, Credo, Sanctus, and Agnus Dei only if the pastors specifically asked the commission if they might. Otherwise, the members should not in any way advance this proposal until Father McManus, president of the national Liturgical Conference in Washington, D.C., provided an official interpretation.[109]

One area where commission members saw clear room for greater improvement was parishioner singing. Very few Catholics sang hymns at Mass. This did not seem so odd at Masses in which the choir sang, but choirs attended only one Mass each Sunday in most parishes, and so all other Masses had no singing.[110] Part of this reluctance came from the hymns themselves, which were often in Latin, but much of it owed to Catholic behavior at Mass. The laity, long excluded from meaningful participation, had developed practices that ran parallel to but apart from the central action taking place in the sanctuary. They often prayed the rosary, for example. Some had begun to read a missal that contained the Latin Mass and an English translation on facing pages. But few knew Latin well enough actually to participate in the responses. The laity, by practice and training, remained quiet throughout the Mass. After all, one could not say the rosary and sing at the same time. By May 1961 Monsignor Pauley asked the Music Committee of the Liturgical Commission to develop a songbook for participated Masses, and Father Getty volunteered to look for "approved English translations" of songs to include in the hymnal.[111]

Enough uncertainty about the structure of new rituals existed a year after the commission began operating for the Participation committee to recommend the development of a directory for the diocese. Here again, the commission's caution stifled significant progress. Father McIlvane pushed to have one guide for the Mass completed within six months and another for all liturgies within a year. Father Rice recommended that the commission use directories from other dioceses as guides, and with this began a yearlong search for useful models. Father Reinhold presented a copy of a directory recently adopted in Manila in the Philippines in March, and the commission added one in use in Marquette, Michigan, at the following meeting. Monsignor Shinar stated in May that he preferred a Canadian directory but wished to wait for its announced translation before using it as a basic text. Father Rice argued in June that the French and Germans were "the pioneers in this field," and suggested that those members working on a Pittsburgh directory use those for models instead. By September Monsignor Shinar proposed that no work be done on the directory until after December, so that they might take advantage of any directories which came out after then.[112]

In the midst of the search for models, Bishop Wright made his desire for a directory for the diocese very clear, and assigned three members of the Liturgical Commission the task of writing one. Monsignor Shinar headed the committee and told the Liturgical Commission in March that he intended to have a guide by the fall. He expressed his desire that Bishop Wright then require every parish Mass to be conducted according to its guidelines and start a program for increased participation. But Shinar's committee had no directory by the fall or even the winter of 1962, when the Council had finished its first session, and Wright could not require pastors to use a form of Mass that did not yet exist.[113]

If the confusion over the Mass form prevented the commission from recommending participation in a specific ritual, members at least pushed for increased participation in general. They worked primarily through the priests, who controlled the ritual in each parish. The commission approached the clergy through a monthly newsletter, priest institutes, priest retreats, and demonstration liturgies.

The newsletter reflected the commission members' desire to ingratiate themselves with the pastors while at the same time pushing them to adopt greater lay participation. Much space went to informing pastors of specific changes in rubrics, but Monsignor Shinar and Father McIlvane, the authors, devoted a good deal of space to persuading and cajoling pastors to support liturgical changes, and gradually spent more time addressing the principles upon which the Vatican based those changes. Not surprisingly, the *Newsletter* highlighted papal support for increased participation. One issue quoted Pius XII's *Mediator Dei*, which instructed the laity that

> to participate in the Eucharistic Sacrifice is their *chief duty* and supreme dignity, and that not in an inert and negligent fashion, giving way to distractions and daydreaming, but with such earnestness and concentration that they may be united as closely as possible with the High Priest.[114]

The *Newsletter* divided participation into "interior" and "exterior," and explained each. A successful liturgy achieved interior participation, "the inner faith and devotion of the worshipping Church, the praise and love and thanksgiving the Mystical Body returns to the Father." Exterior participation, the posture, responses, prayers and chants of the liturgy, served to facilitate interior participation. Exterior participation came in two forms, direct and indirect. Direct participation entailed interaction with the celebrant, and had to be accomplished in Latin so long as the celebrant used Latin. Indirect participation consisted of English recitation and singing done in a Low Mass, which a commentator led. The *Newsletter* argued that direct participation best achieved the exterior participation that led to interior participation. Receiving sacraments, especially the Eucharist, was the most efficacious form of direct, exterior participation.[115]

Even as the Liturgy Commission sought to implement what members understood to be top-down initiatives, they rooted their arguments in part on popular will. The *Newsletter* supplemented its emphasis on papal support from above with assurances of popular reception below. Parishioners would readily embrace the new liturgical practices if properly prepared, it promised. One issue claimed that the "re-evaluation of all 'matters liturgical'" which papal pronouncements required would work well with the modern Catholic, "who now is well equipped to understand and respect the elements of liturgical participation to an astonishing degree." Later reports of one thousand laypeople at the October 1961

Liturgical Day for the laity buttressed this claim. Schoolchildren handled their new role especially well, but the Church had "not given any indication that this [was] for children only." Pastors had to work especially with the adults. A proper presentation of the doctrine of the lay priesthood would make participation easier and give it more meaning. Finally, lay liturgical committees in parishes were certain to produce favorable results.[116]

The *Newsletter* reassured pastors that Latin would remain, but that vernacular translations would help the laity to understand the Mass and move them toward greater union with the priest in the liturgy. The commission's uncertainty about what might be translated permissibly and what those translations might be led the *Newsletter* authors to be cautious. They supplemented their lists of specific prayers that priests might translate with those that they should not. Perfect, interior, direct participation could be achieved only if the laity learned Latin, the authors assumed, because most of the Mass was certain to remain in Latin. But some benefit derived from indirect vernacular participation, and the *Newsletter* urged pastors to encourage this.[117]

Pastors read that the new "participated" Mass spread roles to more than priest and acolyte. It democratized the liturgy. But commission members characterized that democratization as a "restoration" rather than a reform. The December 1961 issue informed pastors that the liturgical changes meant a distribution of roles.

> [As] members of the Mystical Body, we worship together in the liturgy. We have different positions in this one Body. Historically, this has been reflected in the liturgy by assigning different roles in worship. This differentiation became obscured in recent centuries. Some members [the laity] seemed to become almost inactive. Other members [priests] took over what did not rightly belong to them.[118]

Six months later the *Newsletter* reminded the clergy that "the priest-celebrant is not the only member of the Mystical Body," and that a proper Mass recognized different members.[119]

In the months leading up to Vatican II, the commission assured pastors that the slow and tentative steps it had taken so far would be superseded by "revolutionary" changes coming from the world's bishops.[120]

The "demonstration Mass" may have been the most effective mechanism for teaching priests and parishioners about the liturgy. Frederick R. McManus had developed a demonstration Mass for the National Council of Catholic Men (NCCM), which distributed it nationally in order to teach the laity about the ritual in which they participated weekly. The Pittsburgh Liturgical Commission obtained the NCCM booklet and used it on occasion in the diocese. It was a "dramatic presentation" of the Mass, and McManus warned against confusing it with the real thing—which was "not to be thought of as a play or drama."[121]

The Liturgical Commission felt most comfortable introducing reforms at funeral Masses for priests, because these liturgies typically drew large numbers of fellow priests. They created a gathering of people who would not shy from participating, and who in fact considered participation important. Priests readily participated directly in Latin, which they all knew well enough for Mass, and sought the interior experience that the reformed liturgy hoped to effect.[122]

The commission seemed more ambivalent about how to approach the laity directly. Members operated under the assumption that they needed to approach the laity separately from priests, and that they should approach the laity in some way if they were to achieve greater lay participation in the liturgy. But the clergy, who dominated the commission, worried most about winning over the pastors as the most efficacious way to change the liturgy, and so feared alienating the pastors with any action that the pastors might perceive to undermine their authority within their parishes. The commission developed two strategies to approach the laity, and tempered each with concern for the pastors' authority.

The first strategy attempted to attract the laity from all over the diocese to annual "Liturgical Day" workshops and demonstration Masses. These served to educate the laity but implied no obligation to any specific parish reforms. The commission planned the first for October 15, 1961, structured around the theme "Parish Participation in the Liturgy." Members hoped through this program to interest the laity in the liturgical revival then under way. The program took place at Central Catholic High School, located about one block east of the bishop's cathedral. It featured an afternoon of speakers, workshops, and general discussion, followed by a "participated" Mass at Saint Paul's Cathedral.[123] The commission repeated the day in 1962, with the theme "Priesthood of the Laity." For this day the commission brought in the Reverend Howell from England, one of the foremost proponents of lay participation in the liturgy. He emphasized that the laity were "God's people of the New Testament," that they attained this dignity when baptized, "which makes them members of the Mystical Body of Christ." As members, they shared in Christ's priesthood.[124]

The second approach focused on the laity in parishes, and attempted to train leaders who might then act as commentators and infuse their fellow parishioners with a participatory inclination. The commission hoped to work through existing lay organizations, particularly the Holy Name Society and the Diocesan Council of Catholic Women, to engender support for participation. They first planned to do this by setting up an institute to train lay leaders for the Low Mass. The commission intended the institute to give laymen "principles for their work and practical demonstrations." But members worried about pastors' reactions, and stressed that trained leaders would have to respect their pastors' wishes regarding what role, if any, they could actually play in the parish.[125]

The commission established a special committee in 1962 to address the laity specifically and delegated its efforts toward the laity to the committee members.[126] Only laymen and laywomen served on this committee, which sought to "learn to approach the laity." The clerical members of the Liturgical Commission did not seem to take the Lay Organization Committee too seriously initially. None sought to serve on it, and Monsignor Pauley even insisted on appointing as a member a layman who indicated that he would not attend any of its meetings.[127]

But the Lay Committee, after a tentative start, proposed a flurry of measures that members hoped might spur the laity to greater participation. These measures reflected a growing consciousness of the increasing role the laity could play in the liturgy, and in Catholicism more broadly. Committee members offered to recruit and train commentators and leaders, suggested that the commission draw up a reading list for the laity, recommended that the full commission encourage lay teachers to emphasize the liturgy's centrality to their students' lives, and pushed for Mass institute programs at the parish level. The committee also offered its members as speakers on the liturgy to all interested lay groups, and further urged lay organizations "to see to it that speakers of their own be alert to the urgent necessity and importance of having laymen speak to laymen on this subject."[128] The lay members of the Liturgical Commission seemed to catch fire with the task of expanding lay participation in the liturgy. This marked a significant beginning for lay empowerment in the diocese, and therefore a rather profound departure from the still prevailing assumptions about the proper division of authority in Catholicism. Yet these early efforts continued to operate in the "traditional" social context, especially regarding gender roles.

The Liturgical Commission, for example, remained overwhelmingly male and divided tasks along prevailing assumptions of proper male and female roles. When the Liturgical Commission assigned tasks to its members for the first Liturgical Day, they charged their sole female member with providing refreshments. Though this same member served as "chairman" of the Lay Organization Committee, she deferred to a male committee member to report its activities to the full Liturgical Commission after its first meeting.[129]

The Christian Family Movement

If the Adult Education Institute and the liturgical movement in Pittsburgh sought to prepare lay men and women better to assume leadership roles in society some day, the Christian Family Movement actually provided a venue for the laity to exercise such initiatives. The Christian Family Movement (CFM) in Pittsburgh aimed to accomplish two larger objectives in the years surrounding the Second Vatican Council. On the one hand, it sought to make the family and the home the center of devotional activity. In a sense, it attempted to adapt the inherited Catholic devotional culture to the new suburban social context. If Catholic suburbanites could not readily leave their families for devotional exercises in local churches, then families might establish devotional "traditions" in their own homes. On the other hand, CFM attempted to transform the local community to make it more compatible with Christian ideals and, therefore, to be more just. While John Dearden served as Pittsburgh's bishop, CFM's highest-profile activities concentrated on extending the devotional culture into Catholic suburbanites' homes. By the end of the 1950s, however, the CFM social justice agenda emerged more explicitly.

Though Pittsburgh developed an active Christian Family Movement organization, CFM did not originate in the diocese. Pat and Patty Crowley from Chicago emerged early as movement leaders, but historian Jeffrey Burns concludes that two other cities also have legitimate claims to starting the organization. The Pittsburgh CFM traces its roots directly back to Chicago, however, as a young couple who had joined the movement in that diocese came to Pittsburgh in the early 1950s.[130]

Jerry and Barbara Ryan introduced the Christian Family Movement to Pittsburgh when they moved to a South Hills suburb in 1953. The Ryans met while studying at Georgetown University in Washington, D.C., married in 1952, and then went to Chicago so that Jerry could work selling advertising for *Chemical Engineering* magazine. They began expanding their family right away and joined the Christian Family Movement. Jerry's job required that the family move to Pittsburgh after one year, and the Ryans introduced the movement to their new parish in the South Hills.[131]

The movement that the Ryans joined in Chicago and brought with them to Pittsburgh had its origins in the same concern about materialism that so dominated Catholic public discourse in the early 1950s. Burns argues that CFM grew out of young Catholic couples' growing dissatisfaction with lives centered around the search for material security. He states that "couples whose lives had been dominated by an ethos that extolled material success began to see that there had to be more." These couples joined together to infuse their home lives with religious meaning, determined to make the local community more supportive of raising Christian families, and moved eventually to seeking to create a just social order. The impulse to render the culture in which families found themselves more amenable to moral and spiritual development coalesced into an international movement for social justice. In Burns's words again:

> What began as a mere diversion that might enhance one's own family became a transforming experience that drew the couple and their family into a lifetime commitment to make the world a better place for families to live.[132]

This commitment brought young Catholic families to support racial integration, fair housing, gender equality, international peace and justice, and a host of more local issues.

The Christian Family Movement relied upon the theology of the mystical body of Christ and Belgian priest Joseph Cardijn's observe-judge-act method of implementing Catholic Action. In this formula, Catholics were to observe the world around them, judge that environment in the light of Christ's mind, and then act to make it come into compliance with Christian ideals. The last part of the formula, the action, moved young Catholic couples toward active engagement with the world outside of church doors. CFM did not aim to fill stadiums with stalwart Catholics so much as transform the larger community to better reflect Christ's ideals.[133]

CFM spread throughout Pittsburgh's South Hills suburbs to neighboring parishes initially, and gradually began to take on a higher profile in the diocese. CFM members introduced the Cana Conference program to the Pittsburgh diocese in 1954 as a means of making good Catholic marriages better. The diocese held its first CFM general meeting in the fall of 1955, though at this time many seemed uncertain about what the movement hoped to achieve. Long accustomed to Catholic efforts to improve the family itself through various instruction and programs, diocesan officials pitched the movement as another program aimed inward at families themselves. Mission preacher and Saint Philomena pastor Fr. John Frawley, C.Ss.R., told those in attendance that CFM sought to strengthen Catholic families primarily. He pointed out that "once the family becomes aware that others have the same problems as they do, a sense of solidarity is developed that deepens husband-wife relationships and invariably leads to happier families." A year later the *Pittsburgh Catholic* highlighted the Ryan family, at Saint Thomas More parish in Bethel Park, while they implemented the CFM program by practicing family-centered liturgies in their home with their three very young children.[134] In the diocese's eyes, CFM had become a movement to infuse devotions into the families in order to improve family life. As one archbishop explained: "We do a great deal innocently to destroy family life. Even in our spiritual life in the Church we do a great deal to harm family relations. We have men's Communion Sunday, and women's Communion Sunday. We have children's Masses."[135] These served to pull family members away from each other. It would be better to use family-centered devotions and liturgies to draw families together. CFM represented a mechanism for doing just this.

Within a few weeks of celebrating the Ryans' home liturgy, however, the *Pittsburgh Catholic* introduced area Catholics to CFM's observe-judge-act mechanism to achieving social justice. The paper suggested for the first time that CFM sought to use families to improve and transform society. Despite its recognition that social action was "an extremely important part of the Movement's program," the paper stressed that CFM sought "spiritual formation through action." Even as CFM members themselves moved toward social change, diocesan officials framed their movement as a means of sanctifying individuals.[136]

The movement continued to grow over the next couple of years as fully 225 couples from eighteen parishes joined by 1958. Though diocesan officials continued to stress the movement's impact on families and their devotional patterns (greater daily Mass attendance and home-based devotions especially), the CFM emphasis on community action emerged more and more frequently. A November CFM conference in the diocese on creating "happier families" highlighted the focus on solving problems in communities. Fr. Charles Owen Rice's prominent role as a CFM chaplain and speaker at regional and diocesan meetings further enhanced the movement's social justice direction. CFM couples told a meeting of University Catholic Club members at Mount Mercy College that "Mr. Smith went to Mass. He always went to Mass on Sunday. But Mr. Smith went to hell— for what he did on Monday."[137]

Though diocesan officials generally supported CFM as source of renewal among young Catholic families, it also sought to contain it within a broader family life structure that worked primarily through the Holy Name Society and the Diocesan Council of Catholic Women. Bishop Dearden initially appointed the Ryans to head up the diocese's Family Life Committee—or, more precisely, Dearden appointed Jerry Ryan to head the committee, with the assistance of his wife Barbara. Dearden wanted to place CFM, the Cana Conference, and various other family-centered initiatives under the HNS and DCCW committees. Within a couple of years the Ryans had become only advisers to the committee, however, as the diocese sought to establish a more traditional structure with a priest as director and lay deanery leaders who took their directives from him. The diocese then hosted a Family Life Conference with special sessions describing CFM, the Cana Conference, and liturgical customs for the home. The headline session, however, asserted the predominant Catholic hierarchy within the family, as it focused on "The Father as Teacher of the Home."[138]

CFM continued to grow in Pittsburgh, as it expanded in 1959 to four hundred couples in twenty-five parishes. The second annual "Conference for Happier Families" focused even more on social action in the community when it featured a panel on "Political Life and the Christian Family" which included Duquesne University's political science department's chairman.[139]

By 1960 the Pittsburgh members of the Christian Family Movement had integrated fully into the national organization and its growing emphasis on social change. The CFM annual national conference proved so popular that organizers switched to a series of regional conferences to accommodate the demand. Fully twenty-nine Pittsburgh couples attended the New York regional conference that year and prepared for the program's focus on the international life. As this focus indicated, the Christian Family Movement had come to focus less on the internal dynamics of the Catholic family and more on creating an environment in which families could thrive. Jeffrey Burns noted that "CFM would help build a world in which it was easier for families to be good families—not just easier for CFM families, but for all families in the community."[140] Not all CFM members welcomed the increased emphasis on social reform, but the outward engagement with the broader community pushed even those reluctant to look beyond their own domestic arrangements to become at least critical social observers. The Christian Family Movement in Pittsburgh on the eve of the Second Vatican Council had become a popular lay movement for social justice in the diocese.

CONSIDERED INDIVIDUALLY, THE ADULT EDUCATION INSTITUTE, THE liturgical movement, or the Christian Family Movement would not have been sufficient to propel the Church toward a firmer focus on social justice at the end of the 1950s. But these three movements, the renewed emphasis on Catholic Action, and the general support that Bishop Wright offered for progressive causes more generally laid the groundwork for the dramatic transformations that would come from the Second Vatican Council. Church officials entered the 1950s focused on the materialist crisis and persuaded that efforts to achieve social justice would help to resolve the problem. They supported non-Communist unionization, anticommercialism programs, and, a bit later, racial integration as specific remedies for the ills. Each of these strategies required significant lay action and even leadership in order to succeed, and in pushing these efforts the hierarchy necessarily empowered laymen and laywomen. This empowerment sparked a reform impulse that turned back on the Church itself and began to transform lay expectations for, and experiences within, their Church. The lay response to the social justice prescription transcended the original aims and moved lay-women and laymen to work to reform the very religious communities that served as the wellspring for social action. Church officials did not imagine that anything like this would happen when they urged the laity to action in the 1950s, but they would come to understand it fully by the end of the next decade.

PART TWO

Aggiornamento Americano

CHAPTER FIVE

The Second Vatican Council in Rome
and Pittsburgh, 1962–1965

*For those who believe in Christ, who are reborn, not from a corruptible seed,
but from an incorruptible one through the word of the living God, not from
flesh, but from water and the Holy Spirit, are finally established as "a chosen race,
a royal priesthood, a holy nation . . . who in times past were not a people, but
now are the People of God." (1 Pet. 2:9–10)*

—THE PEOPLE OF GOD, *LUMEN GENTIUM*

*Though they differ essentially and not only in degree, the common priesthood
of the faithful and the ministerial or hierarchical priesthood are none the less
ordered one to another; each in its own proper way shares in the one priesthood
of Christ.*

—THE PEOPLE OF GOD, *LUMEN GENTIUM*

*We are back in spirit with the early Christians who met for the Eucharist in the
community assembly hall, those heroic people who were called upon to shed
their blood for their belief in Christ. Our liturgy will not be exactly like theirs,
but it will be closer than ever before in our history. These are special times in
the life of the Church, because the Lord now wants us to do more—for him, for
the Church, for the world which is waiting for the redemption of Christ.*

—COMMENTATORS' TRAINING LESSON

THE SECOND VATICAN COUNCIL IN ROME

Bishops from all over the world met in Rome for the Second Vatican Council during four consecutive autumns to re-examine the Church in light of modern developments. They debated the very principles that undergird the Church and issued documents setting a new course for Catholicism. All Pittsburgh Catholics watched the deliberations carefully, but the Liturgical Commission members paid special attention, and tried to interpret for local pastors and others what the Council was saying, or was about to say. This chapter traces some major developments in Rome and in Pittsburgh during the Council years (1962–65). It examines the changing nature of the Mass, which began the long transformation from sacrifice to celebration in this period, and lays the groundwork for the more substantial changes that came in the years after the Council.

Most Catholics seeking reform looked to the Council convening at the Vatican in 1962 as the best hope for substantive action. The bishops gathered there would no doubt set the course of Catholicism for the foreseeable future, and in so doing would necessarily pass judgment on efforts already under way. But few people, if any, had a secure sense of what the bishops would do. Even the bishops themselves were uncertain. This confusion resulted in part from the manner in which the Council came to be.

Historians are still uncertain why the bishops met. They know clearly that Pope John XXIII called the Council, as only popes can issue such calls, but historians do not know why he called the Council. Most saw John's decision to be some combination of a reaction to the state of the world in the 1950s and the Church's unwillingness or inability to react to those changes. Thomas Bokenkotter emphasized the impossibility of pointing to a single factor as responsible and posited instead that by 1959 "profound scientific, technological, cultural and social developments had so changed the conditions of life that one felt separated from the previous four hundred years by a wide gap." Pope John called the Council to prepare the unchanging Church to meet the challenges of the vastly changed world.[1] Another author suggested that Pope John XXIII did so to combat what he considered to be dangers present in modern society, the materialist concerns that so animated American Church officials. He added later that the bishops' parochialism in the face of a new spirit that had infused the clergy, theologians, lay intellectuals, and Church scholars inspired Pope John to call a Council. He did so

to bring the bishops of the whole world together to let them educate each other as to the true role of the Church in a suffering, morally confused world, two-thirds of it poverty-stricken amid unprecedented plenty in the rest, living in fear of thermonuclear warfare and total destruction, and seemingly unable to disentangle itself from the mess.[2]

Another Council historian provided a similar explanation when he again emphasized the state of the world to be the catalyst for the bishops' gathering:

> After the unfathomable, indigestible horrors of the Second World War, men had emerged from a tunnel to find not peace but further, more diffuse, less tangible hostilities: a cold war that threatened to lock East against West for all the foreseeable future. Protestants were not speaking to Catholics. Jews had not yet recovered from tragedies too deep to face. The outlook was not so much black as merely gray, endless, forlorn.[3]

If the state of the world looked grim, the prospects for the future of the European Church looked bleaker still. Vocational crises in Austria, Italy, and France portended a dire priest shortage unless something dramatic could be done to arrest the decline.[4]

Perhaps because of the pope's central role in calling such Councils, others writing about Vatican II do not even venture theories or guesses as to why the Council met. They leave the explanation to be simply that Pope John called the Council, and that is why it met.[5]

Pope John himself recalled that the idea of a Council was an inspiration he received during a meeting with Cardinal Tardini, Vatican secretary of state. He stated that

> a question was raised in a meeting I had with the Secretary of State, Cardinal Tardini, which led on to a discussion about the way the world was plunged into so many grave anxieties and troubles. One thing we noted was that though everyone said they wanted peace and harmony, unfortunately conflicts grew more acute and threats multiplied. What should the Church do? Should Christ's mystical barque simply drift along, tossed this way and that by the ebb and flow of the tides? Instead of issuing new warnings, shouldn't she stand out as a beacon of light? What could that exemplary light be?[6]

At that instant, he recalled, he determined that the light should take the form of a Council. "Our soul was suddenly enlightened by a great idea that occurred to Us in that moment. One solemn and binding word came to Our lips. Our voice formulated it for the first time—a Council!"[7]

Pope John regularly mentioned that he intended the Council to open the Church up to the modern world. He used the Italian word *aggiornamento* to describe what he meant, which some have defined variously as "bringing the church up to date," "adaptation," "modernization," and "adjustment at any price."[8]

If historians are unclear why Pope John called the Council, they at least write a good deal about how it met. This alone is a significant accomplishment in light of Vatican efforts to keep deliberations and debates secret. The Curia worried that open debates would cause scandal—they would entice Catholics to follow errant thinking because they would suggest that certain issues were open to varying interpretations. Yet the pope insisted on inviting non-Catholic "observers" to the sessions, and some accounts of the Council structure and proceedings tell the Council story very well.

This chapter describes the Council events briefly, highlighting those aspects of the Council experience which seem to have influenced significantly later efforts in the Pittsburgh diocese to implement the changes the Council recommended. Each bishop present at the Council had at least the Council model for bringing changes to his diocese. The bishops did not all replicate the Council in their dioceses, but many drew on the Council experience to inform not only the content of changes they wished to implement, but also the process by which those changes might be implemented. Pittsburgh Catholics attempted to replicate the Council in miniature in the 1971 synod.

The chapter also addresses in some detail the Council's treatment of the laity. The bishops addressed the laity explicitly in three debates, in the Dogmatic Constitution on the Church, the Pastoral Constitution on the Church in the Modern World, and the Apostolate of the Laity. Taken together these decrees elevated and inflated the laity's position in the Church. They empowered the laity to move independently of the hierarchy toward goals that had changed as a result of the Council sessions.

The Council began when Pope John XXIII announced on January 25, 1959, his intention to convene it. His announcement stunned the curial officials on whom Pope John depended to carry out the administrative functions the Council entailed. The Curia largely opposed such a Council as providing too great an opportunity for Pope John or the assembled bishops to do serious harm to the institution over which those curial officials considered themselves the only competent stewards.[9] In fact, Pope John expected his surprise announcement to seventeen assembled cardinals to elicit much talk and interaction, if not excitement and wishes of good fortune. Instead, the cardinals sat in stony silence, as though they had not heard.[10]

Once Pope John called the Council, the Curia acted to delay it as much as possible and to so proscribe the boundaries of debate as to limit severely the Council's opportunity to change anything of significance. The Council proceeded in four phases: antepreparatory, preparatory, the Council meeting itself, and promulgation of the Acts of the Council.[11] The Curia hoped to control each phase, beginning with the first.

Phase one involved sending out questionnaires to all the bishops through-out the world to receive their views on a number of issues. The Vatican also sent questionnaires to the heads of all male religious orders—though not the heads of female orders—and to the faculties of thirty-seven Catholic universities world-wide. The Vatican mailed out about 2,500 questionnaires and received back and catalogued roughly 2,000.[12] The responses were to inform the commissions set up to prepare proposals, or schemas, for the bishops to consider when they finally assembled. Many dioceses borrowed some variation of this approach when they set out to implement the Council's decrees after its conclusion. Pittsburgh, for ex-ample, set up a structure to receive lay opinion on a number of relevant issues and received more than 5,000 suggestions to help the synodal commissions for-mulate diocesan legislation.

The Vatican then formed commissions to produce schemas that the as-sembled bishops were to read and discuss—or, the Curia intended, simply ratify—at the Council itself. The Curia staffed the commissions so that only conservative bishops and theologians would have influence, and then wrote the schemas based upon the traditional interpretations that emerged in the prepara-tory phase. The Curia also appointed only conservative bishops to act as mod-erators for the discussions on the schemas at the Council.[13]

Pope John opened the Council by expressing his desire that the assembled bishops avoid obscure doctrinal debates (which the Curia could control and which would take a lot of time for little practical return) in favor of working to-ward ways of spreading and communicating church teaching—"doctrinal pene-tration and formation of consciences."[14] Pope John's emphasis left more room for variation and made the discussions more accessible to the bishops—most of whom were not adroit theologians.

Early business sessions saw the Curia's attempts to control the Council un-ravel, as the bishops voted first to meet in geographically determined conferences to nominate Council commission members rather than vote immediately from lists of nominations that the Curia provided. Later, the Council voted to discard the Curia's schemas on Revelation, Unity, and the Church. The bishops' debate

The Holy Name Society sponsored outdoor eucharistic rallies in 1930, 1941, 1950, and 1955 at Forbes Field, home of the Pittsburgh Pirates. This 1930 photo indicates the scale of these public rituals. Courtesy of the Archives and Records Center, Diocese of Pittsburgh.

The Holy Name Society marches through downtown
Pittsburgh in conjunction with the 1950 eucharistic rally.
Courtesy of the Archives and Records Center, Diocese of
Pittsburgh.

A procession of altar boys leads the consecrated host, in a monstrance under the canopy. This was the critical moment of each outdoor rally from 1930 to 1955. Courtesy of the Archives and Records Center, Diocese of Pittsburgh.

Float in a parade during the 1955 Holy Name Society convention conveys the society's emphasis on devotional activity. A representative family prays to Mary. Courtesy of the Archives and Records Center, Diocese of Pittsburgh.

THE FAMILY THAT PRAYS TOGETHER STAY TOGETHER

A float from Akron, Ohio, in the 1955 Holy Name Society parade reminds Catholics to keep Christ in Christmas. Courtesy of the Archives and Records Center, Diocese of Pittsburgh.

REMEMBER DEC. 25th

Christ's Birthday

AKRON DEANERY HOLY NAME SOCIETIES

CATHOLIC ACTION

UR 1955 BILLBOARD CAMPAIGN

Fr. Patrick Cullen
of Saint Pius X parish in the
Pittsburgh neighborhood of
Brookline displays the poster
of candidates for the first elected
parish committee. All adult
parishioners, male and female,
were eligible.
Courtesy of the Archives
and Records Center,
Diocese of Pittsburgh.

Bishop Wright addresses
more than 1100 attendees
at a gathering of parish
committee representatives
in the Pittsburgh Civic
Arena, November 1966.
This meeting helped
launch the nation's first
advisory council to a bishop that included signifi-
cant numbers of elected
laymen and laywomen.
Courtesy of the Archives
and Records Center,
Diocese of Pittsburgh.

Exterior view of Immaculate Heart of Mary Church in the Polish Hill neighborhood of Pittsburgh.

Exterior drawing from the parish bulletin of Saint Philomena church and school in Pittsburgh's Squirrel Hill neighborhood.

Exterior view of Saint Thomas More parish church in Bethel Park, a suburb in the South Hills area of Pittsburgh. Its physical space incorporated many principles of the new liturgy.

on liturgy proved Latin to be a cumbersome and awkward language for even the Church "fathers," and brought a resounding 2,162 to 46 majority in favor of roughly the position the liturgical movement advocated.[15] In one of the most significant developments at the Council, the revised schema mandated that significant portions of the Mass should be conducted in the vernacular—thus increasing the likelihood of parishioner participation. The Council determined that

> the use of the Latin language, with due respect to particular law, is to be preserved in the Latin rites. But since the use of the vernacular, whether in the Mass, the administration of the sacraments, or in other parts of the liturgy, may frequently be of great advantage to the people, a wider use may be made of it, especially in readings, directions and in some prayers and chants.[16]

The Constitution on Sacred Liturgy mandated that geographically determined councils should be set up to consider liturgical changes that might aid in popular understanding and participation. These councils were then to submit their recommendations to the pope, who would condone or reject them, before any action to implement them actually took place. Each bishop retained the right to implement the recommendations as he saw fit within his diocese. This opened the way for a continuous consideration of liturgical changes, and came down firmly on the side of liturgical reform.

The bishops' actions at the first session seemed to wrest control from the Curia and empower the episcopacy. One observer noted that the bishops began to realize what the first session's collegial character implied. They

> began to understand that it was not sufficient to wait passively for a charismatic inspiration or to repeat the formulas of scholastic manuals. They must take cognizance of the fact that they were the free instruments used by the Holy Spirit in the spreading of the Christian faith, and that they had been given an immense task which they must accept with humility and courage.[17]

Pope John died before the second session got under way, and this threw the entire Council into uncertainty. Because the first session had closed with the Curia's schemas rejected and commissions formed to devise new ones, the bishops were uncertain what position the new pope might take on these unresolved issues. Pope John had set the tenor for a pastoral and optimistic view of the Church, but his death left even the Council's continuation uncertain. The cardinals elected Giovanni Battista Montini to succeed John XXIII, and he took the name Paul VI. Paul was an Italian cardinal who had spent many years working at the Vatican. He appeared ready to support the Council's liberal bent, especially when he called a meeting of the Curia before the second session began to tell them, and the world, that the Curia was not to block the bishops' actions at future sessions.[18]

The Council opened the second session in October 1963 with debate on the schema *Lumen Gentium* (On the Church), the document that explicated the "Church" constitution. Though a majority of the commission members assigned the task of writing the document intended to re-emphasize the authority of the bishops gathered in Council to share power with the pope, conservatives saw this stress on "collegiality" to be a threat to the pope's sovereignty. The conservatives attempted to block progress in the commission in a sort of filibuster, so that the Council at large might never have a chance to vote on it. Cardinal Suenens, of Belgium, led the four commission moderators in an unprecedented and contrary to Council rules move to present to the entire Council the five questions on which progress halted. The Council coordinating committees balked at the irregularity, and bishops entered negotiations to resolve the situation. They reached a compromise that permitted the questions to reach all the bishops only this once, and the bishops voted heavily in favor of collegiality.[19]

Much debate also centered on the schema's treatment of the laity. Many bishops, particularly liberal European bishops, wished to move the discussion of the "people of God" ahead of the discussion of the hierarchical constitution of the Church so that those reading the document would first encounter the Council's emphasis on the commonality of all Church members. Discussing the hierarchical divisions first implied that the bishops wished to emphasize Church divisions over unity. Conservatives wanted to downplay any discussion of a "universal priesthood" or "priesthood of the faithful" which blurred the clear and important distinctions ordination imposed. They preferred defining the laity in negative terms—they were not priests and not religious (sisters or brothers).[20]

Bishop Wright of Pittsburgh entered the debate firmly on the liberal side. He assured the conservatives that the laity would not become confused and think that membership in the "priesthood of the faithful" meant that the bishops had ordained all Catholics. He stated that "the faithful have been waiting for four hundred years for a positive conciliar statement on the place, dignity, and vocation of the layman." Wright further argued that the laity waited for the Council to declare finally that the Church was not solely the clergy.[21]

The bishops left Rome from the second session largely disappointed. Conservatives succeeded in so slowing debates and impeding progress that the bishops finalized positions on few issues and the Council did not seem likely to end at the next session. Bishop Tracy of Baton Rouge wrote that "too much time had been simply wasted, especially in Commission meetings where, it was felt, there was too much debate and too little action." The bishops did not vote on many issues that they had clearly resolved.[22]

The third session (1964) was more productive, as the bishops promulgated three decrees and debated the decree on the laity. They issued the "Constitution on the Church," "Ecumenism," and "Eastern Churches." But certain papal and curial actions mitigated the bishops' enthusiasm for the work they had accomplished. The session opened with new rules of debate designed, ostensibly, to speed the process, but which had the added and perhaps designed effect of limiting the scope of perspectives that the bishops might hear in the sessions. In addition, Pope Paul added "clarifying" passages to documents that the bishops had already debated and resolved which stressed papal prerogative at the expense of episcopal power.

The Council presidents announced new rules of procedure that limited debate and strengthened the conservative or curial positions. The new rules forbade *periti*, or Council "experts" on certain matters, to lobby or circulate material to bishops designed to influence their opinions on any issues. The *periti* were theologians whom the Council invited to serve as resources for the conciliar commissions and the attending bishops. The *periti* had no voice in sessions, but they might sway debates outside of the business sessions by talking with bishops—many of whom were not theologians themselves. The Curia recognized that a majority of theologians took positions far more liberal than those which the Curia advocated, and feared that the *periti* might influence bishops in the liberal direction. The new rules forbade this lobbying.[23]

The new rules also gave session moderators greater control of the debate. Moderators controlled speaker lists (thereby controlling who could speak), and bishops and cardinals who wished to speak at any session had to submit the text of their speeches five days in advance. If a bishop's speech reflected the views of other bishops, the submitted text had to carry the names of those bishops too, and those who had the longest list of bishops' names on their speeches received priority. Those who had short lists, or no lists, went to the end of the line, and those who the moderators determined wished to express a view already presented did not get to speak at all.[24]

Nevertheless, the bishops did address issues certain to influence the laity's actions and understanding of themselves and others. The bishops discussed religious liberty in session three, though they did not vote on the document until the following session. The debate on religious liberty pitted roughly the same conservatives against the majority of liberals—save for a couple of changes. The American bishops, some of whom had come down regularly on the conservative side, all supported a broad liberty for religion. Some conservative Eastern European bishops favored religious liberty as the only way to ensure their survival in the face of hostile governments.

The conservatives wished to perpetuate a long Catholic tradition that held that error had no rights. Cardinal Ruffini of Palermo argued that civil governments were obligated to recognize Roman Catholicism as the one true religion, and could "tolerate" other religious beliefs out of charity.[25]

The liberal side argued that people should choose their religion freely. Cardinals Cushing of Boston and Ritter of St. Louis argued forcefully that men had the right and duty to follow their honest conscience, that people could not be forced against this, that the state was not competent to judge any religion, that public expression of religion was intrinsic to religious liberty, and that any hint of coercion on the part of Catholics would serve only to drive people away from the Church.[26]

The overwhelming majority of the bishops took the liberal position, and they anticipated voting on this on November 19, 1964. But Cardinal Tisserant, head of the Council presidents, announced that two hundred (conservative) bishops had submitted a petition that asked the presidents to delay the vote. So many changes had been made to the original document, the petitioners argued, that it must be considered a new document and thus debated anew. Tisserant announced that the Council presidents agreed. Since only one day of the third session remained, this delay put off religious liberty for one year. Liberal bishops circulated a counterpetition that garnered one thousand signatures asking Paul VI to intervene on behalf of the majority and hold the vote in session three. Paul demurred, and the Council issued no decree on religious liberty in 1964.[27]

The Council again debated religious liberty in 1965, with U.S. bishops clearly taking the strongest role in support of the new decree. The bishops voted to accept a document that acknowledged both freedom of religious conscience and Catholicism as the one true Church by a majority of 1,997 to 224.[28]

The bishops also debated and reshaped the decree "Apostolate of the Laity" in this session, though they did not finally approve and promulgate this until the final session. The document that the antepreparatory commission prepared numbered seventy pages. The coordinating committee reduced the length twice, first to forty-eight pages and then to fourteen, because material in the original appeared already in the "Constitution on the Church" and in the "Church in the Modern World." The Council first discussed the text in October 1964 and then sent it for revision to reflect a "pastoral" rather than juridical tone. The Council voted on each paragraph between September 23 and 27, 1965, and then again after amendments on November 9, 1965. The bishops voted overwhelmingly in favor of the entire text the following day by a margin of 2,201 to 2.[29]

Bishop Tracy recalled that the debate hinged on a central question: "Did the mission of the layman have its origin in a call or mandate or what-have-you from the hierarchy; or did it have its origin, purely and simply, in the very reception of these sacraments [baptism, confirmation]?" Liberals argued forcefully that baptism initiated the laity in an apostolate of their own, independent of clerical control. (In fact, because Catholic Action was the participation of the laity in the hierarchy's mission, it came under heavy criticism.) One author later argued that the liberals sought a return to the early Church, where all shared in liturgical functions and hierarchical distinctions were minimal. He wrote that "what was sought at the Council was a revindication of the laos as in truth constituting the Church—not a revolt of the laity against the clergy but a new and fuller communion between both elements." Conservatives argued that the laity's greatest aim rightly was doing the clergy's bidding. The liberal view prevailed here as elsewhere, and the final document transformed the lay role in the Catholic church.[30]

The decree the "Apostolate of Lay People" emphasized a clear distinction between the Church and the world, the spiritual and the temporal. The hierarchy had long encouraged the laity to engage themselves in the temporal sphere, and had long understood that the clergy were largely—if not completely—removed from the temporal realm. The Holy Name Society and Diocesan Council of Catholic Women laid down strict guidelines regulating lay behavior in the world, many of which amounted to very particular explications of the general stricture to "avoid sin."

The Council of Bishops in 1964 both pushed the laity into the spiritual realm and broadened their mandate in the temporal. This broadening was in many ways a transformation—so much so in fact that many laypeople (and clergy) could conceive of it as a new realm for lay action. Lay Catholics were not only to lead sinless lives, but to change society, to create a just world. The decree read, in part, that

> the mission of the Church, consequently, is not only to bring men the message and grace of Christ but also to permeate and improve the whole range of the temporal. The laity, carrying out this mission of the Church, exercise their apostolate therefore in the world as well as in the Church, in the temporal order as well as in the spiritual. These orders are distinct; they are nevertheless so closely linked that God's plan is, in Christ, to take the whole world up again and make of it a new creation, in an initial way here on earth.

The bishops were even more emphatic about lay efforts to transform the world later, when they decreed that of all the lay efforts in the temporal realm, "Christian social action is preeminent."[31]

The Council anticipated another of American Catholics' major concerns in the document as well when it addressed the role of women. Their treatment remained general and vague, however. The decree noted that "since in our days women are taking an increasingly active share in the whole life of society, it is very important that their participation in the various sectors of the Church's apostolate should likewise develop."[32] But this was all the Council had to say. The words were promising for women seeking equality within the Church, but also frustratingly ephemeral. The passage seemed to endorse movement toward equal participation with men, but clearly did not do so explicitly. Reluctant bishops had no obligation to recognize any particular model of development.

The fourth and final session opened with the continuation of the debate on religious liberty, and closed with the final ceremony and Paul's message to the bishops as they departed for their dioceses. The bishops published eleven documents in this session, though they had debated and resolved many of these in previous sessions.

All together, the Council promulgated sixteen documents in the four sessions, and then the bishops returned to their dioceses to implement the changes those documents mandated and implied. Francis Cardinal Spellman, the most powerful American cardinal at the outset of the Council, had vowed in 1962 that "no change will get past the Statue of Liberty."[33] But fundamental changes reached every diocese in America. Each bishop remained free to implement them at his own pace, however, and through various means. John Wright moved quickly on some issues and slowly on others. He did not call a diocesan synod until 1968, three years after the Council ended, and the preparation took until 1971.

A brief review of key elements of the Council may help to put it in perspective. The Council sought to evoke a positive, pastoral tone, rather than a legalistic, negative one. It dispersed authority away from the pope to the bishops (and perhaps beyond), recognized religious liberty, and acknowledged that the laity had an independent apostolate within the Church. The gathered bishops defined the Church as the "People of God" rather than the hierarchy, and in so doing elevated the laity to a position never before acknowledged. No longer would the laity look on the hierarchy in quite the same way, and no longer could the hierarchy justly expect them to do so.

In addition, many laymen and -women interpreted the Council's actions as encouragement for more vigorous activity. One such layman wrote that all of us, as lay people, should be sobered by the thought that so far we have fallen short of the total apostolic commitment, in and through life, which the church has now declared to be our duty and our privilege. Before the Council met we may have had some excuse for inaction, such as the lack of clarity in the layman's status. Such excuses can no longer be valid.[34]

A newly empowered and invigorated lay apostolate might move in directions unanticipated, however, and Catholics in Pittsburgh encountered the ecclesiastical tensions that a more active and assertive laity necessarily entailed.

THE SECOND VATICAN COUNCIL IN PITTSBURGH

When Pittsburghers first learned of the Council in January 1959, they expected a grand effort to unify Christianity under the Catholic banner. It was, after all, to be an ecumenical council. As the first such council in nearly a century, people had high hopes for its success. One *Pittsburgh Catholic* columnist anticipated that "it may yet prove to be the best news since the birth of Christ."[35] Only later, and with a tinge of disappointment, did they come to realize that the Council would focus primarily on internal Church matters. And yet this internal focus promised great things as well. Reports of the preparatory process increasingly focused on the likelihood that the Council would redefine the laity's role in light of their increasing significance to the Church's work in the world. Reports from the Council's early sessions confirmed the increasing importance placed on the laity generally, and even noted that the move to introduce more vernacular into the Mass derived from concern that the laity better understand and participate in Catholicism's central ritual.

Pittsburgh (Liturgical Renewal in Light) of Vatican II

While the Council met over the course of four falls, the Pittsburgh diocese moved ahead with liturgical renewal efforts. The Council's clear determination to make significant reform in all aspects of the Church, including the liturgy, bolstered the reform spirit, but also continued the confusion that had permeated earlier efforts. The diocesan Liturgical Commission constantly tried to ascertain what changes the Council had made or would soon advocate, and what specific changes some of the broad principles the Council announced entailed.

The Liturgical Commission worked on two main projects during the Council years, the reform of liturgies outside of the Mass (such as Holy Week, wakes, and confession), and Mass itself. The commission continued its focus on pastors and the laity, but supplemented that with more concerted efforts among the religious, especially women religious, and Catholic school children. The reforms that the commission espoused transformed the Mass from a mysterious remembrance of Christ's ultimate sacrifice which parishioners observed passively, or actively ignored, to a celebration of Christ's resurrection from the dead in which all participated.

Next, we will examine the Liturgical Commission's efforts to reform the liturgies during the years the Council met, the parish responses to these reforms, and the implications these reforms had for race, gender, and ethnicity for Pittsburgh's Catholics. The reforms constitute the first true changes to come from the Council itself.

The Liturgical Commission focused a good deal of attention on liturgies, devotions, and practices that parishioners attended outside of the Mass itself. The commission members addressed reforms in the Holy Week devotions, forty hours devotions, wakes, funerals (particularly priests' funerals), weddings, and reconciliation (confession), and introduced and promoted Bible services. The commission intended to increase lay understanding of, and participation in, each of these rituals by introducing the vernacular and increasing the interaction between the laity and the priest. The transformation of Holy Week provides the best illustration of these efforts.

The commission launched a campaign entitled "Operation Holy Week" in January 1963 to transform existing understandings of Lent and Holy Week. Until this time Catholics focused throughout Lent on Christ's suffering and eventual crucifixion. Parishioners practiced a special penance themselves for the forty days of Lent, in which they often "gave up" some pleasure and attempted to follow the Lenten guidelines that the bishop pronounced. The pleasures that Catholics forwent during Lent often constituted vices in Catholic eyes, so that Catholics gained both through the suffering that they underwent (which brought them closer to Jesus) and by eliminating the bad practice. Alcohol, cigarettes, and candy appeared frequently on the list of pleasures that Catholics surrendered during Lent.

Pope Pius XII had suggested a new Holy Week practice in 1955, and the Pittsburgh diocese had implemented this dutifully. The *Pittsburgh Catholic* reported the reforms, which Church officials insisted were actually "restorations" of early Church practices, as a great success. Many commission members doubted whether parishioners attended, embraced, or even understood the new practices, however. They intended Operation Holy Week to drum up support for the Holy Week structure and to change popular perceptions of Holy Week in general.

Priests learned of these efforts through a variety of sources, including the Liturgical Commission *Newsletter*. On one level, the *Newsletter* provided specific suggestions concerning the new Lenten paradigm. For example, it encouraged pastors to recommend social rather than private Lenten sacrifice. Instead of giving up candy or cigarettes, why not join a civic organization? The editors did not suggest this "to condemn individual personal penance, but to show that there is a constructive, social type of penance as well."[36]

The *Newsletter*'s more important role was to alert pastors to the torrent of information coming through other media in the coming weeks. The commission presented information about the new Holy Week's emphasis from a number of sources to parishioners and pastors alike in an attempt to "touch everyone in the diocese to some extent, however small."[37] Commission members wrote sermon outlines that Bishop Wright distributed to all pastors for use during Lenten Sunday sermons; they wrote articles for the diocesan newspaper, the *Pittsburgh Catholic*; they developed material for children in parochial schools; and they appeared on television shows to discuss the new emphasis. They attempted in each forum to shift the emphasis from Christ's death on the cross to his resurrection from the dead. In this way the commission attempted to shift the long-emphasized lay focus from sin to redemption, to bring home the uplifting message that through baptism Catholics entered the mystical body of Christ as full participants in the Church's efforts to redeem the world. Life was not a lonely individual journey besieged at every turn by sin, but rather a collective social endeavor to make the world whole. The liturgy was an integral part of this effort, and Holy Week was the highlight of the liturgical season.

Teachers told the seventh- and eighth-graders in Pittsburgh's Catholic schools that the solemn ceremonies of Holy Week and Easter were "the greatest liturgical event of the whole year." This was an especially difficult point to argue with children who understood Christmas, the celebration of Christ's birth, to be the greatest event the Church had to offer. The teachers promoted Holy Week's cause with a multilesson plan that extended through at least four days of instruction, one day devoted to each of the four crucial parts of the Holy Week liturgy (Palm Sunday, Holy Thursday, Good Friday, and the Easter Vigil). They addressed the historical origin and development of each day's ceremony and impressed upon their students the importance and relevance of the contemporary liturgies to the students' own lives.[38]

Though the lesson plans stated objectives aimed solely at increasing student awareness of, and participation in, the liturgies, two important themes permeated the instruction. Perhaps the most visible, because of its departure from existing lay experiences in the Church, was an emphasis on hope and happiness.

While the traditional Lenten activities had centered on Christ's death, the terrible agony of his supreme sacrifice, the new emphasis was to be on his resurrection. More properly it was on both the death and the resurrection, but only the new half of this theme stood out. The teacher guide emphasized that "liturgical scholars see that there is a great need to restore the Resurrection to its proper place in the Christian life. We are not redeemed by the death of Christ alone—but by His death and resurrection." Similarly, Catholics emphasized their own sinfulness and unworthiness too much. "Oftentimes we are too conscious of our sinfulness and unworthiness and not enough convinced of our dignity which comes through Christ, from Christ and in Christ. Through Him in Baptism we are made children of God, members of His Body." A new emphasis on baptism at the end of the Easter Vigil was to underscore the positive aspects of the resurrection. "As Christ died, so in Baptism we die to sin: as He rose from the dead, so we rise to a new life of grace and become the 'new people of God.'"[39]

The second theme the teachers taught throughout the sessions was a strong connection between these liturgical values and messages and the students' behaviors outside of church. For example, the Holy Thursday liturgy re-enacted the Last Supper, wherein Christ offered his body and blood to his disciples in the form of water and wine. This was the basis for the Catholic sacrament of Communion, or the Eucharist. Teachers attempted, in their lesson on Holy Thursday, to

> help students realize that the true Christian, through Holy Communion, should become more concerned, for example, about the lonely newcomer to the school, the unpopular or backward classmate, the struggle of the Negro or of the migrant farmer, the plight of the refugee, the millions of persons behind the Iron, Bamboo, or Sugarcane curtain, and the sick.

Further, the teachers emphasized that "our participation in offering Holy Mass ought to be reflected in the way we go out and 'live the Mass' during the day.[40]

If the students listened to the sermons at Sunday Masses during Lent they heard their priests emphasize the same themes. Bishop Wright instructed all priests in the diocese to use the outlines he provided to them to promote understanding of the new Holy Week liturgies and, consequently, engender greater participation.

The outlines stressed the positive aspects of Christ's death and resurrection. For example, the first week's outline noted that "recent Christian piety has sometimes paid excessive attention to the physical details of the Crucifixion," especially in rituals such as the Stations of the Cross. These emphasized too much

Christ's agony and sacrifice at the expense of the benefits that agony brought. Priests were to tell their parishioners that "we must not let the details obscure the fact that the death of Christ is a great triumph and victory." Further, the "crucifixion is a triumphant victory over sin, and the resurrection a triumphant entry into new life. While our attention may focus now on one or the other, it must never be to the exclusion of the other." But no one yet worried about the resurrection excluding the crucifixion. In the commission's and bishop's view, at least, the laity had a "keen sense of sin, and yet a dim sense of how we are become [*sic*] sons of God, or what it is to be a son of God."[41]

The outlines also instructed priests to urge their parishioners to incorporate Christ's redemption into all aspects of their lives. On the third Sunday of Lent priests urged parishioners to look outward.

> Keeping religion within the walls of our churches, schools and homes is, as it were, to limit Christ's redeeming effect. Pius XII said that the "consecratio mundi" belongs to the laity. John XXIII insists that the laity must not lessen but intensify their commitment to the world about them. Christ does not want to bless only our rosary or prayerbook—but the entire world. It is the laity who must extend this blessing by their apostolic efforts.[42]

The commission also put out a television show on channel 2, the local CBS affiliate, which focused on the Easter Vigil itself. The Reverends Larkin and McIlvane, Sister Edward Mary, Brother Neal, and C. Holmes Wolfe held a panel discussion designed to present the views of priests, sisters, brothers, and the laity. The program emphasized those themes developed in the schools and sermons.

The program began with Father McIlvane suggesting that Catholics focused too much on "the Christ of the manger" (Christmas) and not enough on the risen Christ. He continued, "Mind—I don't say that Christians didn't believe in the Resurrection, but without even realizing it they came to emphasize the birth and death of Christ more than the Resurrection." C. Holmes Wolfe, a local attorney, concurred. He said that the "average Catholic today" perceives Christmas to be the most important feast of the Christian year. Sister Edward Mary moved off Christmas but reported that religious teachers emphasize Lenten practices over Easter ones. Brother Neal suggested that Catholics did not rightly understand that Christ's resurrection ennobled all baptized Catholics. He stated that

> Catholics have a great respect for their priests and this is as it should be. Sometimes it is a surprising thing to say—they don't have enough respect

for themselves! What I am trying to say here is this—they don't appreciate the dignity and holiness conferred upon them through a living contact with the risen Christ in the sacrament of Baptism.[43]

The program hit its climax in an exchange between Father Larkin and C. Holmes Wolfe, wherein Father Larkin asked Mr. Wolfe if Catholics "have as yet appreciated the Easter Vigil." Mr. Wolfe replied that the appreciation was on the rise, but that he would not be satisfied "until the Easter Vigil is as well attended as the Christmas midnight Mass." He did not mean to suggest that the presence of bodies alone signified liturgical success, but rather that such a turnout would be an indication that Catholics had "grasped anew the central importance of the Resurrection."[44]

Flushed with the apparent success of Operation Holy Week, the Liturgical Commission devoted the following Lent to "Operation Bible and Liturgy." Pastors read in the *Newsletter* that they "need not wait to begin or to further in our parishes, schools and religion classes the renewed appreciation of the Bible." The commission advocated gradual but steady progress to begin this appreciation through four steps: holding weekly Bible services during Lent; preaching biblical sermons during Lenten homilies; providing short homilies during the daily Masses (something never before done); and keeping well-stocked pamphlet racks with Bible-centered materials in the back of the churches.[45]

February saw four television programs devoted to promoting the Bible and the liturgy and one radio program on each of the six Lenten Sundays. Bishop Wright again distributed sermon outlines, and the commission distributed free to all interested priests in the diocese the text of a talk that Saint Vincent Seminary's rector gave on the "Bible and Liturgy."[46]

The promotion of the Bible resulted from the Second Vatican Council's recognition of biblical sources of divine revelation. This recognition represented a shift away from the long-held position that Scripture and Catholic tradition together constituted the sources of divine revelation, and toward one that accepted that all revelation existed in some form independently in both Scripture and tradition. Such a position moved the official hierarchy closer to Protestants, who considered the Scriptures to contain all revelation. This recognition, really an elevation of Scripture, also entailed a greater emphasis on Scripture during the Mass, which will be discussed a bit later.

In addition to a restructured Holy Week and new effort to introduce Bible services (the nature of which remained loosely defined), the Liturgical Commission promoted greater use of English in forty hours devotions, wakes, funerals, and in 1965, confession. The commission advocated each of these in order to promote lay understanding—the direct participation prized in all liturgies. But each reform also infused the ritual with a "positive" theme that de-emphasized suffering and sacrifice. The reforms imbued the new liturgies with hope and possibilities, with human interaction and understanding.

The commission's advocacy of reform in the wedding ritual marked the first time the commission offered explicit criticism of existing rituals in its promotion of liturgical reforms. Whatever their private beliefs, commission members had always refrained from criticizing existing rituals. Changes were to improve good rituals, never to replace bad ones. This analysis clearly implied criticism of the old, but commission members never stated this criticism until November 1963, when the *Newsletter* recommended greater use of English at wedding Masses. It reported one priest's practice of reading "the word of God" in English immediately after his Latin rendition, and of encouraging all present to participate (sing hymns, respond) fully. The *Newsletter* suggested that wedding parties preferred this wedding to the old "coldly formal one."[47]

The commission also promoted new English rituals for wakes which both enabled those attending to participate knowledgeably and emphasized for the first time that death should be a happy time—when the departed moved closer to eternal life with Christ. Lay members of the commission first sought a new prayer structure for wakes. The commission had not considered this yet because the wake was not a central Catholic liturgy—it had an uncertain status. Mr. Albert Bender reported for the Lay Committee,

> We present, at this time, and for your thought, the hope that a card might be composed with the full agreement of all or many Christian groups, since we of the laity live and die in a society that is basicly [*sic*] Christian though not always Catholic in the Roman Rite sense. It would be difficult to find a better time for Christians to join in prayer together.

The Lay Committee then received two versions of prayers to replace the common practice of saying rosaries. Commission member the Rev. Ralph Roos wrote one. Mr. Bender reported for the Lay Committee at the March 1964 meeting that the two versions were fine, and asked that Bishop Wright recommend them to pastors. Father Roos preferred his own version and asked the commission to adopt it alone. Commission members seemed divided, and Father Reinhold, the only acknowledged liturgical authority on the commission, offered to study them and report back. Roos won out, and later received permission to have "Approved by the Liturgical Commission, Diocese of Pittsburgh" printed on the title page, but the *Newsletter* endorsed both versions.[48]

Roos's prayer service emphasized the positive aspects of death. He wrote in his cover letter to the commission members that his booklet "approaches death in a positive way, rather than negative way. Death is looked upon not as a 'taking away,' but as the entrance of the soul into the eternal life of heaven." Later he reiterated that this service "does not include negative thinking." Roos's wake booklet was very similar in emphasis to the other one that the Liturgical Commission liked, which the Gregorian Institute of America published. This version contained texts that "breathe and inspire Christian hope." It explained that "Christian hope does not palliate the harsh facts of suffering, disease, death and the corruption of the body. Instead it accepts them and then surpasses them." Wakes following this format were to reassure surviving members of the Catholic community that death meant rebirth, that just as Christ was resurrected from the dead, deceased Catholics would begin a new life in heaven (perhaps with a short detention in purgatory).[49]

Despite the great amount of work members expended on these liturgical reforms, the Liturgical Commission reserved its greatest efforts for reform of the Mass. The bishops gathered in Rome cooperated by addressing the Mass first and producing the Constitution on Sacred Liturgy before any other document. This enabled the Liturgical Commission to work on the new ritual with less delay than would have resulted if the Council had focused on the liturgy in one of the later sessions.

The commission worked regularly to break down clerical indifference and hostility to reforms, pushed the laity to become more involved, worked out specific suggestions for various parts of the Mass, produced a diocesan liturgical guide for parishes, began a training program for lay commentators, and implemented reforms mandated at higher levels in the Church hierarchy. Each parish had to implement two major revisions of the liturgy, one mandated by the U.S. Catholic Conference and one by the Vatican. Liturgical Commission members expended a great deal of effort to prepare pastors for these reforms. The Mass changes resulted in a decline in the roles of both priest and choir and a concomitant rise in the role parishioners played in the ritual. Finally, the commission ameliorated the emphasis on sacrifice in the Mass as they had in other rituals.

The commission continued on its tentative course in the early years of the Council as its members waited to see what reforms would emanate from Rome. The commission continued to promote lay participation, and reminded pastors regularly that they should prepare themselves and their parishioners for the changes that would inevitably come from the Council.

The Lay Committee concentrated up through the middle of 1964 on generating interest among the laity for the Mass. The committee purchased a film trilogy on the Mass from the National Council of Catholic Men in the spring of 1963. Each film ran thirty minutes. One focused on the "Meaning of the Mass," another on the "History of the Mass," and the third on a "Demonstration of the Mass." The Lay Committee showed each to the deanery heads of the Holy Name Union and Diocesan Council of Catholic Women in September and asked them to inform their groups about the films. C. Holmes Wolfe reported that the committee had pledges for 106 showings to various groups by April 1964, with each film shown the same number of times.[50]

The Lay Committee also worked to determine the best missal to use for the slightly revised Mass. Various commission members recommended the St. Andrew's Missal, a French missal that would need to be translated, and the St. Joseph's Missal. The commission formed a committee to study a number of missals and then choose one to recommend. Instead, the committee recommended four for adults and three others for children.[51]

But the greatest Lay Committee activity centered on the proper selection, preparation, and evaluation of commentators for Masses. Their role in this came about slowly, however, as the clerical members of the commission did not want to usurp power from pastors. In February 1964 Monsignor Shinar announced that he had received five copies of an extensive commentator "training kit" from the National Council of Catholic Men. He gave one to the Lay Committee. Albert Bender reported at the next commission meeting that the Lay Committee thought the training kit was very good. He advised that the commission should recommend the kit to all pastors and that Bishop Wright should send the kit to each pastor along with a letter "calling the pastor's attention to their duty to provide commentators at Sunday Mass."[52]

But no movement came for months, and C. Holmes Wolfe raised concerns about the need for proper commentator recruitment and training again in July. He worried that many commentators now reading were not spiritually or physically suited to the task. He recommended that Bishop Wright send out a letter on behalf of the commission "directing pastors to select—and to select with great care—the laymen to be given the necessary training." Wolfe then suggested that pastors had neither the inclination nor the opportunity to train commentators, and he volunteered the Lay Committee for this task. The committee estimated that the diocese conducted 1,320 Masses each Sunday, would need at least that many commentators, and so desired to hold the training on a regional basis.[53]

Wright revealed his plans for commentators in August. He wanted "bright young men from the senior year of high school on, so far as age goes" to attend the training and then be available to various parishes for a "proper stipend." He thought that this would best ensure that "the work they do will be done regularly, systematically and with the stability as well as status which such formal training and the detail of a stipend will help guarantee."[54] It also eliminated the pastor's excuse that he could find no qualified or interested layman to do the reading. Wright wished to establish a sort of lay order of commentators commissioned at the diocesan level. This would ensure the high quality of reading that the commission and bishop desired, but not necessarily the level of parishioner participation toward which the reforms had aimed. The commentators would constitute a new class of liturgical experts—albeit lay experts. But Wright's floating pool never materialized. Instead, the commentators worked in their own parishes.

The Lay Committee members had begun to organize the schools for commentators in September, but awaited Bishop Wright's letter to pastors informing them of this. Albert Bender reported at the October Liturgical Commission meeting that 125 parishes would send more than 1,000 men for training in six locations throughout the diocese. Members of the Liturgical Commission began to express concern at this point that the parishes intended to send no women.[55]

The Lay Committee structured the commentator training around the training kits that the National Council of Catholic Men (NCCM) provided. This program consisted of six sessions, five of which called large groups of commentators together from many parishes and the last of which took place in the commentators' parish churches. The training focused on two primary areas: mechanics and spiritual formation. It gave advice on a host of other areas, though, including whom pastors should choose from among the male parishioners to become commentators ("professional men such as doctors, lawyers, teachers and others who have the training and experience needed to speak, lead and communicate effectively with a large group of people").[56] The advice did not include identification of which women would make good commentators.

The NCCM put out a version of the training kit before the Council produced its document on the Sacred Liturgy and then amended it right after the document's release. The Lay Committee had both versions and used the later one.[57] Though parishioners had had many opportunities before to find out about the changes that the liturgical movement and Vatican II favored, this represented the first formal, widespread, and tangible exposure to the new Church which the diocese implemented. All previous efforts to introduce change were persuasive, but they depended upon the pastor's inclination. Many parishioners therefore never saw any transformation in the Mass, or saw only slight changes. But the Lay Committee taught these men the principles of reform in conjunction with specific directions for action within the Mass which transformed the central ritual of Catholic religious practice. The messages these men received, the specific behaviors they rehearsed, represented a reformation of the Mass introduced uniformly across all of America. It is important, therefore, to understand how this transformation began. What did the 1,200 laymen assembled in halls across the diocese learn about the new Mass? What role were the laity to assume? How was the laity to understand the Mass in light of the changes?

The training session provided at least partial answers to these questions. The Mass consisted of two parts and a varying number of subdivisions within each part. If parishioners were passive or distant during the Mass in 1962, they were to be actively involved in an interactive liturgy in 1965. The laity was to understand the Mass as a "dialogue of love" between God and his people.

The training began with an analysis of the old Mass. Session leaders stressed that the pre-reform Mass was antiquated, irrelevant to parishioners' lives. The training material observed that

> worship had become primarily a matter of duty, an obligation which ordinary people fulfilled by being "present" for Mass, while the clergy saw to it that necessary ceremonies and rituals were performed at the appropriate times: The important thing was simply the doing of the rite. These words were to be read. The actions were to be done. The people were to be there, to watch and pray, quietly.

Furthermore, the Mass suffered "from an alarming paralysis with so much of its ritual and formulas completely dependent on past ages." It had become "incapable of providing a living, vital religious experience for modern man." It needed reform.[58]

Parishioners often sought to do something with meaning at Mass, such as "reading a missal," but most practiced individual devotions, rosaries, prayerbook prayers, "a quick Hail Mary." Parishioners sometimes engaged in nonreligious behaviors. "Often enough, the women checked out the new hats and the men checked out the new women."[59]

The reformed Mass would end all this. It consisted of two parts, the Liturgy of the Word and the Liturgy of the Eucharist. The Liturgy of the Word included the entrance rite, reading from Scriptures, and preaching of the Word. (At other times the training sessions also included the "Prayer of the Faithful" in the Liturgy of the Word.) The Liturgy of the Eucharist consisted of the preparation of the gifts (offertory), eucharistic prayer (canon), and Communion. Each part of this Mass included structured parishioner participation, though some parts remained in Latin. The parishioners' most "pointedly logical duty" during Mass was to receive Communion. The entire structure was a dialogue of love between God and parishioners.

The Mass is the most intense point in time and space in which the Father pours out upon his children the fullest force of his love that has been from the beginning. The Mass is that point in which we return our own grateful love in the fullest measure.[60]

The new Mass maximized interior and exterior participation. Especially when preparing to receive the Eucharist, parishioners were to "believe in what [was] taking place," and they were to "strive to assume the mental attitude of Christ—grateful submission to the Father." They could best accomplish this by performing bodily actions (standing, sitting, kneeling, speaking, singing) together. These exterior acts of participation bonded the parishioners into a community and fostered interior emulation of Christ.[61]

Most of the training sessions were devoted to very practical mechanical or technical matters for commentators to consider. These too reflected important values and meanings in the new Mass. Commentators were to use their voices to bring the congregation to greater participation and to impress upon them the importance of this liturgy. Commentators were at all times to be sincere, vigorous ("that is, manly"), and relaxed. They were to be "dignified," yet not a "stuffed shirt." They had to have humility, to approach themselves "with honesty, with tolerance, with understanding, love, and generosity."[62]

Little evidence survives of the commentators' reception of this training. C. Holmes Wolfe did submit a brief initial report to the Liturgical Commission in which he stated that "the response on the part of the men has been excellent." He also reported that some of the men objected to the training format. They had received material to read on their own and then the leaders read the same material aloud at the training sessions. But overall, Wolfe considered the sessions to have been "reasonably successful." The Lay Committee planned a single training day for sisters at Duquesne University later in the month.[63]

The Lay Committee later reported that 1,200 men and 500 sisters took part in twenty-eight sessions conducted in six locations. The men objected to time "wasted" on studying the Mass. They wished to spend all of their time on the mechanics of commentating, but the Lay Committee insisted that they acquire a greater than usual understanding of the Mass. The sisters apparently did not object to the dual emphasis in the training.[64]

The Liturgical Commission continued its emphasis on reaching the pastors in addition to its attempts to educate the laity. Members encouraged pastors to move incrementally toward change. The *Newsletter* recommended that pastors encourage families to attend Mass together, distribute Communion hosts blessed at the Mass in which they are given out rather than rely on stocks of previously transformed hosts, teach people more hymns, use commentators whenever possible, remove excess statues from their churches, and be careful to give proper emphasis to the readings at Mass.[65] Throughout 1963 and the early part of 1964 the commission continued to prod pastors to accept the small changes already recommended and to prepare themselves for the big changes sure to come. In October 1963 the *Newsletter* told pastors that "we must all prepare ourselves in various ways for the liturgical changes which will follow the Council," and three months later it gave even stronger warnings.

> Through all of this there have been priests religious, church musicians and laity who have remained untouched by the renewal in the liturgy. In some cases they expressed open opposition. When they were bishops, pastors or superiors, they saw to it that little or nothing of the liturgical renewal touched their area, except that what was specifically mandated by changes in the missal. . . . Now, however, the battle on the liturgical renewal is over. The Council has unmistakably termed it the work of the Holy Spirit. . . . As a practical consequence, each priest who has to this time opposed the liturgical renewal can do so no longer.[66]

These small reforms aimed at increasing parishioner participation and simplifying the Mass. Father Reinhold, in a series of talks given to the Liturgical Commission itself, repeatedly stressed the need to minimize liturgical actions. He suggested that parishioners look at the host when the priest raises it during transubstantiation but not for too long. He stated that people should not take holy water upon entering and leaving the church for Mass—once was enough, twice was repetitive. He warned against making too many signs of the cross during Mass. The *Newsletter* told pastors that "liturgical scholars all agree that the Roman liturgy over the past several centuries has been the victim of excessive repetition and ornamentation. Now the task is to eliminate what is unnecessary repetition and to prune away what is superfluous ornamentation."[67]

The commission studied the Council's document on the Sacred Liturgy in various meetings and attempted through the *Newsletter* to interpret it for pastors. But the commission heeded Bishop Wright's warning not to "jump the gun" and took no substantial action until the American bishops distributed a standard reform. In March 1964 Monsignor Shinar announced that he had received an official copy of the standard American Mass and that he would distribute it to each commission member. The bishops had decided to introduce the changes in all the dioceses during Advent in 1964, roughly nine months away. This gave the commission most of 1964 to prepare pastors and people for changes they knew would come without revealing any specifics of the ceremony itself.[68]

Finally, in November 1964, the *Newsletter* informed pastors of the changes and devoted an entire issue to making them understandable. The *Newsletter* noted that

> many of us have grown up in what has been characterized as a "clerical" liturgy. Reflecting the theological truth of the Mystical Body, the revised liturgy indicates that the priest is the head of the congregation, but that all God's people are active in the worship of the liturgy.

The *Newsletter* went on to describe the new structure of the Mass, explaining each participant's role as it went.[69]

The first part of the Mass was now officially the Liturgy of the Word, and it consisted of two distinct parts. The first was the "entrance rite," and the second the "Scripture service." In the entrance rite, the parishioners were permitted to recite the entrance chant along with the priest ("Glory be to the Father . . .").[70] Priests were to recite the entrance chant in English, but the collect, secret, and post-Communion prayers remained in Latin. (The commission strongly urged parishes to employ commentators to explain the priest's prayers so that parishioners might understand this part of the Mass.) The *Newsletter* also encouraged pastors to have commentators do the first reading (known formerly as the Epistle, though it was not always from the Epistles). It told the pastors that the Scripture reading "should be one that inspires deep faith and reverence." It was a part of Mass "with a sanctity all its own. The people must be taught to hear, love, and reverence the word of God."[71]

Only priests could perform the second reading, the Gospel, aloud to the congregation. Lay commentators already did this reading in some parishes, and they had to stop. The "homily" followed the Gospel reading. The commission had earlier recommended that pastors pay more attention to the homily, which the *Newsletter* had defined as "a familiar talk between a pastor of souls and the members of his flock, given during a liturgical act upon a biblical text suggested by the liturgy." In November it reiterated that the homily was "a true proclaiming of the word of God, of the 'good news' of Christ," and should never be a "mere catechism." Following the homily, the people were to recite with the priest the Nicene Creed, a statement of Catholic beliefs. This ended the Liturgy of the Word.[72]

The Liturgy of the Eucharist consisted of three major subdivisions: the offertory, the canon, and the last Gospel. In the offertory, the priest received gifts (untransformed Communion hosts, water, and wine), and prayed over them. The commission recommended that two parishioners bring the gifts to the priest in an "offertory procession." They were to take them from a table in the back of the church and carry them the length of the aisle to the priest, who was to greet them at the gate to the sanctuary. This act signified that "the gifts come from the entire community."[73]

The *Newsletter* emphasized that parishioners should sing during the offertory. It related that "a community worship which is recited only (though permissible) would be lacking in the note of celebration which must be the spirit of every liturgical act." This continued the theme of hope and happiness, the emphasis on the benefits of the resurrection, which the Commission had promoted in the reforms of other rituals. For Catholics long used to associating the Mass with the supreme sacrifice, a "note of celebration" constituted a major transformation.

The priest was then to say the "secret prayer" (prayer over the gifts) and the Orate Fratres in Latin while a commentator explained briefly what was happening. Each of the prayers remained in Latin.

Reformers regularly distinguished between those central eternal elements of Mass and those introduced by historical accident. In this view, reformers were to strive to replicate the Mass that early Christian communities had practiced. The liturgical reform movement existed almost to shear the Mass of the trappings it had acquired over time—to rid the Mass of the historical accidents that marred the pure form of the liturgy. Yet at the same time the reformers sought to connect the liturgy to twentieth-century culture, to make it relevant to Catholics in the 1960s. This tension allowed some parts of the Mass to be in English (a nod to twentieth-century needs) but forbade others out of a desire to remain true to early Christian practices. Therefore, the same Liturgical Commission members who advocated English for the Pater Noster accepted as a rationale for keeping the secret prayer and the Orate Fratres in Latin that "liturgists agree that it was never a prayer for all the people to recite."[74]

The canon followed the offertory. It opened with the priest saying prayers in a voice louder than a whisper but too soft for anyone else to hear, and continued on to the congregational recitation of the Our Father in English. It included the subsequent distribution of Communion—still accomplished with parishioners kneeling at the altar rail—while all sang a community hymn. The *Newsletter* stated that this hymn should emphasize the social nature of Communion, that "this sacrament must draw us closer not only to God but to each other. Communion that would not increase our love for our neighbor would be a contradiction." Here, as in other places in the reformed Mass, Catholics were to reorient their liturgical experience from solely vertical, between the individual below and God above, to both vertical and horizontal, to both God and neighbors. The last part of the Liturgy of the Eucharist was the last Gospel. This remained in Latin, and belonged "to the priest and acolytes only."[75]

The new Mass required people to stand much more than they had previously in each part of the Mass. In some places standing replaced sitting, an active posture replaced a passive one. But standing often replaced kneeling. The commission worried that parishioners might understand this to be a retreat from "the most religious posture for prayer." The *Newsletter* therefore pointed out that standing "signifies the honor of reverence to God, and of a willingness to serve." In addition, standing was "the very first posture" that early Christians adopted. By contrast, kneeling came to the Mass in the Middle Ages, when the priest and congregation drifted apart in the liturgy. Kneeling corresponded with "the overemphasis on adoration of the Eucharist and excessive attention to man's sinfulness." The reforms intended to reduce the emphasis on sin by reducing the time parishioners spent on their knees.[76]

The new Mass also moved the commentator officially into the sanctuary and spelled the end of his original role. He now had to be in front of the congregation and face the people while he read. He was no longer barred from the sanctuary. But the commission determined that parishioners would need his instructions for only a couple of months, as the parishioners adjusted to their new routine, and then he might disappear. At the same time, the greater lay role in reading Scripture naturally fell to the commentator, so that he began a transition from commentator to commentator-lector, to finally just lector. Because many parishes hid the commentator in the sacristy, or behind a screen, the *Newsletter* stated twice, once in bold letters, that the commentator should be in front, facing the people, clearly visible to all.[77]

These reforms pertained only to the Low Mass—that which parishes practiced most often. The High Mass, or sung Mass, remained largely unchanged. Pastors could implement some English readings, as in the Low Mass, but they did not have to do so. (As a result, some pastors made all Sunday Masses High Masses, so that they would not have to implement the reforms.)[78]

The *Newsletter* concluded that the reforms just explained represented a "reshaping of our spiritual attitudes and values," and reiterated that they aimed at a "deeper union with Christ on the part of every member of the Church." The reforms represented a significant transformation of the Mass. They had asked Catholics to reconsider their understanding of their central ritual, to perceive the weekly reminder of Christ's terrible ordeal and sacrifice as a "celebration," to appreciate, understand, and actively participate in what had until then been a mystery. Catholics were to put down their rosaries in favor of hymnals and missals that contained not translations to follow silently but dialogue to speak. This new Mass, though intelligible—in part because intelligible—was unfamiliar. But this was not all. The very same issue of the *Newsletter* that explained the new Mass of 1964 warned that "next year, according to newspapers this week, further and more radical changes will take place."[79]

The change came within a few months, as the special commission that the Vatican Council set up to ensure that parishes adopted the new liturgy issued its own document. The *Newsletter* noted that the Pittsburgh Liturgical Commission could "find no contradiction between what the American Bishops have done and what is in this instruction." The Vatican instruction further simplified the Mass. It eliminated some prayers that the priest said alone in Latin and dropped the last Gospel. It decreased the choir's role in favor of congregational singing.[80]

The Vatican reforms sought to make the Mass more consistent with twentieth-century culture. The *Newsletter* reported that "various small adjustments are ordered 'that the liturgical service may exhibit a noble simplicity in harmony with the mentality of our times.'" Recognizing the dramatic transition the new liturgy asked Catholics to accept, the Council also recommended that bishops introduce the changes gradually. The Liturgical Commission concurred with this, and noted that "people cannot accept change that is too violent." Again the *Newsletter* told pastors that more changes lay ahead, that this transitional period would last several years.[81]

The *Newsletter*'s regular attempts to persuade, cajole, and bully pastors into accepting the reforms suggests that some priests rejected the reforms, but evidence of parishioner responses is harder to find. Certainly they did not all reject the changes out of hand. Roughly 1,200 lay commentators underwent six weekly training sessions in the new Mass, and even if they did not wish to study a ritual they had never before analyzed, they completed the program. Furthermore, the February 1965 *Newsletter* reported that a survey of Catholics found that 75 percent approved of the changes. The *Newsletter* tempered this positive response by suggesting that even "ardent" liturgists had to acknowledge the laity's "sharp reaction" to the changes. Moreover, the commission expressed concern for the other 25 percent and worried that a cleavage might develop between the two groups.[82]

An examination of the local parish response to the reforms might be helpful to discerning the broader lay experience. But it is difficult to assess with any precision the ways parishioners in Immaculate Heart of Mary (ethnic), Saint Thomas More (suburban), and Saint Philomena (urban) parishes responded to the reforms. Each parish's bulletins provide clues, however. The Immaculate Heart of Mary bulletin, for example, made no mention of the changes at all. The Saint Philomena bulletin indicated that parishioners responded with enthusiasm to efforts to introduce parishioner participation, save for a reluctance to sing. It thanked parishioners for "having entered so wholeheartedly into the new form of the Liturgy" but urged them to sing more. It assured parishioners that "our Lord will not judge us on the timber of our voice but on the effort we make to render Him our homage."[83] The bulletins made few references to liturgical changes and developments in the ensuing couple of years, and did not acknowledge the changes introduced by the Vatican in Lent of 1965.

Parishioners at Saint Thomas More parish were kept abreast of liturgical developments much better than were parishioners at Saint Philomena and Immaculate Heart of Mary. Fr. Joseph P. Larkin, a Liturgical Commission member, regularly assisted Saint Thomas More's pastor by saying Mass and hearing confession. Larkin kept news of liturgical reform present in the parishioners' lives. For example, in February 1963 he began a series of discussions through the Confraternity of Christian Doctrine (CCD) program on the Second Vatican Council.[84]

Social Implications

Though these reforms aimed explicitly at actions, attitudes, perceptions, and interpretations during the Mass and other Catholic rituals, they had social implications as well. Many reform advocates insisted that Catholics infuse the world outside of the Church with the values the new liturgy embodied. They argued that the new liturgy necessarily included social action in the world. In light of developments under way with Catholic Action, the heightened awareness the civil rights movement brought, and the subordinated position of blacks locally, these reformers called upon Catholics to work for racial justice as a clear extension of liturgical reform. In addition, the re-examination of the principles of liturgical practice sparked a few Catholics to question the role allotted to women in the liturgy. Liturgical reforms inspired and supported social concerns—in large part because the reforms posited a clear connection between the two.

Liturgical Commission members addressed the concern for racial justice more explicitly in these years than they did for equality between the sexes. This can be seen most clearly in an incident within the Liturgical Commission itself, which Fr. Donald W. McIlvane initiated around the end of 1963 and the beginning of 1964.

Father McIlvane was a member of the Pittsburgh Catholic Interracial Council (CIC). The Rev. John LaFarge had formed the Catholic Interracial Council in New York in 1934 as a splinter organization from the Federated Colored Catholics (FCC). LaFarge and a group of FCC members wanted to eliminate the separatist nature of the FCC within the Church because they considered it a hindrance to racial integration in the larger society. Other members of the FCC saw it as necessary for the support of African-American Catholics. This was an especially interesting issue in light of the Vatican's position on other "ethnic" parishes and organizations. How could it deny to African Americans what it gave to Poles? But LaFarge and others saw separation in the FCC as one more pressure delaying or preventing integration in the larger society. LaFarge therefore began the CIC as an alternative to the FCC. By the 1950s, twenty-four American cities had Catholic Interracial Councils, including Pittsburgh.[85]

McIlvane wrote to C. Holmes Wolfe some time around the turn of the new year 1964 to suggest that the Lay Committee of the Liturgical Commission put out a letter with the Catholic Interracial Council calling Catholics to act for racial justice. McIlvane also asked Wolfe to get the Holy Name Society and the Diocesan Council of Catholic Women to join, and suggested that the heads or representatives for each group get together for a photograph to accompany the statement in the *Pittsburgh Catholic*. McIlvane further suggested that members of the Lay Committee participate in the Catholic Interracial Council Day of Recollection as a follow-up to the statement. In order to expedite matters and to demonstrate more clearly what he intended, McIlvane wrote a draft of the statement that the Lay Committee might release.[86]

McIlvane's draft of the statement emphasized the close connection between liturgical renewal and social action. He began with references to Catholic efforts for racial justice, and then moved to the liturgical movement.

> Following as the day from the night, a Christian who is filled with the spirit of the liturgical renewal, must also realize that he must extend this spirit into the community. . . .
>
> No Christian who understands the liturgical renewal can be indifferent to the interracial situation in our country today. Any Christian who would seek to confine the new liturgical spirit within the walls of his parish church would be contradicting himself.

He continued:

> We call upon all our brother Catholics to draw the true Christian spirit from a full and active participation in the liturgy of the Mass and sacraments. We call upon them to live this spirit in daily life by an active participation in

the interracial apostolate. We call upon them to show acts of personal friend-
ship to negro [*sic*] neighbors or fellow workers. We call upon them to help
eliminate discrimination from their neighborhood, their place of employment, and those places where they enjoy recreation.[87]

McIlvane then told J. Ronald Pittman of the CIC that the Lay Committee
was to put out a resolution, and Pittman wrote Wolfe to thank him and invite
Lay Committee members to the CIC Day of Recollection at Saint Paul's Retreat
House.[88]

Wolfe did not respond enthusiastically, however. He reported McIlvane's
letter to the Liturgical Commission but cautioned that he "did not know if we
should start something like this at this time." When other commission members urged the Lay committee to become involved, the committee amended the
statement considerably. Instead of the long and forceful statement McIlvane
had drafted, the Lay Committee wrote that

the work of Vatican II has shown us that the Liturgical Renewal is insepa-
rate from and cannot be in conflict with the doctrine of the Mystical Body.
One part of this doctrine is the realization of the social apostolate. Therefore, all Catholics should extend every effort to further racial equality, acting
personally and in their communities with all men of good will.

The Lay Committee then insisted that the entire Liturgical Commission issue the
statement, and not simply the Lay Committee. Lay Committee members did not
join the Catholic Interracial Council on retreat at Saint Paul's. But their statement
accepted the principle of connecting the liturgical reform to action for social justice. This integrated all aspects of Catholic behavior and further cemented the
new liturgical emphasis on social action rather than private devotion.[89]

Liturgical reforms also sparked—or at least supported—a more active role
for women in the Church. Women made no great strides in the conciliar years,
but they laid the foundation for more substantial progress and greater consciousness about their position in later years. Women religious played the strongest role
in broaching issues of gender in the liturgy, and presenting the hierarchy with
difficult decisions.

Women religious began moving to greater consciousness in the 1950s, in part
in response to papal instructions to examine their ritual practices and in part independently of those instructions.[90] By the 1960s in Pittsburgh, they were the
most enthusiastic supporters of liturgical renewal. This can be seen in their large
turnouts for liturgical days. The Liturgical Commission sponsored liturgical days

for sisters in 1963, 1964, and 1965 which drew 1,000, 1,200, and 800 participants respectively. The commentator training courses drew 500 sisters, despite a general stricture against female commentators in all other settings.[91]

The sisters' greatest leverage for change resulted from the same sex segregation that was intended to insulate them from the outside world. Women religious regularly attended daily Mass in convents, separate from others. Because liturgical reform demanded greater parishioner participation, and because the only "parishioners" present at these liturgies were the sisters themselves, the hierarchy either had to exempt sisters from participation or exempt them from the prohibition against women in leading roles. The Liturgical Commission first broached the issue in October 1964 when a member asked at a meeting why women were not sought out as commentators. Monsignor Shinar, the executive secretary, responded that they could be commentators "under certain circumstances as in a girls' high school or a Motherhouse for sisters." But even in these cases, he warned, they were not to enter the sanctuary. Four months later, when the Liturgical Commission began moving the commentators toward the lector's role, Sister M. Michael asked if women too could assume those roles in girls' high schools and motherhouses. Again the commission agreed that they should be allowed to speak the role but not from the sanctuary. This prohibition held despite the general instruction that lectors and commentators in parishes be in the sanctuary.[92]

When the Council came to a close in Rome, women could serve as commentators and lectors in Pittsburgh only when no males (other than the priest) were present. Still, this represented a step toward full participation and reflected a growing awareness among even the hierarchy that women's subordinated status in the liturgy was inconsistent with the values of the liturgical renewal. Bishop Wright took this recognition a step further when, in September 1965, he asked the Liturgical Commission to establish a Committee on the Sacraments that could get "a woman's opinion on the sacrament of matrimony."[93]

THE MASS IN PITTSBURGH CHURCHES UNDERWENT A PROFOUND transformation between the opening of the first session and the close of the last session of the Second Vatican Council in Rome. A number of other rituals began to change as well. Put in the most stark terms, the Mass moved from a Latin ritual performed by priests aided by acolytes in which no parishioner—save for choir members—participated, to an English ritual that depended for its successful performance on lay participation. In 1962 it was a mysterious and ominous remembrance of Christ's ultimate sacrifice, an alien and distant ritual that Catholics had to attend in groups but during which they practiced private devotions. By the end of 1965 it was a comprehensible social celebration of Christ's death and resurrection. If one of the primary purposes of attending Mass before the reforms was to avoid the sin of missing it, after the reforms it was to receive the grace of Jesus' redemption and to use that grace to redeem the world.

But not all of this was clear to parishioners immediately, and the continued reforms over the next few years ensured that parishioners would grapple with the Mass's meaning for some time. If they took nothing else from the renewal, parishioners understood that the rituals were dynamic in the 1960s, that those habits ingrained over the course of the laity's lifetimes, over generations really, no longer held. The Second Vatican Council had already shaken the foundations of Catholic religious experience by 1965, and the bishops were only then coming home from Rome.

PART THREE

The Post-Conciliar Church

CHAPTER SIX

The Diocesan Pastoral Council

SHORTLY AFTER BISHOP WRIGHT RETURNED TO PITTSBURGH FROM Rome he began significant reform within the diocese. In addition, other members of the Pittsburgh diocese too began work inspired or at least emboldened by Vatican reforms. The diocesan activities represented the official implementation of the Second Vatican Council in the Pittsburgh Church. They lent official assistance to the lay movement away from devotions and furthered the increasing emphasis on social justice. Bishop Wright began two significant processes designed to renew the Church in his diocese. The first was the Diocesan Pastoral Council, and the second was a synod in which Wright sought each Catholic's participation in some form.

The Diocesan Pastoral Council is significant primarily for four reasons. It was a consultative body composed in large part of laymen and laywomen, the first diocesanwide council ever to exist in Pittsburgh—or the nation for that matter. It focused a good deal of its attention on social justice issues, and thereby reflected the growing stature that it held among Catholics relative to devotionalism and separatism. It provided a practice run for the later synod. Finally, it gathered important information about the way Catholics understood and practiced their faith in the wake of the Second Vatican Council. Though Bishop Wright initiated the council, and ultimately controlled its agenda, he could not (and perhaps did not want to) control the voices that emerged in council deliberations. Records of these deliberations therefore afford a window through which to view the changing lay experience of Catholicism and the dynamic Catholic influence on lay experiences in society.

This chapter traces the development and actions of Pittsburgh's Diocesan Pastoral Council in the crucial first years after the last session of the Second Vatican Council. The Pastoral Council was the culmination of Bishop Wright's efforts to transform the Church in the wake of Vatican II, and therefore drew from, interacted with, and inspired many other organizations active in the diocese at this time. An examination of the Pastoral Council necessarily sheds light on the development of Pittsburgh's Catholic Interracial Council, diocesan Human Relations Commission, parish committees, Clergy Council, parochial schools, and Chancery office.

In addition, the council embodied Bishop Wright's vision of the post-Conciliar Church. The council's structure and procedures provide a window through which we can see the Church's predominant values after Vatican II. The issues and areas on which the council focused and the development of the council's deliberations on these issues both reflect the issues central to Catholics after the Vatican Council and shed light on the attitudes, values, and conceptions lay Catholics held in the late 1960s. In short, the Diocesan Pastoral Council is valuable both for itself and because of what it reveals about Pittsburgh's Catholics.

The Pastoral Council's early formation and focus highlighted issues of gender, race, and Church democracy. This chapter addresses each, though it concentrates most heavily on race. Race was the issue on which Catholics most self-consciously and explicitly concentrated their new orientation.

Though Bishop Wright later recalled conceiving the plan for a Diocesan Pastoral Council during the last session of the Second Vatican Council, evidence suggests that he settled on the final model much later. Wright met with five laymen in June 1966 and discussed with them his plan to develop what he called a Diocesan Laymen's Council (DLC). He intended to staff this council with representatives of all-male diocesan organizations,[1] the parish committees, and men whom Bishop Wright would choose at large. Wright envisioned that this council would meet four times a year to discuss an agenda he provided and to make recommendations for action that a yet-to-be-hired coordinator of lay activities would implement. Wright told the gathered laymen that a merger with the Diocesan Council of Catholic Women and groups with mixed male-female membership "might be considered" in the future. He admonished the men to keep his plan a secret and adjourned the meeting.[2]

However, the Diocesan Laymen's Council never came to be. Instead, Bishop Wright began work on a council that drew representatives from the reorganized parish committees, existing lay organizations, the Clergy Council, religious orders, and others. Wright hoped to imitate in many ways the Second Vatican Council from which he had just returned. This body would be a mechanism through which the bishop might learn the clergy's, laity's, and religious's concerns and perspectives on diocesan policy and positions. It would give a voice to the laity in the administration of the Pittsburgh diocese, though the council would have no power.

But no good model existed for such a council within a diocese. The Second Vatican Council had clear precedents and a readily workable structure. Bishops were entitled to attend and act, and no one else save those the bishops invited. The problems organizers faced in Rome were primarily logistical—how to co-ordinate such a large body of individuals. In Pittsburgh, the issue was much more fundamental. Who should serve on such a council? Too many Catholics resided in the diocese to invite them all to serve. Moreover, the Second Vatican Council and national and local social developments had pushed Bishop Wright to steer the Church toward people and causes that demanded a wider group of lay participants than a bishop might have drawn upon before. Bishop Wright could not simply call upon leaders of the Holy Name Society and the Diocesan Council of Catholic Women to serve.

Wright resolved to work toward the council immediately, using steps that allowed parishioners, clergy, and religious of the diocese some input into council membership. The first step was the reformation of parish committees. Until the reform, each parish was supposed to maintain a committee of men upon whom the pastor might draw advice as he saw fit. The parish was to choose members of the committee in elections in which all adult male contributing members of the parish were eligible to vote.

The new parish committees were to be open to all who wished to serve, male and female, eighteen years old and older, who could be nominated and elected. The diocese mandated but may not have enforced a uniform nomination process, but it did make sure that each parish held elections for the new parish committees on the same day. Every parish was required to send out a ballot to each registered male and female parishioner, eighteen years old and older, and to collect those ballots on one Sunday.[3]

The *Pittsburgh Catholic* called this election "a moment of truth." It continued, "For years many of the laity have groused about the exclusivity of the ordained in the running of the parish. That grouse should be routed under the new decree." In addition, many would find "particular significance" in the expanded rights of women, especially in "our day of keen sensitiveness about the place of women in the Church."[4]

Each parish held elections on February 6, 1966, for its Parish Committee, and the *Pittsburgh Catholic* estimated that roughly one-third of the eligible Catholics voted. In some parishes nearly 60 percent of the male and female parishioners voted, but in some, such as the bishop's cathedral parish of Saint Paul's, only a quarter participated. In one parish only 18 percent took part. All parishes installed their new committees on February 13, one week after the elections.[5]

Though women were eligible to participate fully, they did not fare so well in the election process. Women's chances did not look good even before the elections, as few women were nominated to run for office. No comprehensive data on the gender of nominees survives, but evidence of the nominees from two parishes reveals that only two of forty nominees were female.[6]

The *Pittsburgh Catholic* reported a "mixed" reception for women at the ballot box, and listed how women fared in various parishes. Women won 160 seats on parish committees in the elections throughout the diocese, which represented roughly 6.8 percent of all positions available. It is impossible to determine why they did so poorly overall from this, though evidence from a variety of parishes suggests that they could not overcome their exclusion from the nomination process.[7]

Bishop Wright took the second step toward the establishment of a diocesan council in April 1966 when he formed a diocesan Clergy Council. This council, which consisted of thirteen representatives and their alternates, was to meet four times a year with Bishop Wright to "improve communication between [the] Chancery and the diocesan clergy and to serve as a forum for discussing common problems."[8] This council later sent representatives to the Diocesan Pastoral Council.

Wright announced the first of the next two steps in August 1966. He invited all 2,500 newly elected Parish Committee members to attend a meeting in which they would elect from among themselves representatives to the diocesan council.[9]

Bishop Wright was no sports fan, and perhaps for this reason he scheduled the meeting of the Parish Committee members for Saturday afternoon, November 19, 1966—the same afternoon that Notre Dame played Michigan State in a crucial football game televised nationally. The winner was certain to win the national championship, and the ultimate outcome (a tie) testified to how evenly matched the teams turned out to be. Wright himself joked about the stiff competition for the parishioners' interest.[10] Still, 1,182 (47 percent) of the possible 2,500 members attended the meeting held in Pittsburgh's Civic Arena. Those who did come to the meeting met the bishop personally and gathered by deaneries to elect a total of thirteen delegates and thirteen alternates to represent the laity on the diocesan council. Each deanery received one delegate and one alternate. One delegate and two alternates were female, giving them a slightly higher proportion (11 percent of all, 7 percent of delegates) on the diocesan council than among Parish Committee members.[11]

The religious orders working in the diocese elected ten more delegates and alternates to the council the following March.[12] Shortly thereafter diocesan lay organizations elected representatives to the council, and Bishop Wright chose twenty-four at-large delegates personally. Altogether, seventy-two delegates and seventy-two alternates constituted the council, now called officially the Diocesan Council for Consultation on Pastoral Problems and Policies (but known more commonly as the Diocesan Pastoral Council or DPC). Parishioners were able to play some role in choosing twenty-five (35 percent) of the delegates, either through their Parish Committee representatives or by virtue of their membership in and attendance at a special gathering of male and female diocesan organization members in the spring of 1967. A total of forty-eight delegates came to the council by some election or other, and the bishop chose personally twenty-four—almost the same number as the parishioners. The council had twenty female delegates, who constituted 28 percent of the council.[13]

Bishop Wright proudly announced that the Pittsburgh Pastoral Council was the first in America, was far more democratic than the Vatican II document mandated, and would deal with substantive issues, not general principles. Though Wright decided clearly to emphasize Pittsburgh's alacrity in establishing a council and its relatively democratic nature, he just as surely rooted its existence in Vatican II's Decree on the Bishops' Pastoral Office in the Church. The Diocesan Pastoral Council grew directly from the Second Vatican Council.

The Diocesan Pastoral Council met eight times over the next three years to address various diocesan organizations and perceived emergencies on which Bishop Wright desired lay and clergy discussion and advice. The first meeting, held on the weekend of June 16 and 17, addressed the diocese's Catholic schools, the Liturgical Commission, and the Human Resources Commission. This meeting mixed discussion of a traditional Catholic institution, the parochial school, with that of two organizations that reflected the renewal which Vatican II promoted. Even the discussion of the schools touched an issue close to the heart of the reform within the Church: race relations. Bishop Wright declared DPC meetings to be open to the public, and he had Chancery officials specifically invite reporters from the city's two daily papers, the *Post-Gazette* and the *Press*. This first meeting of the Pastoral Council, the first formal attempt by the Pittsburgh hierarchy to consult Catholic "opinion" to determine policy, sheds important light on the popular reception of reforms then under way and the functioning of the new consultative model for Church government. The meeting represented the first official, albeit tentative, step toward the post-Conciliar Church.

RACIAL AND GENDER EQUALITY

Reports in the city papers of the first session of the first meeting focused on proposals to garner greater funding for parochial schools and diocesan high schools. The Council agreed to continue the existing school structure and to raise teacher salaries, but balked at plans to levy an income tax on all adult parishioners to support the schools.[14] But neither the *Post-Gazette* nor the *Press* reported on the controversy surrounding support for a civil rights measure. The measure read:

> Be it resolved that the Diocesan School Board continue its efforts thru education and reasonable action to seek the achievement of full civil rights for all citizens and to seek a solution to the crisis of segregation through parent and student education and through such other programs as the open enrollment policy and continued cooperation with other community agencies, especially the Public School Board.[15]

Sharp debate broke out over the phrase "reasonable action to seek the achievement of full civil rights for all citizens." Some council members saw the term *reasonable action* in particular to be too vague, and pressed their fellow members to adopt a more specific resolution. The debate hinged on previous developments involving the diocesan school board and racial integration.

As whites moved out of the central city to the suburbs, the public schools in areas such as the Hill District, Homewood, and Wilkinsburg became overwhelmingly African American. By contrast, the Catholic schools, especially the high schools, remained overwhelmingly white. The Catholic Interracial Council (CIC) of Pittsburgh pushed the diocesan school board to integrate its schools.

Barely two weeks before the Pastoral Council met for its first session, the CIC Education Committee suggested that the diocesan school board take five steps to alleviate the segregation. It asked the board to provide scholarships to enable African-American families to afford Catholic high schools, especially Saint Augustine High School in Lawrenceville. Saint Augustine's was close to the Hill District and would have been a reasonable place for nearby African-American children to attend. The CIC further asked the board to join Saint John the Baptist parish to the district that Saint Augustine served so that this Hill District parish would funnel its students directly into Saint Augustine's upon graduation from eighth grade. (Roughly 7,400 of the diocese's 230,000 students were African American, and these students were concentrated in the urban grade schools of parishes whose population shifted from white to black.) The CIC's last three suggestions were that the board meet to devise a plan to integrate the Catholic schools, to appoint an African-American member to the school board, and to open school board meetings to the public.[16] The school board did not rush to meet these demands.

The council discussion took place with the Catholic Interracial Council's public criticisms of the diocesan school system fresh in everyone's mind. Most participants in the council discussion accepted, even asserted, that an integrated school was a better school for both black and white students because it best facilitated a "liberal education." The debate opened with speakers pushing for integration. Mr. J. Edward White, of Pittsburgh proper, suggested that the board implement busing between nearby neighborhoods to achieve integration, and noted that the recent large push for state funding of school buses for Catholic schools reflected the Catholics' endorsement of busing in general. He concluded, "I don't see, in all the plans we have had, many progressive, affirmative actions to do away with the segregated education, that does in fact, exist in our schools."[17]

Senator Ernest P. Kline, Minority Leader of the Pennsylvania State Senate from Beaver Falls, pushed the school board even further. He questioned whether this resolution "adequately" answered the criticisms that the Catholic Interracial Council leveled and recommended an amendment to the resolution that inserted after the words *School Board* "and further, that the School Board pursue a policy to racially integrate all diocesan schools through student exchange, busing, and all other legal means available."

The amendment heightened the tension of the discussion quite a bit, as it committed the school board to specific actions to integrate schools. Mr. Thomas Donnelly, of Pittsburgh, opposed the amendment because he worried that asking suburban schools located ten miles from any African-American "citizens" to integrate made no sense at all. Senator Kline replied that Catholic schools in the suburbs might be the only suburban schools that could integrate, because public schools drew students only from within their districts, and Catholic schools should therefore take the lead. He reiterated that "if we're going to say anything on the matter, then I want to say something that is meaningful."[18]

Father Hugo, also a Liturgical Commission member, observed that "the whites have run to the suburbs in many cases, precisely, to avoid contact with negroes [sic]."[19] The suburbs were therefore the "front line of the racial problem today," and the council should endorse Senator Kline's amendment. Frank J. Schneider of Pittsburgh argued,

> I am sure that we are well aware of the lily-white suburbs, and I cannot think of anything that would give me more pleasure on this Council than to see it actively and forthrightly moving in the direction to afford the oppor-

tunities of our colored Catholic children to seek an education in the suburbs, in the atmosphere of the suburbs, in the type of schools that the suburbs have and can afford, in the clean fresh air of the suburbs, from that of
the contaminated city atmosphere that many of them are forced to live in.[20]

The amendment's opponents raised cost concerns (those buses would require additional funds) and turned the tide easily. The council voted down the
amendment by a nearly two-to-one majority (45–25) and adopted the original
resolution. Pittsburgh lay Catholics had once again expressed their lukewarm
support for concerted efforts to break down the racial barrier dividing the diocese.[21] But more than one-third of the delegates on the Pastoral Council sought
to commit the diocesan schools to embrace racial integration. And Bishop Wright
would call the Pastoral Council to a special session within a year to attempt to
devise a more meaningful policy on integration and racial justice in the wake of
Pittsburgh's racial crisis.

The Pastoral Council next took up the liturgy. Monsignor Shinar, liturgical commission executive secretary, presented the results of a liturgical survey recently taken throughout the diocese which indicated that the Pittsburgh parishes
had reformed their liturgical practices dramatically in the five years since the Second Vatican Council opened. The Liturgical Commission had sent out to each
pastor in the diocese a 116-question survey of practices the previous April. Fully
79 percent of the pastors responded. The survey revealed to the Liturgical Commission that the parishes throughout the diocese had very successfully implemented the "external" aspects of liturgical reforms. Some of the results were quite
convincing. Ninety-four percent of the Masses used the English language. Only
5 percent used Latin, and 1 percent used other languages. In 87 percent of the
Masses, the altar was so placed that the priest faced the parishioners. Roughly
85 percent of the Masses had some singing, with 63 percent doing so without a
choir and 22 percent with a choir. When the choir did not sing, 90 percent of the
hymns sung at Masses were in English.[22]

Though the Liturgical Commission had clearly stressed that parishioners
should consider the Mass a communal or social worship rather than a private
devotion, its members remained sensitive to criticisms that the new Mass was
hostile to private devotion. Monsignor Shinar emphasized in his presentation
that more than 90 percent of celebrants paused for a short while after the post-
Communion prayer to allow private devotion. He reported that "we say this helps
to dislodge those who say that, 'You are always talking about communal worship
in the Liturgy and you never give us a chance for a little bit of private devotion.'
Here is the chance."[23]

The survey very clearly established that most parishes had adopted the key aspects of liturgical reform. But the essence of the reform lay in its ability to transform parishioners from passive watchers to active participants. The commission hoped that the changes just reported would also alter the internal experience of the liturgy for parishioners, but they remained doubtful that this had yet occurred. The source of their pessimism was not evident to Diocesan Pastoral Council members, and the Liturgical Commission could provide no satisfactory answer as to how they discerned the degree of parishioners' "internal" participation from a survey that asked pastors to report on their parishioners' external behaviors.

The discussion turned to the subordinated status of women in the liturgy, and the commission members here revealed their uneasiness with the issue. Though the commission had been examining critically the liturgy for seven years, and had confronted the differing roles of women and men in the Mass for at least three years, the commission representatives reacted in the council session as though they had never before considered the possibility of women commentators.

The issue came up in part from a rather offhand remark that Monsignor Shinar made while presenting the survey results. In response to a delegate's question about the use of commentators at daily Masses, Monsignor Shinar replied that this presented a special problem. He pointed out, for example, that "suppose you have ten women at Mass and you are trying to have participation. It is a little difficult, but this can be done." He did not specify why this was difficult with ten women present, but informed delegates understood that such a situation precluded having any commentator. Women were not permitted to fill this role—save for the special exemption for motherhouses, convents, and all-girl high schools.[24]

Some minutes later, after the discussion of daily Mass had ended, Mother Thomas Aquinas approached the microphone and pressed Monsignor Shinar on this point. She reminded him of his statement about the difficulty of generating participation when only ten women were present, and then addressed the unstated principle that made his observation relevant. She pointed out that his observation brought up the issue of women commentators, and told him she thought that "attention needs to be called to the fact that women are still being denied the right to participate as commentators."[25]

Monsignor Shinar hastily called Monsignor Simko, Vicar for Religious, to deal with the question. The council broke into laughter at his quick retreat from the issue, but Shinar persisted. He pressed Monsignor Simko to come forward and answer the question: "Well, how about coming over here. You know the answer to this—the place of women in the Liturgy—since you deal in this problem all the time." Monsignor Simko came forward and said that he determined his policy not from any papal authority but rather a "common sense approach." In a mother house chapel, he said, "it is inconceivable that you would call in the gardener to read to these educated women." So he allowed one sister to remain in her place and do the reading.[26]

Mother Aquinas insisted that Monsignor Simko did not answer her question, and Monsignor Shinar broke in to say that "the same rule applies out in the parishes." He continued that at that point in time "we have no justification for using women as commentators or lectors at all." Mother Aquinas asked Monsignor Shinar if the commission had asked for such justification. Shinar replied, "No. We have enough trouble as it is." At this point Bishop Wright suggested that Shinar should use the word *authorization* instead of *justification,* as Mother Aquinas had suggested that they did have justification for women to serve as commentators and lectors. Shinar agreed. When pressed further to request this authorization, Shinar said that he would "bring it up at the next meeting" of the Liturgical Commission.[27]

But Mother Aquinas was not satisfied that Monsignor Shinar's offer to take it up at the next meeting was sufficient, nor did she think the Pastoral Council should ignore this important issue. She asked Bishop Wright to change the rule adopted to save time in this discussion and allow her to make a resolution that the council might discuss and vote upon. Monsignor Shinar assured her, "We will study that, Sister. Honest we will." At this the delegates and alternates dissolved in laughter, and Bishop Wright remained silent. Another delegate broached a new topic on the liturgy, and the council took no action on women commentators and lectors.[28] But Mother Aquinas had broached a point, reflective of a larger theme, with which the Church would have to grapple in the coming years. How could a religion animated by a quest for social justice deny equal participation and stature to at least half of its members based solely on their gender? The official answer in 1967 was to avoid the issue, though this avoidance also brought with it embarrassment that betrayed Catholic uneasiness with the subject.

Mother Aquinas's unease about the Church's persistent preference for males emerged at the parish level also. Saint Thomas More parishioners decided in the early 1970s to push the diocesan Church to treat men and women equitably in both liturgical roles and education. Their efforts presaged changes in diocesan policy and reflected the laity's growing role in defining the new, post–Vatican Council Church.

The Diocesan Pastoral Council turned once again to race concerns as it considered the Human Relations Commission report. This discussion too highlights the central position race held for Pittsburgh Catholics. The Hon. Harry A. Kramer, Jr., of the Pittsburgh Orphans' Court served as chairman of the Human Relations Commission and rendered its report to the Diocesan Pastoral Council. He recounted how Bishop Wright had founded the commission at his annual Labor Day Mass in the Civic Arena in 1966. Wright had established the commission as part of a larger "united conscience crusade in the whole field of human relations."[29]

Wright chose nineteen Catholics to serve on the Commission, and he asked them to "bring the impartial voice of reason, the objective witness of faith and the constructive role of education, the experience and vision to the task of meeting social tensions." The commission's official purpose was to promote and maintain "civil liberties and social justice," and thereby ensure the "general welfare and common good of all people regardless of color, national origin or creed." Fifteen of the nineteen members were men, five were attorneys, two were from labor, two were priests, and one was a sister.[30]

The commission had spent most of its eight months in existence to this point educating its members about human relations concerns in the diocese. Part of this resulted from the commission members' relative lack of background or experience in human relations. The chairman himself, for example, admitted to giving little study to the race issue prior to starting in his position. In addition to studying the diocese's structure and operations so that they could better identify potential human relations issues, the commission had endorsed Project Equality (to some degree) and Project Understanding, and had encouraged local hospitals to establish miniature human relations commissions of their own.[31]

Judge Kramer concluded his presentation with a not-so-subtle criticism of the Pastoral Council itself. He characterized the Human Relations Commission as an organization that employed a "quasi-judicial" approach to "anticipate and solve human relations problems in the Diocese through investigation and suggestions." He further stated that the commission members will not allow it to be "any kind of rubber stamp, such as you people are apparently turning out to be, but they call the shots as they see them." His observation was probably accurate, though perhaps not in the way that Kramer intended. The Pastoral Council did seem to operate as a rubber stamp, which was not surprising considering that the mechanism that determined membership ensured that most delegates and alternates represented the institutional-hierarchical perspective. In addition, the commission members probably did call the shots as they saw them. That was precisely what worried some council members, for the commission members seemed blind to the city's strained racial situation. Still, it is not clear why Judge Kramer made his criticism, unless he was attempting to pre-empt the sort of charges concerning his commission's inaction which some council members leveled at him in the ensuing discussion. The tension between the Human Relations Commission members present and some council delegates was palpable. Even the council moderator, himself a judge, referred to council questions as "interrogations."[32]

The agenda of the Pastoral Council meeting called for its members to discuss and vote on three resolutions concerning the Human Relations Commission. The first simply asked the DPC to express its support of the HRC. The second asked the council to endorse Project Equality, and the third to welcome participation in Project Understanding.

Right away the council had questions about the Human Relations Commission. Despite the good intentions that may have spurred Bishop Wright to establish this commission, the times called for some serious and meaningful action on racial issues. Some council members questioned whether the commission had accomplished anything meaningful at all. Did the commission act in any way to touch the lives of those it had formed to improve?[33]

Mr. Edward White wanted the council to hear from some of the inner-city pastors "how well this official voice of the Diocese is being heard and how it is evaluated in the inner-city parishes," before voting to support the HRC. Judge Ridge, the moderator, prohibited this until all delegates who wished to speak had been heard first, and no inner-city pastor ever made it to a microphone.[34]

Sister Elizabeth Ann also questioned the "effectiveness of their communication to the faithful." Did parishioners even know what the HRC was doing? Judge Kramer replied that commission member O'Friel, manager of KDKA television station, was working on a "brochure type pass-out thing" that the commission hoped to distribute to all "interested" parishes and parishioners. He then reiterated that though the commission existed in the midst of a turbulent situation, its relative newness meant that members were still "feeling our way."[35]

Despite the pointed questions that individual members aimed at the commission, the majority of the Diocesan Pastoral Council members largely shared the Human Relations Commission's tepid fervor for direct action to bring about racial equality. The council passed the first resolution supporting the HRC.[36]

The HRC ran into more trouble on the second resolution, which called for the council to endorse the diocese's participation in Project Equality. The resolution called upon the council to approve

the recommendations of the Human Relations Commission; that the Diocese as a part of the Conscience Crusade on civil rights called for by the bishop enter into an ecumenically organized form of Project Equality to

promote through education and moral persuasion, equality of job opportunity. It asks the Bishop to report the support of this Council to the Interfaith "[Ad] hoc" Committee, of which he is Chairman.[37]

Council members expressed their concern that the commission had fashioned
partial and half-hearted support for a potentially powerful measure. They worried, in other words, that the commission had devised a way to undermine substantive action with its qualified support of Project Equality.

The bishop's earlier attitude toward Project Equality no doubt informed the
council delegates' concerns. Project Equality was a national movement that called
upon cooperating churches to use only those suppliers and contractors who had
expressed their commitment to hiring regardless of race, ethnicity, or religion.
The churches were to send to each supplier and contractor a questionnaire on
which the companies were to specify that they either discriminated or did not.
No cooperating church was to do business with a company that discriminated
or did not return the questionnaire.

John Flanigan, Robert Eckerle, Laura Joseph, and Molly Rush of the Catholic Interracial Council had presented Project Equality to Bishop Wright in the
summer of 1965, and he had refused to take part in it. He would not involve
the Catholic Church in a movement in which the other area churches and synagogues did not participate. He was aware that the St. Louis diocese had done so,
but he perceived their action to be largely a publicity stunt. The Catholic Interracial Council members were dismayed at Wright's position. Father McIlvane
pointed out in a subsequent CIC meeting that "our diocese has an absolute policy
of not dealing with non-union contracts on construction. . . . is it too much that
we now say. . . . 'show us that you have a fair hiring policy . . . '?"[38]

The CIC considered Wright's action to be shameful and the following summer invited him to participate in Project Equality again. If he refused, the CIC
determined that it would picket his annual Labor Day Mass at the Civic Arena,
the same Mass in which he announced his intention to found the Human Relations Council. Bishop Wright offered to discuss Project Equality again with the
CIC, provided that they devise some way of implementing the project without
coercing suppliers and contractors to provide hiring information. The CIC Board
pointed out that the project simply asked the diocese to check out construction
firms' hiring practices as the diocese already checked out the firms' financial
stability.[39]

Bishop Wright's explanation of the events leading up to this resolution left
out any mention of the Catholic Interracial Council. He stated to the Pastoral
Council that a motion to join Project Equality was raised at the Greater Pitts-

burgh Religion and Race Council, an ecumenical organization of Catholics, Protestants, and Jews. Wright was the only member of that council who had authority to speak for the members' "respective judicatories," as all others were simply staff members to the council. Wright therefore called a meeting of the "top level spokesmen" of the various religious bodies and invited the representatives of Project Equality in Chicago to present the project to these people. No people other than Wright who were qualified to speak for their denominations attended, however.[40]

Wright tried once again to get the principals together by inviting them to his house. They came to this meeting and established a committee of Wright, Mr. Vigdor Kavaler of the Jewish Community Council, and Dr. Kincleloe of the Council of Protestant Churches to organize cooperation. A few of the groups, such as the Episcopalians and Methodists, stated that they had to wait until their annual meetings to determine their members' minds on Project Equality, and so Wright asked the Human Relations Commission to do a similar thing with the Pastoral Council. But some of the groups had already expressed reservations about some parts of Project Equality, and Wright could not guarantee that this ecumenical group would endorse the project in its entirety.[41]

The council delegates' questions to Judge Kramer suggested that they worried that neither the HRC nor Wright endorsed Project Equality in its entirety. Senator Kline seized on the phrase "through education and moral persuasion" as evidence of the commission's intention to avoid significant action. He urged the council to reject the resolution because African Americans were fed up with education and moral persuasion. He relayed that when he took the time to go down into the "negro community,"

> they no longer care about me, and they no longer trust me, even though they know I champion their cause, because I am a white man. And they are sick and tired of dillydallying and getting a lot of phony mealy mouthed resolutions. They want some kind of demonstrative action.

He continued that the HRC, the DPC, and the diocese may be "going down the wrong avenue" until such time that they were ready to "take firm positive action that is really going to mean something." Finally, he asked, would someone explain what the Human Relations Commission meant by education and moral persuasion?[42]

An agitated Judge Kramer responded with an attack on the state legislature and the "so-called leaders" of the African-American community. None of the legislation ever passed that addressed the racial problems in Pennsylvania amounted to anything. Could Senator Kline point to "any neighbor[hood] anywhere in this Commonwealth—let alone this city—that is now integrated that wasn't integrated before that [Fair Housing Bill] was passed?" People managed to find loopholes to get around all the bills the legislature passed.[43]

In addition, the "so-called leaders" of the African-American community were negative. "We are downtrodden; we are underprivileged; we are in the ghetto; we are uneducated. Everything is in the negative." The solution to the legislative futility and the negativity of black leaders was "a program of positive thinking." Barring that, Judge Kramer advocated Project Equality, which he then explained to the council.[44]

Senator Kline was uncertain that he understood Judge Kramer correctly. He asked, "Do you mean some diocesan official? That a Bishop or priest or someone is looking over a contractor who is going to get a million dollar contract and find out that if he discriminates . . . we use friendly persuasion and education or does he cut them off?" Kramer replied that hitting them in the pocketbook was moral persuasion. Kline persisted: "Are you saying, then, that the full force and power of this Diocese will be behind turning down all contractors who are not on the approved list?" Kramer hedged somewhat, leaving open the possibility to buy from a supplier who both discriminated and was the only supplier with a particular product. But given a situation with multiple suppliers, the diocese would choose the one that did not discriminate. He then mentioned, as an aside, that Project Equality would concentrate on suppliers only to start and would not press this on contractors.[45]

Edward White was astounded and pleased. He rose to support the resolution, saying, "I have never yet heard that stand being given as the Diocesan stand." He questioned only one other qualifier in the resolution. The resolution called upon the council to support the diocese's joining an "ecumenical form of Project Equality." White had helped draft Project Equality, and he understood that Project Equality had only one form, a Church either bought the whole package or none of it. What exactly did Judge Kramer mean when he said a "form of Project Equality?" Judge Kramer turned the floor over to Thomas Donnelly, who explained that the diocese would not adopt the project unilaterally. If the major Protestant and Jewish bodies did not go along, neither would the diocese. After Bishop Wright gave his background talk on Project Equality, the council approved the resolution.[46]

The council approved the third resolution, endorsement of a program designed to train lay leaders in human relations, called Project Understanding, with no debate. This concluded the Diocesan Pastoral Council's first session. The patterns established in this session remained for the next three years. The council continued to concern itself with the formal practice of faith and with racial issues, as well as a host of other areas that Bishop Wright deemed worthy of discussion in light of the changes that the Church was undergoing in Pittsburgh. The council examined the decline of devotions, the diocesan newspaper, the Social Services Commission, a professional consulting firm's efficiency report on the diocese structure and operations, school mergers, and finances.

But the Diocesan Pastoral Council never strayed too far from racial concerns. Perhaps the most urgent meeting, and certainly the most urgently assembled deliberation, once again addressed race in the wake of Martin Luther King's assassination.

RACE REVISITED

Race relations in the city, and between the city government and African Americans, were tense in the early spring of 1968. The highly touted Renaissance had produced great gains for the central business district to the exclusion and often the detriment of its adjacent African-American neighborhoods. Small incidents of racial violence had occurred in 1967, which, when put in context of the race riots in other major urban settings, worried the establishment.

On March 30, 1968, the American Civil Liberties Union announced that it would represent five African-American students from Oliver High School whom the school had suspended in the wake of a student disciplinary incident the previous November. The school refused to allow the students back until their juvenile court hearings concluded. When the court deemed the students ready to return to school, three of them had become so disillusioned that they would not go back; they "dropped out." The Northside Christian Ministry asked the ACLU to represent these students, and the ACLU reported, "It seems clear that what little confidence the black community had in the Pittsburgh police force was badly shaken by police handling of the Oliver problems."[47] That same day Governor Raymond P. Shafer too expressed his lack of confidence in the Pittsburgh police's ability to handle racial problems when he announced his plans to call out the Pennsylvania National Guard "if local authorities can't control any possible civil rights disorders this summer."[48]

Martin Luther King's assassination four days later sparked riots in many American cities. Students at Pittsburgh's Schenley High School walked out of the building and into the Oakland section of the city, on the edge of the University of Pittsburgh campus. School administrators decided to continue holding classes anyway. African-American community leaders held assemblies in five other city high schools to reduce racial tension. Mayor Joseph M. Barr ordered the city flag to be flown at half staff, and declared an official state of mourning. Officials called off classes at the University of Pittsburgh, Carnegie Mellon University, and Chatham College. Leaders in the predominantly African-American Manchester section of the city expressed despair, and residents expressed anger. "Down with Whitey," said one.[49]

Charles Harris of the United Negro Protest Committee called on African Americans to remain calm: "I appeal to my people that we give this thing time to work itself out. Let's not take to the streets. Lets hold on and work things out together." But many of Pittsburgh's African Americans could wait no longer. The Rev. Junius F. Carter, pastor of the Church of the Holy Cross in Homewood-Brushton, another African-American neighborhood, told a press conference, "We did not cause white racism, the whites did, and they must end it." He continued, "We are not advocating violence, but we want our rights." The *Pittsburgh Press* worried that the assassin had "given stature to those other fanatics who cry, 'burn baby, burn.'"[50]

Young African Americans ran through the streets of the Hill District, breaking into and looting stores on Fifth, Centre, and Wylie avenues. Someone shot a steelworker in the back as he drove to work through Hazelwood, and police arrested sixty-eight people on charges of disorderly conduct and loitering. Jack Stein, the owner of a grocery on Wylie Avenue, reported that vandals broke into his store and destroyed most of his equipment. Rocks and stones rained down on patrol cars responding to calls.[51]

Hundreds of students from the colleges and universities in Pittsburgh's Oakland section marched from Oakland to downtown the next day, where they entered city hall and sang and chanted freedom songs. The mayor's executive secretary, Burrell Cohen, took four of the leaders into the mayor's office, where he accepted a petition that called on the mayor to make "concrete commitments" toward Dr. King's vision of society, to endorse King's Poor People's Campaign, and to acknowledge "with us, that the crime is not merely one committed by a sick man, but a crime committed by a sick, racist and violent society."[52]

The mayor himself was planning law enforcement strategies for that night's anticipated unrest. Governor Shafer, true to his promise of just a few days prior, sent one thousand National Guardsmen to various armories in Pittsburgh, ready to be deployed. He also closed all state liquor stores, taverns, hotel bars, and beer distributors for three days. The violence returned as darkness fell on the city. Police and firemen responded to over thirty-five fire-bombings in the Hill District and lower Northside. Police began firing on looters, wounding at least one man in the shoulder. Another unidentified person fired a shotgun into a store in the Hill, wounding three people who were not looting. The number of people arrested since Friday night grew to two hundred by Sunday morning.[53]

The *Press* blamed "roving bands of black hooligans on a tear" for the destruction of more stores in the Hill District during the second night after King's assassination. They targeted white-owned stores, but also hit some that African Americans ran. WAMO, an African-American-targeted radio station, broadcast repeated pleas for young African Americans to stay off the streets. Charles Harris once again urged calm: "After seeing what happened Friday night in the Hill District—the damage, the confusion, fortunately no loss of life—use your smarts. The life that is saved may be your own." Many African-American leaders walked the streets throughout the night urging people to be calm, to stay at home.[54]

But the city did not remain calm. Arrests topped seven hundred by Monday morning, and the National Guard had left the armories to patrol the streets. The *Press* estimated damage to be in the hundreds of thousands of dollars, and Mayor Barr ordered a 7:00 P.M. to 5:00 A.M. curfew throughout the city. The *Press* demanded an end to "mobocracy" and "anarchy."[55]

The police attempted to stop a planned memorial march from the Hill District to the Point on Sunday morning. Thousands of people, black and white, gathered in the Hill for the march, but Police Superintendent James W. Slusser ordered the march canceled in response to some morning looting. The march route was to take the group right through the downtown business district. Many turned away when they heard the order, but three thousand refused to comply. Blacks and whites joined hands, and marched twelve abreast toward forty steel-helmeted policemen at Centre and Crawford, the site of the new Civic Arena, which had been built on land that once housed thousands of Hill residents.[56]

Safety Director David Craig tried to negotiate with march leaders to stop, but the marchers themselves told their leaders to go to the back if they were afraid to proceed. Byrd Brown, the head of the local NAACP, told the marchers and police that the march would begin despite the police order. Marchers pushed the police line back, but the line did not break. Some officers attacked marchers and newsmen with nightsticks as the marchers began singing the "We are not afraid" verse to "We Shall Overcome." With tensions mounting rapidly, Police Superintendent Slusser and Safety Director Craig asked for a five-minute delay as they reassessed the situation. Police vans and Special Service units pulled in behind the police and opened their doors, ready to cart away marchers.[57]

March leaders linked arms and started to push through, but the police held the line, then attacked and arrested two African-American youths. Finally, the police moved aside and the march began. It proceeded past the Civic Arena, along

Crosstown Boulevard, and onto Sixth Avenue as the marchers continued to sing "We Shall Overcome." The marchers paused before the Federal Building on Grant Street to emphasize the need for greater federal action on civil rights, and moved to the Point for a memorial service.[58]

Byrd Brown was among the many who spoke at the Point. He relayed that the news media had asked him to cool things down. "I will not do it," he said. "I did not create the situation that exists today. I will not suffer any of the blame for it." He continued that King's dream was still alive, that those surviving must give it new meaning. "I want history to write that we not only eked out a meager existence, but that we did prevail and we did overcome."[59]

That evening, 1,100 Guardsmen occupied the Hill District, while residents lay siege to Police Station number 2 on Centre Avenue, showering police and Guardsmen with rocks and bottles. The Guard was finally able to enforce the curfew by midnight. By Tuesday, over 6,000 Guardsmen and state troopers roamed the city, concentrating in the Hill, the Northside, and Homewood-Brushton. But the city quieted down quickly enough for Mayor Barr to lift the curfew on Wednesday evening and send the troops home on Thursday.[60]

The Mayor's Special Task Force on Civil Disturbances later reported that police arrested a total of 926 people in the course of the rioting, and it estimated total damages and law enforcement costs to be in the millions of dollars.[61] Bishop Wright called a special meeting of the Pastoral Council to devise a strategy to deal with the problems the rioting revealed. Before the general discussion, he asked the delegates to form committees to address and come up with possible courses of action for diocesan departments to address these problems, so that the council might discuss and vote on concrete proposals.

The Pastoral Council met in the middle of June, fully two months after the Pittsburgh riots. Bishop Wright delayed the meeting so that the council could structure the Pittsburgh diocesan response within the framework of the American bishops' proposals, which the U.S. Catholic Conference and National Council of Catholic Bishops formulated in the wake of the Kerner Commission report.

The council meeting began with a forty-minute presentation from Arden Melzor, assistant professor of mental health in the University of Pittsburgh's Social Welfare and Social Work school. Melzor read a scathing critique of the Kerner Commission report, wherein he pointed out that the commission focused overwhelmingly on more efficient and intrusive law enforcement programs as the primary way to resolve racial conflict in American cities. Melzor likened this approach to an attempt to implement flood control by making evacuation procedures more efficient. He found even the panel's recognition of America's enduring racism, a conclusion that had much impressed the American bishops, to be wanting. The primary cause of racial injustice was class inequality, in Melzor's view. The most effective solution to this problem was extensive state economic planning that included income maintenance.[62]

The delegates had no response to the presentation. When the moderator opened the floor to questions and discussion, Monsignor Meenan suggested that Mr. Melzor had read his work very quickly, too quickly for anyone to digest, and requested that members be given a written copy. The chair agreed, thanked Mr. Melzor, and moved on to the next business. Bishop Wright later noted that despite Professor Melzor's particular analysis, he would like the delegates to address ways to alleviate racism in the Pittsburgh diocese. Wright acknowledged the importance of Professor Melzor's class-based analysis, which Wright deemed a "materialist" assessment, but he wished the delegates to address racism as a human and moral concern.[63]

Wright moved, at the discussion's outset, to place this meeting firmly in the Catholic religious context. This was no foray into important yet peripheral ground for a Catholic Pastoral Council to address, for racism was "heresy." Lest anyone miss this crucial point, Wright gave it special emphasis:

> I should not care to take up the battle on any other premise than that of heresy. It is my business to fight heresy, and, therefore, the premise of whatever we do in any other matter is always that it is contrary to the truth and teaching, and the will of God as revealed in Christ Jesus.

He stressed that each diocese, parish, Church agency or organization must ask itself whether "every" aspect of its work supports "truly open, Christian behavior, or does it tend to reinforce the walls of separation and the heresy of white superiority.[64]

At the same time, Wright did not want anyone on the council to address specifically any diocesan shortcomings on the issue of race. He asserted that all Americans were racist, and that no delegate or alternate should point this out about any particular individual or group. This was no doubt in response to the Catholic Interracial Council's most effective tactic: picketing. Bishop Wright himself had founded the Human Relations Council under the pressure of potential pickets at his annual Labor Day Mass, and the CIC had used the tactic in a number of other situations.[65]

Though the council addressed many resolutions, most of the ensuing discussion focused on six resolutions introduced by the various committees. The first called on the diocese to support a parish "twinning" program, wherein a suburban parish would adopt an inner-city parish in order to help the inner-city parish with expertise and finances. The second called for the development of a priest-training program to educate priests about racism. The third asked Bishop Wright to appoint two full-time staff members to the Human Relations Commission. The fourth focused on the formation of a black Catholic prep school designed to provide African-American students with one additional year of high school to shore up any weaknesses that might prohibit them from gaining acceptance at quality colleges. The fifth called for the establishment of an integrated educational program to teach priests *and* laity about racism, and the last urged the diocese to adopt Project Equality. The council passed some of these and rejected others. In so doing the council continued its ambivalent embrace of social justice as manifest in racial justice efforts.

The council readily endorsed and passed the first resolution, which called upon suburban parishes to twin with inner-city parishes. The diocese had nine parishes that qualified as inner-city parishes in need of help, according to Bishop Wright. Further efforts to specify twinning actions, such as exchanging priests, commentators, and lectors, met with mixed response. Bishop Wright flatly rejected one delegate's suggestion that parishes exchange families on a temporary basis because canon law strictly forbade "personal parishes." The discussion moved to other resolutions before the council made clear any specific actions that twinning might entail.[66]

The council had more trouble with the second resolution, which the council discussed in light of its conclusion that local priests simply did not preach about or understand racism. Monsignor Heinrich observed that priests were "afraid of upsetting our parishioners" with sermons on helping blacks, but that "it could be approached very delicately, I think, along with the help we should give to the starving and the naked and the poor in general." When the discussion foundered on specifics and a delegate suggested tabling it, Bishop Wright interjected that this topic was too important to lose at that point. The delegates then modified and passed a resolution that recommended that

> the Bishop invoke the clergy of the diocese for a general conference in which the moral and other problems of the racist mentality will be presented to them by people of every color and background as the beginning of an education program.

Senator Kline introduced the third resolution and elicited great debate. It recommended that Bishop Wright hire two full-time staff members to aid the Human Relations Commission in its work. Kline recommended that one be a priest and the other a layman trained in sociology. Some delegates interpreted this to be an attack on the HRC and opposed this meaning. Others criticized it as too expensive. Still others worried that this resolution intended to change the HRC from a "fact-finding" to an "action" commission. The vast majority of delegates who spoke opposed the resolution, and Bishop Wright endorsed consideration of cost in any resolution introduced.[67]

Sensing that the council was about to kill his resolution, Kline rose again to defend it. He began by expressing his confusion over the turn of the discussion. "I have a difficult time understanding how anybody in this hall could read into that very simple resolution all the things I have heard," he stated. He explained that he wanted a priest and layman to serve because only a priest could gain the clergy's respect, and because he wanted someone trained in this area. He responded to the money question with particular emotion.

> Now, on the question of money. We were called here, and in addition to the regular call, had an urgent letter from the Bishop to be here at great personal sacrifice because of the gravity of this problem, and I can only assume from all that, that this is a very grave problem. And this hardly seems the place to cut short a program because we are worried about money.[68]

Bishop Wright quickly interjected that he did not intend to kill this suggestion on financial grounds and asked that no one consider his earlier statement to be a suggestion that he was so inclined. Further debate ensued, and then the council voted. The chair declared the council to be evenly divided on this, and called upon delegates to stand to indicate their votes. Before this vote took place, however, a delegate suggested that some of the alternates could be moved into the delegate section to vote for their absent delegates. Much shuffling took place, and then the final vote. The council passed the resolution by the narrow margin of 29–27.[69]

This debate marked the turning point in the meeting, as the council voted to kill, table, or withdraw all but one of the resolutions that followed. The council discussed the prep school for African-American students very briefly and then voted on the resolution. The chairman called the voice vote in favor of the resolution. But a delegate disagreed and called for a repeat of the standing vote taken on the HRC staffing resolution. The council voted down the resolution by 24–17.[70]

The next resolution called for the formation of educational teams of blacks and whites to visit suburban parishes and educate them about racism. Much discussion about what and whom the teams would teach followed. One sister insisted that the teams would do best to teach "colored" people "health habits, in sewing, things like that." The transcripts indicate that the discussion simply moved on to other resolutions with no action taken on this at all.[71]

The final resolution concerned the Chancery and Project Equality. Though Bishop Wright had received the Pastoral Council's strong endorsement of Project Equality at the council's original meeting exactly one year before, the diocese had not yet begun to follow its principles. But the diocese was prepared to comply with an ecumenical effort that was set to begin in July. Bishop Wright expressed his concern that a strong endorsement of Project Equality at this point might indicate to some that the Catholic diocese did not support the ecumenical Project Equality about to get under way. Father Sites, the resolution sponsor, was confused and dismayed. He would certainly withdraw the resolution if Wright thought any confusion might result, and he had not intended to undermine the diocese's participation.[72]

Father Hugo shared Father Sites's confusion over how an endorsement might undermine Project Equality. Bishop Wright's reasoning was at best unclear. Given his strong identification with the labor movement and the unions' continuing resistance to integration, his motives may have been less than sincere. This idea takes on added possibilities in light of the direction of the discussion prior to Bishop Wright's intervention, which had focused on the unions. Pittsburgh unions had a long history of either excluding African Americans from membership outright or failing to extend opportunities to join. The result was that major construction projects in the city and region included few, if any, African-American workers. Recent building projects at Carnegie Mellon University and Chatham College resulted in public protests over this issue, with students and faculty lying down before bulldozers in an effort to halt work and force the institutions to demand integrated workforces. The NAACP had released a national study documenting racially exclusionary policies in the construction trades. Father Sites withdrew his resolution.[73]

THE COUNCIL SESSION DEVOTED TO THE ELIMINATION OF THE "heresy" of racism represented the clearest official embodiment of the Church's new emphasis on social justice. That the Catholic Interracial Council more ardently supported racial justice than did the Pastoral Council, and that many Pastoral Council members resisted efforts to promote racial justice entirely, reflects the limits of the transformation in American Catholicism by 1968. But the very existence of the council, and its coming to session in light of racial injustice, suggest that the official Church in Pittsburgh had undergone a remarkable transition. Not only did Bishop Wright and those members present at the meetings consider opposition to racism to be vital to the official Church's acting as a body, but they did not root any of the solutions they debated in the devotional tradition prevalent only a decade and a half before. No one suggested novenas for racial justice, or rosaries to stop inequality. All discussion centered on what action the diocese should or should not take to address race issues. At the same time, the Pastoral Council was simply dumbfounded when presented with a materialist solution to racism. Catholics had not abandoned their opposition to materialism and could not imagine such a resolution to this moral concern.

Furthermore, the council itself reflected Bishop Wright's determination to introduce more democratic, or at least consultative, mechanisms in the determination of official policy. Wright proved adept at steering the Diocesan Pastoral Council to provide the advice he sought, and he certainly would not be pushed in directions he did not intend to go, but he clearly sought to foster an active Church committed to social justice in the Pittsburgh region. The strengths and limits of such a model were evident in the DPC work, and became even more so in the diocese's next significant initiative—the diocesan synod.

CHAPTER SEVEN

Devotional Catholicism in
the Wake of Vatican II

Of what use is it, my brethren, if a man claims to have faith, and has no deeds to show for it? Can faith save him then? Here is a brother, here is a sister, going naked, without means to secure their daily food; if one of you says to them, Go in peace, warm yourselves and take your fill, without providing for their bodily needs, of what use is it? Thus faith, if it has no deeds to show for itself, has lost its own principle of life.

—JAMES 2:14–17

Our practice of religion is too often equated with religious pictures, crucifixes, and other material things; or in lifeless formulas such as prayer at fixed times of the day, novenas, abstinence on Friday, Mass on Sunday without any participation in the Great Act of Sacrifice; and, worst of all, our running away from those places where the Catholic Action should be, or from those persons whom we should be embracing in brotherly love.

—MOTHER VIOLA, 1966, DCCW CONVENTION

THOUGH STRONG EVIDENCE POINTS TO LAYMEN AND LAYWOMEN'S increasing rejection of devotional behaviors in the 1950s, Church officials did not acknowledge any change until the mid-1960s. It is not clear whether Church officials did not see the decline before then or simply chose not to discuss it openly. But in the years after the Council they noted the decline with alarm, and sought to understand and arrest it. This chapter seeks both to chart the further demise of lay devotional behavior and to explore the public response to this knowledge. It focuses on the Diocesan Pastoral Council's investigation of the decline as well as Diocesan Council of Catholic Women and Holy Name Society actions, the Liturgical Commission's continuing efforts to transform Catholic worship practices, and the structure of devotional practices in the parishes. We have explored the causes of the decline in devotions already. This discussion focuses on diocesan officials' discovery of lay disengagement and their attempts to arrest it.

NOTING THE DECLINE IN DEVOTIONS

No one who discussed devotions in the Pittsburgh diocese in the late 1960s doubted that parishioners practiced them less than before. All debate and discussion focused on why devotions declined, how the diocese and parishes might revive them, and even, for some, whether devotions merited popularity at all. Though everyone seemed to agree that devotions declined, the Diocesan Pastoral Council (DPC) formed a subcommittee to determine to what extent this was so and why. The subcommittee conducted a survey of retreat houses and parish pastors to ascertain the state of devotional practice, and this survey indicated that parishioners had begun to abandon devotions before 1968.

Seventy-two percent of the parishes and missions responded to the survey, and they reported an overall decline in devotions. Roughly 64 percent of the pastors who responded to the survey sponsored a retreat of some kind (for men, women, or youth), but 26 percent of these pastors perceived retreats in their parishes to be declining in popularity. Another 15 percent considered their retreats to be improving, and 59 percent perceived them to be about the same. These figures meant that 54 percent of all responding parishes either held no retreats or considered their retreats' popularity to be in decline.[1] The decline was more severe among male parishioners, as the survey report stated that more women's retreats than men's were improving (though it provided no data to support this).

A separate survey taken of retreat masters at eight area retreat houses reported similar results. Of the eight houses, five saw a decline in retreatants over the past five years (1962–67), only two saw increases, and one reported both a decline and an increase. The retreat masters saw a combination of reasons for this decline, though they emphasized most heavily the poor promotions that retreats received in the parishes and increased lay involvement in other areas. The retreat masters uniformly dismissed the possibility that the preaching that retreatants heard while on retreat had any influence on their decisions not to return, and did not address explicitly whether some other aspect of retreats did not attract the laity.[2]

The Benedictines at Saint Vincent's Archabbey and the Holy Name Society retreat leaders took a slightly more sophisticated approach to their own survey two years later. They too had become alarmed at the decline in the laity attending retreats at summer sessions and sought to find out why it had happened. Attendance at Saint Vincent College summer retreats had fallen by over 50 percent between 1960 and 1970, from roughly 2,000 retreatants each summer to fewer than 1,000. The Saint Vincent survey targeted two groups of laity to discern answers to the question. They surveyed 502 laymen who continued to attend retreats regularly and a group of 250 lay leaders that the Pittsburgh diocese had identified for them. Both groups remained active in the Church and their membership may even have overlapped a bit. But the lay leaders favored more "modern" retreats in greater numbers than the retreatants, and they were less interested in traditional retreats. (See fig. 7.1.)

In addition to seeking to understand what kinds of retreat these two groups of laity wanted, the survey asked what kinds of devotions each group wished to participate in while on retreat. The results suggest strongly that the retreatants remained far more interested in devotions generally than did the lay leaders. By 1970, only a third of active lay Catholic leaders sought holy hours and benedictions, and the numbers for rosary recitation, Stations of the Cross, Bible vigils, and adoration dropped below even those levels. The results indicate that even when active lay Catholics were interested in retreats, they did not wish to participate in devotional rituals. (See fig. 7.2.)

The DPC devotional survey revealed that attendance at those devotions that constituted the mainstay of the pre–Vatican II religious practice, such as first Friday devotions, novenas, and forty-hours devotions, was declining in more parishes than it was increasing. In fact, attendance at devotional liturgies declined in at least twice as many parishes as it increased in 1968. (See table 7.1.)

But not all Catholics abandoned devotions. A significant minority of pastors perceived participation in devotions to be about the same in 1968 as it had been in previous years, and a generally smaller but still significant number of priests believed devotions to be on the rise. Perhaps the most interesting question that this survey inspires, but which the surviving summary report cannot answer, is which parishes saw the decline and which did not?

Despite the evidence in 1968 that devotions did not decline in all parishes, all the examinations of devotional life that the subcommittee solicited and the discussion in the Diocesan Pastoral Council took as their premise that the decline was universal.

FIGURE 7.1   Lay Retreat Survey: Retreatants and Lay Leaders (1970)

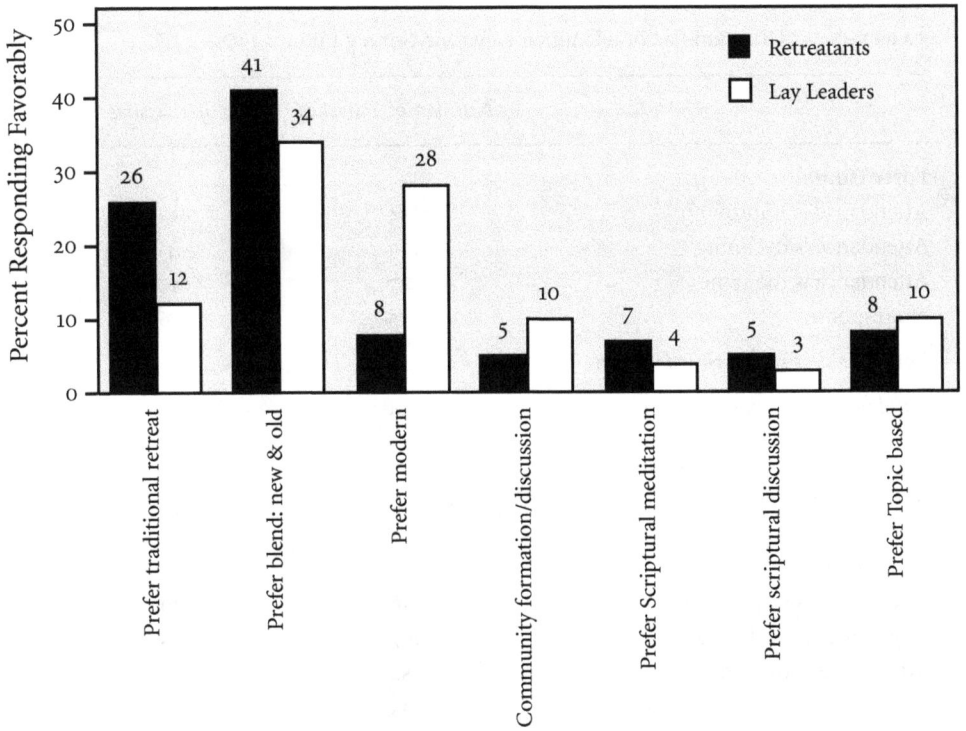

Source: Saint Vincent Lay Retreats file # 48c, Lay Summer Retreats box, Saint Vincent Archabbey Archives.

FIGURE 7.2   Retreats Should Include Specific Exercises
(1970 Survey of Retreatants and Lay Leaders)

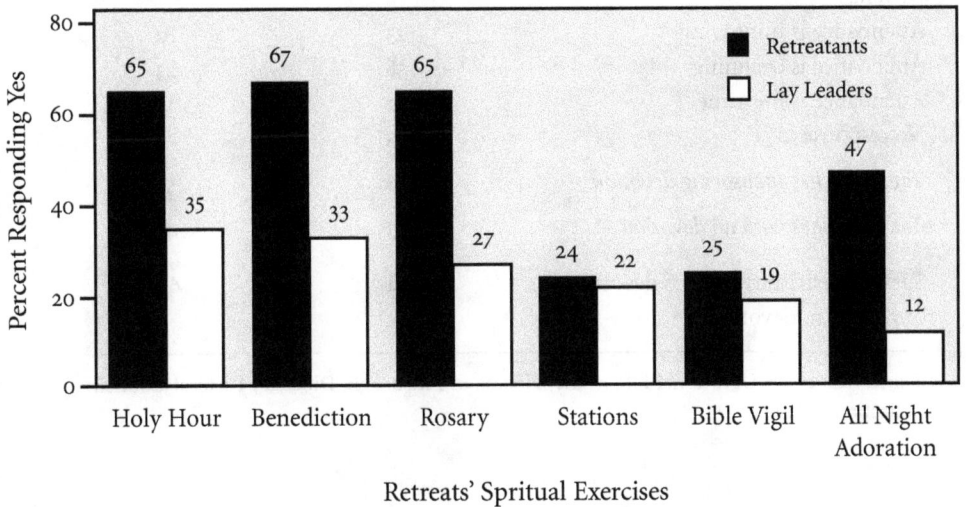

TABLE 7.1   Diocesan Pastoral Council Devotion Survey Results, 1968

	Number of Parishes	% of Parishes
Forty Hours		
Attendance is improving	54	22
Attendance is declining	109	43
Attendance is the same	47	19
No response	15	6
Total parishes sponsoring devotion	225	90
Total parishes with no devotion	24	10
Surveyed parishes with no devotion or decline in devotions	133	53
First Friday		
Attendance is improving	49	20
Attendance is declining	107	43
Attendance is the same	52	21
No response	15	6
Total parishes sponsoring devotion	223	90
Total parishes with no devotion	26	10
Surveyed parishes with no devotion or decline in devotions	133	53
Novenas		
Attendance is improving	23	10
Attendance is declining	58	23
Attendance is the same	42	17
No response	13	5
Total parishes sponsoring devotion	136	55
Total parishes with no devotion	113	45
Surveyed parishes with no devotion or decline in devotions	171	69

Source: Survey on Devotional Life in the Diocese of Pittsburgh, Diocesan Pastoral Council Collection, HADP.

In addition to conducting the survey, the committee sought explanations from various people for the decline in devotions, and then submitted its own analysis. The examinations and analyses the committee solicited and produced itself represent the first explicit study of devotions in the Pittsburgh diocese since at least 1950. No one attempted to fit devotions into the larger context of Catholic life while they flourished, though the laity learned from a wide range of sources that devotions were beneficial, expedient, and even necessary.

The explanations generally agreed that parishioners had undergone, or were currently undergoing, a dramatic transformation in their perceptions of God, themselves, their Church, and the world. They also agreed generally that popular devotions grew from *popular* cultural practices, often with the hierarchy's encouragement, but sometimes not, and that they occupied no official place in official Catholic teaching. The hierarchy did not give retreats, adoration, benediction, and rosary recitation the same status that it bestowed on the Mass, confession, or other sacraments. Yet the hierarchy considered devotions to be in some way intrinsic to proper Catholic formation and deportment. The Rev. Raymond Utz, the Diocesan Spiritual Activities Commission spiritual adviser, noted, "It goes without saying that these devotions are both valid and necessary." The Devotion Committee at least attempted to say why they were valid and necessary when it concluded that "The purpose of true religious devotions is to intensify the soul's dedication to know, love, and serve God."[3]

If the explanations did not all articulate the devotions' purpose, they generally agreed that devotional popularity depended upon forces within and outside of the Church itself. Catholic liturgical reforms filled the void the old liturgy had left with parishioners; they no longer needed "extra-Mass" liturgies for a rich and relevant Catholic experience. The material prosperity Americans enjoyed after World War II filled the physical and material void that poorer Catholics had sought to mitigate through petitional devotions. They no longer had to ask for divine intervention to achieve financial stability or physical healing.

Many explanations for the decline emphasized non-Catholic, or nonreligious causes. For example, the Devotional Committee stressed the Catholics' rise from the laboring and "subjected" class, the relative absence of material and physical needs, and increased competition for leisure time. J. Richard Gomory argued in his explanation of the devotional decline that wars, especially wars that placed significant numbers of Catholics in "battle areas," drew Catholics to "weekly holy hour devotions for the boys overseas." Vietnam did not qualify— there were not enough combatants—and devotional life suffered. The Rev. Raymond Utz expanded Gomory's explanation to suggest that devotions thrived during periods of great distress and need: "War, depression, sickness, even strikes, stimulate these practices."[4] These factors would have dampened devotional participation even had the Second Vatican Council not met.

But these same people rooted other explanations for the devotional demise in a changed religious sensibility as well. The Devotional Committee determined that the new Mass met crucial lay psychological, social, and theological needs to participate in the Church's public prayer life which the old liturgy did not. Raymond Utz noted a "growing apathy toward religion" among all Americans as they shifted from an "ideational value-system" to a "sensate value-system," a more sophisticated theology among the laity which went beyond a "giver-receiver" relationship with God, a new "more refined taste in matters spiritual" which stressed prayers of praise, the correction of devotional abuses (too frequent benediction), and the decline in popularity of those devotions that emphasized quantification (the accumulation of indulgences).[5]

THE MASS IN A POSTDEVOTIONAL CHURCH

The explanations for devotional decline noted a changed lay understanding of religious expression and sensibility, and rooted these changes in the laity's new social and political experiences. To a lesser degree, the explanations noted the laity's greater satisfaction with the newer Catholicism emerging from efforts in the local parishes, lay organizations, the diocesan Liturgical Commission, and, especially, Vatican II. The Second Vatican Council gave a coherent voice to a strong reform impulse among the laity and hierarchy which transformed American Catholicism. A closer examination of the messages Catholics received and the behaviors they undertook in these organizations and parishes clarifies the process by which Catholics came to abandon devotions, and illuminates the new conception of Catholicism from which that abandonment resulted.

The Liturgical Commission entered the Vatican Council years at the forefront of reform, pushing recalcitrant priests toward a more democratic, informed, and participatory liturgy. Bishop Wright, who was largely sympathetic and clearly supportive of the commission, often had to restrain the commission members in their efforts. He was not always successful. But the commission changed its role as well as its composition in 1966, so that over the next few years it served as a "moderate" reform organization that more often criticized reform advocates than entrenched resisters. Though the Liturgical Commission had ardently and actively pushed for a new liturgical understanding and practice in its early years to complement more fully the changing lay religious sensibility, by

1966 the forces it helped unleash had largely passed it by. The dynamo of reform activity moved to the parishes and to the national bishops organization.

The commission continued to present themes it had advocated for half a decade. The laity must participate in and understand the Mass, they must experience internal participation through meaningful external actions. In February 1967, for example, the *Newsletter* argued against introducing a cultivated "sacral language" into the Mass. The commission members worried that some pastors and lectors were attempting to subvert the vernacular movement by creating a sacred English that differed in diction and voice from everyday English. The *Newsletter* announced that

> our position is still that the most sacral language, the speech understood best by God and man, is the language of the commonplace. Language on this level is the "leveler" that reduces all to a common denominator that must be pleasing to God, whether Father, Son or Holy Spirit.[6]

Similarly, the Liturgical Commission pushed for music in Mass that everyone could sing, and urged pastors and choirmasters to eliminate special hymns that originated in the cloistered abbeys.[7]

The *Newsletter* announced and explained the introduction of three major Mass transformations in this period immediately after the Council, each of which introduced more English into the liturgy. In June 1967 the American bishops introduced changes that so reduced the singing at "High Mass" that a distinction between High and Low Mass disappeared officially. This new Mass also reduced the Communion interaction to a shorter, simpler exchange of words. Once the *Newsletter* fully explained the new liturgy it declared that the bishops would introduce no major changes for a long time.[8]

But just four months later the *Newsletter* explained a new role for choirs and Holy Week revisions that constituted a "RADICAL departure from the ways of old," and which confirmed that "our liturgical progress has been so rapid, beyond all expectations, that what was considered progress last year must now be subjugated to just another step in the ladder of liturgical progress."[9] On January 1, 1969, a new "English" Canon, which the bishops designated "Eucharistic Prayers," took effect for all American parishes.[10]

As the Mass became more and more accessible for ordinary Catholics, more understandable, more in line with principles applied universally, the older devotions became less comprehensible. Some, which had long contradicted official canon law, could not withstand the scrutiny Church officials focused on all formal rituals. Efforts to bring them into line liturgically and theologically necessarily entailed changes in some devotions.

But the decline in devotions' popularity did not result so much from official liturgical scrutiny as it did from changed lay perspectives. It came more as a result of the new sensibility that the emphasis on more democratic and participatory liturgies reinforced. Church officials were in a sense catching up to the laity on these matters. The Liturgical Commission helped to meet this new lay understanding of Catholicism through its reform efforts, despite the commission's increasing efforts to moderate the pace and extent of the transformation.

Devotional participation owed its decline as much to changes within those organizations that had long supported devotions as to those that grew up outside the devotional tradition, however. These organizations, such as the Holy Name Society and the Diocesan Council of Catholic Women, came to focus heavily on social justice in part because of the influence that reform bodies such as the Liturgical Commission and the *Pittsburgh Catholic* wielded. But Bishop Wright also steered them consciously toward change.

DEVOTIONAL ORGANIZATIONS IN A POSTDEVOTIONAL CHURCH

Members of the Diocesan Council of Catholic Women met each year for a convention in which they listened to speakers, attended Mass, and interacted in workshops. They produced a yearbook for each convention and dedicated either the book, the year, or a large body of already recited prayers to a person, group, or cause. The DCCW's annual convention yearbook dedications provide a concise outline of the Diocesan Council of Catholic Women's transformation from devotions to social justice, and then, later, its demise as an organization. (See table 7.2.)

A brief examination of these "dedications" sets the tone and parameters of the transformation that the DCCW underwent. The members worked each year from the organization's revival in 1954 until the middle of the 1960s to collect large amounts of prayers for the bishop himself, so that he might expend the power of those prayers toward increased vocations or some other goal that he chose. These gifts of prayers reflected the members' heavy devotional behaviors and the deference this devotional faith produced for ecclesiastical elites. The members donated prayers to the ordinary of the diocese, but limited the bishop's ability to apply them as he chose by further specifying that he should invest them toward garnering additional vocations only. Bishop Dearden was not to use these prayers for world peace or domestic harmony, but rather for

TABLE 7.2   Diocesan Council of Catholic Women Yearbook Dedications

Year	Prayer/Actions	Total Prayers	Recipient/Cause
1954	Rosaries	Many thousands	Bishop Dearden, vocations
1955	Rosaries	20,197	Bishop Dearden, vocations
1956	Rosaries	24,855	Bishop Dearden, vocations
1957	Rosaries	37,051	Bishop Dearden, vocations
1958	Hail Marys	Undisclosed	Bishop Dearden, vocations
1959	Rosaries	Undisclosed	Bishop Wright, his intentions
1960	Rosaries	Undisclosed	Bishop Wright, his intentions
1961	Hail Marys	Undisclosed	Bishop Wright, his intentions
1962	Hail Marys	Undisclosed	Bishop Wright, his intentions
1963	Hail Marys	Undisclosed	Bishop Wright, his intentions
1964	Hail Marys	Undisclosed	Bishop Wright, his intentions
1965	Hail Marys	Undisclosed	Bishop Wright, his intentions
1966	Hail Marys	Undisclosed	Bishop Wright, his intentions
1967	Hail Marys	Undisclosed	Bishop Wright and clergy
1968	Hail Marys	1,000,000	Bishop Wright and brothers and sisters
1969	Hail Marys	1,000,000	Bishop Wright and brothers and sisters
1970	Hail Marys/prayers & cooperation	1,000,000	Bishop Leonard /Auxiliary Bishop Bosco
1971	Prayers and cooperation	Undisclosed	Bishop Leonard for his prayers
1972	Prayers	Undisclosed	Msgr. Schultz on 25th anniversary
1973	Prayers and cooperation	Undisclosed	Priests of diocese
1974	Dedication		Sanctity of all Life
1975	Dedication		Mother Elizabeth Ann Seton
1983	Prayers	Undisclosed	Fr. John Price (DCCW moderator)
1984	Hail Marys	1,000,000	Bishop Bevilacqua
1985	Dedication	Undisclosed	Youth of World (UN Youth Year)
1986	Dedication	Undisclosed	Mother, Good Counsel/Past Presidents
1987	Dedication	Undisclosed	Fr. John Price, year after death
1988	Love, prayers, respect	Undisclosed	Bishop Donald Wuerl

Source: Diocesan Council of Catholic Women Annual Convention Yearbook.

the enlistment of more priests to hear confessions and lead Catholics in devotional rituals.

The DCCW broadened its efforts with the arrival of John Wright as bishop in 1959. Though women still gave their hours of prayer to the bishop, he could do what he wished with them. (No evidence of what he actually did remains.) By 1967 the DCCW members dedicated their prayers to the clergy as well as to Bishop Wright, which reflected the second widening in the members' scope of concern. In 1968 and 1969, the members prayed on behalf of Bishop Wright and all other Catholics in the diocese, and further specified in 1968 that they did so that "we may ever see Christ in one another and love one another as brothers and sisters."[11] These two years, 1968 and 1969, mark the climax of the DCCW's concern for social justice. In addition to the widely addressed dedications, the DCCW newsletter boasted that 700 women attended the 1968 and 1969 conventions, and even more remarkably, 350 women attended the 1969 annual business meeting.[12]

Bishop Wright moved on to Rome in 1969 and his replacement, Bishop Leonard, did not share Wright's keen interest in, and capacity to inspire Catholics to work toward, social justice. Because the Diocesan Council of Catholic Women more than any other lay organization followed the ordinary's directions, the DCCW quickly reverted to a more devotional mode. Members donated prayers only to Bishop Leonard and his newly appointed auxiliary in 1970, and to Bishop Leonard alone in 1971. The 1971 dedication reflected the DCCW's own troubles, as members donated all their prayers to Leonard in the hope that he in turn would devote his prayers back to them.

Even this later devotional tenor carried some of the postdevotional influences, however. DCCW members devoted their prayers to the bishops only in each bishop's first year of service in the diocese, and dedicated other years for causes (against abortion) or people more closely connected to the DCCW itself (moderators, past presidents). But by this time the organization had withered substantially. The devotional emphasis did not attract new members or hold old ones. The DCCW was largely a paper organization in the 1980s with little influence on women's lives in the Pittsburgh diocese.[13]

The move from a devotional emphasis to one on social justice within the Diocesan Council of Catholic Women reveals an important part of this transformation in the Pittsburgh diocese. Though the DCCW had from its revitalization in 1954 emphasized Catholic Action, members had always balanced this with a strong emphasis on devotions such as adoration, retreats, and especially rosary recitation. In addition, the Catholic Action emphasis had centered largely on charitable enterprises and issues that tended to support rather than question ex-

TABLE 7.3   DCCW Annual Retreat Offerings

Year	Number of Retreats	Houses	Total Retreat Days
1955	6	6	18
1956	7	7	21
1957	7	7	22
1958	7	7	22
1959	7	7	21
1960	7	7	21
1961	5	6	15
1962	9	6	27
1963	7	6	21
1964	5	5	15
1965	8	4	24
1966	22	3*	66
1967	24	1	68
1968	32	1	76
1969	25	1	71
1970	42	1	66
1971	17	2	25

*This marks the first year that the Cenacle Retreat House opened for retreats.
Source: *The Echo*, newsletter of the DCCW.

isting institutions and structures (such as hosting foreign students and working for traffic safety). But the DCCW shifted the balance quickly away from devotions during the years the Vatican Council met and by the mid-1960s came to focus almost exclusively on social justice.

The DCCW moved rapidly away from devotions once the Council got under way, so that even by 1963 its newsletter recommended only retreats from among the range of devotional behaviors that it had once supported. Over the course of the next few years, even the number of retreats from which women had to choose declined. (See table 7.3.)

The decline in retreat offerings reversed slightly in 1965, and offerings then rose dramatically in 1966 when Bishop Wright finally succeeded in bringing the Religious of the Cenacle, an order of sisters devoted exclusively to providing retreats for women, to the diocese. But even this retreat revival reflected the new emphasis on acting in, rather than apart from, the modern world. Bishop Wright and the sisters established a retreat center in the heart of the city's Oakland section, on its busiest street, so that women would not have to travel far to attend retreats. Wright relayed to the DCCW women at the 1965 "business meeting" that he and the Religious of the Cenacle had considered "whether it was necessary to locate the retreat house in the country to have a closeness to nature," but decided instead to locate it "in the heart of the diocese which is the Cathedral, thus the Fifth Avenue Address."[14]

Though Wright reported the issue of location only in the context of physical convenience, that women would not find it "hard to get there on snowy Friday afternoons," the choice clearly had implications for the changing perceptions of the Church's role in the world. If until the time of the Council retreats had meant a complete as possible distancing from the modern world, an escape from those very distractions and temptations that made retreats necessary, placing the retreat house in the center of the diocese (and the city of Pittsburgh) represented a strong statement about the nature of the modern retreat. Retreatants at Saint Vincent College in Latrobe or Seton Hill College in Greensburg separated themselves physically as well as spiritually from urban life. These locations provided close proximity to nature in pastoral settings. Bishop Wright and the Religious of the Cenacle considered and then rejected this option in favor of one that stressed connections to the modern world. The new Cenacle retreat house could not get any closer to the urban setting that epitomized "modern" living, and therefore reflected the post–Vatican II efforts to engage this world.

Furthermore, Bishop Wright recast the retreat's role in light of the Council, so that in 1967 he considered retreats essential to the successful implementation of the Conciliar decrees. He told the members assembled at the annual meeting that the Council discussions reflected the bishops' intense concern for the role and place of the laity in the modern Church, and that the new role formulated in the Council depended upon a "devoted, informed, and devout laity." He continued,

> The purpose of the Retreat Movement is to develop this class of laymen, as an elite in the life of the Church. If the Retreat Movement is not successful in this effort, the Council will have no effect on history. To the extent the Council depends on the layman to help make the Church effective in the modern world, so it depends on the Retreat Movement to give us the kind of laymen who are interested and capable of carrying out this mission.[15]

And yet women did not flock to retreats. Though firm attendance numbers are unavailable, the *Echo* asked DCCW members in 1967, "Why are not more people taking advantage of the facilities and benefits of our retreat houses?"[16]

and the Cenacle reduced its offerings by more than half in 1971. The answer to the *Echo*'s question may have been the same as it was before the Council, that women who had demanding responsibilities at home found retreats difficult to schedule. It is also possible that women connected retreats with the devotional style of religious practice that they had come to reject at least a decade earlier.

The DCCW effected this transition to social justice primarily through re-placing its former emphasis on devotions with greater interest in the kinds of Catholic Action it had practiced for a decade and, later, its efforts to analyze criti-cally society's fundamental structure and organization. The DCCW came to ana-lyze society critically over a period of years. The process began with analyses of fundamental inequalities in other societies, particularly in Latin America and India, and the issue of race in America. After working to alleviate the suffering in Latin America and India and seeking a fairer society for all races in Pittsburgh, the women in the DCCW examined their own situations. They did so tentatively and briefly, however, before returning to the more deferential devotional empha-sis in the middle of the 1970s.

The DCCW addressed Latin America regularly in the 1960s. The National Council of Catholic Women launched a nationwide study program on Latin America in 1963 which broached such topics as land reform, urban popula-tion explosions and the poverty it contained, and movements toward democ-racy.[17] The *Echo* told members a few months later that "the world is truly becom-ing smaller. We can no longer ignore the fact that there are problems in Latin America, Africa, Europe, the Near East."[18] The Pittsburgh diocese established a mission in Chimbote, Peru, and the DCCW worked regularly to send clothes and other goods there.[19] The DCCW also supported national Catholic efforts to send food and clothing to Latin America through such programs as the Madonna Plan. This operation supported the efforts of missionaries such as Sister "Dulce" who distributed milk to the Al Agados children of Bahia, Brazil, who lived in huts built upon the garbage dumps of the city.[20]

Dorothy Baker, a Daughters of the Heart of Mary missionary, told DCCW members at the 1964 annual business meeting that women in India had "not yet gotten full equality with men and they are going to have to get up and fight for their rights." The members regularly sent crates of books to India as part of the "Books for India" campaign (originally the catchier "Books for Bombay") to help Indian women "advance" and because Indian women could not use other libraries.[21]

DCCW members concerned themselves primarily with race relations, though, and came to their understanding of inequality chiefly in that realm. Their awareness that American society was not "just" came gradually, peaked at the 1964 and 1965 conventions, declined, revived in 1968, and then largely disappeared. Members learned in 1963 that racism was a "moral issue," and they viewed and/or took part in a number of plays that illustrated its moral dimensions. Members saw *The People Next Door* at the 1963 business meeting, *The Children Are Listening* at the 1963 convention, and the playlet *What the Negro Really Wants* in various settings beginning in 1964.[22] The most emphatic confrontation with racism occurred at the 1964 and 1965 conventions, where members learned that racism was America's most pressing social problem.

Bishop Wright told the DCCW members gathered for the 1964 convention Mass that some Catholics emphasized solely teaching and others only action. He continued that action and teaching "are not parallel things that never meet. They are intermeshed." Total Christian living entailed "action modified by the doctrine" and "doctrine that is revealed by the action." Furthermore, this sort of religious practice rendered the Catholic Church a "servant church" wherein Catholics served each other and the larger community.[23]

J. Edward White told members in the Community Apostolate Workshop that they should work so that "Negroes have equal rights to jobs; fair housing; the admittance to stores, restaurants and business establishments of all kinds." White reminded the women that Pope John had said that Catholics would be judged "not by what we have done, but by what we did not do when we had an opportunity." Ronald Davenport later told members of his terrifying experiences in Mississippi during the recent "Freedom Summer," and then stated that his current white landlord in a Northern white neighborhood mollified neighbors by explaining that Davenport was not dangerous because he was a lawyer.[24]

Women attending the convention the following year heard much the same message, though stated with greater urgency and less optimism. The notion that Catholics must act to relieve injustice in Pittsburgh, the country, and throughout the world permeated each session. James Cunningham, a professor of social work at the University of Pittsburgh, informed members that the Catholic Church had come from behind its walls recently, and especially under John XXIII, to become "a community of men in the world to minister, support, love one another, and to sanctify the world and bring God's Kingdom to all men." This new Church necessitated that Catholics "know the world, its suffering, its peoples."[25]

The DCCW did not long sustain its focus on race, though. Instead, members shifted their concern for social justice back toward more "charitable" works, toward helping the handicapped, the blind, and the mentally retarded at home, and continued their efforts to raise money to support other Catholics working for social justice abroad. The transformation from devotions to action for social justice proved too dramatic, too unsettling for an organization dedicated to absolute deference to the bishop. A social justice orientation necessitated a more independent and critical perspective than a devotional sensibility, and the ordinary did not establish or support the DCCW as an independent organization.

If the DCCW could not establish extensive and long-term programs, could not long center its members' religious behavior around working to alleviate racism, it had equal problems with gender. Members came to consider gender inequality in other cultures before turning back to America, and did so then only tentatively. The first real DCCW discussion of women's subordinated position in any culture came in 1965, during the convention that emphasized so heavily race issues. Mrs. Gladys Tillet, U.S. Representative of the United Nations Commission on the Status of Women, told members,

> Throughout the world, women have not advanced because they are living under ancient and frustrating laws, and we must help these women. We can solve these problems by working together as partners and by understanding the changes that are coming. If we are willing to take our responsibilities, the rights and privileges will come to all women.[26]

Tillet instructed women to conduct seminars on women in other parts of the world, especially South America, and to write to their senators to urge them to ratify "the treaty for human rights."[27]

The DCCW took Tillet's advice but did not limit the scope of study to South America. The *Echo* encouraged women to attend Arlene Swidler's lecture at Saint Mary's Church in Glenshaw on "Modern Women and the Church" in early 1966.[28] The DCCW sponsored a workshop entitled "Women Today and Tomorrow" the following month to kick off a series of lectures on "The Place of Women in the Modern World."[29] The NCCW also worked with the National Council of Jewish Women, the National Council of Negro Women, and the United Church Women on a federal project called Women in Community Service, or WICS, to screen and train vocationally females from poverty-stricken families between the ages of sixteen and twenty-one.[30]

The clearest articulation of women's status and role in American society which the DCCW sponsored came at the 1966 annual convention, when Mrs. Marcus Kilch, past president of the NCCW, discussed the "Christian Woman 1966." Kilch told the assembled members that the modern world made it impossible for those present to duplicate their mothers' lives, "even if we wished." She noted that women had always been subjugated, even in America. But women in modern America had transcended this subjugation and had a wide range of opportunities and resources at their disposal. "We are a new generation of women who have been emancipated from the traditional shackles which kept past generations intimately and almost irrevocably bound to the home hearth." This new generation required a new orientation, though. "If woman is to survive in the modern world she must be trained to be a complete human being, intellectually and spiritually alive. She must be committed to an ideal beyond herself and her family."[31]

Kilch suggested that this commitment ought to come from her role as a member of the body of Christ, manifest in her efforts to eradicate injustice in society. She continued,

> Women will not get all sweet and sentimental today if they are told that all they have to do is say their "beads" each day, and that when they die Our Lady will be waiting with her son to meet them at heaven's pearly gates. We love and venerate our Blessed Mother as much as women of any other generation but if we fail to see her divine son in the Negro, the poor, the sick, the aging, the hungry, and the homeless, we have failed completely.[32]

Kilch outlined some important areas in which women should become involved and then suggested that "perhaps generations to come will rise up and call [the modern woman] blessed." Monsignor Schultz followed this rousing speech with words of caution to the assembled women. When relaying their new role to families and husbands, "break it to them slowly and with a smile," he recommended.[33]

Within a year of Kilch's speech to the DCCW, the local hierarchy rejected efforts to push women out of the home. Though the DCCW continued to endorse efforts to achieve social justice, and sometimes hosted speakers who provided very clear analyses of economic and social disparity between nations and within America, no later speaker or program turned this sort of analysis back on women's roles in America. In fact, at the next annual convention, the Rev. John Seli contradicted Kilch directly. While Kilch saw the need for women to orient themselves beyond self and family as a necessary starting point to living a fully Christian life, Father Seli saw in this a grave danger. He related that "some women feel being a wife, mother or housewife is not fulfilling, that because of this their growth is being stunted." Nothing could be further from the truth. "No other position calls for more devotion, love and skill than the mother's." Women should concentrate on training their children to serve the world.[34]

The DCCW focus on social justice continued in some form up through the 1980s. But by 1970, under Bishop Leonard's lead, the DCCW returned to a far more devotional orientation than it had in the years following the Second Vatican Council. But the return to devotions did not allow the DCCW to flourish.

The DCCW had pushed emphatically for a new understanding of Catholicism rooted in concern and action for all of society's members, and then attempted to return to an older conception rooted in deference and petitions. The initial efforts to change the Catholic understanding proved too successful to allow the return, but not powerful enough to persuade Bishop Leonard to continue it. DCCW conventions never again drew seven hundred members. Whatever dissatisfaction members felt toward the social justice focus of the DCCW, they did not wish to return to the devotional organization.

Though the Holy Name Society had begun a transition away from devotions and toward Catholic Action during the late 1950s and early 1960s, the organization balked at a more complete transformation during the years that the Second Vatican Council met. Bishop Wright attempted to push the Holy Name Society to embrace more completely social justice and liturgical reform, to transform their orientation and practices. The HNS members did not respond sufficiently to this newer orientation, and Wright "reorganized" the society in a way that rendered it peripheral to organized lay activities in Pittsburgh. The Holy Name Society therefore illustrates the experience of a lay organization that decided to resist the transformation from devotional to social justice religious practice.

In order to understand more fully the Holy Name Society experience during and after the Council, it is important to reiterate some important points made earlier. The Holy Name Society was the officially recognized lay male organization in the Pittsburgh diocese. Unlike women and the DCCW, male parishioners actually joined the HNS directly, and these parish-level organizations federated into the diocesan HNS. Bishop Dearden had further designated the Pittsburgh HNS to be the diocesan affiliate to the National Council of Catholic Men. The Holy Name Society had since the early 1950s practiced a heavily devotional Catholicism that emphasized deference to ecclesiastical and civil authority, regular participation in devotions to saints, a strong emphasis on moderation in "secular" thought and behavior, and a regular redefinition of masculinity.

The HNS spiritual director, Father Lackner, and the *News* editors and writers had begun pushing Holy Name members to work actively for Catholic Action in the diocese, and explained Catholic Action in the framework of race relations in America. By the time the world's bishops met in the Second Vatican Council, the Holy Name Society in Pittsburgh had begun the ideological transformation from devotional to active, laid the groundwork for ecumenical interaction, and supported the growth of the Christian Family Movement.

Once the Council got under way, diocesan officials attempted to effect the transformation more dramatically by changing the diocesan, deanery, and parish meeting format to create "grass roots" participation in liturgical and social efforts. The new meetings combined the study of biblical readings with closely directed societal analyses and resolutions for action. Members read a passage provided by the diocesan office, discussed the relevance of that passage to the world (most frequently Latin America), and then resolved to act in some way to further the meaning of the biblical passage in the modern context. Father Lackner admitted to members that this new format was "somewhat revolutionary," but he considered such a revolution necessary if the Holy Name Society was to "grow and be a dynamic force in the community and in the parish."[35]

The new format did not effect the transformation Bishop Wright had intended, however, and by 1966 evidence of strain between the bishop and the society emerged in the *Newsletter*. HNS President James Sullivan, of Saint Rosalia parish, told members that he would have liked to have brought more than three representatives to the NCCM convention but that Bishop Wright would not spend the money. Sullivan reported his disappointment the following month that Bishop Wright had to cancel his planned attendance at a "very important meeting" of the HNS in May because Wright had to go to Rome to represent the North American bishops at the commemoration of *Rerum Novarum*.[36]

Three months later, in September 1966, Bishop Wright announced that he was reorganizing the Holy Name Society. The reorganization shifted the society's emphasis more explicitly to social justice and demoted it to the status of one among many lay organizations rather than as the premier male lay organization. Wright stripped the Holy Name Society of its official status as diocesan affiliate to the National Council of Catholic Men and instead allowed the society to elect representatives to a "diocesan council of laymen" (which became the Diocesan Pastoral Council). Wright further expressed his displeasure with the national Holy Name Society devotional emphasis when he told Pittsburgh HNS members that he would allow them to draw "inspiration and guidance" from national headquarters, but that he expected the diocesan organization to "set its own objectives, to develop its own programs, to acquire its own momentum, and to play its own part in diocesan organized Catholic Action."[37]

The Holy Name Society did not flourish under this new organizational format. HNS President Guy Pirro noted "poor attendance at Area meetings, absence of the Area officers and Commission Chairmen, lack of interest and weak Public Relations" in the Pittsburgh HNS. He urged members to shoulder some of the blame themselves, to cease in their "unjust" criticisms of the diocesan office, but he was fighting a losing battle. The new Holy Name Society did not draw the allegiance of the old members, and the younger men did not come to an organization long associated with devotional behaviors.[38]

The Holy Name Society had resisted the transformation even more than had the DCCW. In so doing it severed its most nurturing connection. Bishop Wright finally decided to marginalize the society rather than deal with its intransigence, and the society had thrived because of its close proximity to the official hierarchy. Wright was so successful at demoting the society (no great feat for an organization whose most persuasive recruiting tool had been the bishop's insistence that men join) that it could not revive in its devotional form under Bishop Leonard. The HNS continued to exist through the 1980s but only as an organization that sponsored trips to professional sporting events.

THE TRANSFORMATION IN CATHOLIC UNDERSTANDING FROM devotional to social justice marked the end of those lay organizations unable to embrace the change. Raymond Utz suggested that the liturgical reforms did not draw lay Catholics as quickly or completely as reformers had expected, but that it did open the door for Catholics to escape from devotions that no longer held attraction for them. He did not recognize that the flight preceded the reforms. This leaves open the question of what Catholics wanted from their Church. How did they understand their religion? For some, such as members and supporters of the Catholic Interracial Council and the Liturgical Commission, the answer was clearly a Church grounded in concern for social justice. For others, perhaps most, the answers can be approached through an examination of the Pittsburgh synod.

CHAPTER EIGHT

The Promise of a Democratic Church

The Laity and the 1971 Pittsburgh Synod

VATICAN II HAD ENDED, THE LITURGICAL REFORMS WERE WELL ON their way to implementation, the Diocesan Pastoral Council was up and running, but the diocese had yet to take stock and implement the reforms in a systematic and comprehensive way. Accordingly, Bishop Wright determined in 1968 that the diocese should have a synod to implement the Second Vatican Council reforms in the Pittsburgh area. Vatican rules required each diocese to hold a synod at least once each decade, but Pittsburgh had not held one since 1954. A synod is an episcopal proclamation of ecclesiastical laws governing the diocese which holds until the bishop amends them or until he (or one of his successors) promulgates a new synod. The bishop holds absolute power in his diocese. He acts as legislator, executive, and final arbiter. Canon law required bishops to consult only a limited number of priests when promulgating a synod.[1] Most lay Catholics never knew that the diocese even held synods, much less what they were. But Vatican II had so changed the process of government on the episcopal level that few bishops sought to repeat the traditional synod process. Instead they desired to incorporate a broader degree of advice on diocesan legislation, much as they had been consulted at the Vatican Council.

Many dioceses had already held their synods by 1968, and Pittsburgh sought to benefit from their experiences. Bishop Wright looked particularly to Detroit, Bishop Dearden's diocese. Though Dearden had gone to Rome for the Vatican Council sessions as a staunch conservative, he returned a changed man. He became convinced that the laity should be consulted on pastoral matters, and established an elaborate consultative structure to tap parishioner desires and ideas at the outset of the synod's preparation phase.

Wright sent a delegation of priests to Detroit to study the Detroit synod as a model for the coming Pittsburgh efforts. The group returned generally enthusiastic, though they had some reservations about Pittsburgh's ability to duplicate Detroit's process. The Detroit diocese had an extensive adult education program in place that enabled the laity to provide "informed" suggestions. The Adult Education Institute in Pittsburgh did not measure up to the task, in the delegates' eyes. The delegates, and other key figures in the Pittsburgh synod preparation structure, worried that Pittsburgh's laity was not knowledgeable enough to participate in the process. But the delegation was sufficiently impressed to draw up a model for a Pittsburgh synod that followed the Detroit experience very closely.[2]

Bishop Wright intended to draw the laity into the preparatory process as much as possible, but he also wanted to consult a broad range of priests. The priests already had a deliberative body that Wright consulted on pastoral matters, and he wanted them to endorse and cooperate fully on the synod preparation. He offered to give them a full review of synod proposals that he too would review, and even asked Father Maida, who had responsibility for drawing up the Pittsburgh synod consultation process, to present his plan to the Clergy Council to get their approval. Maida proposed the Detroit plan to the council and they rejected it unanimously.[3]

The Clergy Council members thought the Detroit plan consulted the laity too much, and they did not think the laity capable of contributing valuably or efficiently to the preparation. The clergy worried that the laity were not sufficiently informed about Catholic doctrine, or disciplined enough as a body, to participate in such a grand enterprise. Father Maida returned to the Clergy Council at their next meeting. Though he understood that the priests were reluctant to give the laity a significant role in the synod, Maida also knew of his own and Bishop Wright's desires to involve them as much as was practicable. He presented the Clergy Council with a modified plan that involved the laity. The council was not pleased. Despite Maida's assurance that the General Coordinating Board for the Synod (of which he was a member) had "ruled out that we would have any wide participation or education of the laity" at the Clergy Council's request, the plan did try to involve the existing Parish Committees.[4]

Father Grundler reminded Maida that the Clergy Council had discussed and rejected ("unanimously, as far as I can recall") "grassroots" participation. He told Maida that the synod would not work if the laity were involved, and added for emphasis, "If they framed the Constitution of the United States this way, we still wouldn't have one. It sounds good, but it won't work." Maida tried to placate Grundler, suggesting that this proposal differed so substantially from the Detroit model that it constituted a new plan that the Clergy Council had not yet rejected and which would work. Grundler was not mollified. If the diocese attempted to involve the laity the synod would not be complete until 1990, he asserted, and he termed the whole idea of lay participation "humbug." But the Clergy Council relented, finally, after members received assurances that the elaborate preparation plans would not obligate any priests to participate.[5]

Once Bishop Wright had the Clergy Council's endorsement, however reluctant, he still needed to devise and carry out the synod preparations. He assigned the task to a General Coordinating Board for the Synod (GCBS), which consisted of eleven members. Most of the activity, and therefore the authority, lay in two officers' hands, though, the president and the executive director. Msgr. John C. McCarren served as synod and GCBS president, and Fr. Leo Vanyo as executive secretary.[6] After a long period of discussion, and ongoing amendment, the GCBS settled on a plan for synod preparation which Bishop Wright approved.

A five-tiered, pyramidlike structure handled the preparations. Bishop Wright stood at the top. The board members regularly reminded each other and the other participants in the preparation that Bishop Wright was the sole legislator in the diocese and that all preparation served as advice only. The General Coordinating Board served directly below Bishop Wright, though in practice Father Vanyo and Monsignor McCarren acted as almost another level between the board and Bishop Wright. Eleven Synodal Commissions addressed distinct categories upon which the synod preparations focused. A Laity Commission studied the laity, and then solicited, modified, proposed, and justified legislation that addressed the laity, for example. A Worship Commission addressed the liturgy.[7] The commissions proved subordinate to the GCBS, though the GCBS suggested regularly throughout the three years of preparation that the commissions had ultimate responsibility for devising and writing the final legislation (subject to the bishop's review).

Each deanery formed a committee that passed proposals on to the commissions, and these deaneries formed the second-lowest tier. The deanery committees drew six members from each parish that participated, and divided the representatives into three separate groups to evaluate proposals from the parishes. The parishes constituted the bottom tier, the grassroots level. The GCBS asked each parish to form a synod Committee, or to use the existing Parish Committee to work on the synod preparations. In addition, the GCBS asked each parish to host a general meeting on each of the eleven areas of focus, and encouraged each to form special study groups to pursue any particular areas of interest in more detail. The diocese sent out specially chosen priests with prepared talks on each area to run the general meetings. In addition to parishes, independent groups of

Catholics could apply for "special group" status and forward any proposals they developed to the commissions directly.[8]

The GCBS settled on a plan that satisfied Bishop Wright in July 1968. The plan called for a three-stage process that took place first on the parish level, then the deanery, and then the commission. The grassroots involvement concentrated in the first stage, within the parishes. It entailed a variety of means of educating parishioners about the synod process and then soliciting from them proposals that parish committees and participants in the deanery and commission level evaluated in their deliberations.[9]

Parish committees received proposals from parishioners, discussed and voted on them, and then passed them along to the deanery committees. Though the original plans called for proposals that did not receive a majority of favorable votes in the parishes to die there, parishes passed along many—perhaps all—of the proposals that they voted down.[10]

Parishes sent proposals to the deanery for the second level of the synod preparations. Each of the thirteen deaneries formed a twelve-member committee that received and then polished the proposals from the parishes. These committees focused on language only, and refrained from editing the proposals' contents. The deanery committees then handed the proposals to a second group of deanery-level committees composed of six parishioners drawn from each parish in the deanery. The deaneries divided this large body of parishioners into thirds, ensuring that two of each parish's six appointments went to each committee. Each third examined and then voted on a third of the polished proposals, so that they could process the proposals quickly and with little burden. The deaneries then passed all of the proposals on to the relevant commissions.[11]

The commissions received the proposals from the deaneries as one of a few sources of information they had to write the synod legislation. They also conducted research on their areas and invited "experts" to discuss the topic with them. Once the commissions had examined the proposals, completed their research, and consulted their experts, they wrote out legislation to reform and guide the diocese in their particular area. The commission had to root each piece of legislation it submitted in a clearly identified passage from the Vatican II documents. The members then submitted their work to the General Coordinating Board, which evaluated the work and was supposed to return it to the commissions for revision. From there the legislation was to go to Bishop Wright, who was to make any revisions he wanted and then promulgate them.[12]

The organization and plan for the synod preparations was extremely complex and required great skill and cooperation. Even if everyone understood and embraced the process and his or her role in it, the preparation would have required a great deal of coordination and cooperation. And everyone did not understand and accept the structure and process. The Clergy Council opposed grassroots participation, particularly any parishioner involvement that required clerical exertion. Many parishioners did not understand or believe their new role in diocesan policy formation. Father Vanyo noted in an early Coordinating Board session that he was having great difficulty staffing the commissions. People just did not want to serve, or did not believe that the bishop would respect the commission's work. One layman turned down a request to chair a commission because, in his words, "I personally doubt that the voice of the layman will be heard and acted upon to the extent I would desire if I were to act as chairman." Others simply neglected to return Vanyo's letters, or said they were too busy. Roughly 23 percent of the parishes assigned no delegates to the deanery committees.[13]

Perhaps most unsettling to the entire process, Bishop Wright moved to Rome during the preparations to fill his new role as prefect for the Congregation of the Clergy. Bishop Leonard, his successor, did not share his enthusiasm for the democratic process.

The lay and clerical reluctance to embrace the synod wholeheartedly might also have resulted from their confusion about the process. The GCBS did not settle on a final plan for almost a year, and then modified that as it went along. The parishes and deaneries did not follow the plan exactly, and the commissions attempted to change their composition to get more representation from minority views as the preparations progressed.[14] This confusion manifested itself in the proceedings at the various levels. This was so particularly for the commission level, where members moved tentatively at first in their roles.

THE LAITY SPEAKS THROUGH THE SYNOD

But the synod preparations did call for and receive extensive lay participation despite the confusion and hesitancy many laymen and laywomen felt. If 23 percent of the parishes did not participate in the preparations directly, 77 percent did. The *Pittsburgh Catholic* ran a series of pages about each of the eleven synod foci with forms attached that parishioners filled out and returned to the paper. Parishioners mailed in 3,000 proposals on worship alone from all but twelve parishes in the diocese. In addition, a number of lay organizations, particularly women's groups, asked Father Vanyo to come talk about the synod. Perhaps the best measure of parishioner enthusiasm and involvement was the number

TABLE 8.1   Parish Proposals in Preparation for Pittsburgh Diocesan Synod (1969)

Proposal Subjects	Number of Proposals	Percent of Total
Clergy	210	21
Liturgy, Mass	157	16
Education, schools	155	16
Laity	144	14
Power	129	13
Age	116	12
Sacraments	66	7
CCD	65	7
Gender	35	4
Nuns, sisters	33	3
Democracy	31	3
Ecumenism	21	2
Bishop	21	2
Devotions	14	1
Race	12	1

of proposals they submitted to reform the Church. The commissions received 5,150 proposals from the deaneries. This represented only a portion of all the proposals submitted because parishes eliminated duplicates before sending them to the deaneries, and the deaneries combined like proposals from different parishes into single proposals before counting them.[15]

Not all the proposals that the commissions received have survived, but those from the Beaver, Butler, and Southeast District 1 deaneries do remain. In all, they total 994, or roughly 20 percent of all the proposals submitted. These deaneries contained 22 percent of all parishes.[16] The proposals reveal a great deal about the lay concerns in the late 1960s and the ways that laypeople wanted to shape their Church.[17] A careful review of each proposal reveals that laymen and laywomen focused on a range of themes and subjects. A few stand out from the others. (See table 8.1.)

TABLE 8.2   Proposals That Address Devotions

Category	Number
Rosary	7
Mary	6
Novenas	5
Forty hours	1
Retreats	6
Total	*14*

Parishioners expressed little interest through their proposals to return to the insular, devotional Church that existed in the early years of the 1950s. This is evident in the way that they addressed (or did not address) devotions and those pillars of Catholic separatism that characterized the Church in those years. Given an opportunity to imagine what their Church should be, the laity spoke powerfully in the late 1960s that it should not be the Church of their parents and their youth. They wanted a more democratic Church, responsive to their concerns and needs, and in which their voices mattered considerably.

LAY REJECTION OF DEVOTIONS AND SEPARATISM

The proposals provide powerful commentary on the distance the laity had moved from just ten or fifteen years earlier. Despite the dramatic transformation in devotional practices over the previous decade and a half, parishioners addressed only 14 of 994 proposals to devotions. Judging by the relative absence of proposals on devotional practices, one might reasonably conclude that laymen and laywomen concerned themselves little with such matters. They were largely content with the state of devotional activity in their parishes and the diocese. Those proposals that did address devotions spread across five areas.[18] (See table 8.2.)

One main theme emerges from the handful of proposals on devotions. Parishioners who addressed novenas, the rosary, and Mary wanted to increase devotional offerings and to generate renewed interest among lay Catholics. They expressed their desires simply and typically in very general terms. A parishioner from one of the diocese's southern parishes, for example, suggested that the diocese "encourage increased devotion to Blessed Mother through the Rosary and special devotions." Another parishioner from Our Lady of Peace in Beaver County recommended "that each week each parish have devotions in honor of Our Blessed Mother." A Butler County parishioner noted that devotions "are all very necessary and we should not be too quick in dropping these services." Two of the fourteen proposals addressing devotions recommended that the laity exercise greater control during the rituals. Five of the six proposals related to retreats focused on clergy retreat experiences, not lay. Parish committees and deanery committees generally voted in favor of the suggestions, save for when they recommended additional nocturnal or forty hours devotions. Overall, however, the laity's lack of interest in devotions stands out most, with only 1 percent of the proposals focusing on what was once a central defining characteristic of Catholic life.

Laymen and laywomen focused more on certain Church strictures, rules, and experiences that impinged on the separate Catholic culture than they did on devotions. They addressed Catholic separatism directly when they mentioned schools and marriage, but ignored such areas as movies and literature which had loomed so large in Catholic public discussions the previous decade. No proposal called for the Legion of Decency's return, or recommended ways to regulate Catholic access to literature. The only proposal relating to censorship, movies, and literature was garbled in transcription and reveals no discernible perspective on these issues.[19] Catholics did have much to say about schools and marriage, however.

Fully one hundred proposals addressed Catholic schools in one way or another, and another fifty-five focused on education more broadly. In these the laity overwhelmingly rejected the school as an instrument of Catholic separatism. The suggestions about schools ranged over a number of issues, from specific curricular concerns to teacher qualifications to the availability of special needs instruction. But a plurality, forty-four in all, addressed financial concerns in one way or another. The central message, delivered in a variety of forms, was that the system burdened parishes, the diocese, and families too much as it existed currently, and that some compromise of the comprehensive K–12 system should be adopted. As discussed earlier, the cost of maintaining such a comprehensive structure strained Catholic resources dramatically. The necessary increase in lay teachers promised to worsen the situation. Many parishioners focused on ways to alter funding or reduce costs.

The most often proposed solution, one repeated seventeen times in one variation or another, was to eliminate some or all of the existing schools. One parishioner suggested that "a central office have the authority to close or merge schools when necessary." Another recommended that "the Catholic schools be eliminated and use the facilities for Catholic studies and C.C.D. programs." Still another proposed that "the parochial schools be eliminated and the present buildings be converted into Catholic high schools." One recommended that the diocese "phase out our parochial schools."

The second most common solution to the problem was a change in the funding strategies then employed to reduce the burden on a particular constituency, usually the parish from which the proposal originated. Because of the almost hodgepodge way in which Catholic schools developed, some parishes had no schools, some had K–8 parochial schools only, and some had both K–8 and high schools. The diocese generally left support of K–8 schools to the parish itself but used a variety of funding strategies for the high schools. Parish high schools drew their students from the parish primarily, and perhaps a bit from neighboring parishes. They relied for support on tuition, parish subsidies, and the subsidized labor that members of religious orders offered. A system of regional high schools also existed which drew students from a number of parishes within their areas. Religious orders sponsored some of these, and the diocese operated others. The diocese assessed one tax on parishes with no high school to support the regional schools, and another lower one on parishes that maintained their own high schools. The more recently founded of these admitted boys and girls, but many that had existed for years and decades served only boys or girls. The diocese used funds from the high school tax to support all of the coed schools, and the all-boys schools, but did not provide assistance to those that taught only girls. Parishes felt the high school tax acutely as it drained resources from other parish costs and activities.

Parishioners who felt the pinch of the tax sought a tax assessed equally regardless of whether a parish maintained its own high school, or a shift of the burden to those parents whose children attended the school. In an ironic turn of the argument that area Catholics had long used about taxes to support public schools, these parents argued that they should not have to pay to support a school that benefited only a portion of the community. One Catholic from a remote rural parish proposed that parishes "that do not have access to a Catholic High School, *should not* be assessed." Raise the tuition for those parents who wanted to send their children to a Catholic high school, many maintained. Another proposal urged that "the Catholic school system be supported entirely by tuition."

When laymen and laywomen addressed aspects of Catholic schools other than finances, they pushed to reduce the power and authority that pastors held and to increase the influence of the laity in schools. One parishioner framed a suggestion to reduce the pastor's role as follows: "Pastors shouldn't have the added burden of running a school for which they know little or nothing about and have no training for the role." Often the parishioners sought to move school policy making away from the pastor to the diocesan level or to parish school boards on which pastors sat but which included other members who had votes on school matters as well. Overall, fifteen of the proposals sought either to reduce the pastor's authority in schools or to increase lay power (or both).

Catholics felt similarly about marriage. Eight of thirty proposals regarding marriage called for greater latitude in marriage rules or enforcement. Some wanted to ease the rules regarding mixed marriages by either allowing them to take place in Protestant churches, eliminating the promises required of the non-Catholic spouses, having the church recognize any marriage that the state recognized, or allowing divorced Catholics to remarry. A Catholic from Saint Bernard's in the suburb of Mt. Lebanon proposed, "Any marriage considered valid by the state, should be recognized by the Church, provided neither party has a living spouse by a prior marriage." Another from Saint Conrad in Butler County suggested that "the dispensation for a marriage, when one partner is not a Catholic, be eliminated. In this day and age, we should be practicing Ecumenism, this is one thing we could do away with. Dispensation may be necessary where there is some serious reason, but not in all cases." Others sought to soften the marriage tribunal (the diocesan board that ruled on Catholic requests to have marriages annulled) by placing laypeople—especially couples—on it.

Seven proposals addressed marriage preparation classes or married couple classes. Five of these recommended giving laypeople, especially married couples, more prominent roles in these classes.

The most common specific proposal relating to marriage, repeated six times, was to allow priests to marry. Other proposals addressed this obliquely, such as the one that recommended freezing priests' salaries until they were able to marry. One parishioner from Mater Dolorosa parish in Butler County asserted, "Priests should marry if they so desire. It is ridiculous that the few who have married are excommunicated. God made rules that say no wives for priests, did he? There would be more priests if they were allowed to marry." Three proposals called for continued priestly celibacy, and one of those claimed that a survey taken in the parish revealed that 60 percent agreed with this position.

If laymen and laywomen did not wish to retrieve the Church of the early 1950s, what did they want? What kind of Church did they seek to construct when given the extraordinary opportunity in the late 1960s? The answer can be found both by examining the specific themes and subjects that the laity identified and by looking very broadly at all of the proposals. Overall, Catholics in the Pittsburgh region sought to create and sustain a more liberal Church than existed in 1968. An analysis of proposals reveals that parishioners submitted more liberal

FIGURE 8.1   Proposals by Type (Liberal, Conservative, Neutral)

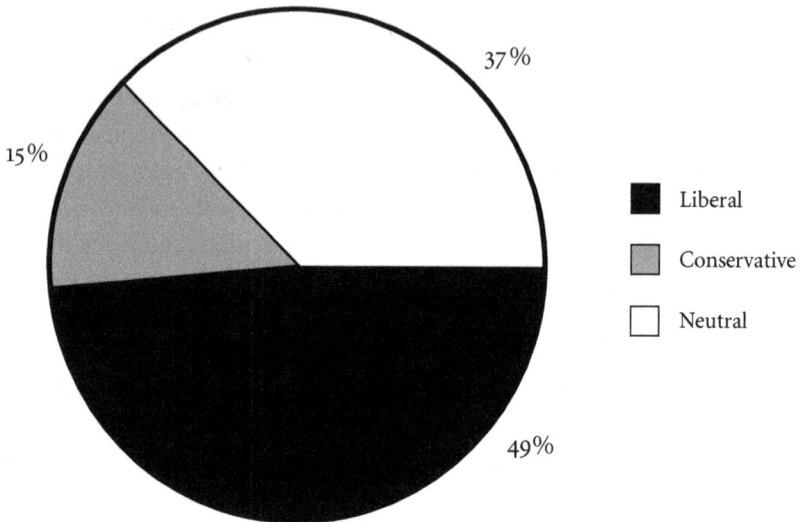

37%

15%

49%

Liberal

Conservative

Neutral

proposals than conservative. (See fig. 8.1.) In fact, only 15 percent of the proposals Catholics submitted sought conservative ends, while 49 percent sought liberal and 37 percent sought neutral.[20]

Moreover, parish committees voted in favor of 74 percent of the liberal proposals they evaluated, and deanery committees favored only 53 percent. This suggests that parishes supported liberalizing the Church more than did the deanery committees. Put in another way, those furthest from the center of power within the diocese favored liberalizing the Church more than did those closest to the center. The same pattern held for neutral proposals, where the parish committees favored 71 percent of those that they evaluated and the deanery committees favored only 49 percent. Parish committees favored a significantly lower percentage of the conservative proposals, only 61 percent. But the deanery committees favored even fewer (36 percent), suggesting that even the deanery committees favored liberal proposals more than conservative.

What did this mean specifically? We have already determined that the laity demonstrated little interest in those themes that dominated the public discussion of Catholicism in the 1950s. They worried little about devotions and did not seek to sustain a separate K–12 Catholic school system, especially in light of the drain on other projects and endeavors that the schools represented. But what did parishioners seek to accomplish with the 210 proposals that focused

TABLE 8.3   Proposals Addressing Priests

Topic	Frequency	Percent
Rationalize priest assignments	24	11
Increase priests' salaries	16	8
Increase priests' control over assignments	12	6
Limit/eliminate priests' role in social concerns/demonstrations	12	6
Reduce/abolish stipends for funerals, weddings, etc.	10	5
Make priests more accessible to parishioners	9	4
Increase priests' role in teaching CCD and religion classes in schools	8	3
Reduce/eliminate priests' financial role in parish	7	3
Priests should focus on parish's spiritual aspects	7	3
Provide more generously for priests' retirement	7	3
Improve homilies	6	3
Let priests marry	6	3
Provide/require professional development for priests	6	3

on the clergy? What suggestions did they make about the liturgy? What issues of power and age concerned the laity?

Clergy

The parishioners' proposals regarding the clergy addressed a wide array of areas, though many of them clustered around some common subjects or themes. The parishioners' model for the priesthood in the late 1960s emerges out of the proposals, and it reveals a tension over the changed role from the 1950s. Many laymen and laywomen saw priests as spiritual beings who should not engage in the mundane concerns that consumed others in society. Part of this seemed to come from a sense that priests were largely incompetent in these worldly areas, but it also derived from a sense that priests ought to focus on higher, spiritual concerns. Others saw the priests' religious training as giving them special competence in the social justice arena and applauded their efforts to improve society. Parishioners revealed this not through general statements about model priests, but through their proposals targeted at very specific concerns. (See table 8.3.)

The greatest concentration of concerns clustered around priests' personnel and employment issues. Prior to the late 1950s, pastors often served for life in their parishes. They worked as assistants in a handful of places until they achieved their first pastorate, but once there they often stayed until they died. The *Pittsburgh Catholic* regularly contained obituaries for pastors who had served for decades in the parish in which they resided at their deaths. But in the late 1950s the bishops began rotating pastors as well as assistants on a regular basis. This allowed priests to experience a variety of settings and worked to discourage pastors from becoming too entrenched with cliques in their parishes. But it also created upheaval for pastors and parishioners when bishops transferred the priests. Consequently, parishioners wanted to rationalize the mechanism by which the bishop assigned priests to parishes. In particular, they wanted the bishop to seek a good fit between priest and parish, to allow priests to have significant say in where they ended up and when they moved, to provide a voice for the laity in the assignments, and to establish an appeal mechanism to allow priests to challenge assignments. Some of these proposals seemed to come from parishioners who wanted their priests to move on, and some came from parishioners who wanted to hold onto their priests. Both groups felt they had little influence in the process and conveyed the desire to leverage some control by empowering priests, parishioners, or both. Parishioners were largely dissatisfied with the current system. One parishioner proposed a very specific process:

> It is proposed: that a "board" be appointed or established to assist the Bishop in making a judgment on the suitability of a priest for the administration of any parish. All recommended qualifications should be taken into consideration, such as piety, apostolic zeal and the ability to communicate with parishioners and assistants. Seniority alone is not sufficient reason for a priest to be assigned to administer a parish.

Others asked simply to raise the voices of those most affected by the process. A number recommended simply that "the priest concerned should be consulted by the bishop prior to an assignment." Three proposals, such as this one from suburban Saint Bernard parish, recommended a greater voice for the laity: "The laity should be consulted on transfer and assignment of parish priests."

Parishioners also wanted their priests to receive higher salaries. Part of this concern related to the difficulties of living with little income, but much of it came from parishioner unhappiness with paying priests out of pocket to perform sacramental duties. Laywomen and laymen seemed particularly unhappy with paying priests to perform weddings and funerals. This connected power-fully with the clear sentiment to distance priests generally from financial matters and allow them to concentrate almost entirely on spiritual and other community concerns. The laity wanted to separate these powerful spiritual moments from fee-for-service transactions. The payment reminded parishioners that priests too worried about mundane matters. One Saint Christine parishioner proposed that "priests' salaries should be increased and stipends for weddings, funerals and masses be discontinued."

The distaste for connecting priestly duties with cash transactions reflected a powerful desire to reduce or eliminate the priests' role in parish finances more generally. Though parishioners might debate whether priests should engage in demonstrations and marches, they achieved consensus that priests should not be leading building programs and paying the bills. Some of these proposals seemed to derive from a sense that priests held little competence in these areas. One, for example, stated that "if the priest is to remain as the temporal as well as the spiritual manager of the parish, he should be required to take additional training in finances, property planning, etc." Another called for the diocese to conduct an annual audit of parish books. At least one parishioner framed the issue as a matter of justice: "Give the layman control of the Parish Finance, where it belongs. They have to raise the money. It is time they give them [their] rightful duty." But most suggested that parishioners valued the priests for their spiritual role and saw the financial responsibilities as unwanted intrusions into time that could be spent on the parishes' spiritual needs. Each hour that a priest spent doing the books deprived parishioners of an hour of marriage counsel-ing, youth work, or CCD instruction. The financial role constituted an oppor-tunity cost. One Saint Veronica parishioner recommended relieving "priests of the financial responsibility of governing the Parish in order that they have more time for Spiritual duties." A Saint Andrew parishioner asserted,

> The responsibility of the parish priest should be only spiritual. Planning, de-signing, building, financing, etc., should be the responsibility of the elected directors of the parish. A priest cannot possibly be schooled in all these fields. Also, he would have more time to act as counselor and adviser to individu-als who have no one to consult.

Parishioners did not necessarily believe that priests excelled at their spiritual work—the proposals suggest much the opposite—but they did believe that priests' work ought to be spiritual. Laymen and laywomen wanted priests to preach better homilies at Mass, to visit the sick, to teach religion in parochial schools and in the CCD program, to make themselves more accessible to parishioners, and to develop their own spirituality. One parishioner relayed that

> every Sunday I hear sermons that are not particularly soul searching or even based on the scriptures. Since Christ and what He says through the Bible is the only valid reason for a congregation to assemble, I propose that the clergy read, contemplate and study God's word in the Bible and, in turn, reach out to help people find God for themselves.

Another stated, "We propose that the priests take more time to visit the sick parishioners. This is when the priest can comfort them and give them a little attention in their homes." Still another recommended that "the authority and responsibility for all parish functions, not directly concerned with spiritual Life, be vested in the Parish committee so that the parish priests have more time to concentrate on spiritual problems."

Much of the parishioner ideal for priests as a people set apart for spiritual purposes can also be seen in the response to priests becoming more engaged with the laity. Some parishioners recommended that priests be barred from demonstrations and marches, that they keep their hair cut short, dress in black, and return to the rectory by midnight. One particularly irate parishioner urged that

> when it comes to matters not directly related on [sic] concerning the Roman Catholic Church, priests and nuns should refrain from picketing, marching and various other types of demonstrations. A severe punishment should be given to those members of the clergy who participate in such actions.

The emphasis on punishment reveals a strong sentiment, evidenced in other proposals as well, that priests should defer to higher authority and model that obedience to the larger community. In fact, one proposal clearly placed obedience to ecclesiastical and civil authority as the essence of the priests' role:

> The clergy should be our inspiration, leaders and ideals. Though I realize they are human, I expect more of them—less pettiness, more honoring of authority (both Church and Civil), more living up to their vows. If their conscience is to be their guide, instead of their duly, authorized superiors, then perhaps they'd better find another profession and support themselves.

Other parishioners applauded the activist priest, however. One parishioner recommended that "priests and parishioners should be more active in political

TABLE 8.4   Proposals Addressing Laity

Proposal Theme or Subject	Frequency	Percent
Empower laity	73	51
Solicit lay opinions	16	11
Laity should control finances	14	10
Restrain laity	8	6
Increase lay role in CCD programs	6	4
Increase lay voice in pastor selection	5	3
Increase women religious–lay interaction	5	3

and social controversies." These parishioners clearly saw the priest as a useful resource to help transform society, and they saw such participation as a reasonable outcome to the priest's continuing development as a human being. In opposition to calls for mandatory clerical garb, one parishioner urged that "the dress of the clergy and religious should be a matter of reasonable choice of the individual."[21] Another parishioner placed the entire matter of priestly behavior in terms of their individual consciences in insisting that "no infringement be placed on priests' decision to act in good conscience in peaceful demonstrations supporting social causes." These parishioners did not seek to compel priests to work actively for social change but to allow this should priests seek to do so. They assumed that priests should reach their own determination of appropriate behavior rather than simply follow directives from higher authority.

The same tension over authority, obedience, competence, and conscience permeated the proposals addressed to the laity and to power.

Laity

The lay concern about authority and power within parishes and the diocese comes across very strongly in the proposals directed at the laity. Though the proposals varied across a wide range of specific topics, fully 51 percent sought to empower the laity in some way, while only 6 percent sought to restrain the laity. (See table 8.4.) The wide range and specificity of proposals make it difficult to group the suggestions into larger categories. The laity proposed that they lead devotional rituals, distribute Communion, have greater roles in generating nominations for parish committees, be allowed to join parishes without residing within their boundaries, go hatless in Mass, and be better appraised of the synod preparation progress. They wanted to halt the publication of parishioner contributions in the parish bulletins, enlarge women's roles within the Church, and give sermons in Masses. They clearly turned the insistence that the laity be active in the broader society back onto the Church itself. The laity sought greater and more meaningful roles in Church governance and rituals. They wanted to diminish the power that the clergy wielded in many areas of parish life, to contain them within the realm of spiritual concerns.

The most commonly identified means of empowering the laity which emerges from the proposals came from suggestions to increase consultation. One parishioner recommended that "the pastor and parish committee should attempt to find out the parishioners opinions on many church related subjects on a regular basis through questionnaires distributed at least twice a year." Some specified areas for consultation such as the assignment of priests to parishes and even the bishop's selection. One parishioner urged that "efforts be made to solicit, on a continuing basis, the preferences of parishioners regarding sermon topics, Mass Schedules, C.C.D. times, etc." Another wanted a "visitation committee" to be formed to "visit families and gather opinions on C.C.D., Mass schedules, sermons, etc." Most of these proposals did not bind the hierarchy to follow lay opinion, but simply to consider it. They did not threaten to undermine the fundamental power structure within the parish or diocese, only to make those in power more responsive to the people of God.

One means to greater responsiveness was to increase the interaction between the laity and the clergy, which the proposals recommended in a variety of settings. The desire for greater consultation and interaction between the laity and those who took religious vows extended to women religious as well. The laity expressed keen interest in spending more time with nuns and sisters. One parishioner proposed that "the Nuns of the parish be permitted to attend CFM meetings, visit the homes of parishioners and joining them in a meal if so invited." Another suggested that "Religious Sisters should be able to serve on committees in the Parish and make home visits." Still another recommended that "the laity be informed that the religious are members of the community and may have an opinion and should have all rights accorded other citizens." Expanding contact between women religious and laymen and laywomen likely worked to transform power relations within parishes, though the proposals did not reveal this as an aim.

The laity were more assertive in other areas. They clearly wanted to direct their parishes' financial activities. We have already encountered this idea in the discussion of the clergy proposals above, and it requires little elaboration. But it bears repeating because the laity clearly saw this as an area where they could exercise authority more wisely, efficiently, or responsibly than the clergy. Here they did challenge the clerical prerogative and asserted very emphatically that the clergy ought not to hold power in this area.

Parishioners sought to share rather than usurp power in the area of religious education, especially in the CCD program. One parishioner recommended that "there should be more lay involvement in the religious education of children in the parish." But others sought to ensure that priests did not disengage entirely from this role. One suggested that priests and nuns were best qualified for this role when insisting that "CCD classes be taught by priests and nuns and not by laymen." Another was slightly more open in urging that "we should have better qualified CCD instructors. Preferably nuns or seminarians, although salaried laymen may be necessary."

Power

A sixth of all proposals, 129 in all, dealt directly with issues of power in the Church. They ranged from the very general ("Give people more say in the changes") to the very specific ("In church-affiliated lay organizations, priests may serve as chaplains, advisors or consultors, but that laymen govern their own organizations"). These proposals confront very important principles of authority, subsidiarity, and democracy, and provide the laity's answers to critical questions swirling about the Church. Should the people of God exercise more power within the Church? What should constitute the basis for authority? Should the Church seek to implement subsidiarity throughout its structure? Many of these issues have been addressed implicitly in the discussion above, but they merit explicit discussion here as well. (See table 8.5.)

Eighty of the 129 proposals, roughly 62 percent, dealt with the power relationship between the laity and the hierarchy, while 33 (26 percent) focused on power relations within the hierarchy itself. Those that addressed power relations within the hierarchy concentrated on conflicts between diocesan and religious authorities and on the bishop's power over priests within the diocese. One dealt with the relationship between the bishop and Rome: "That Bishop Leonard do all in his power to convince the Bishops of the United States that the power of the Curia is a threat to the Church."

Most of the proposals regarding priests and bishops sought to resolve issues of obedience and freedom regarding priests' behaviors. One parishioner from Saint Christine parish wanted the bishop to prohibit priests "from wearing

TABLE 8.5   Proposals That Address Power

Proposal Subject or Theme	Frequency	Percent of All Power Proposals
Address power within hierarchy	33	26
Address power between laity and hierarchy	80	62
Favor power concentration in bishop, pastor	24	19
Favor dispersing power away from bishop, pastor	85	66

extreme haircuts." Another urged the bishop to force each priest to return to "the rectory by mid-night except for special occasions." One parishioner from Saint Thomas More parish in suburban Pittsburgh urged bishops to "take a firm stand against activities of the so-called 'maverick' or 'militant' priests in civil affairs." Another wanted priests and nuns to "obtain permission from their superiors and be advised as to the procedure to be used before appearing on TV, Radio, and in public press and 'March Demonstrations.'" But a slightly greater number sought to empower priests in their relations with the ordinary. One parishioner recommended that "the Priests select the Dean of a District rather than the Bishop."[22] Another recommended that "the dress of the clergy and religious should be a matter of reasonable choice of the individual." A Butler County parishioner proposed that "priests may accept invitations to teach or deliver [lectures] in non-Catholic educational institutions or before non-Catholic religious groups without the permission of the Ordinary."

A greater number of proposals focused on the power relations between the laity and the hierarchy, and here the vast majority sought to empower the laity in new ways. Table 8.5 reports all those proposals that sought either to concentrate power in the hierarchy (bishop, pastor, priests) or disperse power away from the hierarchy. It includes those proposals that dealt with power relations between priests and bishops as well as those that focused on the laity and the hierarchy. These proposals reveal a strong sentiment to move power down the hierarchy and toward the laity. Parishioners proposed concentrating power in the bishop, pastor, or priests in 19 percent of all proposals. They favored dispersing power in 66 percent of the proposals.[23] If we examine only those proposals that address the power relations between the laity and clergy (including the bishop), the disparity becomes even greater. (See table 8.6.) Nine of every ten

TABLE 8.6   Proposals That Address Power Relations Between Laity and Hierarchy

Proposal Subject or Theme	Frequency	Percent
Reserve power in hierarchy	8	10
Empower laity	72	90
Total	*80*	*100*

TABLE 8.7   Themes of Proposals That Address Power Relations Between Laity and Hierarchy

Proposal Subject or Theme	Reserve Power in Clergy	Empower Laity
Parish governance	6	39
School / CCD governance	2	12
Parish finances	1	14
Ritual (liturgy, devotions)	3	16

proposals sought to empower the laity relative to the clergy, while only one in ten sought to reserve power with the clergy.

These proposals addressed power relations primarily in four contexts, with each revealing a strong preference for increased lay power. (See table 8.7.) The laity were poised in the late 1960s to assume greater responsibility and authority in their parishes. They sought this responsibility in part because they wanted to free priests for spiritual work, in part because laymen and laywomen considered themselves to be more competent in their parish's temporal matters, and in part because they saw this arrangement as more consistent with democratic ideals.

Laywomen and laymen referred directly to democratic ideals or rooted their specific proposals in democratic assumptions thirty-one times. Four of these dealt with clergy relations with bishops, and twenty-seven addressed the laity in a democratic context. Of the twenty-seven that focused on the laity, fully twenty endorsed democratic governance and only two sought to restrain the democratic impulse.[24] In most proposals, the laity sought to expand democratic processes.

In some cases they attempted to widen the pool of participants in existing democratic processes. For example, one parishioner from Saint George parish on the Southside of Pittsburgh wanted "the present system of nominations for the parish committee [to] be changed so all parishioners 21 or over, if they so desire, can become candidates and the names printed on the ballots." Another parishioner from a Butler County parish recommended that "for the elections of the parish committee, everyone of high school age or older, who use church envelopes be permitted to vote." Still another urged that "in electing parish committeemen all eligible to vote participate in the nomination as well." In other cases parishioners sought to expand the purview of democratically chosen representatives. One Saint Basil parishioner proposed that "some of the financial decisions associated with running the parish should be taken away from the pastor and more of the responsibilities be given to the elected parish committees." Another suggested that "parish decisions of administrative and financial policy should be made by the Church Committee together with the priest. The decision of the majority should be binding." Some parishioners sought to use popular referendums to make significant parish or diocesan decisions. One Saint Andrew parishioner proposed just such a procedure for the synod itself:

> If a diocese is to have certain statutes, they should first be presented to all Catholics in the diocese for a vote. Those statutes that have been found acceptable, then, should be adhered to in all parts of the diocese and not revised or altered to suit the needs or wishes of individual parishes or priests.

The fact that Pittsburgh Catholics in the 1960s took as an assumption that their parish, and sometimes diocesan, structures ought to follow democratic principles shows how powerful a transformation had taken place in the preceding two decades. A culture so thoroughly steeped in deference and obedience to authority had given way to one infused with assertions of rights and prerogatives. The vast majority of these assertions came in the realm of "temporal" concerns, but the laity sought more significant roles in the liturgical arena as well.

Liturgy

The laity recommended expanding their role in the liturgy in 21 of the 157 proposals that they offered, and failed even once to recommend that their role be diminished. They sought to distribute Communion, receive Communion in the hand, offer homilies, and consult with pastors on Mass times and homily topics.

TABLE 8.8   Proposals on the Liturgy by Type

Type	Frequency	Percent
Liberal	79	50
Conservative	28	18
Neutral	50	32
Total	*157*	*100*

Did the laity embrace the liturgical changes already undertaken? Did they seek to restore the old liturgy? An examination of the type of proposals that parishioners offered suggests that laymen and laywomen endorsed the reforms already implemented and wanted even more. (See table 8.8.) Half of all the proposals that parishioners made sought liberal ends. They pushed for things such as further translations into English, greater roles for the laity, freedom from obligations, and stronger voices in liturgical decisions. Less than a fifth of proposals sought conservative ends, such as the restoration of reformed or abandoned practices, the abolition of folk Masses, or the halt to any future changes. The rest of the proposals sought neutral ends, such as the development of age-based liturgies and homilies explaining Catholic practices.

Parishioners directed their liberal, conservative, and neutral proposals over a number of subjects connected to the liturgy, with a clustering around the themes identified in table 8.9. Liberal proposals dominated in each of the categories as parishioners sought to continue the movement of liturgical reform already under way. This can be seen in each of the subjects listed in the table, though a brief discussion of lay proposals on homilies and obligations conveys lay desires for the liturgy.

The most powerful message that laywomen and laymen sent out regarding homilies was their dissatisfaction with their current experiences. Regardless of whether they sought liberal, conservative, or neutral solutions, the laity agreed unanimously that homilies could and ought to be better. Some parishioners sought to remedy the situation by eliminating the homily. One, for example, recommended that "there be no homily on Holy-days." One suggested that there be no homily, "at the first mass on Holy Days." Most sought to improve rather than eliminate the homily, though. Some gave very mild suggestions, such as the Saint Canice parishioner who proposed merely that priests ought to "try to improve homilies." A Saint Winifred parishioner urged "that an effort be made on

TABLE 8.9   Liturgical Proposal Themes and Subjects

Proposal Subject	Frequency	Percent
Homilies	25	16
Obligations	15	10
Music	12	8
Communion	12	8
Age	14	9
Gender	9	6
Language	8	5

the part of all priests toward more soul stirring sermons to provoke serious thought on the part of the congregation." A Saint George parishioner wanted the homilist to "be well prepared to lend the maximum of instruction to the faithful."

Others sought more specific routes to improvement. Here the disposition toward liberal changes emerges more clearly. A number sought to widen the source of homilies beyond the parish priest. One proposal called for "readings from writers of distinction during homilies." Another recommended that "qualified laymen be permitted to render sermons at Mass." Still another urged "that the religious be given an opportunity to prepare and deliver appropriate homilies on special and occasional Sundays, and Holydays of obligation." For these Catholics, the insistence that only priests give homilies deprived the community of good preaching.

Parishioners also sought to improve homilies by more carefully directing priests toward specific subject matter or styles. One noted that

> because for so many, the weekly Mass is the chief means of instruction, priests should make every effort to relate the gospels, epistles and prayers at Mass to our daily lives, so that we are fortified and strengthened to live and act as Christians throughout the week.

Another wanted sermons to "relate to important issues of the day. A definite stand against social injustice is needed for the church to be more functional in today's world." One parishioner from Our Lady of Loretto parish suggested that "as a change from the Sunday sermon priests should use other means of instruction such as: discussion, questions, films, etc., to draw from, involve and educate the people of the parish."

A number of parishioners recommended that priests seek out sermon topics from the laity. This consultation would better match parishioner interests with the priests' efforts, and presumably lead to more relevant homilies delivered to more attentive Catholics. Some parishioners recommended that priests accomplish this through home visitations, while others suggested that questionnaires would suffice.

Parishioners regularly expressed opinions on various liturgical "obligations" under which they lived, and a decisive majority urged the hierarchy to loosen or eliminate them. The most prominent was the obligation to attend weekly and Holy Day Masses. Catholics lived under the clearly stated expectation that they attend Mass every Sunday and on eight additional "Holy Days" throughout the year. Priests insisted that missing Mass on any of these days without good reason constituted a sin against God and placed an individual's soul in danger of eternal damnation. A number of parishioners proposed changing this. Some sought incremental changes, such as the Resurrection parishioner who wanted Catholics to be able to "fulfill the obligation to attend Mass by attending either on Sunday or on any day of the week other than Sunday." Similarly, another parishioner wanted the "Sunday Mass Obligation [to] be fulfilled by attending Saturday Mass." One suggested that attendance at Mass on Thanksgiving count for Mass the following Sunday. Others sought more profound change, such as the parishioner from Saint Basil who urged that "the weekly Mass obligation be eliminated entirely." Another recommended that "attendance at Mass on Holy Days should be voluntary." Whether parishioners sought incremental or profound changes, most of them sought to lessen externally imposed obligations and place more responsibility for formal worship participation on individual Catholics.

Gender

Thirty-five of the lay proposals addressed gender issues directly, with a vast majority of them focused on women and their roles in the Church. As in other areas, the laity favored liberal rather than conservative positions. What did they seek specifically? Fifteen of the thirty-five proposals sought to reduce or eliminate gender distinctions, and twelve of the proposals recommended empowering women within the Church. For example, one parishioner from Saint Anne's parish in the South Hills urged the diocese to "take immediate steps to effectively enlarge the role of women in the life of the Church, including liturgical celebrations."

TABLE 8.10   Proposals Addressing Gender

Type	Number
Liberal	22
Conservative	9
Neutral	4
Total	35

Another suggested that "women be encouraged to assume liturgical roles now usually held by men, such as Lector, commentator, cantor, server." Still another asserted that "women should be equal to men in Liturgical functions." Other suggestions included eliminating the disparity between diocesan support for boys' and girls' high schools, allowing women to forgo wearing hats in church, and allowing women over forty years of age to practice birth control. Some parishioners sought to ensure that women be represented on parish committees. (See table 8.10.)

Those proposals that sought conservative ends urged the Church to continue single-sex organizations, to reserve male privilege in liturgical functions ("that no one be permitted in the sanctuary but the priest and males"), and to require women to continue to wear distinctive garb. One sought to head off any further changes by recommending that "any programs to the end of eventually having women ordained to the priesthood be discouraged."

DEVISING LEGISLATION

The synod preparation process afforded Pittsburgh's lay Catholics an extraordinary opportunity to articulate a vision for their Church in the midst of a great transformation. The laity responded with a powerful call to continue moving in the direction that Vatican II clearly aimed the Church. The task then fell to the synod commissions to distill that vision into formal documents to guide the diocese over the coming decades.

The commissions labored long to fashion the proposals they received from the parishes, along with the information they had derived from their study and experts, into their own proposals for new legislation. For a short while the synod promised to reflect a wide range of Catholic opinion and will, to be truly a "democratically" derived program for Catholic life and governance in the diocese. And to a certain extent the very enlightenment and empowerment the laity received from their own study and discussion made them more critical and self-conscious about their faith. But the synod's great promise dissipated in the last stages of synod preparation, promulgation, and implementation.

The demise of the democratic ideal came initially with Bishop Wright's elevation and transfer from the diocese. His replacement, Bishop Leonard, did not share Wright's affinity for grassroots influence on episcopal concerns. Wright had pushed for a principled Catholic presence in the physical world, a forthright and dynamic encounter with the world to reshape it along Christian ideals. He sought to empower the laity through formally democratic structures, particularly the Parish Committee, to gain a greater control over, and therefore a larger stake in, their Catholic community. In many ways, he epitomized the liberal Catholic bishop in a time of liberal reform.

Bishop Leonard was not so inclined. He took a more personally pastoral approach to diocesan governance. Wright's grand plans were certainly exciting, but Leonard saw little value in them for the Pittsburgh Church. What did parish committees have over rosary recitation? How did Diocesan Pastoral Councils engender a greater love for Mary? Leonard was uncomfortable with the intellectual and theological concerns that animated Bishop Wright and the synod process, and he made this plain to the General Coordinating Board for the Synod. He indicated in late 1970 that he was concerned most with the actual legislation, the rules and laws, and not with the theological foundations that had preoccupied the commissions for so many months. When the GCBS put together the final synod book, he wanted a short introduction and concise theological statements.[25] The final synod book reflected the two bishops' disparate concerns and values. Bishop Wright's December 1968 announcement that the synod would take place took six pages of the book, while Bishop Leonard's foreword to the final product ran only a page and a half.[26]

Early the next year Fr. Kiernan Stenson wrote to the GCBS from the Chancery, in a tone making clear that he wrote on Leonard's behalf, that the synod was not to establish new programs without Bishop Leonard's prior approval (which Stenson suggested was not forthcoming). He then went on to criticize many of the synod preparation's findings to date. Community Affairs had recommended hiring people to effect social justice in the larger community. It would be better that priests, religious, and the laity articulate the diocese's position on such issues. The efforts to decentralize and democratize the Church, which the synod embodied, ran counter to Stenson's interpretation of Vatican II documents. In Stenson's (and Leonard's) view, "The concept of democracy in the Catholic Church does not in any way reduce the singular and historically-conditioned authority of a bishop. If we develop an administrative, democratic procedure, do we begin to erode away these powers which have been part of the sustaining force of our Church?" Further, was the Church more properly a social work agency or "an institution for the teaching of the Word of Jesus Christ?" Stenson argued that it could not be both and had to be the latter. Finally, Stenson saw in the growing emphasis on professionalism within the Church an effort to transform the institution into a corporation. "It is a fleeting feeling, but one based on experience, and it is the feeling that L.T.V. [steel corporation] has taken us over and we now serve another purpose—the purpose of structural systems as the essence of the diocese."[27]

Father Stenson reflected Bishop Leonard's concern that the synod pushed the Church too far from the shepherd or parish model of the diocesan Church wherein the ordinary held firm but benign control. The bishop was to lead his flock, not consult them. Moreover, the extensive bureaucracy that a more democratic Church required necessarily depersonalized the institution, or did so from the bishop's perspective at least. Bishop Leonard's concerns did not bode well for the synod.

The next factor undercutting the democratic spirit and origin of the synod preparation came about because of the unwieldy nature of the broad consultative process. Everything took longer and finished later than the timetable had allotted, and the General Coordinating Board found itself in the uneasy position of asking Bishop Leonard for an extension to complete a project for which he held little enthusiasm. The GCBS felt pressed for time even with the three-month extension Bishop Leonard granted. Delays in all aspects of the process meant that the commissions did not submit their reports on schedule, and the GCBS members became increasingly frustrated with the commissions as a result. Only two of the eleven commissions submitted their reports on time (Religious and Property, Finance and Planning), and the rest came weeks, sometimes months, late.[28] The GCBS became increasingly critical of the commissions as the promulgation date approached. Father Vanyo expressed his frustration with the commissions in a long letter to a representative of the Columbus, Ohio, diocese, which had asked for his advice for their own synod. He relayed that "our greatest weakness was our Commission membership."[29] Commission members did not care to shoulder all the blame for the delays, however, and told the GCBS so. Ted D. Taubeneck, chairman of the Ecumenism Commission, attached a note to his commission's submission stating that the GCBS should share the blame for the late report because it performed crucial duties late, delaying the commission's work.[30]

The tension between the GCBS and the commissions proved so great that the GCBS felt justified in abrogating earlier agreements that they would return the amended commission proposals to the commissions for comment and further revision (and perhaps negotiation). Perhaps more importantly, the GCBS altered the commission work dramatically. When commission members caught wind of this development they objected. But the GCBS held firm. The Rev. John Cassella told Vanyo that a GCBS member told him that they would not send the amended materials back to the commissions because "'you guys sent in a lot of junk.'" Cassella deemed this attitude and policy a "gross violation of charity." Vanyo replied that many of the submissions were "of inferior quality" and required extensive GCBS revision. He saw no practical way of returning the material to the commissions and still meeting the deadline.[31] The GCBS changed the commission reports and then sent them to Bishop Leonard, who made his own suggestions, and then returned them to the GCBS. Father Vanyo then wrote the entire document based upon the drafts and suggestions that came out of the GCBS alterations and Bishop Leonard's comments.[32] The final document often departed dramatically from what the commissions had submitted.

Many commission members were astounded and furious. Sr. Elizabeth McMillan wrote to Father Vanyo,

> I know that many responsible people who worked on the Commissions were disillusioned, not to say scandalized, at how much of their work was disregarded. I hope you can see that there is more to the issue than their feeling unappreciated. The wholesale revision of the documents by the Steering Committee (and Bishop Leonard) makes a farce of the much-advertised "participation."[33]

Msgr. Jerome McKenna told Monsignor McCarren that the GCBS and Leonard revisions replaced good material with one section that "in our estimation was quite frankly trite and banal as well as poorly constructed." As for its author, "It is plainly evident that he is not familiar with the most recent developments in the theology of the religious life."[34] James Cunningham, chairman of the Community Affairs Commission, wrote to Bishop Leonard that "the final document came as a large surprise to us [commission members]. It seems but a pale shadow of the sturdy report submitted." C. Holmes Wolfe, Jr., who served on both a deanery subcommittee and the Pastoral Government Commission, told Vanyo that the final document ignored the deanery work, which was "particularly disappointing." In addition, the GCBS-Leonard revisions of the commission work did not sit well. "I do not believe that we have been treated fairly." The GCBS had the commission report for four months and never consulted the commission on revisions. "The procedure followed ... will lend itself to great disenchantment, even indignation."[35]

The General Coordinating Board and Bishop Leonard had largely discarded almost three years of widespread lay, clerical, and religious consultation and work in favor of an expedient end to a long preparation process. In effect, they had rejected the new model of Catholicism emanating from the Second Vatican Council. Many participants resented this. But even so, the final product departed from the previous synod legislation dramatically. It encouraged and applauded lay participation in the liturgy and parish governance.

Bishop Leonard promulgated the synod in a dramatic ceremony in Saint Paul's Cathedral but appointed no commission to implement the legislation. Father Vanyo had expected and hoped that Bishop Leonard would appoint him to run an office dedicated to implementing the synod legislation. Leonard did not. The diocese implemented some aspects of the synod and not others. The existing diocesan departments adopted some programs and ignored others. Bishop Leonard made no concerted effort to "implement" the synod. Father Vanyo recalled,

> I think Bishop Leonard was glad it was over. You know, this was not his style. But he was like Pope Paul VI, he had no choice. Paul VI had to continue the Council, Bishop Leonard had to continue the Synod. . . . But he did not bring the same enthusiasm to the synod that Bishop Wright did.[36]

In his final analysis, Father Vanyo believed that the synod would have been better had the synod commissions and the Coordinating Board initiated the legislation and the parishioners reacted to it. He suggested that parishioners could have originated some ideas in reaction to the commissions' and board's legislation in this scheme as well.[37]

The synod's final stages disappointed a great many laywomen and laymen, particularly those who worked closest to the project. Bishop Leonard's determination to downplay the synod effectively stifled the opportunity for significant structural reforms in the diocese for the next three decades, and may have cost the diocese its opportunity to regenerate the Church in Pittsburgh. But the preparation itself provided an impetus for lay involvement in the local and diocesan Church which had never before existed. It spurred the laity to think about their religion and its role very self-consciously. It encouraged those who wished to continue the Vatican reform spirit in the local parishes to persevere, and it provided a rare opportunity for Catholics to assess their parish and personal religious beliefs and behaviors. Parishioners wanted a Church that shifted power in local parishes from pastors to the laity, and in the larger diocese from the bishop to priests and the laity. They pushed the Church to embrace democratic structures, to support more fully and enthusiastically liturgical reform, and to lessen the gender inequities that then existed. They wanted little part of the heavily devotional, insular Church of the 1940s and early 1950s. Though they did not seem to advocate unequivocally the broader social justice role for the Church in the broader society, they certainly embraced those principles within the Church itself. The parishioners did not succeed in persuading the diocesan hierarchy on all aspects of these positions, but they emerged from the synodal process with a clearer sense of how they would shape the Church themselves.

THE 1971 PITTSBURGH SYNOD MARKED THE APEX OF DEMOCRATIC participation in Pittsburgh diocesan government. It drew more lay participation than did the Diocesan Pastoral Council, and for a brief time seemed capable of transforming the very nature of Catholic relations in Pittsburgh. The laity responded energetically to Bishop Wright's sincere request for consultation on pastoral aims and structures for the diocese, and appeared for a short while to have won over those in the diocese who continued to perceive the laity's role to be to "pray, pay, and obey." The extensive consultation that Wright implemented for the synod promised a new, more egalitarian Church. The bishop sought to change the diocesan legislation as the parishioners wanted it changed. But the heady promise of lay consultation proved short-lived, and the synod ended with dashed lay hopes and a great deal of bitterness on the part of those laywomen and laymen most active in the synod preparations.

Yet the synod endorsed a heightened lay position within the diocese, reformed diocesan programs, and pulled many laymen and laywomen into more active roles within the Church. It encouraged the laity to view the institution in ways largely unfamiliar. It suggested that the Catholic Church was potentially a democratic institution, responsive to the needs and desires of its adherents. In the course of its deliberations, the synod asked for and received thousands of proposals from the laity on ways to reform the Church which shed a great deal of light on lay desires and perceptions in the immediate wake of the Second Vatican Council. Whatever its ultimate limitations for lay empowerment, it enabled the laity to speak to future generations about their concerns in 1969.

CHAPTER NINE

The Post-Conciliar Parishes

THE DIOCESE SERVED AS THE MOST EXPLICIT AND DETERMINED interpreter of the Second Vatican Council reforms in Pittsburgh. It had the resources and the impetus to translate the reforms into official programs. Moreover, the Council had elevated the bishops' stature and authority within the hierarchy, had made the bishops aware of the opportunity and responsibility to translate the reforms actively. But ordinary parishioners continued to encounter the organized Church primarily in the parish. They apprehended the Vatican reforms through various media, but experienced and confronted them through the parish structure. This book has visited three parishes at various points to explore more fully the local lay experience, and in this chapter looks more comprehensively at the parishes in light of the Vatican II changes.

Parish officials in each of the three parishes—Immaculate Heart of Mary, Saint Philomena, and Saint Thomas More—actively supported devotional Catholicism in the years before the Second Vatican Council even as parishioners themselves began to abandon such practices. The ethnic and urban parish continued to provide the structures for formal devotion to a greater degree than did suburban Saint Thomas More parish. The differences between parish experiences widened in the years after the Council. The suburban parish enmeshed itself in the world, to the extent that it defined itself as an actor in the larger society. The urban parish moved more gingerly in that direction, and foundered on liturgical changes. It became almost two parishes, and as such expended much of its energy reconciling differences rather than moving clearly in one direction. The ethnic parish leaders held onto the forms of the devotional tradition, bolstered in its aims by economic and demographic constraints. In their attempt to retain the formal devotional traditions, though, they foundered.

One can see in these stories the general decline in devotional practices in the parishes, the rise of a democratic-egalitarian parish governing structure, and the transformed liturgy. The three parishes that practiced largely similar rituals, and structured experiences in roughly the same way outside of those rituals in the early 1950s, began to diverge as the Conciliar changes reached the parish level. By the middle of the 1980s, suburban, urban, and ethnic parishes differed significantly in the way they sought to structure formal worship and parishioners' experiences outside of the liturgy.

The Diocesan Pastoral Council helped focus the debates and developments under way in the local parishes in a session devoted to the parish committee and parish council. Parish committees, and later parish councils, represent the most significant change in lay experience outside of the formal liturgy. The diocesan reform of 1965 sought to increase the scope of consultation and decision making in the parish from the pastor only to all adult parishioners (through formally elected representatives). Bishop Wright intended the parish committees to "provide a means to the common counsel needed for the common planning in discharge of common responsibility toward the common good of the parish."[1] The parishes moved unevenly toward that goal.

The Lay Activities Office of the diocese conducted a survey of pastors in 1968 in preparation for a Diocesan Pastoral Council meeting on parish committees. Each parish had held elections for members two years before the survey, and Bishop Wright deemed that long enough ago to ascertain the parish committees' effectiveness throughout the diocese. The survey and subsequent Pastoral Council discussion revealed that parish committees did not address the scope of parish experience that Bishop Wright had hoped that they would. Committees varied in composition, purpose, and procedure across the diocese. For example, though the new diocesan statute required ten laymen or laywomen for each parish committee, 7 percent of parishes had only four, 33 percent had six, 46 percent had eight, and only 14 percent had all ten. Furthermore, 18 percent of parish committees used committee votes to arrive at all decisions, 46 percent arrived at their decisions by consensus, and 36 percent used some combination of consensus and voting.[2]

Most importantly, though, and most disappointing to Bishop Wright and the *Pittsburgh Catholic,* parish committees focused predominantly on building and maintenance and finances. They did not sufficiently broach the liturgy, community affairs, and religious education. (See table 9.1.)

The parish committees had not increased lay participation on the whole range of issues vital to parish life, but rather gained voice in areas in which pastors were willing to concede that some laymen had greater "expertise." This very issue shaped clerical and popular debate on parish committees. Many Catholics, particularly but not exclusively priests, sought only competent, or expert,

TABLE 9.1   Parish Committee Survey Results, 1968
(Percentage of Committees That Discussed These Topics)

Frequency	Building Maintenance	Liturgy	Community Affairs and Ecumenism	Finance	Religious Education
Never	2	13	38	5	17
Seldom	1	16	20	6	12
Occasionally	5	25	14	5	19
Frequently	4	5	2	3	10
Always	88	41	26	81	42

Source: Pittsburgh Catholic, 22 March 1968.

advice on parish governance, while others saw democratic participation to be the key principle that parishes should use to guide their activities. The debate raged fairly strongly in 1968, though those advocating "expertise" clearly had the upper hand. For example, a quarter of all parishes did not announce Parish Committee meeting places and times publicly, 62 percent kept upcoming meeting agendas secret, and 55 percent never told parishioners what the Parish Committee had decided.[3]

IMPACT OF THE PARISH COUNCIL

One can see in the experiences of the three parishes the impact of an active Parish Council on parish life. Saint Thomas More, a suburban parish, had an engaged Parish Council that enabled the parish to move more responsively and rapidly toward greater lay involvement in a wide range of areas—including the liturgical, temporal, and social. The other parishes had far less active councils and moved only fitfully toward recognizing the greater role the laity wished to play, and would play eventually throughout the diocese. The urban and ethnic parishes suffered as a reasult.

Saint Thomas More Parish

Saint Thomas More parishioners moved to incorporate the model of a democratic and active Parish Council very deliberately. They established democratic procedures for electing the council, held open and well-publicized meetings, and sought to address a range of issues critical to parish financial, liturgical, and spiritual life.

The council met about once a month during the fall, winter, and spring, and less regularly in the summer. It ranged over a number of issues and periodically undertook studies of the parish to assess how well it fulfilled the parishioners' needs. Monsignor Rooney was under no obligation to follow the council's recommendations, but he almost always did so. When he sensed that the council was moving in a direction that he did not countenance, or which might cause problems in the Chancery, he convinced the council to table its discussion. But his position on the Executive Committee and his influence among council members allowed him to head off those situations before they reached such a stage. The council remained active and vibrant throughout the 1970s, and served as a limited popular means of parish governance.

Many of the council's actions come to light in the focus on Saint Thomas More's encounter with the Vatican II reforms in the liturgy and in the community. The council expressed its concern with the liturgy immediately, and maintained a high interest throughout the 1970s.

Jules Coelos, Worship Committee chair, told the council in its second meeting that the committee had several long-range plans for the parish, and expanding the role of women topped the list. Coelos read five proposals at the following meeting, four of which expanded female roles in the liturgy. The committee wanted women commentators and lectors to be able to hold the paten under parishioners' chins as they received Communion. Male lectors and commentators did this when not enough altar boys were present, and the committee thought women should be allowed to do so also. The committee further recommended that females be permitted to serve as acolytes, as ushers, and as eucharistic ministers. The parish council approved by an 18–12 vote the recommendation to allow women to hold the paten, by a 12–8 vote to allow girls to serve as acolytes, by an unrecorded vote to allow women ushers, and then foundered on the eucharistic minister suggestion.[4]

The diocese of Pittsburgh had announced in February that lay parishioners would be permitted to distribute Communion at Masses. Though many Catholics saw this nationwide development to be a further elevation of the laity—a recognition on the part of the hierarchy that parishioners should fill as many roles as possible in the Church—the hierarchy carefully proposed eucharistic ministers as a short-term response to the temporary priest shortage. They were to distribute Communion only because not enough priests existed to meet the great demand. The Saint Thomas More bulletin informed parishioners that eucharistic ministers would function only "at our more crowded Masses, together with our staff of priests." When the bulletin announced the names of the first six eucharistic ministers, it listed three necessary conditions for them to function. They could distribute Communion when the minister was not available, when he was unable (through sickness, age, or otherwise engaged pastorally), or when relying solely on the priest would "unduly prolong" the Mass. Only males could serve as eucharistic ministers, and these unordained males would lose the privilege as soon as vocations increased sufficiently to make them unnecessary.[5]

Because the eucharistic minister role empowered the laity in one of the Church's most sacred acts, excluding women underscored their inferior status within the Church. Furthermore, the very shaky theological grounds for permitting nonordained males to do this (necessity) did not exclude women on the face of it. The necessity existed for more people to distribute Communion, and these people held no special qualifications other than their membership in the mystical body of Christ. Women too were members of that body.

The Worship Committee debated this issue heatedly in the weeks before the September council meeting. Jules Coelos reported to the Executive Committee that the issue "created much discussion" at the Worship Committee meeting, and that most of the people were opposed or "apathetic" (perhaps indifferent) to the idea. Thirty-one council members served on the Worship Committee, including eleven women. Mr. Coelos further reported that the committee was less opposed to female acolytes, and the idea of female ushers "created negative opinions."[6] Mr. Coelos reported the recommendations to the larger council the following week, reporting that the committee had "tabled" the issue of women eucharistic ministers until later.

Monsignor Rooney asked Auxiliary Bishop Bosco whether women might hold patens, and Bosco replied that he thought they might do so "at exceptional times, or in case of necessity," and that the Chancery had given permission for this. Bosco also stated that girls could not serve as acolytes. Rooney then reported to the next council meeting that women could hold the paten, that "it was not feasible at this time to contact the Bishop on the matter of girl Acolytes," and that women could serve as ushers. The issue of women eucharistic ministers remained tabled.[7]

A council subcommittee on eucharistic ministers studied the issue and then reported in favor of commissioning females. The council debated the recommendations at its March 1974 meeting. After much discussion, the council recommended unanimously to Monsignor Rooney that women be permitted to serve in this role. But the issue remained at that stage for more than a year, until Rooney reported to the Executive Committee in May 1975 that a movement existed in the diocese to allow specially trained nuns to distribute Communion. He sent Jules Coelos and Sister Michelle (the parish social services minister) to the training to observe it. The two told the Executive Committee that the training made women more knowledgeable about distributing Communion, and Rooney then recommended three women (including Sister Michelle) for appointment. Two months later Rooney informed the Executive Committee that the diocese had decided to permit women to serve as eucharistic ministers, and that Rooney's three nominations were acceptable. These three women became the first female eucharistic ministers commissioned in the Pittsburgh diocese. The parish continued to expand its number of eucharistic ministers at a ratio of one female for every new male appointed, so that by January 1979, eight of the twenty-four ministers were female.[8]

The Parish Council addressed the liturgy in a number of other ways as well, including sponsoring, participating in, or supporting three formal studies of the parish liturgical experience during the 1970s. The Worship Committee worried throughout the period that the liturgy did not generate sufficient parishioner participation or reflect parishioner involvement in planning. A 1976 survey of parishioners revealed that the parishioners themselves desired "improved ways to solicit parishioners' opinions and to communicate with parishioners through a variety of media." The Parish Council released five recommendations for an improved liturgy in 1977 based upon a study of the parish which Saint Thomas More did in conjunction with Catholic University of America. The CUA study spurred the Parish Council Executive Committee to debate and then abandon efforts to hire an independent professional agency to conduct a more formal study of the parish liturgy.[9]

The council also replaced a temporary crucifix in the new church with a risen Christ, an act that reflected the new emphasis of the Mass on the redeeming benefits of Christ's resurrection over the agony of his crucifixion.[10] The new church, which the parish opened in 1968, did not display a statue of Mary prominently, and the Altar Society pushed to get one in the church. This attempted return to a devotional emphasis in the new church did not fare well, however. The Worship Committee at first endorsed the idea, studied various statues for months, and then rescinded its endorsement.[11] The post–Vatican II Church was not, in the view of the Worship Committee and the larger Parish Council, a devotional meetinghouse.

The post-Conciliar parish was a community that interacted with the larger society to transform it. Saint Thomas More parishioners became involved in a number of ecumenical, charitable, and political efforts, sponsored educational activities, and engaged in civil protest. Many of these efforts took on clear and explicit intentions to work for social justice within the diocesan church, the local community, and the national society. Some even looked beyond national boundaries to the poor and suffering in other parts of the world, particularly Latin America, and sought to alleviate the conditions. Three parish efforts illustrate well the parish's willing though uneasy transition from the insular devotional community to the interactive proponent of social justice.

The first focused within the Church itself, on the parish's and the diocese's attitudes and policies on gender. During the same period the Parish Council discussed female eucharistic ministers, the diocese changed its means of funding Catholic high schools. The schools were single-sex institutions, and the diocese sponsored directly South Hills Catholic High School. In late 1973 the diocese introduced a subsidy plan that required each parish within the boundaries of its three regional boys high schools to pay a set portion of parish income to the schools. The Parish Council debated and then rejected the diocese's scheme, citing it as inequitable because it slighted female Catholic secondary education. The parish had thirty-seven girls in female Catholic high schools that year, and only twenty-two boys at SHCHS. The council recommended that the diocese develop a plan that supported all Catholic secondary schools. Bishop Leonard told Monsignor Rooney that it was too late to change the system for that year, and assessed the parish 2.2 percent of its income.[12]

The Parish Council persisted in its objection to the funding scheme, however. Instead of dividing the 2.2 percent among male and female schools, it divided the subsidy to SHCHS by the number of students from Saint Thomas More parish, and then subsidized the female high schools that educated parishioners at the same per student rate. The assessment came out to two hundred dollars for each boy at South Hills Catholic, and the parish sent two hundred dollars to each female high school for each student from Saint Thomas More whom they had enrolled.[13]

The issue came up again the following year, when council member Tom Beck recommended dividing support between South Hills Catholic High School and Fontbonne Academy (the closest girls high school). The council debated Beck's proposal, with some members objecting to the larger subsidy that SHCHS would reap (Fontbonne had thirty-six students, SHCHS only twenty-one), and some worried that the parish was focusing too narrowly on the two schools. A motion to table Beck's proposal met defeat, and the council passed it by a vote of 11–8.[14]

Bishop Leonard decided to reinstate the 2.2 percent assessment of parish income to support boys high schools in November 1975, and to supplement that with a 1.8 percent subsidy of female Catholic high schools. The parish had thirty-three students in female Catholic high schools, and only sixteen boys in

SHCHS in 1975. The enrollment pattern further exacerbated the inequitable distribution that the diocese mandated. Hugh Finneran motioned to send subsidies directly to the female high schools, to bypass the diocese entirely. The council passed the motion unanimously. The council then rescinded its earlier determination to fund only SHCHS and Fontbonne Academy, and to distribute the funding on a per student basis.[15] The council had decided to defy diocesan authority over an issue of social justice. The diocese's decision to favor males over females was unjust, in the council's eyes, and members opted in favor of justice over obedience.

The second case proved more complicated, and forced the parish to define more clearly the shape of its notions of social justice. It involved parish attempts to rectify some of the damage America had done in Vietnam. The parish considered and then decided to "adopt" a family from South Vietnam. The Apostolate Committee of the Parish Council responded favorably to a diocesan program to encourage parishes to adopt Vietnamese families. The committee recommended in September 1975 that the Parish Council fund the adoption, which entailed finding housing for the family and finding a job for the "breadwinner." They expected the commitment to last roughly four or five months. The council adopted the proposal after ensuring that the funds to support the family would be separate from the general parish funds (they were concerned about a drain on the budget).[16]

The short-term commitment stretched into months and months, however, as the Vietnamese family of ten found it impossible to adjust to life in suburban Pittsburgh. Local landlords evicted the family from the homes the parish located for them, and the diocese discouraged any long-term parish commitment to the family. After fifteen months, persistent problems locating housing, mounting Catholic school tuition bills, and little success in the family's becoming economically self-sufficient, the parish located a home for the family outside of its boundaries and shifted financial responsibility for the family to the state. Rather than accept the new arrangement, the family moved to the more hospitable environment of California.

The parish had set out to alleviate the suffering a family experienced caused in large part by American actions in Vietnam. Parishioners saw the adoption plan as a means of becoming active in the world community in ways more meaningful than simply writing checks for overseas relief. Parishioners welcomed a family displaced by a war associated intimately with the parish (at least three parishioners lost their lives in Vietnam), and hoped to share the benefits and wealth of suburban life. Parishioners anticipated a quick adjustment and short-term support. When the months stretched into years, however, parishioners tired of their commitment. A later opportunity to sponsor a family from Cambodia provided the parish with an opportunity to reflect on its experience with the Vietnamese family. Council members recalled the great amount of money that the first family required, but focused instead on other aspects of support. They remembered that "the dollar amount is insignificant, the sacrifices made by the people involved was [sic] great, the total experience was both good and rewarding—a positive experience." The council voted unanimously to adopt the Cambodian family but vowed to approach the venture differently. They resolved that "our goal is to help them become independent so that they can do their 'thing.' We should not dictate but help them find themselves."[17] In so doing, parishioners too were finding themselves as a community dedicated to social justice. Though the Vietnamese family's experience did not seem the great success the parishioners recalled, it was an opportunity for the parish to fill its emerging role as actor in society for social good.

The largest effort that the parish expended to help transform the world focused locally. The parish built an apartment building near the parish to house elderly people who could not afford rents in the existing buildings in the area. The project began with Saint Thomas More parishioners in mind but expanded to encompass any resident of Allegheny County. The parish had to confront its mission when the change became necessary. The change in scope meant that parishioners had to look beyond the parish to the larger community, to expend considerable parish efforts on the broader society.

The issue arose when Sister Michelle and Monsignor Rooney realized that a number of older Saint Thomas More parishioners who lived in local buildings could no longer afford the rent. The parishioners' children were subsidizing their rents in some cases, and in others the parishioners had to move out of the apartments. Monsignor Rooney brought a housing expert to the Parish Council Executive Committee meeting in April 1978 to generate support for a parish-sponsored building.[18] The parish hired a local real estate company with experience in elderly housing to handle the project once the parish received the bishop's permission, but parishioners still had to do quite a bit of work to set it up.[19]

The parish decided to build the apartments through a special Housing and Urban Development program that required the parish to put up a small amount of money and handle all the administrative details. Parishioners began to worry about HUD involvement because it made clear to many for the first time that the project could not be limited to Saint Thomas More parishioners. Some were uncertain that they wanted to undertake a broader housing development, and others worried about minorities coming to the suburbs. In a brief discussion of the proposal in the Parish Council some members grilled the realty representative on the government's role. One expressed his disbelief that the government would not want to control occupancy selection. Another was less tactful. "Wouldn't we be forced to have blacks?" the questioner demanded. The realty representative admitted that some units would have to be set aside for minorities, based upon their proportion of the population in the larger community.[20]

Parishioners consulted with HUD five times over the course of the next few months, met with an Allegheny County housing representative and three HUD-recommended consultants, and held a number of committee meetings.[21] They then presented their findings to the Parish Council. Some council members again expressed concern over the type of people who would live there. One member insisted that the committee make clear when presenting this to the parish the "low income" aspect of the project. Mr. Coelos wondered if the parish could make the 20 percent minimum number of units that had to be reserved for low-income residents a maximum as well. Andrew Sedley responded that they could limit the poor spaces to 20 percent, but that they could also devote 100 percent of the spaces to the poor.[22]

Andrew Sedley's suggestion revealed the transformation that those parishioners who had worked intimately on the project had undergone in the last few months. The project had been transformed in their eyes from a way to help older parishioners to an effort to fill a broader societal need. The apartment building was a significant way to serve the larger community, and particularly those members of the community most in need.

Mr. Coelos was surprised at Mr. Sedley's suggestion. "Is the Committee dedicated to 100% Section 8 occupancy?" he asked. Monsignor Rooney replied that they were. Coelos reminded the council that the original proposal was to help elderly parishioners who were not poor but who had trouble meeting their expenses. This was a very different idea. Did the committee intend to limit residency to the parish or neighborhood? Andrew Sedley said that parishioners would get priority, but that the building would then be open to all county residents. Coelos asked about "affirmative action." Mr. Sedley replied that HUD required the parish to set aside 10 percent of the units for minorities.[23]

Council members again expressed concern about the new purpose of the project. Mr. Greiner wondered what the parish was hoping to accomplish: "Was the intent that housing would be provided for parishioners or the low-income elderly of the county?" Mr. Sedley finally stated explicitly the project's aim. The project began with the intent of helping parishioners, but "the committee ultimately decided that as Christians the parish should look to the good of all."

Mrs. Plantes reiterated Andrew Sedley's point: "We are very blessed and we have an obligation to think of those who are not as blessed. This would be an opportunity for Christian witness." The council approved the proposal and built Saint Thomas More Manor.[24]

Saint Thomas More parish effected its transformation from an insular, devotional community aimed toward each member's personal salvation to a community that sought to live out the Christian ideal of service for social justice in the larger society. The members did not all agree on each undertaking or even participate heartily. But they decided to act in the larger society as a force for justice, for the transformation of their local, national, and world society along Christian ideals.

Saint Philomena Parish

The urban Saint Philomena parishioners moved in the same direction but much more slowly and with greater resistance. They established a Parish Council and Executive Committee in 1974, but neither addressed the sorts of issues that Saint Thomas More's council and Executive Committee addressed. In fact, the two bodies more often served to kill ideas and proposals than to generate them. The parish's sesquicentennial history reported very dryly that the council's committees took four years to "refine their aims."[25] Even three years after that the bulletin reported that the council was still trying to "become the coordinating and leadership group it is mandated to be."[26] Two sets of events best illuminate Saint Philomena's tenor of Catholicism in the years after the Second Vatican Council.

The first set affected the parish's devotional tradition in ways virtually unique to Saint Philomena parish but involved little lay activity. Parishioners had to respond to developments more than generate them. The Vatican officially reviewed its calendar of saints and removed Saint Philomena from the list in 1961. Two years later the Vatican beatified John Neumann, an early pastor of Saint Philomena parish, and then canonized him in 1977. Within just a few years the parish both lost and gained a saint. Parishioners made little note of Philomena's demotion, and determined to keep her as the parish's patron saint.[27]

Many parishioners took great pleasure at John Neumann's beatification and canonization, however. Regina Kelly flew to Rome for the beatification ceremony and wrote a long report for the Diocesan Council of Catholic Women. The parish introduced a statue of Neumann at a time when most parishes were removing statues from their churches. But the parishioners played little role in the great political process that sainthood entailed in the later twentieth century. Redemptorist Father Francis X. Litz, who had official responsibility for lobbying on Neumann's behalf, estimated the cost of the movement to be in the hundreds of thousands of dollars, and recalled that "theologians, lawyers, medical men, historians, Vatican officials, cardinals [and] the pope" put in a vast amount of hours in the ninety-one-year effort to canonize Neumann.[28] Though parishioners took a great deal of pride in Neumann's canonization, they did not begin a regular Neumann novena or start an elaborate devotional tradition around the parish saint.

The lack of devotional apparatus surrounding Neumann's canonization reflected the parishioners' movement away from a highly devotional faith. Yet they had not fully embraced the Vatican Council reforms, particularly the liturgical reforms. The second set of events that crystallized the parish's experience of the reforms came with the transfer of a young assistant priest to Saint Philomena's in the late 1970s, and centered around the liturgical changes he introduced.

Fr. Francis Gargani came to Saint Philomena parish in 1978 and was given responsibility for the liturgy and youth. He established or invigorated a host of parish organizations, ranging from the Respect Life Committee, which focused primarily (though not exclusively in these years) on efforts to stop abortions, to programs for the elderly. Most dramatically, however, he set out to increase lay participation in the Masses by encouraging singing, making the liturgy more vibrant (active, colorful), and by prodding parishioners to become involved. He recruited various parishioners to help carry out the more elaborate liturgical practices, and infused the Mass with longer and more contemporary songs.[29]

Father Gargani also made changes to the sanctuary design and the interior of the church. He moved most of the statues from the church to the hallway that ran along its eastern wall. Many parishioners appreciated, applauded, and assisted in these changes. They welcomed the more colorful and celebratory tone of the new Mass, and saw it to be more in keeping with the Vatican II reforms, which they supported. These were, by most accounts, the "newer" parishioners at Saint Philomena's.[30] Because many parishioners had lived in the parish for their entire lives, they saw those who moved into the parish after completing grade school to be "new." Enough old parishioners remained to make this a significant division in the parish. A 1981 parish census revealed that 37 percent of Saint Philomena parishioners had resided in the parish for twenty years or more, and 46 percent of these parishioners had lived in the parish for more than forty years.[31] The newer parishioners seemed to favor the liturgical and architectural changes.

Those who objected to the changes were predominantly "old" parishioners. One parishioner recalled their response in very personal terms: "The statues being moved were likened to that of a stranger coming to a persons home as a guest and rearranging the furniture while the host was out." The old parishioners referred to the hallway that then housed the statues as the "hall of the saints," and considered the saints to be "hostages" in their new home.[32] The older parishioners' anger turned to hostility as Gargani covered the crucifix in the sanctuary with banners for special occasions in an effort to make the Mass celebration "less sad."[33]

The older parishioners responded in a couple of ways. Many stopped coming to the parish, and instead attended Mass at other parishes that did not emphasize parishioner participation so much.[34] The parish census fell from 1,189 to 855 between 1981 and 1983, a decline of roughly 28 percent, as parishioners left because of the controversy. (It rose to 1,350 by 1983, however, once the priests had departed.)[35] Overall Mass attendance did not suffer at all throughout 1981, however. Others called the Redemptorist provincial to put a stop to this, to force Father Gargani and Father O'Rourke, the pastor, from reforming the liturgy. Two provincial representatives came to the parish for a parish meeting, during which deeply divided parishioners on both sides of the issue aired their grievances. In the wake of the meeting, and at or near the normal time when the Redemptorists reassigned priests, the provincial transferred both Fathers Gargani and O'Rourke to other parishes. The newer parishioners were upset, and again called the provincial. The provincial then extended Father Gargani's tenure at Saint Philomena for six months, but let Father O'Rourke's transfer stand.[36] Father O'Rourke's replacement resigned six months later, due to the continuing division within the parish and the stress it caused.[37] His replacement left two years later, giving the parish four pastors in a period when they were likely to have had only one or two.

Within six years of the divisive split among parishioners over the saints' removal and the banners obscuring the parishioners' view of the crucifix, a subsequent pastor removed the crucifix permanently in favor of a risen Christ. Parishioners resolved the division somewhat by attending separate Masses. The older parishioners took the 8:00 Mass Sunday mornings, where no one sang and the priest entered and exited the church through side doors next to the sanctuary. Those who wanted more active participation attended the 10:00 Mass Sunday mornings, which had a great deal of singing and lasted fifteen or twenty minutes longer than the 8:00 Mass. The other Masses, Saturday evening and Sunday at noon, fell somewhere in between, with less singing than the 10:00 but more participation than the 8:00.

Immaculate Heart of Mary Parish

Immaculate Heart of Mary priests determined that their post–Vatican II parish would remain insular, dedicated to the preservation of the Polish Catholic community. They did so in the context of race relations, that area of social action on which the diocese had focused so much of its attention. The parishioners confronted the issue twice, once with school integration, and a second time with their involvement in the Model Cities program.

Fewer and fewer students attended Immaculate Heart of Mary school from the 1950s onward. By 1969 the enrollment had declined by more than half from its 1951 level, and it showed no signs of rising.[38] The Catholic Interracial Council noted in 1969 that the parish turned away black students who sought admission, on the grounds that the admission would have diminished the school's (and parish's) ethnic integrity. The Catholic Interracial Council sought a HUD investigation, but a CAP lawyer convinced them to go easy on the parish.[39] The parish had decided not to open its doors to blacks despite a compelling need for students because it persisted in valuing the parish as an insular community, set apart from the world. Its social obligations ranged across the Atlantic Ocean to Poland, but not to the adjoining neighborhoods of the Hill District or Homewood. Parishioners continued to view the parish and not society as the proper realm of concern.[40]

The second opportunity for the parish to implement the new Vatican II understanding of the parish's social mission involved the parish's civic organization and race. The parish had formed the Polish Hill Civic Association within a program that encouraged local Pittsburgh neighborhoods to found such groups to work for community solidarity and neighborhood improvements. The Polish Hill organization affiliated with the Model Cities Program. But its members soon grew suspicious of the Model Cities program and pulled out altogether when all of their four nominations for area representative on the governing board were turned down in favor of a non-Pole. A leader of the Polish Hill Civic Association reiterated the community's need for the services the Model Cities program was supposed to provide: "We want to get the community on its feet. We want better streets and better garbage collection. We need recreation facilities, a library, a health center." The young did not stay, and the neighborhood was becoming older and older. But, a Civic Association leader explained, "The original Model Cities program of community action was never put into practice. We were being subjugated to black power and militancy."[41] The Civic Association remained active in the community. It drew its members from parishioners, met in church buildings, and served as a sort of secular arm of the parish.

But it did not expand its membership, its orientation, to other residents of Polish Hill. The parish and the organization understood their concern to be the ever-shrinking number of parishioners, not all residents of the neighborhood or city.

THE LITURGY BEFORE THE COUNCIL SESSIONS HAD UNDERGONE SOME minor adjustments, but remained largely the same as that set out in chapter 7. Parishioners in Immaculate Heart of Mary, Saint Philomena, and Saint Thomas More parishes attended the same Mass, wherein the priest performed the same ritual. The Mass was a ritual reproduction of Christ's supreme sacrifice, a serious and somber event that emphasized the parishioners' sinful nature and unworthiness, but which offered the redemption that Christ's crucifixion permitted.

Though architectural peculiarities made the stage for each ritual enactment somewhat different, the basic structure and themes remained largely similar in each church. Straight rows of pews lined the rectangular interior of each room, facing a sanctuary separated from the rest of the room (and the parishioners) by a Communion or altar rail. A main altar with a prominently displayed crucifix took the center position on the back wall of the sanctuary in each church, flanked by other altars to saints. Immaculate Heart of Mary's sanctuary placed Mary above the crucifix, so that she, rather than her son, dominated the altar structure. But the crucifix was present. (Immaculate Heart of Mary supplemented this smaller crucifix with a larger one placed on a pillar away from the main altar, though still in the front of the church.) Parishioners attending Mass in these churches noted the presence of the sacred images of saints in the church as well, and often expended the time spent at Mass focused on one or more of them, particularly Mary.

Parishioners at all three parishes viewed the Mass action from a separate sphere. They did not understand the language, see much of the ritual performance (because the priest shielded it with his body), or take part in "sacred" acts performed therein. Parishioners had come more and more to receive Communion, to partake actively in one part of the ritual, though a majority of Catholics still did not. The choir sang hymns during the High Mass, and the organ played at others. Few, if any, parishioners sang hymns, and those hymns they sang did not regularly complement the priest's actions or the liturgical calendar.

The Mass was really two different sets of actions, performed on different sides of the Communion rail. Parishioners said rosaries, prayed novena prayers, recited other prayers, tried to follow the priest's actions with the help of an English-language translation (missal), or daydreamed on one side of the rail.

Priests accomplished the sacred acts on the other. The parishioners benefited from their proximity to the holy, by their physical nearness to the sacred acts performed.

But the Second Vatican Council transformed the liturgy. The tenor of this transformation can be seen in the architectural norms the Council initiated, and which each parish adopted at some point in time, to varying degrees. The most dramatic transformation came for Saint Thomas More parishioners, who built a new church entirely in the wake of the Council.

ARCHITECTURAL CHANGES

The old Saint Thomas More church was a relatively small aluminum and glass rectangular structure. Though its features were more plain than either Saint Philomena's or Immaculate Heart of Mary's, parishioners understood as they entered that they came into a sacred space. Statues of Joseph and Mary flanked the crucifix along the back wall of the sanctuary, and a metal Communion rail separated the pews from the sanctuary.

Father Logue, and after his death Monsignor Rooney, decided to build a new church because the old one could not accommodate the rapidly expanding parish population. The pastors hired an architect and worked out a set of plans, which they showed to parishioners at various stages of development. The construction companies finished work in 1968, when parishioners first attended Mass in the new church. The Mass in this new church differed dramatically from that in the old.

Though parishioners still drove to church, their experience changed dramatically from the years before the Council. Parishioners attending Mass at the old church approached a relatively low, one-story building as they drove toward the church parking lot. After 1968 they came to an impressive multistory octagonal edifice with a towering twenty-six foot cross perched at the exact center. The building rested on the highest point in the church property, so that parishioners exiting their cars, especially from the school parking lot, walked up to the main doors. They entered a foyer as they passed through the outside doors, and then the church itself.

Once inside they encountered a wide open space, configured horseshoe-like around the main altar and sanctuary. The term *main altar* had become a misnomer here, though, as the church contained only one altar. The architect placed this altar at the exact center of the entire building, in fact, to signify the centrality

FIGURE 9.1
Saint Thomas More Parish Church, 1950s

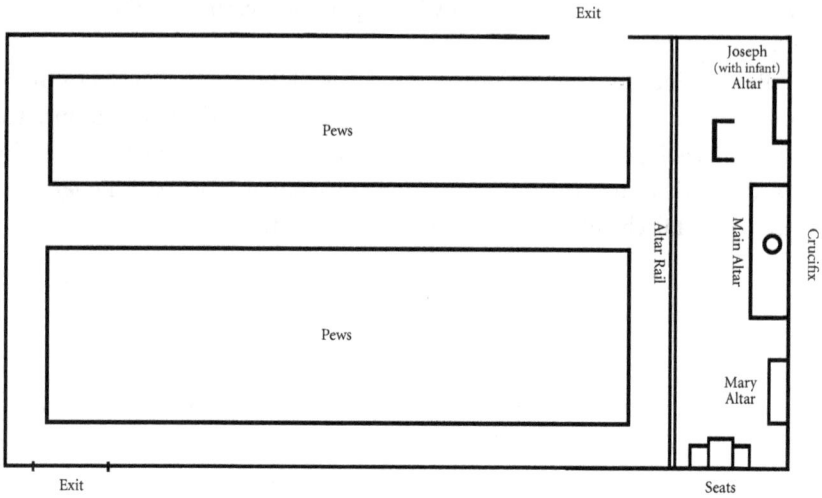

Saint Thomas More Parish Church, 1968

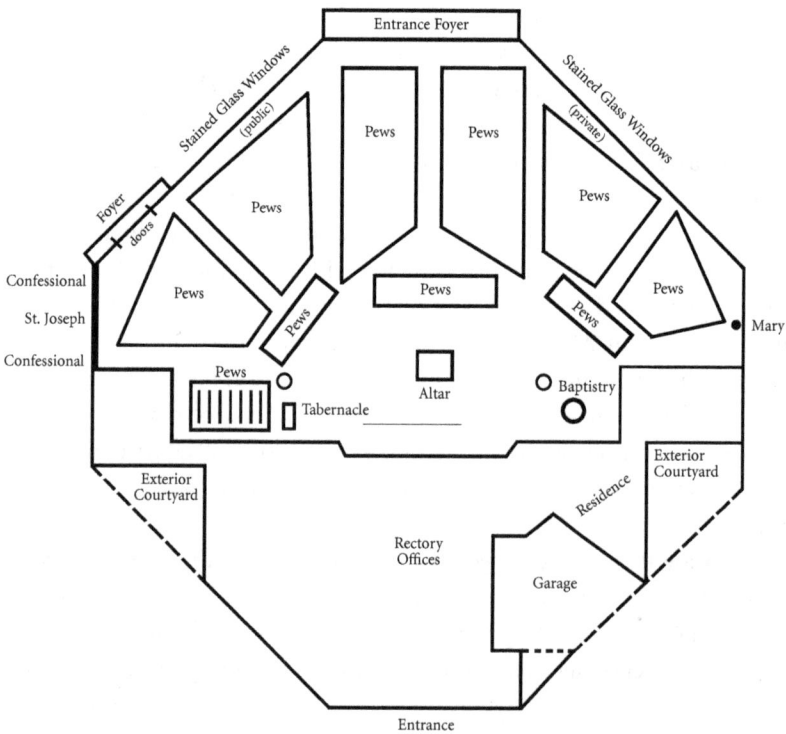

of the eucharistic celebration to all the community's functions and endeavors. All emanated from Christ, brought to the parish in the Mass, at the altar. The cube-shaped altar stood away from the sanctuary wall, in the center of a slightly raised platform. No statue or crucifix adorned the altar here. A crucifix hung on the back wall of the sanctuary, behind the priest during Mass, when the parish finished construction. But a Parish Council committee chose a statue of a resurrected Christ to replace the crucifix within a few years. Though the sanctuary was raised a couple of steps above the church floor, no altar rail separated the parishioners from the sanctuary.

The pews fanned out from the altar on three sides, separated by wide aisles. Parishioners taking seats anywhere in the pews had a clear view of the obvious focal point of the room, the altar. Behind the pews, on either side of the entrance foyer, two large rectangular stained glass windows depicted scenes from Saint Thomas More's life. One window faced Fort Couch Road and the very large South Hills Village shopping mall on the other side. This window depicted scenes from Saint Thomas More's public life: lion guardant (which represented England), sword (knighthood), crown, scepter, book of laws (chancellor), Tower of London, headsman's ax (imprisonment, martyrdom), papal keys (loyalty), merited crown (sainthood). The other side faced trees and undeveloped land in 1968, and consisted of images of Saint Thomas More's personal life: cross, rings, daisies (marriage in Christ, his four children), host and chalice (Communion), scales of justice (lawyer), book, pen, tulip (influence of Erasmus), cross and hairshirt (penitential life), lute (interest in music), cock in the field (More coat of arms). In the 1980s, however, these images faced a mall too, as commercial development virtually surrounded the church grounds.

The windows defined as public those acts performed explicitly for, by, or in regard to the state, and as personal all realms within which parishioners were likely to act: work, family, religious worship, education, and leisure. The windows, though presented in a very modern, metaphorical way, reflected the persisting understanding of the parish role as insulated and separate from public, societal interaction. The parish was not an actor in the world, was not "the witness which the Christian must bear to his neighbor when his neighbor is in need," but rather a locus for personal encounter with the divine, distinct from any explicit societal implications. These windows, in an otherwise "modern" Catholic church, reflected the incompleteness of the transition from devotion to social action by 1968.

Transparent windows lined a slightly smaller octagon perched above the pews and sanctuary, providing generous lighting during the day. An extensive lighting system kept the church bright for evening services as well.

A baptistry stood to one side of the altar, and the tabernacle to the other.[42] A statue of Mary occupied a spot along the wall between the sanctuary and baptistry. Otherwise no images distracted parishioners from the altar. The altars to Mary and Joseph from the old church did not come to the new. The stained glass windows of Saint Thomas More were behind the worshiping parishioners, and not easily seen unless parishioners turned to look behind themselves or across the congregation at the wall on the other side of the church.

The new church followed architectural guidelines designed to facilitate parishioner participation and to train parishioner focus on the altar, the Eucharist. The people at worship were to be aware of each other, to be a conscious community gathered for a common purpose, to honor God and to affirm community. The pew structure kept every parishioner close to the altar and placed other parishioners in easy view.

However, parishioners who remembered the old church considered the transition to the new rather unremarkable. "I don't think we thought very much about it, frankly," recalled one.[43] Another stated, "Unless you were an architect, or into building in some respect, I doubt that you [thought about it]."[44] Some did note the difference in size, that the old church was intimate because it was small, especially at the popular 10:00 Mass. But they did not perceive the new church to be impersonal, either.[45]

Parishioners at Saint Philomena parish did not see the same scale of architectural change as those at Saint Thomas More, but they saw dramatic change nevertheless. The first change was significant but did not arouse much parishioner response. The pastor turned the altar around to face the people in keeping with diocesan regulations. For many years this was all that changed. But in 1980 a new assistant priest arrived full of enthusiasm for liturgical renewal, and the pastor allowed him to implement changes throughout parish life.

Father Gargani, the assistant, rapidly removed the altars for Saint Gerard and Saint Philomena from the sanctuary, took down the altar rail, removed statues of Saint John Neumann to the hall, and draped a large curtain across the back wall of the sanctuary, shielding from view the crucifix. Father Gargani placed the statues in the hall that ran along the side of the church room. Parishioners contested many of these changes, however, and the interior changed regularly over the course of the decade. As noted earlier, a subsequent pastor removed the large crucifix and put in its place the image of the risen Christ.

Parishioners attending Mass in the late 1980s at Saint Philomena parish saw a much simplified church. In addition to the changes listed above, the parish moved the confessionals to the rear, under the choir loft, removed the pews that

FIGURE 9.2
Saint Philomena Parish Church, 1950s

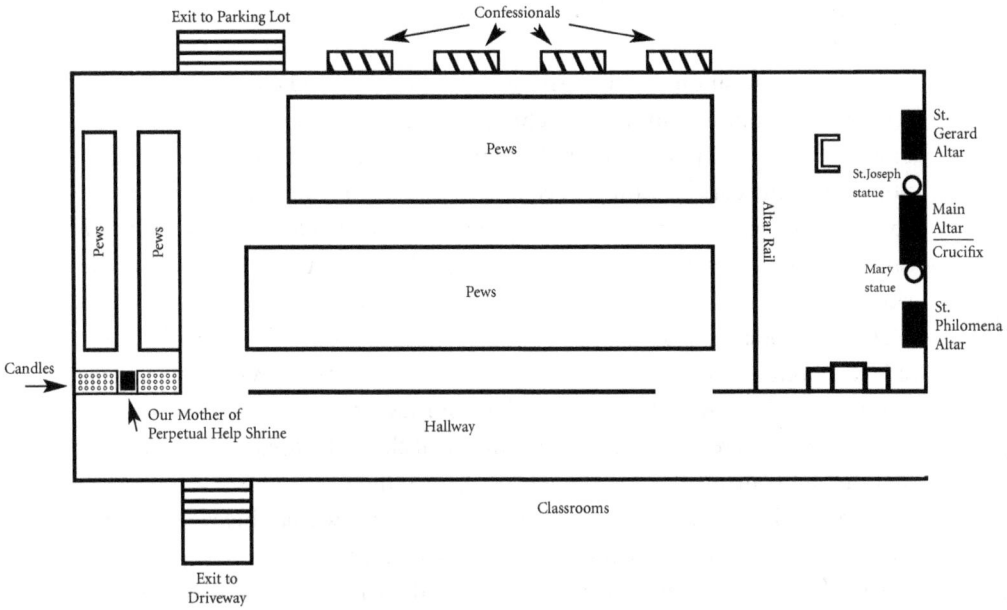

Saint Philomena Parish Church, 1980s

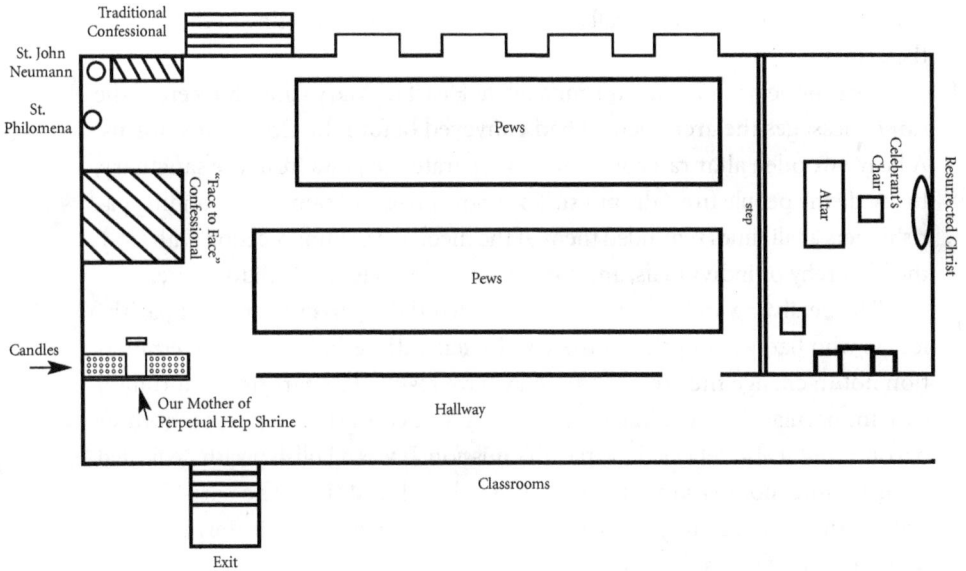

faced the shrine for Our Mother of Perpetual Help, and replaced three of the traditional confessionals with one that accommodated the new "face to face" ritual structure.

But the parishioners relatively stable population and consequent lack of resources did not permit major architectural renovations or the construction of a new church building. Within the limits of a stretched budget and a divided population, the parish accomplished a significant transformation of its worship space. Parishioners continued to sit in rows of pews stretching back from the sanctuary, but that sanctuary contained a very plain altar, under the image of the risen Christ. No rail separated the sanctuary from the pews. Save for a statue of Mary to the side of the sanctuary, all images of saints were either in the hall outside the room or behind the pews. The altar to Our Mother of Perpetual Help remained, but the pews that faced that altar, and suggested an alternative focus to the main altar, were gone. The new arrangement clearly focused parishioners' attention on the main altar and the acts performed there.

Immaculate Heart of Mary parishioners who came to Mass before the Council and in the late 1980s encountered little architectural change. The pastor did put a new altar in the sanctuary, so that he faced the people as he performed the sacred transubstantiation ritual, but this change did not move the church toward the simplified, main altar–focused model that came from the Second Vatican Council. Rather, the pastor accommodated diocesan policy by adding yet another piece to the heavily adorned church. The church remained the same otherwise, with saints occupying every wall and the crucified Christ hanging in the front of the church.

Parishioners who entered Immaculate Heart of Mary Church received the same messages the architecture had conveyed before the Conciliar reforms. A heavy wooden altar rail continued to separate the pews from the sanctuary, to divide the people from the priest. The many images of saints surrounding parishioners at all times reminded them of the mediated communication with God, the hierarchy of individuals, and the variety of models to which to aspire.

The persisting architecture also connected these parishioners with parishioners who had worshipped in these walls generations before. The determination not to change the architecture may have resulted in part from exorbitant cost. Immaculate Heart of Mary parishioners were clearly the poorest of the three parishes, but it also reflected the parish's mission. It was a Polish parish dedicated to sustaining, not discarding, ethnic and cultural tradition. The parishioners' stated pride in the beauty of their church interior suggests their unwillingness to modernize if given the opportunity.[46]

FIGURE 9.3
Immaculate Heart of Mary, 1950s

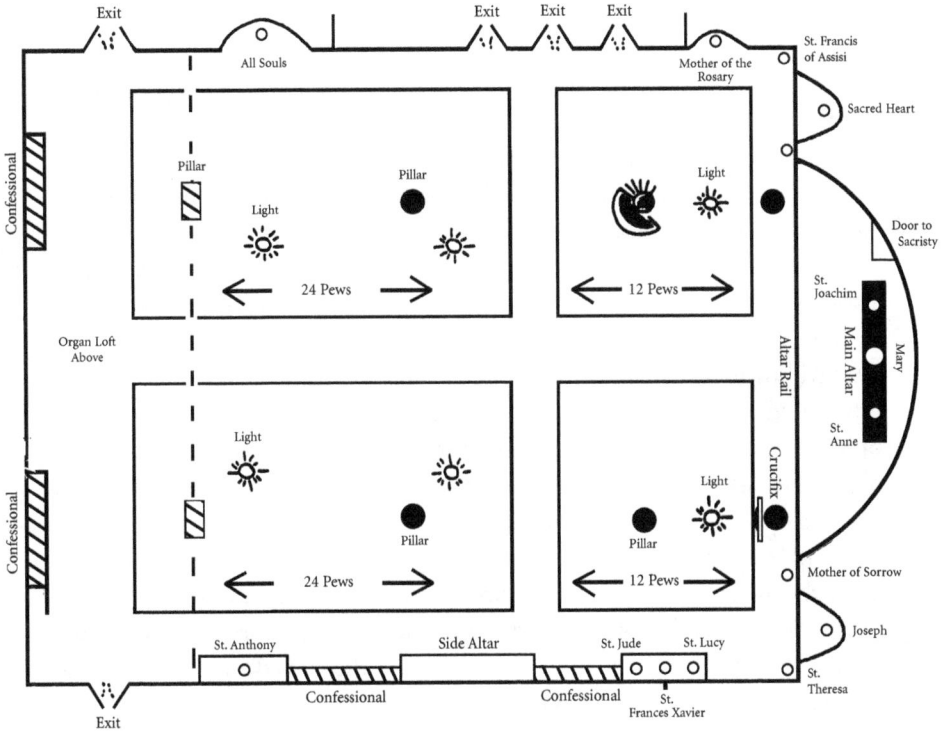

Immaculate Heart of Mary, 1980s

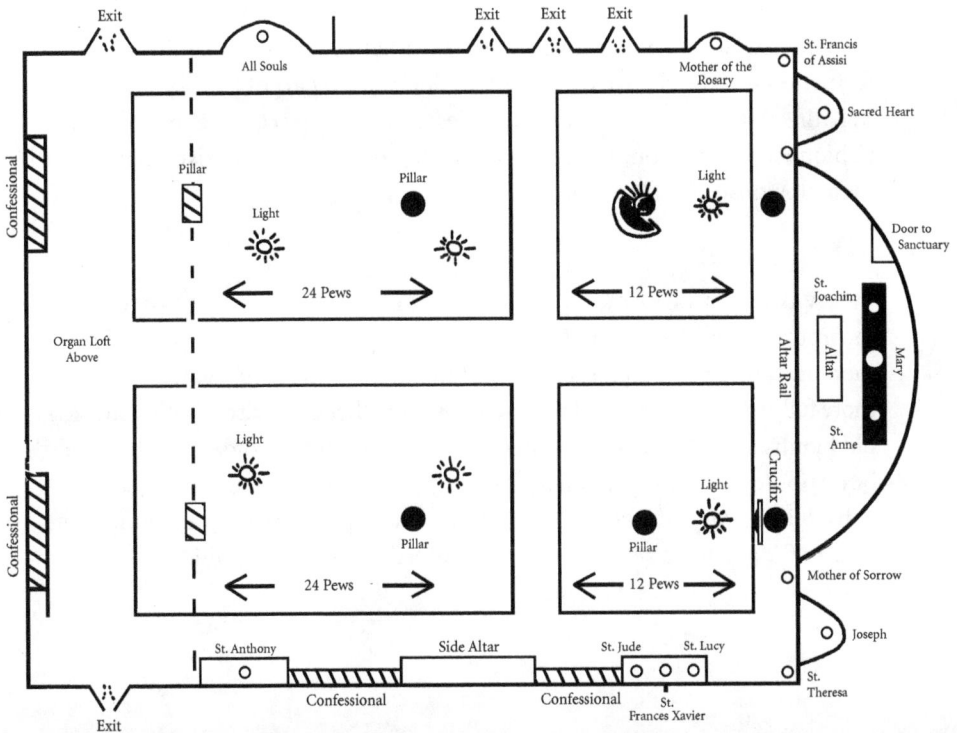

Liturgical Changes

The liturgy itself underwent a dramatic transformation in light of the Conciliar reforms, but the parishes did not implement the changes in the same ways or to the same degree. Not only did the parishes differ architecturally after the Council, but they differed in the actions they performed inside the church as well. Saint Thomas More parish adopted liturgical changes much more quickly and fully than did Saint Philomena and Immaculate Heart of Mary parishes. Saint Thomas More parishioners expressed no outward resistance to the changes, and even pressured the pastor and diocese to adopt some changes sooner than they were willing to do. Parishioners at Saint Philomena's divided over the changes introduced by Fathers Gargani and O'Rourke, and long-time Immaculate Heart of Mary parishioners supported Father Jendzura in his resistance to diocesan pressure to change, as younger parishioners moved away from the neighborhood and parish.

The Mass that emerged from the long period of reform consisted of three parts: the Introductory Rites, the Liturgy of the Word, and the Liturgy of the Eucharist. The American bishops prescribed the basic structure and specific options within that structure, so that every Mass in the United States would be essentially the same. The parishes did not have a lot of latitude in how they might structure their Masses, though they used the existing flexibility to such an extent that different Masses provided different experiences.

The new Mass was celebratory rather than somber, comprehensible rather than mysterious, and interactive rather than isolating. The most significant transformation was the change from Latin to English. No part of the Mass remained in Latin by the 1980s. Everything the priest said was now comprehensible to parishioners. In addition, the priest interacted directly with parishioners more than previously. Parishioners took active roles in the liturgy.[47]

THE VARIATIONS BETWEEN MASSES REFLECTED THE PARISHIONERS' incorporation of the Vatican II reforms. Those parishes that incorporated more modern music embraced the tone and themes of the Second Vatican Council more fully than did those that resisted song altogether or persisted with centuries-old hymns. Though part of the architectural continuity in older parishes could be attributed to waning financial resources, the change in musical practices involved little or no additional expenditure. Those parishes, such as Immaculate Heart of Mary and a significant portion of Saint Philomena, which resisted the "new" music, valued tradition over change. The disagreement over musical practices suggested more than artistic preference, though. It reflected fundamental differences in the perception of what the "Church" ought to be and do. It was either a haven from a sinful and corrupt world, or an integral part of a larger community seeking after the Kingdom of God on earth. It either called men, women, and children away from the dangers outside its walls, or pushed them out to engage and transform the world.

Conclusion

THE CATHOLIC CHURCH IN AMERICA CHANGED DRAMATICALLY
between 1950 and 1972, beginning almost a decade before the Second Vatican
Council and continuing right through and beyond the Council. The laity began
to move away from the devotional Catholicism that had so powerfully shaped
their lives for a century by 1950, but it is not certain where they were headed.
The Council helped to chart the direction. Most Catholics consider Vatican II to
be a critical moment in the Church's history, and the study of Pittsburgh Catholics confirms this—though perhaps not in the way generally understood. The
Council did not represent an abrupt change imposed from above. In fact, contemporary Catholics did not perceive the Council's changes to be so much a
shock to the unchanging Church that they had inherited from their parents, but
rather as official recognition of the currents of change already under way.

The story of the transformation in Pittsburgh, as related in these chapters,
is dramatic. Pittsburgh Catholics entered the 1950s in the midst of what Church
officials understood to be a material crisis. They saw materialist threats in Communism, unbridled capitalism, sensuality, indecency, and commercialism. Church
officials worried about Catholics falling away from the Church and worked hard
to insulate the laity from anything that might lure them away—even, and perhaps especially, from family members who stepped outside the Catholic cultural
and social boundaries.

To combat the threat, the Catholic discourse prescribed three primary solutions. Catholics were to become even more devotional than they had been.
They were to continue to build and maintain a separate Catholic social and cultural world, a Catholic "ghetto," as contemporary commentators referred to it.
They were to shun the growing faith in things scientific, and they were to work
for social justice. The laity seemed to respond well to these prescriptions in the
early years of the decade as they flocked to large public rituals, packed their chil-

dren into ever-expanding parochial schools, and supported unions and public officials who sought to ameliorate economic exploitation.

But by the middle of the decade laymen and laywomen began to chart a different course. They continued to attend Mass, but they no longer practiced devotional rituals as they had before. They swelled Catholic school enrollments, but they packed into public schools even more. They married outside the faith, socialized with Protestant and Jewish neighbors, and eagerly joined the consumer/ commercial revolution sweeping the nation. Perhaps most importantly, Catholic women entered the public sphere more fully as they gained material power through wage work. Though the laity did not reject the call to social justice, many struggled with its growing emphasis on racial equality and seemed more eager to turn their critical gaze back on the Church itself.

At just this moment the Church hierarchy convened the Second Vatican Council in efforts to take stock of the Church in light of the modern world. They too responded to the reform impulse and began to reshape the Church. Both bishops and laity, it seemed, asked how the institutional Church might become more democratic, just, and responsive to the needs of its members. Church officials and laymen and laywomen agreed for a brief moment in the 1960s that the parishes and dioceses ought to be more democratic than they had been for decades, and they cooperated in a common effort to devise a path toward that goal. In Pittsburgh, they joined for two years of hard work preparing for the 1971 synod in ways that ensured that lay voices would be heard. The laity clearly called for a larger voice in parish and diocesan affairs and for a more democratic Church generally. This shared vision did not last.

This book does not fully explore the reasons for the demise, though it clearly derived in some degree from a growing fear among those in authority that the changes under way undermined their stewardship. During the 1970s, 1980s, and 1990s, the common vision dissipated, and Church officials sought to reject the emerging model of the democratic Church. The laity had moved too far to return to the Church of the 1950s, however. Perhaps the economic dislocation that swept through the diocese in the late 1970s and 1980s muted the optimism already dampened by the failures of reform efforts within and outside the Church. Whatever the causes, the decades following the 1970s saw more retrenchment than expansion, more fear than confidence.

EPILOGUE: THE PITTSBURGH DIOCESE AT THE END OF THE MILLENNIUM

The stories of the three parishes and of the diocese itself in the 1980s and 1990s reflect the struggles that the Church throughout the nation has undergone in recent decades. Immaculate Heart of Mary parish saw a dramatic decline in parish population and the aging of its remaining members. Buffeted as well by economic hard times, the parish remained committed to its Polish identity. As its school population dwindled, it decided to resist racial integration as a means of bolstering enrollments or implementing a social justice vision. Though the parish was able physically to restore its magnificent dome, it was forced to close its school. The parish survived the diocese's consolidation process intact, but in a much diminished state.

Saint Philomena parish suffered a fate far worse. It too saw a decline in its school population and a growing financial deficit as the parish struggled to keep the school afloat. The Redemptorist order that ran the parish decided to close the school in order to stop the financial distress. They did not realize, perhaps, that diocesan guidelines mandating parish subsidies to neighboring schools meant that the parish reaped no financial relief from their decision. The result was that the parish ran an annual deficit equal to that from when they supported their own school. The diocese called in the debt, and then closed the parish on the last day of the fiscal year 1993. The Redemptorists made millions from the sale of the property.

Saint Thomas More suffered no such economic setback. Continued population growth in the South Hills suburbs resulted in the formation of new parishes from within the parish boundaries, but Saint Thomas More continued to support itself comfortably. When it required a new roof in the 1990s, it took the opportunity to redesign its worship space yet again. But Saint Thomas More suffered the scourge that would cause scandal throughout the nation and world for the Catholic Church. One of its priests preyed upon the altar boys who served the community and was eventually convicted in criminal court of child molestation.

The optimism had disappeared in these parishes, as well as in the diocese as a whole. In the early 1990s the diocese decided to conduct a massive self-study aimed at closing and consolidating parishes. Saint Philomena's was in the midst of this process when the diocese closed its doors. All told, the diocese closed or merged more than one hundred parishes by the time Bishop Wuerl announced that he would convene the nineteenth diocesan synod for the Jubilee Year 2000.

The nineteenth synod included little of the lay participation so prized in the eighteenth. Though Bishop Wuerl established commissions to consider new regulations, no member came via a democratic election. If Bishop Wright could boast that two-thirds of all the 1971 Synodal Commission members arrived at their position through some election, Bishop Wuerl could proclaim that he personally appointed every single member of the 2000 Synodal Commission. The commissions did not poll the laity for their ideas and recommendations, but rather invited them to respond to drafts of working papers written by appointed authors. The 2000 synod prized efficiency over democracy.

The lay and clerical common effort to create a more democratic Church did not survive into the twenty-first century. The laity remained far more supportive of this model than did the clergy. Church demographics and the recent pedophilia crisis may force a return to the more democratic model, however, as the rapidly shrinking priesthood and the still growing laity has already produced numerous priestless parishes whose ranks will grow dramatically in the near future. The experiences of the 1950s and 1960s may prove instructive at this moment.

Notes

Preface

1. "What the Council Did," *Newsweek*, 20 December 1965, 60; John K. Jessup, "New Currents Swirling Around Peter's Rock," *Life*, 17 December 1965, 27; "Ite in Pace" *New York Times*, 9 December 1965, 46.

2. Stanley I. Stuber and Claud D. Nelson, *Implementing Vatican II in Your Community: Dialogue and Action Manual Based on the Sixteen Documents of the Second Vatican Council* (New York: Guild Press, 1967), 11; Douglas J. Roche, *The Catholic Revolution* (New York: David McKay, 1968), xviii; Donald J. Thorman, foreword, *The Catholic Revolution*, by Douglas J. Roche (New York: David McKay, 1968), ix; John Tracy Ellis, *American Catholicism*, 2nd ed. rev., Chicago History of American Civilization Series (Chicago: University of Chicago Press, 1969), 163; David J. O'Brien, *Renewal of American Catholicism* (New York: Oxford University Press, 1972), 3; Sidney Ahlstrom, *A Religious History of the American People* (New Haven: Yale University Press, 1972), 1017; John Cogley, *Catholic America* (New York: Dial Press, 1973), 116. John Cogley understood the decade of the Council to be a time when the Catholic Church "throughout the world underwent more change than it had experienced in centuries, and nowhere was its impact more consequential than in the United States."

3. Theologians and clerics especially held this to be true. Thomas Bokenkotter echoed *Life* magazine's initial assessment when he wrote that the Second Vatican Council "was undoubtedly the most important religious event of the twentieth century." Harvey Cox, author of the widely read 1960s classic *The Secular City*, wrote in 1984 that the Council changed "something of major proportion" and calculated its impact to be "enormous." Catholic theologian Frans Josef van Beeck argued that Vatican II "inaugurated a significant rearrangement of the themes and emphases of the Catholic faith and identity experience." Joseph Cardinal Bernardin, archbishop of Chicago, reflected twenty years after Paul VI dismissed the last session that the "Council has had a powerful impact on the Church and society throughout the world," and added that it "also had significant influence in Church developments in the United States." Thomas Bokenkotter, *A Concise History of the Catholic Church* (Garden City, N.Y.: Image Books, 1979), 421; Harvey Cox, *Religion in the Secular City: Toward a Postmodern Theology*

(New York: Simon and Schuster, 1984), 108; Frans Josef van Beeck, *Catholic Identity After Vatican II: Three Types of Faith in the One Church* (Chicago: Loyola University Press, 1985), 4; Joseph Cardinal Bernardin, foreword, *Vatican II Revisited by Those Who Were There,* ed. Alberic Stacpoole (Minneapolis: Winston Press, 1986), 3; Kenneth E. Untener, "Cardinal Dearden: A Gentleman of the Church," *America,* November 26, 1988, 434.

4. Bokenkotter, *A Concise History,* 421; Cox, *The Secular City,* 108; van Beeck, *Catholic Identity,* 4; Bernardin, foreword, *Vatican II Revisited,* 3; Untener, "Cardinal Dearden."

5. Martin E. Marty, *Pilgrims in Their Own Land: 500 Years of Religion in America* (New York: Penguin Books, 1984), 466; James Hennesey, *American Catholics: A History of the Roman Catholic Community in the United States* (New York: Oxford University Press, 1981), 314; Jay P. Dolan, *The American Catholic Experience: A History from Colonial Times to the Present* (Garden City, N.Y.: Doubleday, 1985), 425, 426. Dolan noted that the Council did not come out of nowhere, though: it "emerged from a general reform movement that had been sweeping through Roman Catholicism" (425).

6. Andrew M. Greeley, *The American Catholic: A Social Portrait* (New York: Basic Books, 1970), 137, *American Catholics Since the Council: An Unauthorized Report* (Chicago: Thomas More Press, 1985), 21–22. Greeley remained impressed in 1985, however, at how much "stability and continuity" American Catholics exhibited in the face of this transformation. Twenty years later the transformation impressed him more. Andrew Greeley, *The Catholic Revolution: New Wine, Old Wineskins, and the Second Vatican Council* (Berkeley: University of California Press, 2004); Jim Castelli and Joseph Gremillion, *The Emerging Parish: The Notre Dame Study of Catholic Life Since Vatican II* (San Francisco: Harper and Row, 1987), 1, 196; George Gallup, Jr., and Jim Castelli, *The American Catholic People: Their Beliefs, Practices, and Values* (Garden City, N.Y.: Doubleday, 1987), 1.

7. See especially Joseph P. Chinnici, O.F.M., "The Catholic Community at Prayer, 1926–1976," 70–81, and Paula M. Kane, "Marian Devotion Since 1940: Continuity or Casualty?" 116–17, in James M. O'Toole, ed., *Habits of Devotion: Catholic Religious Practice in Twentieth-Century America* (Ithaca, N.Y.: Cornell University Press, 2004), 9–87; Mark S. Massa, *Catholics and American Culture: Fulton Sheen, Dorothy Day, and the Notre Dame Football Team* (New York: Crossroad, 1999); Charles R. Morris, *American Catholics: The Saints and Sinners Who Built America's Most Powerful Church* (New York: Times Books, 1997); and John T. McGreevy, *Parish Boundaries: The Catholic Encounter with Race in the Twentieth-Century Urban North* (Chicago: University of Chicago Press, 1996). Other scholars continued to present the 1950s as a period of lay enthusiasm for the Church they inherited from their parents. See, for example, Chester Gillis, *Roman Catholicism in America* (New York: Columbia University Press, 1999), 77; Ralph McInerny, *What Went Wrong with Vatican II: The Catholic Crisis Explained* (Manchester, N.H.: Sophia Institute Press, 1998), 7–12. Even McGreevy suggests that the laity were largely "unprepared for sweeping changes" (160).

8. They find support for their concerns in recent works that argue for the continuing popularity of traditional devotional Catholicism until the moment that

Council-inspired reformers pushed the laity to abandon their cherished practices. See especially Robert Orsi's work on popular devotions to the Madonna of 115th Street in Harlem and Saint Jude. Though he does not trace changes in devotional participation rates over time, and therefore does not seek to identify periods of fervor and uninterest, Orsi suggests that the lay attachment to the devotions persisted into the 1960s and that reformers met significant resistance when they tried to alter these popular pietistic practices. Robert A. Orsi, *Thank You Saint Jude: Women's Devotion to the Patron Saint of Hopeless Causes* (New Haven: Yale University Press, 1996), 32–35, *The Madonna of 115th Street: Faith and Community in Italian Harlem, 1880–1950* (New Haven: Yale University Press, 1985).

9. For a thorough discussion of the debates now raging in the Church, see Thomas P. Rausch, *Reconciling Faith and Reason: Apologists, Evangelists, and Theologians in a Divided Church* (Collegeville, Minn.: Liturgical Press, 2000); Joseph A. Komonchak, "Interpreting the Council: Catholic Attitudes Toward Vatican II," in *Being Right: Conservative Catholics in America,* ed. Mary Jo Weaver and R. Scott Appleby (Bloomington: Indiana University Press, 1995); Robert J. Egan, S.J., "Two Versions of History," *Commonweal,* September 8, 2000, 7–8; and Peter Steinfels, *A People Adrift: The Crisis of the Roman Catholic Church in America* (New York: Simon and Schuster, 2003), 32–36. For a strident presentation of the more conservative position, see McInerny, *What Went Wrong with Vatican II.* A less strident but still vigorous critique of the post–Vatican II changes can be found in David Carlin's *The Decline and Fall of the Catholic Church in America* (Manchester, N.H.: Sophia Institute Press, 2002). Carlin sees Vatican II as only one of three causes of this change. The other two are the opening of the Catholic ghetto and the social and cultural revolution against authority which swept through America generally.

10. Joseph P. Chinnici, O.F.M., "American Catholic Spirituality: What Practices Tell Us About the Church" (unpublished paper provided to the author in April 1999), 5. Chinnici's synthetic interpretation, "The Catholic Community at Prayer, 1926–1976" is the most thorough discussion of the changes before Vatican II on the American scene.

CHAPTER ONE.   Pittsburgh Catholics and the Materialist Crisis

1. See Ben Marsh and Pierce Lewis, "Landforms and Human Habitat," in *A Geography of Pennsylvania,* ed. E. Willard Miller (University Park: Pennsylvania State University Press, 1995), for an introduction to the physical geography of the region.

2. For more information on Pittsburgh's rise as an industrial city, see Sylvester K. Stevens, "The Hearth of the Nation," in *Pittsburgh: The Story of an American City,* ed. Stefan Lorant (1964; Lenox, Mass.: 1988), 177–205. See Francis G. Couvares, *The Remaking of Pittsburgh: Class and Culture in an Industrializing City, 1877–1919* (Albany: SUNY Press, 1984), for a discussion of workers in the industrial city.

3. Kenneth J. Heineman, *A Catholic New Deal: Religion and Reform in Depression Pittsburgh* (University Park: Pennsylvania State University Press, 1999).

4. An "incline" is an enclosed car that travels up and down the side of a steep hill on a track similar to that of an uphill portion of a roller coaster. Unlike a roller coaster, however, the cars move up and down the hillside at the same slow speed.

5. Quoted in Joel A. Tarr, "Infrastructure and City-Building in the Nineteenth and Twentieth Centuries," in *City at the Point: Essays on the Social History of Pittsburgh*, ed. Samuel P. Hays (Pittsburgh: University of Pittsburgh Press, 1989), 215.

6. Bob Regan, *The Bridges of Pittsburgh* (Pittsburgh: The Local History Co., 2006), 39–41.

7. John Bodnar, Roger Simon, and Michael P. Weber, *Lives of Their Own: Blacks, Italians and Poles in Pittsburgh, 1900–1960* (Urbana: University of Illinois Press, 1982).

8. The city's natural boundaries have played a role in the battle over racial integration. In the city's heavily Catholic and virtually all-white Southside, for example, parents recently succeeded in revoking the school board's long-standing practice of busing to achieve racial integration by focusing on these divides. The parents argued not that they opposed integration or even busing, but rather that they would no longer stand for the board busing their or anyone else's children "across a river." The board could not integrate schools in the Southside without busing whites northward across the Monongahela or blacks southward.

9. Roy Lubove, *Twentieth Century Pittsburgh: Government, Business and Environmental Change* (New York: John Wiley and Sons, 1969), 1, 2.

10. Robert Dvorchak, "Saturday Diary: Pittsburgh, the Once and Future City," *Pittsburgh Post-Gazette*, 30 October 1999, A-15.

11. "Pittsburgh Welcomes You!" (1958), in "This Is Pittsburgh—1953" file, American Service Institute Collection, Archives of Industrial Society, University of Pittsburgh, Pittsburgh, Pennsylvania (hereinafter to be cited as AIS).

12. "This Is Pittsburgh—1953," *Pittsburgh Sun-Telegraph*, 8 November 1953, 1.

13. Ibid.

14. Ibid., p. B, p. 1.

15. Ibid.

16. Michael P. Weber, *Don't Call Me Boss: David L. Lawrence, Pittsburgh's Renaissance Mayor* (Pittsburgh: University of Pittsburgh Press, 1988), 247, 253.

17. For a fuller discussion of the environmental clean-up efforts, see Sherie R. Mershon and Joel A. Tarr, "Strategies for Clean Air: The Pittsburgh and Allegheny County Smoke Control Movements, 1940–1960," in *Devastation and Renewal: An Environmental History of Pittsburgh and Its Region*, ed. Joel A. Tarr (Pittsburgh: University of Pittsburgh Press, 2003), 145–74.

18. Bodnar, Simon, and Weber, *Lives of Their Own*, 187; and U.S. Department of Commerce, Bureau of the Census, *U.S. Census of Population and Housing, Pittsburgh, PA* (Washington, D.C.: U.S. Government Printing Officer, 1950, 1960, 1970, 1980).

19. One cannot measure actual Church membership very easily for Pittsburgh because the Census Bureau did not record Church affiliation beyond 1926 and no other group maintained a count of Church members. These figures come from the *Pittsburgh City Directory* for 1940 which lists churches by denominations (and then puts the remainder under the heading "miscellaneous") but adds no further data other than

street address. *Polk's Pittsburgh (and Allegheny Co.) City Directory* (Pittsburgh: R.C. Polk and Co., 1940).

20. *Polk's Pittsburgh City Directory, 1950.*

21. *Polk's Pittsburgh City Directory, 1960.* By 1960 the *City Directory* no longer reported churches by individual denomination but did provide the following breakdown: 348 Protestant, 86 Catholic, 28 Jewish, 26 Orthodox. By 1970 the *Directory* reported church totals for all of Allegheny County (1,131) only, though it listed only 497 individual churches in the city.

22. The Pittsburgh diocese encompasses Lawrence, Butler, Beaver, Allegheny, Washington, and Greene counties, and so does not coincide even with the Pittsburgh Standard Metropolitan Statistical Area (SMSA), which consists of Beaver, Allegheny, Washington, and Westmoreland counties.

23. I say probably because the source for this data is not completely reliable. These figures come from the *Official Catholic Directory*, which is an annual compilation of Church statistics for each diocese Vicariate Apostolic in America. Leaving alone the very imprecise quality of Church data in general (how does one accurately define let alone measure Church membership), the specific numbers in the *Catholic Directory* are suspect. The publishers depend upon the parishes and the diocese to report to them, and often carry data from year to year when no changes get reported. The *Directory*'s reporting of general population numbers from the U.S. Census varies from the figures the Census Bureau published. But one can get a reasonable sense of trends from the data, and I have never found the data reported to be wildly inaccurate. *The Official Catholic Directory* (New York: P.J. Kennedy and Sons, 1940, 1951, 1960, 1965, 1970, 1975, 1980).

24. This popular view is shared by academics as well. See, for example, Andrew Greeley, *The Catholic Revolution: New Wine, Old Wineskins, and the Second Vatican Council* (Berkeley: University of California Press, 2004), 17–18; David Carlin, *The Decline and Fall of the Catholic Church in America* (Manchester, N.H.: Sophia Institute Press, 2003), 25.

25. It is difficult to state with precision the percentage or number of Catholics who read the various publications, or to determine how they read the material when they did see it. But we do know that the total circulation of Catholic periodical publications increased dramatically during the twentieth century and especially in the 1950s. This trend existed in Pittsburgh as well. The *Pittsburgh Catholic* reported that presses turned out one issue of a Catholic periodical for every three Catholics in 1925, one for every two Catholics in 1950, and one for every 1.5 Catholics in 1953. The *Pittsburgh Catholic* circulation reached roughly one quarter of the diocese's 202, 347 families in 1954. "'Catholic' Attains Record," *Pittsburgh Catholic*, 10 February 1955, 4; the Rev. Richard Ginder, "Catholic Press Directory Summarizes Number, Kind of Periodicals," *Pittsburgh Catholic*, 10 February 1955, 9.

26. For a brief discussion of how historians might incorporate literary critical methods, especially the new historicist focus on "discourses" in historical work, see Joseph Kelly and Timothy Kelly, "Searching the Dark Alley: New Historicism and Social History," *Journal of Social History* (Spring 1992): 678–94.

27. The 1907 edition of the *Catholic Encyclopedia* defined *materialism* specifically as "a philosophical system which regards matter as the only reality in the world, which undertakes to explain every event in the universe as resulting from the conditions and activity of matter, and which thus denies the existence of God and the soul." This seems to be the working definition that Catholic prelates and contributors to the *Pittsburgh Catholic* used to inform their positions. Constantin Gutberlet, "Materialism," in *The Catholic Encyclopedia*, vol. 10 (New York: Robert Appleton, 1907), 41.

28. "Intensified Mission Work Called for by Pope to Save World from Materialism," *Pittsburgh Catholic*, 21 June 1951, 1. A former missionary to China agreed, stating that Communism "denies that man is a creature who owes allegiance to God, it places emphasis on material things only, and it denies man the freedom of decision and action." "Some Opposition to Communism Has Wrong Basis, Priest Asserts," *Pittsburgh Catholic*, 2 August 1951, 3. See T. J. Blakeley for a Catholic interpretation of dialectical materialism. Blakeley argues that as an ideological system, Marxism would be dialectical materialism, a variation from classical materialism that is "materialist" in that it is rationalist and based upon the premise that natural science must be the foundation for all human knowing. "Materialism, Dialectical and Historical," in *The New Catholic Encyclopedia*, vol. 9 (Washington, D.C.: Catholic University of America Press, 1967), 445. Denis R. Janz argues that American Christians took no notice of Marxism before 1917, a fact supported by the lack of any reference to Marx in the 1907 *Catholic Encyclopedia* discussion of materialism. By 1967 dialectical materialism merited an extended entry in the *New Catholic Encyclopedia*. Janz disagrees with Blakeley's assessment of Marxism's materialism, and identifies Marx's greatest challenge to religion as its denial of an unchanging "natural law." Denis R. Janz, *World Christianity and Marxism* (New York: Oxford University Press, 1998), 52.

29. Philip Jenkins advances this argument in his recent book on the Cold War in Pennsylvania. See especially pp. 166–76 in *The Cold War at Home: The Red Scare in Pennsylvania, 1945–1960* (Chapel Hill: University of North Carolina Press, 1999).

30. *Holy Name Newsletter* (June–July 1956), 9, Box 11, Holy Name Society Collection (hereinafter to be cited as HNS Collection), Historical Archives of the Diocese of Pittsburgh (hereinafter to be cited as HADP).

31. John Collins conveyed his concerns to readers regularly between 1950 and 1954, when Bishop Dearden bought the paper and put his own editor in charge. Though Collins addressed issues ranging from political, social, and cultural developments in the United States to papal pronouncements on intimate personal matters, he never strayed too long or far from Communism's threat. One year he devoted over a third of his columns to the Red menace. Collins usually addressed between three and six subjects in each weekly column. I sampled the March columns in each year from 1950 to 1954 . He wrote least about Communism in March 1952 (13 percent) and most frequently about it in 1954 (35 percent). See John Collins, "To the Point," *Pittsburgh Catholic*.

32. Rice argued in one column, for example, that no government agency should strip unions of their rights simply because the government suspected the union of being Communist. However, he was perfectly happy with jailing the Communist leaders and removing their civil rights, because "that does not endanger the human rights

of American workers in general." The Rev. Charles Owen Rice, "The Condition of Labor: Logical," *Pittsburgh Catholic*, 31 January 1952, 5.

33. Collins was not alone in his concern for principled anti-Communism. A debate raged within the Catholic Press Association which resulted in the members' adopting a resolution to refrain from smearing individuals and offering space for accused individuals to defend themselves. "CPA Adopts Code, Guide," *Pittsburgh Catholic*, 2 June 1955, 1.

34. Fr. Richard Ginder already had a national reputation by the time he began writing for the *Pittsburgh Catholic*. He had been contributing for fifteen years to the nationally distributed conservative weekly *Our Sunday Visitor*, where he also served as an associate editor. In addition, he edited *The Priest, My Daily Visitor*, and *The Catholic Choirmaster*. Ginder's columns in *Our Sunday Visitor* dripped with contempt for liberals, Democrats, and anyone Ginder thought might be a Communist. He especially blamed Franklin Roosevelt and Harry Truman for selling the nation out to the Soviet Union, but he attacked a range of public figures for their lack of diligence in opposing Communists. A number of Fr. Richard Ginder's *Our Sunday Visitor* columns have been collected and republished under the title *Right or Wrong*, a series that runs to at least four volumes. See *Right or Wrong: Essays by Father Richard Ginder, Columnist for Our Sunday Visitor*, ser. 1, 2, 3, 4 (Huntington, Ind.: Our Sunday Visitor Press, 1959, 1961).

35. "True Justice," *Pittsburgh Catholic*, 14 June 1951, 4. "In the Spotlight," *Pittsburgh Catholic*, 23 May 1952, 2. "Bishop's Statement Is Warning: America Must Recover Moral Strength or Face Fate of Rome," *Pittsburgh Catholic*, 22 November 1951, 1.

36. "Real Christian Social System Explained as Collaboration, Not Conflict, of All Elements," *Pittsburgh Catholic*, 29 December 1950, 1; "In Directive to Priests, Pope Calls for Vigorous Application of Social Teachings of Church," *Pittsburgh Catholic*, 28 September 1950, 1; "Pope's Exhortation to Priests Covers Entire Field of Work," *Pittsburgh Catholic*, 5 October 1950, 1.

37. For a recent treatment of the Pittsburgh Catholic encounter with capitalism and social justice in the Great Depression, see Kenneth J. Heineman's *A Catholic New Deal: Religion and Reform in Depression Pittsburgh* (University Park: Pennsylvania State University Press, 1999).

38. William H. Mooring, "'Disneyland' a Blatant Nightmare," *Pittsburgh Catholic*, 28 July 1955, 10. Mooring would later publicly recant his criticism, suggesting that Walt Disney had somehow managed to pull off the commercialization with integrity.

39. The quote comes from a speech that Oklahoma senator Monroney gave on the Senate floor in December 1954. The *Pittsburgh Catholic* quoted from it extensively in its December 16 editorial condemning Sunday shopping. "'Sunday Shopping' Problem," *Pittsburgh Catholic*, 16 December 1954, 4. John Collins, "To the Point: Advent and Christmas," *Pittsburgh Catholic*, 30 November 1950, 4. Catholics did not battle Christmas's commercialization alone.

40. The Rev. Robert J. McBride, "In the Spotlight: Without This Chain," *Pittsburgh Catholic*, 27 April 1950, 2. "Defeat Today's Materialism by Return to Christianity of Early Centuries, Pope Urges," *Pittsburgh Catholic*, 20 May 1954, 1.

41. Fr. Hugh Wilt, O.S.B., "The Layman Through the Years," *Holy Name Newsletter*, February 1956, 11, Box 11, HNS Collection, HADP.

42. Pope Pius XII and Cardinal Stritch of Chicago did point to the likely dangers of immodest dress. Pius XII urged the world's bishops in 1954 to "take action against immodesty in dress, which has 'spiritually ruinous effects, especially on young people,' and is a most serious plague of the present time." Cardinal Stritch called women's dress "shocking and immoral," and asserted that "modesty is that virtue which stands guard over the path which may lead to a violation of chastity." "Immodesty in Dress Serious Moral Problem, Pope Says," *Pittsburgh Catholic*, 9 September 1954, 8; "Cardinal Calls Modern Dress 'Shocking,'" *Pittsburgh Catholic*, 2 December 1954, 6. The Very Rev. John J. McDonough, "Man Versus the Machine," *Pittsburgh Catholic*, 7 December 1950, 6. McDonough's article came from a longer piece that the *Pittsburgh Catholic* serialized for several weeks in its pages.

43. The Rev. Robert McBride, "The Weaker Sex Is Not Always So," *Pittsburgh Catholic*, 9 September 1951, 2; John Collins, "To the Point: Christmas Parties," *Pittsburgh Catholic*, 11 December 1952, 1; "Those 'Office Parties,'" *Pittsburgh Catholic*, 30 December 1954, 4; "Pope Reviews Church Teaching on Obligations of Married Life," *Pittsburgh Catholic*, 8 November 1951, 1.

44. "Bishop Dearden New National Chairman on Decent Literature," *Pittsburgh Catholic*, 25 November 1954, 1.

45. "'Progressives' Have Brought Chaos to Education, Cardinal Declares," *Pittsburgh Catholic*, 12 November 1953, 1. John Collins, "To the Point: John Dewey," *Pittsburgh Catholic*, 5 June 1952, 4.

46. John Collins, "To the Point," *Pittsburgh Catholic*, 23 October 1952, 4. Collins's surprise at these numbers (a *mere* 95 percent believe in God) seems quite odd from the distance of nearly half a century, but it speaks to the power of the crisis discourse.

47. *Pittsburgh Catholic*, 19 November 1953, 5.

48. The Rev. Paul M. Lackner, "From the Director's Notebook," *Holy Name Newsletter*, June–July 1958, 10. "Pope Pius Warns Against Peril of 'Man-Made World,'" *Pittsburgh Catholic*, 13 June 1957, 1.

49. "In the Spotlight," *Pittsburgh Catholic*, 27 July 1950, 2.

50. John Collins, "To the Point: Pittsburgh Cool," *Pittsburgh Catholic*, 2 October 1952, 4; John Collins, "To the Point: Evangelist Leaves," *Pittsburgh Catholic*, 9 October 1952, 4. Fr. John E. Kelly insisted later that Catholics who take part in Graham's crusades "are endangering their Faith." "Billy Graham's 'Partial Gospel' 'Danger to Faith,' Priest Says," *Pittsburgh Catholic*, 2 May 1957, 1.

51. John Collins, "To the Point: Leakage and Converts," *Pittsburgh Catholic*, 1 April 1954, 4; "Protestant Survey Shows Catholic 'Losses' Called Unreliable," *Pittsburgh Catholic*, 19 March 1959, 1. For the first poll, the *Christian Herald* mailed surveys to 25,000 Protestant ministers and asked how many converts they had within their congregations. It received replies from 2,219 and extrapolated from these responses a figure for the nation as a whole. In the second, the paper mailed surveys to 10,000 Protestant ministers asking about conversions in the past three years, and received 917 results.

The Catholic poll went out to pastors in Buffalo and Detroit, with results reportedly coming from 99 and 67 percent of pastors.

52. John Collins, "To the Point: Echoes," *Pittsburgh Catholic,* 4 December 1952, 4. Ed Steimer, "Justice Scores Anti-Catholic State Charter," *Pittsburgh Catholic,* 4 April 1957, 1. John Collins, "To the Point: Going Respectable?" *Pittsburgh Catholic,* 20 August 1953, 4; Fr. Richard Ginder, "Jehovah's Witnesses Refuse to Render Caesar His Due," *Pittsburgh Catholic,* 23 February 1956, 5.

53. "POAU 'Hate' Meeting Attacks Catholicism," *Pittsburgh Catholic,* 21 February 1957, 6. The *Pittsburgh Catholic* reported on POAU activities and pronouncements regularly. Sixth United Presbyterian Church in the Squirrel Hill section of Pittsburgh, for example, hired as minister in 1960 a man who reportedly urged those attending a Cleveland POAU meeting to "vote as you please—if it's not for a Catholic." "Prize Package," *Pittsburgh Catholic,* 20 October 1960, 4.

CHAPTER TWO.   **Anti-Communism and the Decline of Catholic Devotionalism**

1. On Musmanno's activities, see Michael P. Weber, *Don't Call Me Boss: David L. Lawrence, Pittsburgh's Renaissance Mayor* (Pittsburgh: University of Pittsburgh Press, 1988), 282–86. In contrast to the vehement anti-Communism that other Catholics practiced, Lawrence, the city's most prominent Catholic, supported an accused Communist sympathizer in one of the city's highest profile public hearings. See Philip Jenkins, *The Cold War at Home: The Red Scare in Pennsylvania, 1945–1960* (Chapel Hill: University of North Carolina Press, 1999): 166–76, for an overview of the Catholic response to Communism in the 1950s.

2. "Passion Sunday Set by Pope for World Crusade of Prayer," *Pittsburgh Catholic,* 16 March 1950, 1. Pius XII entitled the encyclical "Anni Sacri."

3. Stefan Lorant, *Pittsburgh: The Story of An American City* (1964; Lenox, Mass.: Author's Edition, 1988), 355, 370.

4. See Paula Kane's "Marian Devotion Since 1940: Continuity or Casualty?" in *Habits of Devotion: Catholic Religious Practice in Twentieth-Century America,* ed. James M. O'Toole (Ithaca, NY: Cornell University Press, 2004), 89–130, for a thorough discussion of the post–World War II Marian devotion of which rosary recitation is a central part.

5. The Rev. Robert J. McBride, "In the Spotlight: Without This Chain," *Pittsburgh Catholic,* 27 April 1950, 2; "In the Spotlight: Fifteen Minutes," *Pittsburgh Catholic,* 24 August 1950, 2; John Collins, "To the Point: United in Faith," *Pittsburgh Catholic,* 7 September 1950, 1.

6. John Collins, "To the Point," *Pittsburgh Catholic,* 14 September 1950, 4.

7. Jay P. Dolan, *The American Catholic Experience: A History from Colonial Times to the Present* (Garden City, N.Y.: Doubleday, 1985), 220–21.

8. "Eucharistic Night Brings Record Gathering of Men in Demonstration of Faith," *Pittsburgh Catholic,* 14 September 1950, 1, 4.

9. Ibid.

10. Ibid.; "As the Eucharistic Night Comes to a Close," *Pittsburgh Catholic*, 14 September 1950, 3.

11. "Eucharistic Night," 4.

12. The Rev. Robert J. McBride, "In the Spotlight: Impressions," *Pittsburgh Catholic*, 14 September 1950, 2.

13. "Mt. Mercy College Plans Mary's Day Observance May 1," *Pittsburgh Catholic*, 29 April 1951, 1; "Expect Thousand College Students for 'Mary's Day,'" *Pittsburgh Catholic*, 30 April 1953, 6. For a discussion of other American pageants on May 1, see chapter 3 of Richard M. Fried, *The Russians Are Coming! The Russians Are Coming! Pageantry and Patriotism in Cold-War America* (New York: Oxford University Press, 1998).

14. The rally was technically outside of the Pittsburgh diocese. Pius XII had just that year carved out four counties from the Pittsburgh Diocese to form the Greensburg diocese, and Saint Vincent College fell within the new see. The Greensburg diocese was so new at the time of the Marian Eucharistic Rally, in fact, that it did not yet have its own bishop. Westmoreland County's seventy-two parishes sponsored the event for their women, so few, if any, of the participants came from the Pittsburgh diocese. But it made front-page news in the *Pittsburgh Catholic*.

15. "Expect 6,000 Women to Attend Marian Rally Sunday, August 19," *Pittsburgh Catholic*, 2 August 1951, 1; "Over 15,000 Women Take Part in Eucharistic Rally at Latrobe," *Pittsburgh Catholic*, 23 August 1951, 1.

16. *Holy Name Newsletter*, May 1956, 3.

17. "For the Record . . . ," *Holy Name Newsletter*, December 1959, 10. In 1956 Bishop Dearden was quoted as saying that the Holy Name Society represented "some 100,000 men" in the Pittsburgh diocese. "The Good People Are Not a Minority," *Holy Name Newsletter*, December 1956, 7. Pittsburgh's male Catholic population stood at about 430,000, which included boys not eligible for membership.

18. *Holy Name Newsletter* (no month listed, 1954), 7; February 1957, 4; August–September 1957, 12.

19. *Saint Vincent College Journal* 40 (February 1931): 134.

20. John Collins, "To the Point: Retreat Movement," *Pittsburgh Catholic*, 11 June 1952, 1.

21. Typewritten materials entitled "Act of Reparation to the Sacred Heart." Saint Vincent Lay Retreats file no. 48c, Lay Summer Retreats Box, Saint Vincent Archabbey Archives, Latrobe, Pennsylvania.

22. "Deanery Rally on June 17," *Holy Name Newsletter*, June–July 1956, 15.

23. "Good Friday Cards," *Holy Name Newsletter*, February 1968.

24. "7–Church Walk Scheduled in Diocese," *Holy Name Newsletter*, March 1968, 1, 7.

25. The *Newsletter* ran ads for the Good Friday cards every year of its publication in the issues for the months preceding and containing Easter. Though it is difficult to measure participation in these devotions, the Holy Name Society did once publish information about how many cards they sold. In 1959 the society distributed sixteen thousand cards, but by 1968 they were down to slightly more than four thousand. *Holy Name Newsletter*, March 1969, 2.

26. Here and There Around the Diocese," *Holy Name Newsletter,* February 1956, 13; Essay Winners Given Awards," *Holy Name Newsletter,* June–July 1959, 9, Box 11, HNS collection, HADP. Three other prizes were a statue of Blessed John of Vercelli, a Manual Missal, and a ticket to a Pirates game; Paul Lackner, "From the Director's Notebook," *Holy Name Newsletter,* January 1960, 11.

27. Dolan, *American Catholic Experience,* 387.

28. For an example of papal blessings see "Here & There Around the Diocese," *Holy Name Newsletter,* February 1956, 13; quote, Fr. Hugh Wilt, "The Layman Through the Years," February 1956, 11.

29. Paul Lackner, "From the Director's Notebook," *Holy Name Newsletter,* November 1958, 10.

30. *Holy Name Newsletter,* April 1958, 10.

31. "A Successful Convention" and "Convention Resolutions," *Holy Name Newsletter,* December 1957, 4, 5. A concelebrated Mass had more than one celebrant (priest) preside over it. *Holy Name Newsletter,* 6 March 1969, 4.

32. The Pittsburgh Diocesan Council of Catholic Women newsletter claimed that more than 9 million women belonged to the NCCW nationally in 1956. "An Invitation," *News,* June 1956, 1, Box 1, Diocesan Council of Catholic Women Collection (hereinafter to be cited as DCCW Collection), HADP. Citations for DCCW material refer to box numbers that I have assigned and may not be accurate any longer. I transported the DCCW material from the DCCW office to the diocesan archives, and the archivist had not yet had the opportunity to reorganize the material to store it permanently. The materials resided in two unmarked boxes in his office when I first wrote this chapter, and I have assigned them numbers 1 and 2.

33. "History of the Pittsburgh DCCW," *1954 Convention Book,* 61, Box 2, DCCW Collection, HADP.

34. Mary Jo Weaver, *New Catholic Women: A Contemporary Challenge to Traditional Religious Authority* (San Francisco: Harper and Row, 1986), 119, 120.

35. "Why DCCW?" *News,* December 1956. Just as the *Holy Name Newsletter* changed names a number of times, the Diocesan Council of Catholic Women's monthly communication also changed names. Roughly the same pattern of newsletter quality can be detected for the DCCW and HNS, which experienced a brief period of great success (as measured by many pages and glossy paper with photographs) in the late 1950s and early 1960s and then a trailing off to finally just typewritten photocopied pages in the late 1970s and 1980s. The DCCW newsletter never approached the quality of the *HNS Newsletter* at its height, though it has outlasted its counterpart. The DCCW publication was originally the *News of the Pittsburgh Diocesan Council of the National Council of Catholic Women,* then *The Echo, DCCW Communique,* and finally *Dear Member.* I will cite the first title as simply the *News.*

36. Cecilia Guehl, "Organization and Development," *News,* February 1958, 1.

37. The Rev. Raymond T. Schultz, *News,* June–July 1960, 1.

38. "Digest of Committee Workshops," *News,* November 1959, 3. The article suggested this was a reasonable fear, because "it is a fact, whether we like to admit it or

not, that there are some women who have the unhappy faculty of aggravating and agitating everyone with whom they come in contact."

39. "From Our Spiritual Moderator," *News,* April 1956, 1. "The Pittsburgh DCCW Is Now 100% in the Number of Federated Groups," *News,* February 1957, 1.

40. M. Regina Clare, "A Strategic Retreat," *News,* November 1959, 4; Regina G. Kelly, "Let's Make a Retreat," *News,* April 1959.

41. The Rev. William P. Weirauch to the 1954 Pittsburgh DCCW Convention, *1954 Convention Book,* 7, Box 2, DCCW Collection, HADP.

42. The *News* reported individual group's gifts at times, such as when CDA. Court Monaca contributed 228 rosaries to Bishop Dearden's 1955 convention gift. "Catholic Action Highlights," *News,* October 1955, 3.

43. DCCW *Convention Book,* 1954, 1955, 1956, 1957, and 1958. A Message from Our Most Reverend Bishop," *News,* February 1956, 1; "Christmas Spiritual Bouquet for Our Bishop," *News,* November 1956; "A Thank You from Bishop Dearden," *News,* February 1957, 1.

44. Pat O'Neill, "50,000 Catholics Salute Christ," *Pittsburgh Post-Gazette,* 1 October 1955, 1; "135,000 to March in Catholic Procession," *Pittsburgh Press,* 1 October 1955, 3. "Holy Name Directors Plan for Convention," *Pittsburgh Catholic,* 1 September 1955, 11; *Holy Name Newsletter,* November 1955, 13.

45. "Procession Floats Show Religious Themes," *Pittsburgh Catholic,* 8 September 1955, 11; "Holy Name Timetable Compiles Directions," *Pittsburgh Catholic,* 15 September 1955, 11; "Best Convention Honors Holy Name," *Pittsburgh Catholic,* 6 October 1955, 1.

46. *Holy Name Newsletter,* November 1955, 5.

47. James O'Toole, "The Church Takes to the Streets," paper delivered at the American Catholicism in the Twentieth Century Conference, University of Notre Dame, November 1990, pp. 8–10.

48. "Eucharistic Rally Fifth in History Here," *Pittsburgh Catholic,* 29 September 1955, 3.

49. The actual turnout is difficult to determine, because reports varied widely. The *Pittsburgh Catholic* suggested at one point that 100,000 actually showed up. The *Pittsburgh Post-Gazette* reported 35,000 in Forbes Field and an additional 15,000 on vantage points in nearby Schenley Park, for a total of 50,000. The *Pittsburgh Press* reported only 30,000, all of whom were in Forbes Field. Pat O'Neill, "50,000 Catholics Salute Christ," *Pittsburgh Post-Gazette,* 1 October 1955, 1; John Troan, "Catholic Rally Prays for World Peace," *Pittsburgh Press,* 1 October 1955, 1; "HNS Buys 80,000 Candles," *Pittsburgh Catholic,* 15 September 1955, 11; "135,000 to March in Catholic Procession," *Pittsburgh Press* (1 October 1955), 3; "John F. Laboon to Lead Procession," *Pittsburgh Catholic,* 29 September 1955, 7; "Call for Crusade Heralds Rally, Parade by 125,000," *Pittsburgh Catholic,* 29 September 1955, 1; "Holy Name Timetable Compiles Directions," *Pittsburgh Catholic,* 15 September 1955, 11.

50. "10,000 to Pray at Deanery 'Family Hour,'" *Pittsburgh Catholic,* 4 August 1955, 7; "5,000 Attend Family Hour of Prayer," *Pittsburgh Catholic,* 18 August 1955, 3.

51. The Rev. Charles F. Moosmann, "The Sodality of Our Lady," *Pittsburgh Catholic,* 30 October 1952, 2.

52. The Rev. Charles F. Moosmann, "The Sodality of Our Lady," *Pittsburgh Catholic,* 1 October 1953, 2; 25 February 1954, 2.

53. "Lent and Daily Adoration," *Pittsburgh Catholic,* 17 February 1955, 4; "Diocese to Begin Daily Eucharistic Adoration," *Pittsburgh Catholic,* 3 February 1955, 1, 2; "Deaneries Plan Adoration," *Pittsburgh Catholic,* 10 February 1955, 1.

54. "Lent to Begin Wednesday with Eucharistic Adoration," *Pittsburgh Catholic,* 17 February 1955, 1. "Adoration Devotions Crowded," *Pittsburgh Catholic,* 3 March 1955, 1. "Laity Fill Churches to Pray," *Pittsburgh Catholic,* 24 February 1955, 1.

55. "Inspiration from Pittsburgh," *News,* March 1955, 1; *Holy Name Newsletter,* February 1955, 4; "The Presence of Christ," *News,* April 1955, 1.

56. Parish Bulletin, 20 February 1955, Immaculate Heart of Mary Parish Records (hereinafter to be cited IHM records), Pittsburgh, Pennsylvania; Parish Bulletin, 20 February 1955, Saint Thomas More Parish Records (hereinafter to be cited STM records), Bethel Park, Pennsylvania; Parish Bulletin, 20 February 1955, Saint Philomena Parish Records (hereinafter to be cited SP records), Pittsburgh, Pennsylvania. (In 1992 Bishop Donald Wuerl suppressed Saint Philomena's parish, and instructed the parish to move its records to Saint Bede's parish, also in Pittsburgh.)

57. "Daily Eucharistic Adoration," *News,* May 1955, 1.

58. Parish Bulletins, 6 March 1955, 17 April 1955, IHM records; *Holy Name Newsletter,* December 1955, 4.

59. "Are We Promoting Eucharistic Adoration?" *News,* June 1955, 1; "Daily Eucharistic Adoration," *News,* July 1955, 3; "Parishes to Increase Eucharistic Adoration Participation," *Pittsburgh Catholic,* 12 January 1956, 1.

60. Parish Bulletin, 5 February 1956, STM records; "Summer Highlights from Committee Suggestions," *News,* June 1956, 2; "Daily Eucharistic Adoration," *News,* February 1957, 2; "Eucharistic Adoration Reminder," *Pittsburgh Catholic,* 14 March 1957, 8.

61. Fr. Paul Lackner, "Daily Eucharistic Plan to Increase Vocations, Insure World Peace," *Pittsburgh Catholic,* 10 October 1957, 8.

62. Fr. Paul Lackner, "Holy Name Column: Daily Eucharistic Adoration," *Pittsburgh Catholic,* 15 October 1959, 6.

63. Richard P. McBrien, ed., *The HarperCollins Encyclopedia of Catholicism* (New York: HarperCollins, 1995), 650. For a fuller explication of the Our Lady of Perpetual Help devotion, see Timothy Kelly and Joseph Kelly, "Our Lady of Perpetual Help, Gender Roles, and the Decline of Devotional Catholicism," *Journal of Social History* (Fall 1998): 5–26. For more on the nineteenth-century devotion, see the Rev. Michael Muller, C.Ss.R., *Our Lady of Perpetual Help in the Work of Our Redemption and Sanctification* (Baltimore, 1873). The Rev. Thomas B. Roche, "The Redemptorists in Pittsburgh, Pennsylvania One Hundred Years, 1839–1939," "Old St. Philomena's 1839–1925," "New St. Philomena's 1921–1939," 47; SP records. The Very Rev. Joseph McDonough, C.Ss.R., "Fifty Years in Squirrel Hill, St. Philomena's Parish 1921–1971," St. Philomena Parish Archives.

64. Lorant, *Pittsburgh*, 355. Saint Philomena Annual Report, 1942, p. 6, Redemptorist Provincial Archives, Baltimore Province, Brooklyn, N.Y. For brief discussions of wartime rationing, see John Mortun Blum, *V was for Victory: Politics and American Culture During World War II* (New York: Harcourt, Brace, Jovanovich, 1976), 23; and William L. O'Neill, *A Democracy at War: America's Fight at Home and Abroad in World War II* (Cambridge: Harvard University Press, 1993), 136.

65. "10,230 Attended Retreats in Year," *Pittsburgh Catholic*, 28 September 1950, 1; *Pittsburgh Catholic*, 6 January 1955, 9. I am less confident of this data than I am for the evidence on male participation levels for a number of reasons. First, the *Pittsburgh Catholic* was clearly less interested in reporting female activities and did so only sporadically. It is quite possible that the editors simply did not know about each women's retreat. Second, no equivalent female group organized retreats in the way that the Holy Name Society did for men, and so records were harder to obtain at the time and in retrospect. Men concentrated their retreats in four locations throughout the 1950s, 1960s, and 1970s. Women's retreats took place at a number of locations, and these places changed regularly. Though the DCCW sought to organize retreats in the later 1950s in ways similar to the HNS, the women's organization never managed to establish a comparable retreat program.

66. Dolan, *American Catholic Experience*, 220–21.

67. John Collins, "To the Point: Principle," *Pittsburgh Catholic*, 4 May 1950, 4.

68. Anonymous, "Through a Kind Friend . . . ," *Our Lady of Perpetual Help* 1 (Autumn 1937): 3. Catholics often use Our Mother of Perpetual Help in the place of Our Lady of Perpetual Help. No clear pattern distinguishes the use of one over the other; rather they seem interchangeable.

69. McDonough, "50 Years in Squirrel Hill," 13.

70. James T. Paterson, *Grand Expectations: The United States, 1945–1974* (New York: Oxford University Press, 1996), 320. See also Landon Y. Jones, *Great Expectations: America and the Baby Boom Generation* (New York: Coward McCann, 1980), 66.

71. A number of sources convey this postwar affluence. For clear graphical presentations, see Wallace C. Peterson, *Silent Depression: The Fate of the American Dream* (New York: Norton, 1994), 36, 38. Robert Heilbroner and Aaron Singer, *The Economic Transformation of America, 1600 to the Present*, 3rd ed. (New York: Harcourt, Brace, Jovanovich, 1994), 323. See James K. Galbraith, *Created Unequal: The Crisis in American Pay* (Chicago: University of Chicago Press, 1998), 144–49, especially fig. 8.2 on p. 146 for wage disparity data. The disparity began to grow again in the 1970s before expanding dramatically in the 1980s and 1990s.

72. John Bodnar, Roger Simon, and Michael P. Weber, *Lives of Their Own: Blacks, Italians, and Poles in Pittsburgh, 1900–1960* (Urbana: University of Illinois Press, 1982), 250.

73. U.S. Department of Commerce, Bureau of the Census, *Sixteenth Census of the United States, 1940: Population*, vol. 2, *Characteristics of Population, Part 6, Pennsylvania–Texas*, C-41 (Washington, D.C.: U.S. Government Printing Office); U.S. Department of Commerce, Bureau of the Census, *1950 U.S. Census of Population*, vol. 2,

Characteristics, Part 38, Pennsylvania, 38–116, 38–334; U.S. Department of Commerce, Bureau of the Census, *United States Census of Population: 1960,* vol. 1, *Characteristics of the Population, Part 40, Pennsylvania,* table 73; U.S. Department of Commerce, Bureau of the Census, *1970 Census of Population, Characteristics of Population, Part 40, Pennsylvania.*

74. U.S. Department of Commerce, Bureau of the Census, *Sixteenth Census of the United States, 1940: Population,* vol. 3, *The Labor Force, Part 5, Pennsylvania–Wyoming,* table 5; U.S. Department of Commerce, Bureau of the Census, *1950 U.S. Census of Population,* vol. 2, *Characteristics, Part 38, Pennsylvania;* U.S. Department of Commerce, Bureau of the Census, *United States Census of Population: 1960,* vol. 1, *Characteristics of the Population, part 40, Pennsylvania,* tables 72, 73, 96.

75. Margaret Marsh, *Suburban Lives* (New Brunswick, N.J.: Rutgers University Press, 1990), xiv, 74–89; William Dobriner, *Class in Suburbia* (Englewood Cliffs, N.J.: Prentice-Hall, 1963), 64–65.

76. Sam Bass Warner, *The Private City: Philadelphia in Three Periods of Its Growth* (Philadelphia: University of Pennsylvania Press, 1968), 174; id., *Streetcar Suburbs: The Process of Growth in Boston 1870–1900* (Boston: Harvard University Press, 1962; New York: Atheneum, 1976), 154; E. Gartly Jaco and Ivan Belknap, "Is a New Family Form Emerging in the Urban Fringe?" *American Sociological Review* 18 (1953); Clark, *The Suburban Society,* 152–54; Clifford E. Clark, Jr., "Ranch-House Suburbia: Ideals and Realities," in *Recasting America: Culture and Politics in the Age of Cold War,* ed. Lary May (Chicago: University of Chicago Press, 1989), 172. See also Herbert J. Gans, "Effects of the Move from City to Suburb," in *The Urban Condition: People and Policy in the Metropolis,* ed. Leonard J. Duhl (New York: Basic Books, 1963), 186–87, 190 .

77. John Modell, "Suburbanization and Change in the American Family," *Journal of Interdisciplinary History* 9, no. 4 (Spring 1979): 640–45.

78. See, for example, Kenneth T. Jackson, *Crabgrass Frontier: The Suburbanization of the United States* (New York: Oxford University Press, 1985), 279. Even works that seek to downplay any distinction in community interaction between urban and suburban living highlight the greater amount of energy and time suburban residents devote to private, family-centered activities—especially work on the house and yard: Gans, "Effects of the Move," 184–87. S.D. Clark, *The Suburban Society* (Toronto: University of Toronto Press, 1966), 161. Frederick A. Shippey wrote to counter the secularization model, though he did conclude that the suburbs presented special challenges to Christian religious belief and practice: *Protestantism in Suburban Life* (New York: Abingdon Press, 1964).

79. David L. Birch, "The Economic Future of City and Suburb," Center for Economic Development Supplementary Paper No. 30 (New York: Committee for Economic Development, 1970), 18–19; William Issel, *Social Change in the United States, 1945–1983* (New York: Schocken Books, 1987), 87–88. Though Americans moved to the suburbs in significant numbers beginning in the 1940s, the five years between 1950 and 1955 brought more suburban growth than the preceding decade. See Conrad Taeuber and Irene B. Taeuber, *The Changing Population of the United States* (New York: John Wiley & Sons, 1958), 109. The Allegheny County suburban growth figures can be

found in the Pennsylvania State Planning Board's "The Population of Pennsylvania, a Social Profile: An Analysis of Recent Demographic Trends Emphasizing Inter-County Comparisons" (September 1963), 33.

80. The ten urban parish schools were: Saint Paul's Cathedral, Holy Trinity, Saint Philomena, Sacred Heart, Saint George, Saint John the Evangelist, Guardian Angels, Saint Gabriel, Nativity, and Saint Peter. I selected the sample randomly, save for ensuring that parishes from each of the three sections of the city (Northside, Southside, and Central City) made it into the sample in the proportion in which the sections housed parishes. The ten suburban parish schools, which I also selected randomly from a list of those suburban parishes that maintained schools in 1951, were: Sacred Heart in Emsworth, Saint Alphonsus in Wexford, Saint Bernard in Mt. Lebanon, Saint Irenaeus in Oakmont, Saint Joseph in Verona, Saint Theresa in Perrysville, Saint Althanasius in West View, Saint Elizabeth in Pleasant Hills, Saint James in Sewickley, and Saint Ann in Castle Shannon. See *Catholic Directory* (New York: P. J. Kennedy and Sons).

CHAPTER THREE.   Catholic Separatism and the Opening of the Catholic Ghetto

1. Charles R. Morris, *American Catholic: The Saints and Sinners Who Built America's Most Powerful Church* (New York: Times Books, 1997), 164.

2. In fact, Paula Kane suggests in her study of Boston Catholics in the early decades of the twentieth century that Catholic separatism provided a path to the American middle class absent the discriminatory roadblocks that full immersion necessarily entailed. See *Separatism and Subculture: Boston Catholicism, 1900–1920* (Chapel Hill: University of North Carolina Press, 1994), 2–3.

3. Paula Kane argues that American Catholics had made it as "insiders" by the 1950s, which suggests that efforts to sustain the separate Catholic sphere in that decade would inevitably feel alien to the Catholic laity. Kane, *Separatism and Subculture*, 10.

4. Later, in the 1960s, 1970s, and 1980s, one might identify a distinctively Catholic perspective on health care. This would fall primarily in the areas of birth control, abortion, and euthanasia. But no association of health care workers advocated any of these in the 1950s.

5. John M. Neeson, "Mythical All-Catholic Football Team Picked," *Pittsburgh Catholic,* 2 December 1954, 10. Marquette head coach F. L. (Frosty) Ferzacca chose the team. The Pittsburgh Pirate players were: Roberto Clemente, Bob Garber, Dick Hall, Jerry Lynch, Danny Murtaugh (coach), Eddie O'Brien, Bob Purkey, Jim Trimble, Frank Thomas, Lee Walls. "Eight Catholics on Pirate Squad Add Power to Pennant Pursuit," *Pittsburgh Catholic,* 14 June 1956, 10.

6. John Collins, "To the Point: 'Inter-Faith' Meetings," *Pittsburgh Catholic,* 15 July 1954, 4. Collins pointed out that this ban did not extend to cooperation on non-religious matters of common concern.

7. Fr. Daniel H. Brennan, "The Question Box: Isn't the Anglican Church Close to the Catholic Church?" *Pittsburgh Catholic,* 11 July 1957, 4.

8. Fr. Daniel R. Brennan, "Question Box," *Pittsburgh Catholic,* 7 March 1957, 4.

9. "'Massive Disobedience,'" *Pittsburgh Catholic*, 18 June 1959, 4.

10. Fr. Richard Ginder, "The Catholic School: What Advantages Do Pupils Receive?" *Pittsburgh Catholic*, 23 August 1956, 1.

11. Bishop Dearden proclaimed this statute (119, paragraph a) in the 1954 synod. The *Pittsburgh Catholic* published the reminder annually during Dearden's reign. See, for example, "Your Eternal Truant Officer," *Pittsburgh Catholic*, 13 September 1956, 4; "Know Your Duties," *Pittsburgh Catholic*, 21 March 1957, 4.

12. "Catholic Education a MUST," *Pittsburgh Catholic*, 15 May 1958, 4.

13. Fr. Daniel H. Brennan, "The Question Box: Catholic Education Required?" *Pittsburgh Catholic*, 7 August 1958, 4; "The Catholic School," *Pittsburgh Catholic*, 25 April 1958, 4.

14. "Catholic Colleges Are Best," *Pittsburgh Catholic*, 7 July 1955, 4.

15. "Cardinal Stritch Says Catholics Should Attend Catholic Colleges," *Pittsburgh Catholic*, 14 August 1952, 1; McDowell, "Catholic Colleges," 4. McDowell did not exactly offer a rousing endorsement of these same institutions when he stated of Catholic colleges: "They are fully accredited. They are staffed by competent professors. They do not try more than they can handle." Fr. Avery R. Dulles, S.J. "What Are the Dangers to Catholic Students in Secular Colleges?" *Pittsburgh Catholic*, 21 June 1956, 5; the Very Rev. Vernon F. Gallagher, "Advantage of Catholic Colleges," *Pittsburgh Catholic*, 2 June 1955, 5; "Bishop States Dangers of Secular College Training for Catholics," *Pittsburgh Catholic*, 17 August 1950, 5.

16. The Very Rev. Thomas J. Quigley, "Man Seeks Beauty, Truth, Goodness, Through Fine Arts," *Pittsburgh Catholic*, 25 August 1955, 3.

17. "Trained in Absolute Truth," *Pittsburgh Catholic*, 14 June 1956, 4.

18. "Scientists and Morality," *Pittsburgh Catholic*, 28 November 1957, 4.

19. "'No. 1 Student' Quits Science to Be Jesuit," *Pittsburgh Catholic*, 7 August 1958, 2.

20. "One-fifth Average Parish Only 'Nominally' Catholic, According to New Survey," *Pittsburgh Catholic*, 6 September 1951, 1; "His Example Most Important for Modern Times," *Pittsburgh Catholic*, 14 March 1957, 14.

21. John Collins, "To the Point: Invalidly Married," *Pittsburgh Catholic*, 22 July 1954, 4; Fr. Daniel H. Brennan, "The Question Box: May Gifts Be Given to Catholics Outside the Church?" *Pittsburgh Catholic*, 20 June 1957, 4.

22. Fr. Daniel H. Brennan, "The Question Box: Attendance at Invalid Weddings," *Pittsburgh Catholic*, 2 July 1959, 4.

23. John Collins, "To the Point: Ralph Kiner," *Pittsburgh Catholic*, 4 October 1951, 4.

24. Fr. Daniel H. Brennan, "The Question Box: Why Does Church Refuse Burial?" *Pittsburgh Catholic*, 18 July 1957, 4; Fr. Daniel H. Brennan, "The Question Box: Burial of Non-Catholics in Catholic Cemetery," *Pittsburgh Catholic*, 18 July 1957, 4.

25. Thomas P. Brennan, "What Is a Catholic Man?" *Holy Name Newsletter*, September 1956, 8, 9, Box 11, HNS collection, HADP.

26. Msgr. Irving A. DeBlanc, "Two Final Suggestions by Which Christians May Live a Full Life," *Pittsburgh Catholic*, 13 March 1958, 5.

27. The Rev. Thomas W. Jackson, "Church Music," *Pittsburgh Catholic,* 6 July 1950, 7; "Church Music," *Pittsburgh Catholic,* October 1950, 7; "Church Music," *Pittsburgh Catholic,* 30 March 1950, 7; The Rev. Thomas W. Jackson, "Church Music," *Pittsburgh Catholic,* 7 December 1950, 7.

28. "Ask Stores Here to Aid 'Modest Dress' Campaign," *Pittsburgh Catholic,* 27 March 1952, 3.

29. "Confraternity of Christian Mothers," *Pittsburgh Catholic,* 10 April 1952, 11.

30. "Here's the Rule for '55—It's Smart to Be Modest," *Pittsburgh Catholic,* 10 February 1955, 14. See Kathryn Jay's history of the "Supply the Demand for the Supply" movement among Catholic teenage girls in El Paso, Texas, for an insightful history of a more organized effort to accomplish the same goal. " 'In Vogue with Mary': How Catholic Girls Created an Urban Market for Modesty," in *Faith in the Market: Religion and the Rise of Urban Commercial Culture,* ed. John M. Giggie and Diane Winston (New Brunswick, N.J.: Rutgers University Press, 2002), 177–98.

31. The Rev. Charles F. Moosman, "The Sodality of Our Lady," *Pittsburgh Catholic,* 9 April 1953, 2.

32. *News,* June 1955, n.p.: "Food for Thought from Inspiring Talks Given at Recent Open Deanery Meetings," *News,* July 1955, n.p., Box 1, DCCW Collection, HADP.

33. "Cardinal's Robes to Be Simplified," *Pittsburgh Catholic,* 11 December 1952, 1.

34. John Collins, "To the Point: Short Stuff," *Pittsburgh Catholic,* 24 June 1954, 4.

35. "The Pope Speaks on Fashion," *Holy Name Newsletter,* April 1959, 14; Box 11, HNS Collection, HADP.

36. John Collins, "To the Point: To Meet the Crisis," *Pittsburgh Catholic,* 28 February 1952, 1.

37. "Regulations for Lent, Diocese of Pittsburgh," *Pittsburgh Catholic,* 8 February 1951, 1.

38. "Fast and Abstinence Rules Have 'Important Modifications,' " *Pittsburgh Catholic,* 21 February 1952, 1.

39. "Lenten Guide for Fast and Abstinence," *Pittsburgh Catholic,* 17 February 1955, 1.

40. Fr. Richard Ginder, "Church Never Dilutes Doctrine to Please Unbelieving Persons," *Pittsburgh Catholic,* 12 December 1957.

41. "Virginity Glorifies Marriage When Given as Gift to God," *Pittsburgh Catholic,* 22 May 1958, 5. "Pope Reviews Church Teaching on Obligations of Married Life," *Pittsburgh Catholic,* 8 November 1951, 1.

42. Clement Simon Mihanovich, Br. Gerald J. Schnepp, S.M., and the Rev. John L. Thomas, S.J., *A Guide to Catholic Marriage* (Milwaukee: Bruce Publishing Co., 1955), 53.

43. Martin J. Scott, S.J., *Marriage* (New York: Paulist Press, 1930), 3.

44. Mihanovich, Schnepp, and Thomas, *A Guide to Catholic Marriage,* 70.

45. Kay Toy Fenner, *American Catholic Etiquette* (Westminster, Md.: Newman Press, 1961), 338.

46. "Steady Dating in High School Found Harmful," *Pittsburgh Catholic,* 14 October 1954, 11.

47. "In the Spotlight," *Pittsburgh Catholic*, 30 August 1951, 2; "Teenagers Are Warned Against Steady Dating," *Pittsburgh Catholic*, 24 March 1955, 1.

48. "Pope Reviews Church Teaching on Obligations of Married Life," *Pittsburgh Catholic*, 8 November 1951, 1; the Rev. Charles F. Moosmann, "The Sodality of Our Lady," *Pittsburgh Catholic*, 9 July 1953, 2.

49. John Collins, "To the Point: 'Birth-Control' Sheet," *Pittsburgh Catholic*, 25 May 1950, 4; "Social Justice, Not Birth Control, Is Needed, Wheeling Bishop Says," *Pittsburgh Catholic*, 26 July 1952, 3; "'Overpopulation' Temporary Issue, Sociologists Say," *Pittsburgh Catholic*, 15 January 1953, 3; J.J. Gilbert, "World Feeding Progress Blow to Birth Control," *Pittsburgh Catholic*, 11 November 1954, 6; John Collins, "To the Point: Gandhi Is Dead," *Pittsburgh Catholic*, 4 December 1952, 4; "Birth Control Propaganda Real Problem," *Pittsburgh Catholic*, 30 May 1957, 7; "Birth Control Pills Ruin Man's Dignity," *Pittsburgh Catholic*, 25 September 1958, 6; "Land of Liberty or License?" *Pittsburgh Catholic*, 21 August 1958, 4. The entire birth control discourse presumed that the debate addressed use among married couples, and seemed not to entertain the possibility that it might encourage premarital intercourse.

50. A copy of the code can be found in Steven Mintz and Randy Roberts, eds., *Hollywood's America: United States History Through Its Films*, rev. ed. (New York: Brandywine Press, 1993), 142–52.

51. On the formation of the Legion of Decency, see Gregory D. Black, *The Catholic Crusade Against the Movies, 1940–1975* (New York: Cambridge University Press, 1998), 17–28; Frank Walsh, *Sin and Censorship: The Catholic Church and the Motion Picture Industry* (New Haven: Yale University Press, 1996), 66–94; and Morris, *American Catholic: The Saints and Sinners*, 204–09.

52. "Against Offensive Films: Pledge of Legion of Decency to Be Renewed Here Sunday," *Pittsburgh Catholic*, 7 December 1950, 1. This is actually the "short version" of the pledge. The "long version" contains a statement of intent formally to join the Legion and a fuller condemnation of indecent movies. The long version can be found in Chester Gillis, *Roman Catholicism in America* (New York: Columbia University Press, 1999): 224–25.

53. "Legion Film Ratings by Phone Anytime," *Pittsburgh Catholic*, 13 June 1957, 1.

54. "Condemned Film Showing Here," *Pittsburgh Catholic*, 8 January 1953, 1.

55. John Collins, "To the Point: Dirty Film Here," *Pittsburgh Catholic*, 19 August 1954, 4.

56. For a good brief history of the NODL, see Una M. Cadigan, "Guardians of Democracy or Cultural Storm Troopers? American Catholics and the Control of Popular Media, 1934–1966," *Catholic Historical Review* (April 2001): 252–82.

57. "Father Ginder Specifies Duties of Book Censor," *Pittsburgh Catholic*, 17 February 1955, 2.

58. "Decent Literature Organization Opens New Chicago Office," *Pittsburgh Catholic*, 31 March 1955, 6.

59. "Decency Legion Pledge Will Be Renewed Sunday," *Pittsburgh Catholic*, 6 December 1951, 1; "Drive Cleaning Up Books, Movies Here," *Pittsburgh Catholic*, 2 December 1954, 1; "Legion of Decency Pledge Sunday," *Pittsburgh Catholic*, 9 December 1954, 1.

60. "Home and School," *News*, June 1956, "Decent Literature Campaign," *News*, September 1956.

61. "That 'Comic' Book 'Cleanup,'" *Pittsburgh Catholic*, 30 September 1954, 4.

62. Sr. M. Aurelia, O.S.F., "Catholic Girls," *Pittsburgh Catholic*, 31 August 1950, 5.

63. Msgr. Irving DeBlanc, "Vocation of Women Is Role of Motherhood," *Pittsburgh Catholic*, 13 September 1956, 12.

64. Ibid.; "Pope Lauds Womanhood, Criticizes 'Pagan' Abuses," *Pittsburgh Catholic*, 18 October 1956, 1, 2.

65. Msgr. Irving DeBlanc, *Pittsburgh Catholic*, 29 August 1957, 5.

66. "North Side Girls Prepare for Careers," *Pittsburgh Catholic*, 1 November 1956, 13.

67. "The Ideal Catholic Teenage Girl," *Pittsburgh Catholic*, 31 October 1957, 7.

68. Patricia Wargetz, "Forum of Youth Opinion: A Girls' School," *Pittsburgh Catholic*, 28 November 1957, 7.

69. "Sharp Rise in Working Wives Disregards Papal Teachings," *Pittsburgh Catholic*, 18 August 1955, 6.

70. Alexandra Hill, "Working Wives and Mothers Sacrifice True Role as Heart of Home," *Pittsburgh Catholic*, 13 March 1958, 11.

71. "Sharp Rise in Working Wives," 6.

72. Hill, "Working Wives and Mothers," 11.

73. "The Pope Speaks to Women," *Pittsburgh Catholic*, 5 June 1958, 11. This column appeared intermittently throughout the later 1950s. The original source of the quote is the papal encyclical *Women's Duties in Social and Political Life*, 1945.

74. Msgr. Irving A. DeBlanc, "'Rights of Women' Carefully Considered, Not Really Confusing," *Pittsburgh Catholic*, 6 December 1956, 11.

75. Anthony T. Padovano, "No Turning Back: Pilgrim Church Has Ventured Beyond the Fortress," *National Catholic Reporter*, 12 November 1999, 3.

76. "'Spectacular' Growth of Church in U.S. in Fifty Years Revealed," *Pittsburgh Catholic*, 9 February 1950, 1; "U.S. Catholics Number 27,766,441, Gain of More Than Million in Year," *Pittsburgh Catholic*, 1 June 1950, 1; "Catholic Growth Here Far Exceeds General Population Increase," *Pittsburgh Catholic*, 14 June 1950, 1. One should view the Catholic population statistics somewhat cautiously. The reports of Catholic population come from pastors' estimates, and pastors more readily added names to the parish registers than removed them. The *Pittsburgh Catholic*, ironically, warned readers that this process probably depressed the reports below the true numbers.

77. "U.S. Catholic Hospitals Had Over 7,000,000 Persons Under Treatment in Past Year," *Pittsburgh Catholic*, 24 July 1952, 1; "Catholic Papers, Magazines Achieve Record Circulation," *Pittsburgh Catholic*, 31 July 1952, 3.

78. The dip in enrollment between 1951 and 1952 reflects the formation of the Greensburg diocese out of four counties from the Pittsburgh diocese.

79. "School Report Shows Continued Increase in Enrollment; Now 90,060," *Pittsburgh Catholic*, 18 January 1951, 1.

80. Catholic university and college enrollments actually declined in the early 1950s.

81. Timothy Walch, *Parish School: American Catholic Parochial Education from Colonial Times to the Present* (New York: Herder and Herder, 1996), 170. Walch addressed the Catholic parochial school system nationally, and the characterization certainly applied to Pittsburgh.

82. "Catholic School Program of Nation Keeps Abreast of Growth in Population," *Pittsburgh Catholic*, 26 June 1952, 1.

83. "Schools Graduate 11,000," *Pittsburgh Catholic*, 2 June 1955, 1.

84. *Fifty-fifth Annual Report of the Catholic Schools, Diocese of Pittsburgh, 1959–1960* (Pittsburgh, 1960): 23; *Fifty-eighth Annual Report of the Catholic Schools, Diocese of Pittsburgh, 1962–1963* (Pittsburgh, 1963), 19. For two years during the period (1956 and 1957) the number decreased, but it rose again in 1958 and 1959.

85. Fr. John B. McDowell, "Should Catholic Schools Abandon First Four Grades?" *Pittsburgh Catholic*, 28 June 1956, 1, 3.

86. Msgr. John B. McDowell, "The Facts About Our High Schools," *Pittsburgh Catholic*, 20 February 1958, 1; "Catholic High Schools Drop 100 Students," *Pittsburgh Post-Gazette*, 14 February 1958, 17.

87. Fr. John B. Sheerin, C.S.P., "'Madness' Over Missiles Presenting New Danger to Liberal Education," *Pittsburgh Catholic*, 16 January 1958, 4.

88. "Scientists and Morality," *Pittsburgh Catholic*, 28 November 1957, 4.

89. "Have Faith in Our Schools, Don't Panic over Sputnik," *Pittsburgh Catholic*, 5 December 1957, 1.

90. Msgr. John B. McDowell, "Did Red Sputnik Put U.S. Schools in 'Dog House'?" *Pittsburgh Catholic*, 19 December 1957, 1.

91. "Keep Science, Arts Balance, Diocesan Teachers Told," *Pittsburgh Catholic*, February 1958, 9.

92. "Expanding Duquesne University Shuns 'Sputnik Hysteria,'" *Pittsburgh Catholic*, 3 April 1958, 2.

93. Other concerns should make us cautious about reaching conclusions from this data. The seven-year lag between baptism and enrollment allow for a great deal of change in the nature of the population—people could have moved in and out of the diocese quite a bit in the intervening years. The infant baptism count follows a calendar year, while school enrollments are reported for school years. Children born after September in each year may have been baptized that same year but might not have been eligible to enroll in first grade until the following year. I used the seven-year lag because the diocese encouraged parents to enroll their children at age seven in first grade. Not all Catholic schools maintained kindergartens in the 1950s and 1960s, so kindergarten enrollments are not good measures of commitment to Catholic education.

94. Words of caution should guide us here as well. This graph does not track true retention rates, because it simply compares enrollment totals for each class as it progresses toward graduation. It does not follow specific students to see whether they remained in the area and chose not to enroll in Catholic schools. The increasing rate of decline could be explained by a net exodus of Catholic school-age children from

the diocese, or by a significant movement of students from places within the diocese where Catholic schools existed to places that had no schools.

95. Msgr. Irving A. DeBlanc, "'56 College Graduate Must Meet Religious, Civil, Social Challenges," *Pittsburgh Catholic*, 7 June 1956, 5. DeBlanc's answer was that the laity should fully engage in the family life apostolate. Donald McDonald, "'Apathy' of Catholic Laity Disturbing Bishops, Clergy," *Pittsburgh Catholic*, 4 November 1954, 5.

96. Sixty students took advantage of the scholarships in 1955. "Diocese Trains Lay School Teachers," *Pittsburgh Catholic*, 21 July 1955, 1.

97. "Lay Teachers Needed in Catholic Schools," *Pittsburgh Catholic*, 16 September 1954, 2; "Schools with Increased Enrollment Need Lay Teachers," *Pittsburgh Catholic*, 22 August 1957, 2.

98. Other explanations for the low marriage rate exist. Because demographers establish the marriage rate by calculating the number of marriages for every thousand people in any given year, years with disproportionately high numbers of people in the typical marrying ages (twenty to thirty) will have high rates and those with unusually low numbers in that age cohort will have low rates. Thus, the 1950s pattern may have resulted from the low birthrate during the Depression. The *Pittsburgh Catholic* speculated in 1952 that the low national marriage rate in 1951 derived from the dearth of "young persons reaching marrying age" because of the Depression's low birthrate. "Lowest Divorce Rate for Years, Is 1951 Record," *Pittsburgh Catholic*, 26 July 1952, 8.

99. "Christian Family Life in Danger, Archbishop Alter Tells Conference," *Pittsburgh Catholic*, 27 March 1952, 1; Msgr. Irving A. DeBlanc, "Lack of Preparation Found First Factor in Marriage Breakups," *Pittsburgh Catholic*, 25 July 1957, 5; "Lawyers Told of Moral Law on Divorces," *Pittsburgh Catholic*, 3 July 1958, 2.

100. "So You're Going to Marry?" *Pittsburgh Catholic*, 19 January 1956, 4.

101. Msgr. Irving A. DeBlanc, "Teen-Age Marriages Result in Problems," *Pittsburgh Catholic*, 2 February 1956, 13.

102. "Men Should Wait to 25 to Marry; Women, 23," *Pittsburgh Catholic*, 19 July 1956, 1.

103. The *Official Catholic Directory*, the source for this information, reports numbers provided by each diocese. Dioceses did not report mixed marriages that took place outside of the Church's purview, as they had no reliable and systematic way of tracking these. Therefore, the total for exogamous marriages is likely to be higher each year than that reported in the *Catholic Directory*. Andrew Greeley has argued that national data from the National Opinion Research Center suggest that Catholic exogamous marriage patterns have remained steady at about a third of all marriages involving one Catholic partner for every generation born from the 1920s through the 1970s. If his report is accurate for the nation and for Pittsburgh itself, perhaps the *Catholic Directory* data reflect merely a greater tendency for Catholics in mixed marriages to include the Church in their weddings. Andrew Greeley, "Just the Facts, Man: Catholics Still Marry Catholics," *Commonweal*, 17 December 1999, 14–15.

104. "Conference Stresses Laity," *Pittsburgh Catholic*, 1 November 1956, 3.

105. "'Shop Weekdays Only' Appeal in 'Keep Sunday Sacred' Drive," *Pittsburgh Catholic*, 25 February 1955, 1, 2.

106. "Send Religious Cards For Christmas Greetings," *Pittsburgh Catholic*, 28 November 1957, 9; "Nativity Scenes Help Keep Christ in Christmas," *Pittsburgh Catholic*, 20 December 1956, 1.

107. "Christ Back in Christmas Here," *Pittsburgh Catholic*, 29 December 1955, 4.

108. Black, *Catholic Crusade*, 143–44; Walsh, *Sin and Censorship*, 266–68; Garth Jowett, "A Significant Medium for the Communication of Ideas," in *Movie Censorship and American Culture*, ed. Frances G. Courvares (Washington, D.C.: Smithsonian Institution Press, 1996), 258–76.

109. Black, *Catholic Crusade*, 144; Walsh, *Sin and Censorship*, 269–70.

110. This explanation is further complicated by the conclusion that the PCA reached in the early 1930s that the Legion of Decency held little influence with moviegoers even then. The PCA came to this determination after an informal survey that included an assessment of the Pittsburgh market, where a concerted Legion campaign against immoral films did not diminish movie attendance at all. The Legion may never have been effective in policing lay Catholic behavior, though it clearly influenced Hollywood with the threat that lay Catholics would follow Legion directives. See Gregory Black, *Hollywood Censored: Morality Codes, Catholics and the Movies* (New York: Cambridge University Press, 1994), 187.

111. Una Cadigan suggests that Catholics understood the censorship differently than did other Americans through at least the 1950s. Catholics differentiated between freedom and unrestrained license, and saw the efforts to curtail unrestrained license as supportive of democracy and true freedom. Cadigan, "Guardians of Democracy," 269–75.

112. Black, *Catholic Crusade*, 145–47.

113. *Pittsburgh Catholic*, 17 February 1955, 3.

114. "'Storm Center' Film Draws Bleak Legion Classification," *Pittsburgh Catholic*, 12 July 1956, 11.

115. William Mooring, "Film Rating Difference Shows Freedom," *Pittsburgh Catholic*, 2 February 1956, 14.

116. "Catholic Critics Tell Readers Why Films Are Class 'B,' 'C,'" *Pittsburgh Catholic*, 7 November 1957, 13; "Adolescents' Needs Change Legion Ratings," *Pittsburgh Catholic*, 28 November 1957, 1.

117. "Pa. Movie Censor Board Near End After 41 Years," *Pittsburgh Catholic*, 9 February 1956, 1.

118. "Pa. High Court to Hear Appeal on Seized Film," *Pittsburgh Catholic*, 13 March 1958, 1; "Are Americans Indecent?" *Pittsburgh Catholic*, 20 March 1958, 4; "Jury Indicts 2, Condemns Film," *Pittsburgh Catholic*, 27 March 1958, 1; "Condemned Film Being Shown Here by 7 Drive-ins," *Pittsburgh Catholic*, 19 June 1958, 1.

119. "Senate Bill 373," *Pittsburgh Catholic*, 16 April 1959, 4.

120. "D. A. Promises Strong Stand Against Filth," *Pittsburgh Catholic*, 9 July 1959, 1.

121. "Your Pledge for Decency," *Pittsburgh Catholic*, 11 December 1958, 4.

122. "Official," *Pittsburgh Catholic*, 10 December 1959, 1.

CHAPTER FOUR. **Social Justice and Reform**

1. For copies of the two encyclicals, see David J. O'Brien and Thomas A. Shannon, *Catholic Social Thought: The Documentary Heritage* (New York: Orbis Books, 1992) This volume sets the encyclicals in the context of Catholic thought on social justice. In another publication, O'Brien provides a brief overview of the American hierarchy's developing positions on economic and social justice issues which frames the encyclicals' roles in American Catholic social thought very well. David J. O'Brien, "The Economic Thought of the American Hierarchy," in *The Catholic Challenge to the American Economy: Reflections on the U.S. Bishops' Pastoral Letter on Catholic Social Teaching and the U.S. Economy,* ed. Thomas M. Gannon, S.J. (New York: Macmillan, 1987): 27–41.

2. John Collins, "To the Point: Holy Justice," *Pittsburgh Catholic,* 5 October 1950, 1.

3. "Sixtieth Anniversary of Encyclical Recalls Problems That Inspired It," *Pittsburgh Catholic,* 3 May 1951, 1; John Collins, "To the Point: Toward Social Justice," *Pittsburgh Catholic,* 10 May 1951, 1.

4. For Boyle's early life and career I have relied on John B. McDowell's recent biography, *Water, Death, and Grace: The Life and Works of Hugh Charles Boyle, Priest, Pastor, Bishop* (Pittsburgh, 1999).

5. See David McCullough, *The Johnstown Flood* (New York: Simon and Schuster, 1968) for an extended story of the flood.

6. Despite his beginnings in a family with modest means and extraordinary tragedy, Boyle did not remain poor throughout his career. He left an estate valued at $160,000 when he died, an amount that translated to roughly $1.1 million in 2000 dollars.

7. The quote came from a Chicago priest speaking at the archdiocese's annual Labor Day Mass. "Catholic Who Is Poor Trade Unionist Is Poor Catholic, Father Mase Says," *Pittsburgh Catholic,* 14 September 1950, 5.

8. John Collins, "To the Point," *Pittsburgh Catholic,* 31 July 1952, 4.

9. "Taft-Hartley Law 'Tyrannous,' Bishop Haas Tells Convention," *Pittsburgh Catholic,* 18 May 1950, 1.

10. See, for example, John Collins, "To the Point: Long Siege?" *Pittsburgh Catholic,* 19 October 1950, 4; John Collins, "To the Point: Still Silent," *Pittsburgh Catholic,* 26 October 1950, 4; John Collins, "To the Point: Store Strike," *Pittsburgh Catholic,* 14 December 1950, 4; the Rev. Charles Owen Rice, "The Condition of Labor: Railroaders," *Pittsburgh Catholic,* 21 December 1950, 5.

11. Charles J. McCollester, "Introduction," *Fighter with a Heart: Writings of Charles Owen Rice, Pittsburgh Labor Priest,* ed. Charles J. McCollester (Pittsburgh: University of Pittsburgh Press, 1996); Patrick J. McGeever, *Rev. Charles Owen Rice: Apostle of Contradiction* (Pittsburgh: Duquesne University Press, 1989), 52–54.

12. Rice focused so intently and doggedly in the 1950s on combating Communism within the labor movement that Charles McCollester, who edited a collection of Rice's columns, saw anti-Communism as the central theme in Rice's columns from the period. McCollester, pp. 59–123.

13. The Rev. Charles Owen Rice, "The Condition of Labor: Whose Ox?" *Pittsburgh Catholic*, 17 April 1952, 5; "To the Point: Steel and Justice," *Pittsburgh Catholic*, 17 April 1952, 1.

14. See David Brody, *Steelworkers in America: The Nonunion Era* (Cambridge: Harvard University Press, 1960), chap. 12; Jeremy Brecher, *Strike!* (San Francisco: Straight Arrow Books, 1972), chap. 4; Paul Krause, *The Battle for Homestead 1880–1892* (Pittsburgh: University of Pittsburgh Press, 1992); and Arthur G. Burgoyne, *The Homestead Strike of 1892* (1893; Pittsburgh: University of Pittsburgh Press, 1979), chaps. 10 and 11.

15. John Collins, "To the Point: For a Ride," *Pittsburgh Catholic*, 18 January 1951, 4; "To the Point: 'Control' Item," *Pittsburgh Catholic*, 8 March 1951, 4.

16. "Archbishop Lucey Opposes Move to Cripple Public Housing Plan," *Pittsburgh Catholic*, 22 March 1951, 6.

17. "Rent Control Morally Justified During Shortage, Official Says," *Pittsburgh Catholic*, 11 September 1952, 5.

18. John Collins, "To the Point," *Pittsburgh Catholic*, 10 April 1952, 4; John Collins, "To the Point: Rent Control," *Pittsburgh Catholic*, 7 August 1952, 1.

19. The pastor made his recommendation in the parish bulletin in July 1950. The *Pittsburgh Catholic* then carried the recommendation in its July 27 issue. "Parishioners Encouraged to Join Hazelwood 'Housing Co-operative,'" *Pittsburgh Catholic*, 27 July 1950, 3.

20. John Collins, "To the Point," *Pittsburgh Catholic*, 9 August 1951, 4; "'Socialized Medicine' Not Wrong, Pope Says," *Pittsburgh Catholic*, 19 July 1951, 1.

21. "'Shop Weekdays Only' Appeal in 'Keep Sunday Sacred' Drive," *Pittsburgh Catholic*, 24 February 1955, 1.

22. "North Side Fights Sunday Sales," *Pittsburgh Catholic*, 12 April 1955, 1.

23. "Santa Claus or Christ?" *Pittsburgh Catholic*, 9 November 1950, 3. The column appears to be a print advertisement placed by the Catholic Cultural Center in Pittsburgh; "'Put Christ Back into Christmas' Campaign of Christian Mothers to Be Aided by Trolley Posters," *Pittsburgh Catholic*, 30 November 1950, 1.

24. John Collins, "To the Point: Advent and Christmas," *Pittsburgh Catholic*, 30 November 1950, 4.

25. John Collins, "To the Point," *Pittsburgh Catholic*, 22 October 1953, 4.

26. The National Council of Catholic Men published the pledge initially in their monthly newsletter, and the *Pittsburgh Catholic* reprinted it in the December 16, 1954, edition on p. 9.

27. "That Christmas Shopping," *Pittsburgh Catholic*, 20 November 1958, 4.

28. "Warns Against Pre-Christmas 'Office Parties,'" *Pittsburgh Catholic*, 14 December 1950, 1; "Avoid Excesses at Office Parties, Mayor Requests," *Pittsburgh Catholic*, 18 December 1952, 1.

29. Mary Tinley Daly, "Office Christmas Party Can Be—Well, Almost Anything," *Pittsburgh Catholic*, 15 December 1955, 13.

30. U.S. Department of Commerce, Bureau of the Census, *U.S. Census of Population and Housing, Pittsburgh, PA* (Washington, D.C.: U.S. Government Printing Office, 1950, 1960, 1970, 1980); John Bodnar, Roger Simon, and Michael P. Weber, *Lives of Their*

Own: Blacks, Italians and Poles in Pittsburgh, 1900–1960 (Urbana: University of Illinois Press, 1982), 30, 187.

31. U.S. Department of Commerce, Bureau of the Census, *U.S. Census of Population and Housing, Pittsburgh, PA* (1950, 1960, 1970, 1980).

32. "Negroes Crowded in Ghetto," *Pittsburgh Post-Gazette*, 15 February 1954, "Housing Situation in Pittsburgh Clippings" file, ASI, AIS; "Facts and Figures on City of Pittsburgh's Housing for Negroes: Is the Hill District Doomed?" *Pittsburgh Courier*, 29 April 1950, "Housing Situation in Pittsburgh Clippings" file, ASI, AIS.

33. "Is the Hill District Doomed?" *Pittsburgh Courier*, 29 April 1950, "Wretched Slum Returns Huge Profit to Owner," *Pittsburgh Post-Gazette*, 12 April 1954, "Housing Conditions in Pittsburgh Clippings" file, ASI, AIS.

34. "Negroes Crowded in Ghetto," *Pittsburgh Post-Gazette*, 15 February 1954.

35. "Is the Hill District Doomed?" *Pittsburgh Courier*, 29 April 1950.

36. City of Pittsburgh, Mayor's Special Task Force on Civil Disturbances, *Progress Report*, in *Pittsburgh*, ed. Roy Lubove (New York: New Viewpoints, 1976), 239.

37. Pittsburgh Chamber of Commerce, "Pittsburgh," *City Directory 1970*.

38. "Angry 16th Ward Voters Attack Housing Project Before Council," *Pittsburgh Post-Gazette*, 28 September 1950, "Housing Situation in Pittsburgh Clippings" file, ASI, AIS.

39. For the purposes of this analysis, I have included any article that featured African Americans or Africans, or addressed an issue of racial cooperation, segregation, or discrimination. I included any article that dealt with the Catholic Interracial Council, missionary activity in Africa generally, or the situation in South Africa. I have not included articles that dealt with Asian missionary efforts or reports on Korea, Vietnam, or Latin America, nor did I include articles that addressed Hispanic Americans or Asian Americans (which were negligible in number).

40. The *Pittsburgh Catholic* ran eleven articles on Louisiana integration battles and only five articles on race in Pittsburgh.

41. "Ripe for the Harvest," *Pittsburgh Catholic*, 30 August 1956, 4.

42. Conservative critics testified to Wright's place as a liberal Catholic prominent on the American cultural scene when they attacked him specifically for positions that he took. Boston-based Jesuit conservative priest Charles Feeney launched such attacks from his position at the Saint Benedict Center for Catholic students at Harvard University in the late 1940s. See Mark S. Massa, *Catholics and American Culture: Fulton Sheen, Dorothy Day, and the Notre Dame Football Team* (New York: Crossroad, 1999), 28, 29.

43. Russel W. Gibbons, "Conflicts in Catholicism . . ." *Nation*, 8 December 1962, 392.

44. David J. O'Brien, "When It All Came Together: Bishop John J. Wright and the Diocese of Worcester, 1950–1959," *Catholic Historical Review* (April 1999):187–89.

45. For example, in one 1954 article in *The Voice of St. Jude*, Wright argued that Catholics must assent to all papal teachings in public addresses, including his utterances on radio broadcasts. "Papal Addresses, Letters Cannot Be Ignored, Bishop Wright Asserts," *Pittsburgh Catholic*, 15 July 1954, 8.

46. "The Citizenship Filter Test," *Pittsburgh Catholic*, 5 November 1959, 4.

47. "Promise Seen in Law Against Discrimination in Pittsburgh Housing," *Pittsburgh Catholic*, 14 January 1960, 1; Fr. Paul Lackner, "How Important Are Smokers?" *Pittsburgh Catholic*, 18 February 1960, 11; Fr. Charles Owen Rice, "Negro Workers," *Pittsburgh Catholic*, 10 March 1960, 4.

48. "East Liberty's Challenges," *Pittsburgh Catholic*, June 1960, 4.

49. Paul Lackner, "From the Director's Notebook," *Holy Name Newsletter*, October 1958, 6, 7. The *Newsletter* varied the capitalization of the word *Negro* throughout its issues, sometimes using a capital *N* and sometimes not. I have followed the *Newsletter*'s usage in all quotations.

50. Ibid.

51. Arthur B. Sullivan, "The Mystical Body and Integration," *Holy Name Newsletter*, May 1959, 3, 4.

52. Robert A. Dumas, "The Church and Integration," *Holy Name Newsletter*, June–July 1959, 3–5.

53. Arthur Alonso, O.P., *Catholic Action and the Laity*, trans. by Cornelius J. Crowley (St. Louis: B. Herder, 1961), 103.

54. Jeremiah Newman, *What Is Catholic Action? An Introduction to the Lay Apostolate* (Dublin: Gill, 1958), 2.

55. Donald McDonald, "Catholic Action Duty of Alert Newspaper," *Pittsburgh Catholic*, 7 October 1954, 5.

56. HNS *Newsletter*, February 1955, HNS Collection, HADP.

57. HNS *Newsletter*, January 1955.

58. HNS *Newsletter*, February 1955.

59. Lackner followed mainstream Catholic thought in this. See R. P. Chenu, O.P., *Restoring All Things: A Guide to Catholic Action*, ed. John Fitzsimons and John McGuire (New York: Sheed and Ward, 1938), esp. chap. 1, "Catholic Action and the Mystical Body."

60. John A. Hardon, *Pocket Catholic Dictionary* (Garden City, New York: Doubleday, 1985), 275–76.

61. Mel Piehl, *Breaking Bread: The Catholic Worker and the Origin of Catholic Radicalism in America* (Philadelphia: Temple University Press, 1982), 85–88; Mel Piehl, "The Politics of Free Obedience," in *A Revolution of the Heart: Essays on the Catholic Worker*, ed. Patrick G. Coy (Philadelphia: Temple University Press, 1988), 202; "Liturgical Commission Members, 1 November 1960," "Liturgical Commission Folder," Box 7, Mr. C. Holmes Wolfe, Jr., Personal Papers (hereinafter to be cited as Wolfe Papers), HADP.

62. John Collins, "To the Point," *Pittsburgh Catholic*, 24 December 1953, 4.

63. "Those 'Office Parties,'" *Pittsburgh Catholic*, 30 December 1954, 4.

64. "Your Heart . . . His Manger," *Pittsburgh Catholic*, 22 December 1955, 4.

65. Daly, "Office Christmas Party," 13.

66. "Here Are the Rules," *Pittsburgh Catholic*, 7 October 1954, 8; "Prizes for Top Crusaders," *Pittsburgh Catholic*, 7 October 1954, 8; "Circulation Crusade Ends in Rush," *Pittsburgh Catholic*, 4 November 1954, 1.

67. "St. Lawrence Boy First Prize Winner in Campaign by Schools of Diocese," *Pittsburgh Catholic,* 9 December 1954, 1. Paul placed in the top three finishers each of the first three years of the contest.

68. "Pittsburgh Catholic New ABC Member," *Pittsburgh Catholic,* 5 April 1956, 1, 2.

69. Virginia Kenny, "Want to Buy or Sell a House? Catholic Ads Get Results," *Pittsburgh Catholic,* 3 July 1958, 1.

70. *United States of America v. Murray Kram,* Crim. No. 14777, United States District Court for the Western District of Pennsylvania, 145 F. Supp. 662; 1956 U.S. Dist. Lexis 2654.

71. It is not clear who initiated the complaints. Later articles suggest that some recipients of the solicitation complained to the Post Office. But those who testified in court against Kram seem to have realized that Kram was running a for-profit business only after the Post Office or the U.S. Attorney's Office contacted them regarding plans to prosecute.

72. *United States of America v. Murray Kram.*

73. Alvin Rosensweet, "Marjorie Matson, Lawyer, Well-Known Civil Libertarian," *Pittsburgh Post-Gazette,* 24 November 1980, 10. Matson's papers are housed in the University of Pittsburgh Archives Service Center, but they are unorganized and appear to begin with her work in the early 1960s. I could locate no references to the Kram case in these papers. Matson may have been particularly sympathetic to Kram in this case because she had been the target of a Catholics' crusade just a few years before. Judge Musmanno made Matson the focus of an anti-Communist purge effort in 1951, as he sought to have her fired from her position with the district attorney's office. For a discussion of this episode, see Weber, *Don't Call Me Boss,* 284–86.

74. *United States of America v. Murray Kram;* "'Junk Dealer' on Trial Here," *Pittsburgh Catholic,* 14 June 1956, 1; "40 'Gimmick' Victims Testify at Kram Trial," *Pittsburgh Press,* 13 June 1956, 4; "Religious Gimmick Trial Begins," *Pittsburgh Press,* 12 June 1956, 1.

75. "Religious Gimmick Trial Begins," 1; "Religious 'Junk' Convicts Kram," *Pittsburgh Catholic,* 21 June 1956, 1, 2.

76. Ibid.

77. "Kram Loses His Plea for Acquittal," *Pittsburgh Press,* 14 June 1956, 2.

78. *United States of America v. Murray Kram;* "Religious 'Junk' Convicts Kram," 1, 2.

79. "Kram Loses His Plea for Acquittal," 2.

80. Ibid.

81. *United States of America v. Murray Kram;* "Religious Gimmick Trial Begins," 1; "Religious 'Junk' Convicts Kram," 1, 2.

82. "Kram Gets 3 Months, $4,500 Fine for Fraud," *Pittsburgh Catholic,* 22 November 1956, 9.

83. "Kram Cleared of Fraud," *Pittsburgh Post-Gazette,* 10 September 1957, 6.

84. *United States of America v. Murray Kram,* No. 12162, United States Court of Appeals Third Circuit, 247 F.2d. 830; 1957 f U.S. APP. LEXIS 3754.

85. "'Junk Dealer' on Trial Here," 1; "Religious 'Junk' Convicts Kram," 1; "Religious Junkmen Busy Again," *Pittsburgh Catholic,* 27 September 1956, 1

86. "Religious 'Junk' Dealer Denounced," *Pittsburgh Catholic,* 21 August 1958, 1.

87. Parishes often depended on sales of such items to support their work, and Kram's efforts may have threatened the viability of their efforts. Barbara Kane Pilliod makes just this point in her reminiscences about parish life in 1950s New York City: "The Way We Were," *Commonweal,* 12 September 2003, 32.

88. "Christmas Junk," *Pittsburgh Catholic,* 27 October 1960, 4.

89. Bill Fichter, "No Double Standard in Religious Junk," *Pittsburgh Catholic,* 10 November 1960, 5.

90. Mrs. W. J. McCarthy, "Disputes Editorial on Religious Junk," *Pittsburgh Catholic,* 17 November 1960, 5.

91. "Milwaukee Firm Answers Editorial," *Pittsburgh Catholic,* 8 December 1960, 5.

92. "Lay Action Vital, Archbishop Says," *Pittsburgh Catholic,* 23 April 1953, 1. The archbishop was Boston's Richard J. Cushing.

93. Msgr. Thomas J. Quigley, "Catholic Doctrine and Practice in Human Relations," *Pittsburgh Catholic,* 10 September 1953, 1; "No Age Limit at Adult Education Institute," *Pittsburgh Catholic,* 13 January 1955, 16.

94. "Adult Education Term Ends; 449 Were Enrolled," *Pittsburgh Catholic,* 4 December 1952, 1.

95. Quigley, "Catholic Doctrine and Practice," 1.

96. "Adult Education Term Ends"; "Adult Education Courses Report Big Registration," *Pittsburgh Catholic,* 4 February 1954, 1; "1,100 in Adult Study Courses," *Pittsburgh Catholic,* 18 February 1954, 1; "1600 Adults Set Education Class Record," *Pittsburgh Catholic,* 28 October 1954, 1; "1,420 Attend Adult Courses at Central," *Pittsburgh Catholic,* 4 October 1956, 8.

97. Karen Sue Smith, "The Man from Collegeville: Michel Blows His Horn, Social Justice and the Liturgy," *Commonweal,* 8 September 1988, 457. Keith Pecklers, author of *The Unread Vision: The Liturgical Movement in the United States of America: 1926–1955* (Collegeville, Minn.: Liturgical Press, 1996), agrees with this assessment for Michel and extends it to the movement more generally.

98. Ernest Benjamin Koenker, *The Liturgical Renaissance in the Roman Catholic Church* (Chicago: University of Chicago Press, 1954), 1–6.

99. Because the NCWC charter strictly forbade any involvement in the liturgy on the grounds that this would infringe on the sovereign power of each individual bishop to run his diocese as he wished, the bishops established the committee as a committee of the American Hierarchy, independent of the NCWC. McManus, *Thirty Years of Liturgical Renewal, Statements of the Bishops' Committee on the Liturgy* (Washington, D.C.: United States Catholic Conference, 1987), 6–7.

100. McManus, *Thirty Years of Liturgical Renewal.*

101. Robert J. McClory, "John Dearden's Legacy of Collegiality Lives On," *National Catholic Reporter,* 12 August 1988, 2; "Catholics Mourn Death of Cardinal Dearden," *Pittsburgh Catholic,* 5 August 1988, 1.

102. "List of Representatives to Liturgy Week," Liturgical Commission file, Wolfe Papers, Box 7, HADP; Bishop John J. Wright to C. Holmes Wolfe, Jr., Liturgical Commission file, Wolfe Papers, Box 7, HADP.

103. The Diocesan Archives contain a copy of the questionnaire sent to each priest, but no returns. References in later meetings and correspondence indicate that the commission received at least two hundred returns and tabulated responses. "The Liturgical Commission Questionnaire," Liturgical Commission file, Wolfe Papers, Box 7, HADP; LC Minutes, 10 March 1961, Liturgical Commission file, Wolfe Papers, Box 7, HADP.

104. William G. Storey, "Questions Value of Latin," *Pittsburgh Catholic,* February 1960, 5.

105. Mrs. James F. Young, "Explains Reaction to Dialogue Mass," *Pittsburgh Catholic,* 14 April 1960, 5.

106. P.J. Meier, "Sees Pit-Falls in the Vernacular," *Pittsburgh Catholic,* 14 April 1960, 5.

107. Mrs. Michael Strasser, "Urges Mass Change to Vernacular," *Pittsburgh Catholic,* 23 June 1960, 5.

108. P.V.D., "Cites Irishmen's Love of Latin," *Pittsburgh Catholic,* 5 May 1960, 5.

109. LC Minutes, 13 January 1961, Liturgical Commission file, Wolfe Papers, Box 7, HADP.

110. Saint Philomena had only one choir Mass, for instance, as did Saint Thomas More. Interview with Jane and Dan Quinn, 7 November 1989.

111. LC Minutes, 12 May 1961, Liturgical Commission file, Wolfe Papers, Box 7, HADP.

112. LC Minutes, 9 March 1962, 20 March 1962, 11 May 1962, 8 June 1962, 14 September 1962, Liturgical Commission file, Wolfe Papers, Box 7, HADP.

113. LC Minutes, 20 March 1962, Liturgical Commission file, Wolfe Papers, Box 7, HADP.

114. *Liturgical Commission Newsletter* (hereinafter to be cited as *LC Newsletter*), 1, May 1961, 1, Liturgical Commission file, Wolfe Papers, HADP.

115. Ibid.

116. *LC Newsletter,* 1, June 1961, 1, November 1961, 2, January 1962, 2, October 1962, 2, December 1962.

117. *LC Newsletter,* 2, February 1962, 2, March 1962, 2, May 1962, 2, September 1962.

118. *LC Newsletter,* 1, December 1961.

119. *LC Newsletter,* 2, June 1962.

120. *LC Newsletter,* 2, July 1962, Liturgical Commission file, Wolfe Papers, HADP.

121. The Rev. Frederick R. McManus, "Demonstration of Holy Mass Script and Explanation," Liturgical Commission Publications file, Wolfe Papers, Box 7, HADP.

122. LC Minutes, 15 December 1961, Liturgical Commission file, Wolfe Papers, Box 7, HADP.

123. Flyer advertising "Diocesan Liturgical Day," Liturgical Commission file, Wolfe Papers, Box 7, HADP; LC Minutes, 9 June 1961, Liturgical Commission file, Wolfe Papers, HADP; LC Minutes, 21 April 1961, 1 September 1961; Liturgical Commission file, Wolfe Papers, HADP.

124. LC Minutes, 8 June 1962, 12 October 1962, 12 October 1962, Liturgical Commission file, Wolfe Papers, HADP.

125. LC Minutes, 21 April 1961, Liturgical Commission file, Wolfe Papers, HADP.

126. The commission established other subcommittees as well, so that in 1962 it had committees for sacred music, sacred art and architecture, participation, and lay organizations.

127. LC Minutes, 9 February 1962, Liturgical Commission file, Wolfe Papers, HADP.

128. Lay Organization Committee Minutes, 5 April 1962, Liturgical Commission file, Wolfe Papers, HADP.

129. LC Minutes, 1 September 1961, 15 December 1961, 9 March 1962, Liturgical Commission file, Wolfe Papers, HADP.

130. Jeffrey M. Burns, *Disturbing the Peace: A History of the Christian Family Movement, 1949–1974* (Notre Dame, Ind.: University of Notre Dame Press, 1999), 18–19.

131. "Liturgical Customs Practiced in Home," *Pittsburgh Catholic,* 18 October 1956, 12.

132. Burns, *Disturbing the Peace,* 1, 2.

133. Cardijn introduced the observe-judge-act approach initially with Catholic workers and students in Europe, and then in America with the Young Christian Workers and Young Christian Students organizations.

134. "CFM Brings Awareness of Others," *Pittsburgh Catholic,* 15 September 1955, 12; "Liturgical Customs Practiced in Home," Mr. and Mrs. Gerry Ryan, "Catholic Family Customs," *Holy Name Newsletter,* November 1956, 7.

135. "Materialism Said Ruining Family Life," *Pittsburgh Catholic,* 10 August 1961, 12.

136. "Christian Family Movement Motto 'Observe-Judge-Act,'" *Pittsburgh Catholic,* 25 October 1956, 12.

137. "'Conference for Happier Families' Nov. 23," *Pittsburgh Catholic,* 13 November 1958, 11; "Model Group Presents Christian Family Theme," *Pittsburgh Catholic,* 26 March 1959, 8.

138. The Rev. Paul M. Lackner, "Family Life Group Adds Chapter," *Pittsburgh Catholic,* 2 April 1959, 5.

139. "Convention Scheduled by CFM for Nov. 22," *Pittsburgh Catholic,* 5 November 1959, 3; "Msgr. Leonard to Give Convention Keynote," *Pittsburgh Catholic,* 12 November 1959, 9.

140. "Pittsburghers Attend CFM Meet in N.Y.," *Pittsburgh Catholic,* 11 August 1960, 8; Burns, *Disturbing the Peace,* 102.

CHAPTER FIVE.   **The Second Vatican Council in Rome and Pittsburgh, 1962–1965**

1. Thomas Bokenkotter, *A Concise History of the Catholic Church* (Garden City, N.Y.: Doubleday, 1977; Garden City, N.Y.: Image Books, 1979), 411; Henri Daniel-Rops believed the Church to be fine but the world in bad shape—hence the Council. *The Second Vatican Council: The Story Behind the Ecumenical Council of Pope John XXIII,* trans. Alastair Guinan (New York: Hawthorne Books, 1962), 123.

2. Xavier Rynne, *Vatican Council II* (New York: Farrar, Straus and Giroux, 1968), 3, 21. Robert Blair Kaiser argued that John sought a Council as a way to get the Church to confront the world: *Pope, Council and World: The Story of Vatican II* (New York: Macmillan, 1963), 14. G.C. Berkouwer also agrees with this perspective generally: G.C. Berkouwer, *The Second Vatican Council and the New Catholicism*, trans. Lewis B. Smedes (Grand Rapids, Mich.: Eerdmans, 1965), 11–33.

3. Henri Fesquet, *The Drama of Vatican II: The Ecumenical Council, June, 1962–December, 1965*, trans. Bernard Murchland (New York: Random House, 1967), xv.

4. "Priest 'Pool' Begun in Europe to Ease Dearth," *Pittsburgh Catholic*, 14 July 1960, 9; "Italy Loses 2,000 Priests in 8 Years," *Pittsburgh Catholic*, 17 May 1962, 8; "Vocations Drop Sharply in France," *Pittsburgh Catholic*, 24 May 1962, 12.

5. See, for example, Robert E. Tracy, *American Bishop at the Vatican Council* (New York: McGraw-Hill, 1966), 13–14.

6. Peter Hebblethwaite, *Pope John XXIII: Shepherd of the Modern World* (Garden City, N.Y.: Image Books, 1987), 316.

7. Msgr. James I. Tucek, "Best Forecast for Vatican Council Found in Words of Pope John," *Pittsburgh Catholic*, 9 August 1962, 3. Later, in his opening statement to the Council, Pope John expanded on this epiphany explanation: "It was completely unexpected, like a flash of heavenly light." "Pope John's Address Opening 2nd Vatican Council . . . the Text," *Pittsburgh Catholic*, 18 October 1962, 5.

8. Jay P. Dolan, *The American Catholic Experience: A History from Colonial Times to the Present* (Garden City, N.Y.: Doubleday, 1985), 424; Hebblethwaite, *Pope John XXIII*, 387; Oscar Cullmann, "The Reform of Vatican Council II," in *Vatican Council II: The New Direction*, trans. James D. Hester (New York: Harper & Row, 1968), 76; Mario Von Galli, *The Council and the Future* (New York: McGraw-Hill, 1966), 124.

9. Bokenkotter, *A Concise History*, 412; Rynne, *Vatican Council II*, 30; Hebblethwaite, *Pope John XXIII*, 325–27.

10. Hebblethwaite, *Pope John XXIII*, 322.

11. Bokenkotter, *A Concise History*, 412; Hebblethwaite, *Pope John XXIII*, 325; Rynne, *Vatican Council II*, 29.

12. Rynne, *Vatican Council II*, 27–28.

13. Ibid., 32.

14. Ibid., 47.

15. Ibid., 57, 60, 76–84, 100–103, 109–11; Bokenkotter, *A Concise History*, 413–16.

16. Austin P. Flannery, ed., *Documents of Vatican II* (Grand Rapids, Mich.: Eerdmans, 1975), 13.

17. Rynne, *Vatican Council II*, 131.

18. Pope John died June 3, 1963, from an illness he had had for quite some time. His advanced age and illness had spurred him to push for a short preparation period for the Council against the Vatican bureaucracy's advice of a rather long period to prepare—perhaps as long as one or two decades. Bokenkotter, *A Concise History*, 416–17; Rynne, *Vatican Council II*, 151–53.

19. Bokenkotter, *A Concise History*, 417–18; Tracy, *American Bishop*, 113–19.

20. Rynne, *Vatican Council II*, 192–93.

21. Ibid., 193.

22. Tracy, *American Bishop*, 152.

23. Rynne, *Vatican Council II*, 293–94.

24. Ibid.

25. Ibid., 299–300.

26. Tracy, *American Bishop*, 159–61; Rynne, *Vatican Council II*, 300–303.

27. Tracy, *American Bishop*, 170–72.

28. Ibid., 173–74. John Courtney Murray, a Jesuit professor of theology at Woodstock College in Maryland is generally acknowledged to be the intellectual leader of the religious liberty movement, and his *We Hold These Truths: Catholic Reflections on the American Proposition* (Kansas City, Mo.: Sheed and Ward, 1960) is the classic work that sets out the arguments in favor.

29. Patrick Keegan, Foreword, in *Laymen: Vatican II's Decree on the Apostolate of the Laity*, ed. Peter Foote, John Hill, Lawrence Kelly, John McCudden, and Theodore Stone (Chicago: Catholic Action Federations, 1966), 4.

30. Gary MacEoin, *What Happened at Rome? The Council and Its Implications for the Modern World* (New York: Holt, Rinehart and Winston, 1966), 61. *Laos* was Greek for people, or laity; Tracy, *American Bishop*, 186–88.

31. Flannery, *Documents of Vatican II*, 772, 774.

32. Ibid., 777.

33. John Cooney, *The American Pope: The Life and Times of Francis Cardinal Spellman* (New York: Dell Books, 1984), 349.

34. Keegan, Foreword, 5.

35. Fr. John B. Sheerin, C.S.P., "Hope Seen in Ecumenical Council," *Pittsburgh Catholic*, 12 February 1959, 4.

36. *LC Newsletter*, February 1963, Liturgical Commission Publications file, Box 7, Wolfe Papers, HADP.

37. *LC Newsletter*, February 1963.

38. "Catholic Schools, Diocese of Pittsburgh, Operation Holy Week Teacher Guide," 1–15, Liturgical Commission Publications file, Wolfe Papers, HADP.

39. All quotes from "Teacher Guide, Operation Holy Week," 14.

40. Quotes from "Teacher Guide, Operation Holy Week," 9.

41. Lenten Sermon Outlines, 1963, Operation Holy Week, Liturgical Commission Publications file, Wolfe Papers, HADP; First Week in Lent and Fourth Week in Lent.

42. Lenten Sermon Outlines, Third Week in Lent.

43. The quotes and references here are from a plan for the show wherein each member set out his or her role, even to the point of stating dialogue. "Preliminary Outline for 'Operation Holy Week' Program for Sunday February 17," Liturgical Commission file, Wolfe Papers, Box 7, HADP.

44. Outline for Holy Week Program.

45. *LC Newsletter*, January 1964. This issue of the *Newsletter* also listed five books that pastors might consult to appreciate better the biblical renewal themselves.

46. *LC Newsletter,* February 1964.

47. *LC Newsletter,* November 1963.

48. Liturgical Commission Minutes, 14 June 1963, 13 March 1964, 10 July 1964, Liturgical Commission file, Box 7, Wolfe Papers, HADP (hereinafter to be cited LC Minutes).

49. Ralph Roos, "Wake Prayer Booklet," Liturgical Commission Publications file, Box 7, Wolfe Papers, HADP; "Bible Vigil for Use at a Wake," Liturgical Commission Publications file, Box 7, Wolfe Papers, HADP.

50. LC Minutes, 19 April 1963, 14 June 1963, 11 October 1963, 10 January 1964; "A Film Trilogy on the Holy Sacrifice," Liturgical Commission Publications file, Box 7, Wolfe Papers, HADP.

51. LC Minutes, 10 May 1963, 14 June 1963; *LC Newsletter,* July–August 1963. For adults, the commission recommended the *Saint Andrew Bible Missal,* the *Saint Andrew Daily Missal, The Layman's Missal, Maryknoll Missal;* for children, *Frere Jacques Missal, Children's Prayer Book,* and the *Saint Christopher Missal.*

52. LC Minutes, 14 February 1964, 13 March 1964, 12 June 1964.

53. LC Minutes, 10 July 1964. The Lay Committee members based their estimate on the number of Masses each Sunday by multiplying by four the number of parishes in the diocese (330).

54. LC Minutes, 7 August 1964.

55. LC Minutes, 11 September 1964, 9 October 1964.

56. "Course Director's Manual for the Training Program for Commentators and Lectors," Training Program for Commentators and Lectors folder, Liturgical Commission Publications file, Box 7, Wolfe Papers, HADP.

57. The sessions focused on the following areas: session one, the importance of liturgical renewal; session two, the layman's role at Mass; session three, the structure of the Mass; session four, commentator's duties; session five, delivery and technique; session six, dress rehearsal for a Mass. The Wolfe Papers contain both versions, though the later one shares a folder with notes, names, and letters regarding the sessions which indicate that the Lay Committee used the latest version for the training. The earlier version was less critical of the "old" Mass than the later kit. The release of the document may have emboldened the NCCM and the Liturgical Conference (the national version of the Liturgical Commission), which put the training kits together.

58. "Training Session I," 2, 6–7, Training Program for Commentators and Lectors folder, Liturgical Commission Publications file, Box 7, Wolfe Papers, HADP.

59. Training Session II," 9.

60. "Training Session II," 9, 11; "Training Session III," 3.

61. "Training Session IV," 8–9.

62. "Training Session V," 3; "Training Session II," 12.

63. "A Report on Behalf of the Lay Committee," 13 November 1964, Training Program for Commentators and Lectors folder, Liturgical Commission Publications file, Box 7, Wolfe Papers, HADP; LC Minutes, 13 November 1964.

64. *LC* Minutes, 11 December 1964.

65. *LC Newsletter,* January 1963, April 1963, May 1963, June 1963, September 1963, October 1963, December 1963.

66. *LC Newsletter,* January 1964.

67. LC Minutes, 13 March 1964, 11 September 1964, 8 January 1965; *LC Newsletter,* July 1964.

68. LC Minutes, March 1964.

69. *LC Newsletter,* November 1964.

70. Ibid.

71. Ibid.

72. *LC Newsletter,* March 1964.

73. *LC Newsletter,* November 1964. Later reforms dropped the last Gospel but retained the tripartite structure in the liturgy of the Eucharist. It became the offertory, canon, and Communion (reception among parishioners).

74. *LC Newsletter,* November 1964.

75. Ibid.

76. *LC Newsletter,* December 1964.

77. Ibid.

78. Ibid.

79. *LC Newsletter,* November 1964.

80. *LC Newsletter,* February 1965.

81. Ibid.

82. Ibid. The *Newsletter* further reported that many of the 75 percent who supported the changes would not support more radical reform, though it gave no evidence for this.

83. Saint Philomena Parish Bulletin, 27 December 1964, Saint Philomena Rectory, Pittsburgh, Pennsylvania.

84. Saint Thomas More Parish Bulletin, 3 February 1963, Saint Thomas More Rectory, Bethel Park, Pennsylvania (hereinafter to be cited STM Bulletin).

85. Martin A. Zielinski, "Working for Interracial Justice: The Catholic Interracial Council of New York, 1934–1964," *U.S. Catholic Historian* 7 (Spring–Summer 1988): 234, 235, 247. See also John McGreevy's *Parish Boundaries: The Catholic Encounter with Race in the Twentieth-Century Urban North* (Chicago: University of Chicago Press, 1996), 40–47, for a thorough discussion of the CIC founding.

86. The Rev. Donald McIlvane to C. Holmes Wolfe, n.d., Liturgical Commission file, Box 7, Wolfe Papers, HADP.

87. Proposed Joint Statement of the Lay Committee and Catholic Interracial Council, Liturgical Commission file, Box 7, Wolfe Papers, HADP.

88. J. Ronald Pittman to C. Holmes Wolfe, 21 February 1964, Liturgical Commission file, Box 7, Wolfe Papers, HADP.

89. LC Minutes, 10 January 1964, 14 February 1964, 13 March 1964.

90. Patricia Curran, *Grace Before Meals: Food Ritual and Body Discipline in Convent Culture* (Urbana: University of Illinois Press, 1989), 133–36. Mary Jo Weaver, *New*

Catholic Women: A Contemporary Challenge to Traditional Religious Authority (San Francisco: Harper and Row, 1986), 76–83.

91. LC Minutes, 13 September 1963, 11 September 1964, 11 December 1964, 8 October 1965.

92. LC Minutes, 9 October 1964, 12 February 1965.

93. LC Minutes, 10 September 1965.

CHAPTER SIX.   The Diocesan Pastoral Council

1. The organizations were: Catholic Physicians' Guild, Catholic War Veterans, Holy Name Society, Knights of Columbus, Saint Thomas More Society, Saint Vincent de Paul Society, and the Serra Club. Though some of these organizations did not specifically exclude women, Wright envisioned choosing only males from their membership.

2. "Proposed Minutes of Meeting of 6/18/66," Diocesan Pastoral Council Correspondence file, Box 1, Pastoral Planning Collection, HADP.

3. "Revision and Updating of Statute No. 130 of the Diocesan Synodal Decrees," DPC Studies and Recommendations file, Box 1, Pastoral Planning Collection, HADP.

4. "Challenge to Parish Involvement," *Pittsburgh Catholic,* 16 September 1965, D.P. Council P.C. Clippings file, Box 1, Diocesan Pastoral Council (1967–1970) Collection (hereinafter to be cited DPC Collection), HADP.

5. "Parish Committee Elections Held Around Diocese; Installations Set," *Pittsburgh Catholic,* 10 February 1966, D.P. Council P.C. Clippings file, Box 1, DPC Collection, HADP. The *Pittsburgh Catholic* surveyed forty parishes to see what the turnout was like, and reported results from only eighteen.

6. See the photo accompanying an article entitled "Religious Ruled Eligible to Vote in Parish Committee Elections," *Pittsburgh Catholic,* 3 February 1966, D.P. Council P.C. Clippings file, Box 1, DPC Collection, HADP, and the STM bulletin, 12 December 1965.

7. A statistic from one parish was very telling. Seventy-one of the 398 parishioners who voted in Holy Rosary parish in Homewood wrote in the names of candidates not nominated on the official ballot. In all, these 71 voters cast votes for 133 different parishioners, 101 (76 percent) of whom were female. None of these women garnered sufficient support to win, however, and even the two incumbent female committee members lost their seats. One of these seats went to Joseph Pace, the diocese's first African-American Parish Committee member. "Diocese Implementing Council's Decisions," *Pittsburgh Catholic,* 18 August 1966; "Parish Committee Elections Held Around Diocese; Installations Set," D.P. Council P.C. Clippings file, Box 1, DPC Collection, HADP. The article did not explain how two women already sat on the committee despite female ineligibility to vote.

8. "Clergy Council Organization Completed," *Pittsburgh Catholic,* 21 April 1966, D.P. Council P.C. Clippings file, Box 1, DPC Collection, HADP.

9. "Diocese Implementing Council's Decisions."

10. For an interesting discussion of the game's significance for American Catholic history, see chapter 9 in Mark S. Massa's *Catholics and American Culture: Fulton Sheen, Dorothy Day, and the Notre Dame Football Team* (New York: Crossroad, 1999).

11. "Parish Committee Gathering to Bring 2,500 to Civic Arena," *Pittsburgh Catholic*, 10 November 1966; "Parish Committees Elect 13 Delegates to Diocesan Council," *Pittsburgh Catholic*, 23 November 1966, D.P. Council P.C. Clippings file, Box 1, DPC Collection, HADP.

12. "Ten Religious Order Delegates Named to Diocesan Council," *Pittsburgh Catholic*, 16 March 1967, D.P. Council P.C. Clippings file, Box 1, DPC Collection, HADP.

13. "Diocesan Council Members Announced," *Pittsburgh Catholic*, n.d., D.P. Council P.C. Clippings file, Box 1, DPC Collection, HADP.

14. "Catholic School Finance Plan OKd," *Pittsburgh Post-Gazette*, 18 June 1967; "Up Teachers' Pay, Catholics Asked," *Pittsburgh Press*, 18 June 1967, D.P. Council P.C. Clippings file, Box 1, DPC Collection, HADP.

15. "Diocesan Pastoral Council Summary of Agenda Items and Motions Passed June 1967 thru March 1969," DPC Agendas-Resolutions, etc., file, Box 1, Pastoral Planning Collection, HADP.

16. Education Committee Report, Board of Directors Minutes (hereinafter to be cited as Board Minutes), 6 June 1967, Box 1, Catholic Interracial Council of Pittsburgh Collection (hereinafter to be cited as CIC Collection), Archives of Industrial Society (hereinafter to be cited AIS), University of Pittsburgh Libraries.

17. Diocesan Pastoral Council Meeting Transcripts (hereinafter to be cited as DPC Transcripts), 17 June 1967, Box 2, DPC Collection, HADP.

18. Ibid., 41–42.

19. I have followed the capitalization of the term *Negro* as it appears in the sources throughout this book. If it appears in these pages with a small *n*, that is because it appeared that way in the source from which I quote.

20. DPC Transcripts, 17 June 1967, 41–43, Box 2, DPC Collection, HADP.

21. Ibid., 43–47.

22. DPC Transcripts, 18 June 1967, 65–70, Box 2, DPC Collection, HADP. The survey reported responses as a percentage of Masses, rather than parishes. This meant that 1,275 of the 1,338 Masses that respondents reported took place each week were in English.

23. Ibid., 74–76.

24. Ibid., 84.

25. Ibid., 90.

26. Ibid.

27. Ibid., 91.

28. Ibid., 93–94.

29. Ibid., 154–55.

30. Ibid., 155, 156, 160.

31. Ibid., 160–66.

32. Ibid., 166.

33. See John McGreevy's thorough history of Catholics and racial issues in northern cities to gain a fuller understanding of growing tensions within the church over race. *Parish Boundaries: The Catholic Encounter with Race in the Twentieth-Century Urban North* (Chicago: University of Chicago Press, 1996). Note especially chapters 8 and 9.

34. DPC Transcripts, 18 June 1967, 171, Box 2, DPC Collection, HADP.

35. Ibid., 172–73.

36. Ibid., 173–74.

37. Ibid., 174–75.

38. Board Minutes, 10 August 1965, Box 1, FF #3, CIC Collection, AIS.

39. Board Minutes, 30 June 1966, 28 September 1966, Box 1, FF #3, CIC Collection, AIS.

40. DPC Transcripts, 18 June 1967, 188–90, Box 2, DPC Collection, HADP.

41. Ibid., 188–90.

42. Ibid., 177–78.

43. Ibid., 179–80.

44. Ibid., 181.

45. Ibid., 182–83.

46. Ibid., 184–186, 192.

47. "ACLU Blasts Oliver High and Police," *Pittsburgh Press,* 1 April 1968.

48. "Shafer Plans Use of Guard in Any Riot," *Pittsburgh Press,* 1 April 1968, 10.

49. "Prayer Calms School Tension," *Pittsburgh Press,* 5 April 1968, 1; "Black, White Alike Mourn King Here," *Pittsburgh Press,* 5 April 1968, 1. Duquesne University canceled classes on the day of King's funeral. "Stunned Negroes Now Looking 'For a Joshua,'" *Pittsburgh Press,* 5 April 1968, 2.

50. "Black, White Mourn King," *Pittsburgh Press,* 5 April 1968, 2; "End Racism Now, Negro Tells Whites," *Pittsburgh Press,* 5 April 1968, 4; "The King Assassination," editorial, *Pittsburgh Press,* 5 April 1968, 18.

51. "Uneasy Calm in Hill After Looting Spree," *Pittsburgh Press,* 6 April 1968, 1, 2.

52. "College March Honors Dr. King," *Pittsburgh Press,* 6 April 1968, 4. The *Press* itself made no such acknowledgment. Instead it reserved all its ire for "hooligan opportunists, seizing an excuse to plunder and destroy, to maim and kill." "A National Emergency," *Pittsburgh Press,* 7 April 1968, sec. 2, p. 2.

53. "State Stores, City Bars Shut to Nip Violence," *Pittsburgh Press,* 7 April 1968, 1.

54. "Hill Rampage Saddens Responsible Adults," and " 'Be Cool' Youths Urged," *Pittsburgh Press,* 7 April 1968, 2.

55. "City Blames Young Hoodlums for Rioting, Fire-Bombings," *Pittsburgh Press,* 8 April 1968, 1.

56. "A Dream, a Song Spur March Here," *Pittsburgh Press,* 8 April 1968, 1.

57. Ibid.

58. Ibid.

59. Ibid.

60. "Patrols Keep Lid on Hill," *Pittsburgh Press*, 8 April 1968, 1, 6; "6000 in City Battle Hit-Run Vandals," *Pittsburgh Press*, 9 April 1968, 1; "City Lifts Curfew but Keeps Guard Up," *Pittsburgh Press*, 10 April 1968, 1; "City Patrols Ending, Bars Open," *Pittsburgh Press*, 11 April 1968, 1.

61. Mayor's Special Task Force on Civil Disturbances, "Civil Disorder, 1968," in *Pittsburgh*, ed. Roy Lubove (New York: New Viewpoints, 1976), 238.

62. DPC Transcripts, 15 June 1968, 3–24, Box 2, DPC Collection, HADP.

63. Ibid., 27–28, 42, 43.

64. Ibid., 36.

65. Ibid., 32; The Catholic Interracial Council had, for example, widely publicized two priests' membership in the Pittsburgh Athletic Association (an elite social organization) after they refused to resign despite the PAA's determination to continue barring African Americans from membership. Board Minutes, Box 1, FF #3, CIC Collection, AIS.

66. DPC Transcripts, 15 June 1968, Box 2, DPC Collection, HADP.

67. Ibid., 56–67.

68. Ibid., 67–68.

69. Ibid., 72–75.

70. Ibid., 5–8. The page numbers reflect the start of the evening session, which the transcriber used to start numbering again. The vote also reflects the loss of a number of delegates from the afternoon session.

71. Ibid., 10–21.

72. Ibid., 25–30.

73. Ibid.

CHAPTER SEVEN.   **Devotional Catholicism in the Wake of Vatican II**

1. "Survey on Devotional Life in the Diocese of Pittsburgh," December 1968, Diocesan Pastoral Council Collection (hereinafter to be cited DPC Collection), HADP. The Diocesan Archives house only the report of the survey, and I have been unable to locate the data upon which the summary was based.

2. Pittsburgh Pastoral Council, Committee on Devotional Life, "Tabulation of Results from the Questionnaire Regarding Retreats," Box 2, DPC Collection, HADP.

3. Raymond Michael Utz, "Some Notes on Devotional Life," and "Report of the Devotional Life Sub-Committee to Diocesan Pastoral Council," December 1968, Box 2, DPC Collection, HADP.

4. "Devotional Life Sub-Committee Report"; J. Richard Gomory, "Devotional Life"; and Utz, "Some Notes on Our Devotional Life," 5, DPC Collection, HADP.

5. "Devotional Life Sub-Committee Report"; Utz, "Some Notes on Our Devotional Life," 6.

6. *LC Newsletter*, February 1967, 1.

7. *LC Newsletter*, June 1967, 1. The liturgical reform movement in America originated in the abbeys, where monks developed patterns of congregational participation.

8. *LC Newsletter,* June 1967, October 1967.

9. *LC Newsletter,* February–March 1968, 1.

10. *LC Newsletter,* December 1968, 1.

11. Diocesan Council of Catholic Women convention yearbook, *To See God's Image in Every Man, 1968,* DCCW Collection, Box 2, HADP.

12. *The Echo,* October 1968, August 1969, October–November 1969.

13. This can be seen in the quality of the newsletter, which became mimeographed typewritten pages and started to come out bimonthly rather than monthly in 1969.

14. "DCCW Annual Business Meeting," *The Echo,* July 1965, DCCW Collection, Box 1, HADP.

15. "The Retreat Movement Today," *The Echo,* January 1967.

16. "Promotion . . . How? When? Why?" *The Echo,* April 1967. The *Echo* suggested that women did not attend because members did not advertise well enough.

17. *The Echo,* February 1963.

18. "Day for International Understanding," *The Echo,* May 1963.

19. They sent an incubator for premature babies, for example, and supported the maternity hospital with annual financial donations.

20. "Sister Housebreaker," *The Echo,* February 1963.

21. "Annual Business Meeting," *The Echo,* July 1964.

22. *The Echo,* July 1963, October 1963, June 1964.

23. "Theme Presented," *The Echo,* October 1964.

24. "Racial Issues Highlighted" and "Fear in Mississippi," *The Echo,* October 1964.

25. "War Without Arms," *The Echo,* October 1965.

26. "Below the Equator and Around the World—A Job for Women," *The Echo,* October 1965.

27. Ibid.

28. "For Women Interested in Their Role in the Church," *The Echo,* February 1966.

29. "Women Today and Tomorrow," *The Echo,* March 1966.

30. "Women in Community Service," *The Echo,* May 1966, October 1966.

31. "Christian Woman 1966," *The Echo,* November 1966. Despite the very provocative speech Kilch made, the Pittsburgh DCCW's traditional bent can be seen in the terms it continued to use throughout its publications. *The Echo* refered to Mrs. Kilch only by her husband's name (Marcus), and for the next several years continued to use the term *man* to denote men and women (and, on occasion, when the reference clearly included only women).

32. "Christian Woman 1966," *The Echo,* November 1966.

33. Ibid.

34. "Responsibility for Family Enrichment," *The Echo,* October 1967.

35. HNS *Newsletter,* March 1963, 3.

36. "Presidential Plaudits," HNS *Newsletter,* May 1966; "Presidential Plaudits," HNS *Newsletter,* June 1966.

37. "Official," HNS *Newsletter,* September 1960.

38. Guy Pirro, "Shades of Progress," HNS *Newsletter,* May 1967.

CHAPTER EIGHT.   **The Promise of a Democratic Church**

1. Bishop Wright's synod was the diocese's eighteenth—the diocese had held one roughly every seven and a third years. The twentieth century saw eleven synods by 1954 (one for every five years), which meant that the fourteen-year gap between the seventeenth and eighteenth synods stood out dramatically. Ecclesiastical laws regulated the administration of sacraments, regulations regarding priestly responsibilities, and similar matters. They also set rates for clerical stipends (how much a priest could charge for a wedding or funeral), and so had to be updated regularly enough to prevent a decline in clerical income. The 1971 synod abolished stipends, however. The bishop was constrained to keep his diocesan legislation consistent with Vatican canon law, and lawyers helped him do this. Bishop Wright also noted his obligation to "call" the vicars-general, diocesan consultors, the seminary rector, rural deans, a deputy from each collegiate church, pastors of the synod host city, one superior from each clerical and religious institute in the diocese, and at least one pastor from each deanery. Bishop John Wright, "Formal Call of the Synod," *Eighteenth Synod of the Diocese of Pittsburgh* (Pittsburgh: Diocese of Pittsburgh, 1971), v.

2. Interview with Msnr. John C. McCarren, September 1988, Pittsburgh, Pennsylvania. McCarren served as the president of the Pittsburgh Synod, and was a member of the original delegation that Wright sent to Detroit. The synod's executive director, Fr. Leo Vanyo, wrote to and received information from a number of other dioceses that had already held synods, including the following: London, Ontario; Kansas City–St. Joseph; Atlanta; Fall River, Massachusetts; Manchester, New Hampshire; Baltimore; and Evansville, Indiana. Current Correspondence, files, 1968–70, "Proceedings of the Eighteenth Diocesan Synod, 1971" Collection (hereinafter to be cited as Synod Collection), Box 6, Historical Archives of the Diocese of Pittsburgh (hereinafter to be cited as HADP).

3. "Clergy Council Minutes of Meetings," 22 May 1968 (hereinafter to be cited CC Minutes), Box 7, Synod Collection, HADP.

4. CC Minutes, 19 August 1968.

5. Ibid. The clergy seemed to object as much to the efforts they would have to expend to get the laity involved as they did to the consequences of lay involvement themselves. They received assurances that they would not be responsible for generating lay participation, and so softened in their opposition.

6. More than half of the GCBS members were officers of one kind or another. They served as president, executive director, executive secretary for the synod, secretary of the GCBS, treasurer, general chairman for the synod, and vice president.

7. The eleven commissions were: laity; worship; community affairs; religious orders; property, finance and planning; clergy; education; communication; ecumenism; spiritual life; and pastoral government.

8. The special groups posed a problem for the GCBS. Bishop Wright had expressed anxiety about "pressure" groups that would use the synod to subvert the Church in its exposed and open time. Father Vanyo initially understood Wright's concern to be about Pittsburgh radicals, and he tried to limit their access (though he was uncertain how to identify them). When Wright discovered this, he told Vanyo that

only national groups such as the Liturgical Conference worried him, and Vanyo relaxed his guard. Only a handful of groups applied for special status, and all received the designation. They were: the Association of Pittsburgh Priests (a liberal priest organization formed to counter the more conservative Clergy Council), Thomas More Society, Office of Lay Activities, Diocesan Human Relations Commission, Lay Group of Saint Elizabeth, Pleasant Hills, Mount Mercy College (later Carlow College), Catholic Interracial Council, and the Religious Education Forum. General Coordinating Board for the Synod Meeting Minutes (hereinafter to be cited GCBS Minutes), 13 November 1968, Box 7, Synod Collection, HADP; Bishop Wright to Father Vanyo, 24 October 1968, GCBS Minutes.

9. GCBS Minutes, 6 July 1968; Father Vanyo to the Reverend Bryce, 31 July 1968, GCBS Minutes, July 1968, file, Box 7, Synod Collection, HADP.

10. Father Vanyo to the Reverend Bryce, 31 July 1968, GCBS Minutes, July 1968, file.

11. The Rev. Leo V. Vanyo to "Reverend and Dear Father," 7 August 1968, Material Concerning the Organization of the Synod—Charts, Reports, Etc. file, Box 7, Synod Collection, HADP; Father Vanyo to the Reverend Bryce, 31 July 1968, GCBS Minutes, July 1968, file.

12. GCBS Minutes, 13 August 1969.

13. Ibid.; Patrick K. McCarren to the Reverand Vanyo, 15 May 1969, Current Correspondence, May 1969, file, Box 6, Synod Collection, HADP; GCBS Minutes, 13 August 1969; GCBS Minutes, July 1969. It is difficult to discern whether the parishes did not participate because parishioners did not want to participate or because they did not know about it, or because of clerical skepticism. Seventy-seven percent participation is very good, but it still leaves almost a quarter of the parishes outside the reform efforts. However, the 77 percent participation figure comes from a GCBS report that 267 of the diocese's 346 parishes formed synod committees. The Catholic Directory suggests that the diocese had only 321 parishes in 1970, and this number remained about the same for a thirty-year span. If 267 parishes did participate, and the diocese really had only 321 parishes, then fully 83 percent of the parishes participated.

14. The GCBS did not react favorably to this and generally refused to comply.

15. The Rev. Leo Vanyo to chairmen [of Parish Synodal Committees], 26 November 1969, Current Correspondence, November 1969 file, Box 6, Synod Collection, HADP. Terry Brock, the *Pittsburgh Catholic* editor, sent the proposals to Father Vanyo, who forwarded them to their parish of origin. They then entered the regular parish-level process. Father Vanyo received at least ten requests from female groups, particularly Guilds and Christian Mothers, in the summer of 1969. Current Correspondence, August 1969, file, Box 6, Synod Collection, HADP. The Rev. Leo Vanyo to Joseph Williams, n.d., Current Correspondence, March 1971, file, Box 1, Synod Collection, HADP.

16. Additional proposals from special groups, such as the women religious of the diocese, have also survived. They are located in the Historical Archives of the Diocese of Pittsburgh.

17. Many proposals addressed more than one theme or subject, so the column totals more than 100.

18. The total number of proposals that address devotions is smaller than the sum of individual devotional practices because proposals sometimes addressed more than one devotion.

19. The proposal text reads as follows: "It is proposed: that the Diocese involved [*sic*] in encouraging censorship in entertainment, records and literature."

20. I have used the following criteria for placing proposals into the liberal, conservative or neutral category:

Liberal: Proposals that seek change in the current practices that will shift power to the laity, increase lay roles, democratize procedures, or loosen strictures generally. [Examples: (1) "It is proposed that qualified laymen be permitted to render sermons at Mass"; (2) "Head covering in church should be at discretion of individual"; (3) "Women should be equal to men in liturgical functions."]

Conservative: Proposals that seek to prevent change, to restore practices changed during the past decade, or to tighten strictures on behavior. [Examples: (1) "That activities be established in high schools and colleges analogous to those of parish societies such as St. Vincent de Paul Society, Holy Name, etc., to counteract SDS-type activities and encourage later participation in parish functions"; (2) "That the present calendar of Holy Days of Obligation be maintained"; (3) "We propose that Priests should be prohibited from wearing extreme haircuts."]

Neutral: Proposals with unclear intent, that seek change that has no clear liberal or conservative impact. [Examples: (1) "That Youth organizations be organized wherever possible on an interparish basis"; (2) "The diocese formulate and regulate the football league for grades 4, 5 and 6. A gentleman feels the league is not regulated enough, although men are well meaning. Should have more supervision"; (3) "It is proposed: that, all parishes be assessed to support our diocesan High Schools, except when supporting a parish high school."]

21. As further illustration of the greater embrace of liberalism among parishes than among deanery-level committees, the parish committee endorsed this proposal 6–0, while the deanery committee voted the opposite, 0–15.

22. Deans served as administrators of geographic subdivisions of the diocese. They had little actual power (the bishop reserved that to himself), but served as intermediaries in the chain of command.

23. These numbers include proposals that dealt with power relations between bishops and priests as well as those between priests and laity.

24. The other five proposals sought to ensure that certain groups, such as women, religious, or youths, achieved representation on elected bodies. Since they constrained democracy by seeking to limit parishioners from exercising unlimited voting choices, I chose not to include them among those proposals that sought to expand democratic practices. But they did not directly challenge or seek to undermine democratic bodies either.

25. GCBS Minutes, 13 November 1970.

26. "Eighteenth Synod of the Diocese of Pittsburgh," iii–xi.

27. Kiernon Stenson to Father Vanyo and members of General Coordinating Board of the Synod, 5 March 1971, Current Correspondence, March 1971, file, Box 1, Synod Collection, HADP.

28. GCBS Minutes, 13 November 1970.

29. The Rev. Leo V. Vanyo to John [no last name], 8 January 1971, Current Correspondence, January 1971, file, Box 1, Synod Collection, HADP. Vanyo thought this could be remedied with greater efforts in selecting members. "I think it is imperative that time be devoted to the selection of people. Particularly in respect to the laity, there are abundant skills available, but one has to take the time to determine who these people are."

30. Ted D. Taubeneck to Fr. Leo Vanyo, 14 January 1971, Current Correspondence, January 1971, file.

31. The Very Rev. John J. Cassella to the Rev. Leo Vanyo, 9 February 1971, Current Correspondence, February 1971, file, Box 1, Synod Collection, HADP; the Rev. Leo Vanyo to the Very Reverend Cassella, 12 February 1971, Box 1, Synod Collection, HADP.

32. Father Vanyo in turn sent his drafts to a seminary professor for editorial comments before sending them to the publisher. In some cases, such as the new legislation on Christian burial, Vanyo wrote the legislation from scratch himself. The Reverend Vanyo to the Rev. Msgr. Leonard J. Fick, 11 February 1971, Current Correspondence, February 1971, file, Box 1, Synod Collection, HADP. Interview with Msgr. Leo Vanyo, 8 September 1988, Pittsburgh, Pennsylvania.

33. Sr. Elizabeth McMillan to the Rev. Leo Vanyo, 28 March 1971, Current Correspondence, March 1971, file, Box 1, Synod Collection, HADP. McMillan continued that she was worried that "while we are holding to outmoded ways of exercising authority, that very authority is losing credibility."

34. The Very Rev. Jerome McKenna to the Rev. Msgr. John C. McCarren, 31 March 1971, Current Correspondence, March 1971, file, Box 1, Synod Collection, HADP.

35. C. Holmes Wolfe, Jr., to the Reverand Vanyo, 6 April 1971, Current Correspondence, April 1971, file, Box 1, Synod Collection, HADP.

36. Interview with Msgr. Leo V. Vanyo, 8 September 1988, Pittsburgh, Pennsylvania.

37. The diocese essentially adopted Vanyo's preferred method when it conducted its next synod in 1999–2000, save for that it provided little real opportunity for significant lay reaction to the committee-generated documents.

CHAPTER NINE.   The Post-Conciliar Parishes

1. Bishop John Wright, "Prefatory Note," Diocesan Pastoral Council meeting transcripts (hereinafter to be cited as DPC transcripts), 23 March 1968, Box 2, Diocesan Pastoral Council Collection (hereinafter to be cited as DPC Collection), HADP.

2. DPC transcript, 23 March 1968, 119–23.

3. DPC transcript, 23 March 1968, 125, DPC Collection, HADP.

4. Saint Thomas More Parish Council Minutes, 24 June 1973, 23 September 1973 (hereinafter to be cited STM Council Minutes), Minutes—General Meetings 1974 file, Saint Thomas More Rectory, Bethel Park, Pennsylvania.

5. STM bulletin, 4 February 1973. To underscore further the temporary and emergency nature of the eucharistic minister, the appointments were for short periods, usually one year, and eucharistic ministers were to be recommissioned to continue in the role. In actual practice, eucharistic ministers continued serving beyond their formal appointment period without further commissioning.

6. Saint Thomas More Executive Committee Meeting Minutes of the Parish Council, 10 September 1973 (hereinafter to be cited as STM Executive Committee Minutes), Saint Thomas More Rectory, Bethel Park, Pennsylvania.

7. STM Executive Committee Minutes, 14 October 1973; STM Council Minutes, 6 January 1973.

8. STM Council Minutes, 24 March 1974; STM Executive Committee Minutes, 15 May 1975; STM bulletin, 14 January 1979; STM Executive Committee Minutes, 8 July 1975. Two of the eight female eucharistic ministers were women religious, so that lay women constituted 25 percent of all in this year.

9. STM Council Minutes, 26 February 1976; STM Executive Committee Minutes, 19 May 1977; STM bulletin, 24 April 1977. The council wanted to train lectors and commentators better (in ways to use the microphone, for example), to generate more singing by "soft-pedaling" the organ and toning down the folk group, to get better participation in all spoken and sung responses, to locate the Communion stations better for more efficient traffic flow during Communion, and to get the Worship Committee more involved in preparing the liturgy.

10. STM bulletin, 28 September 1975.

11. STM Executive Committee Minutes, 13 September 1977, 18 April 1978, 9 May 1978.

12. STM Executive Committee Minutes, 11 November 1973, 9 December 1973.

13. STM Council Minutes, 21 May 1974, 23 June 1974.

14. STM Council Minutes, 26 March 1975.

15. STM Council Minutes, 23 November 1975.

16. STM Council Minutes, 28 September 1975.

17. STM Council Minutes, 27 September 1981.

18. STM Executive Committee Minutes, 18 April 1978.

19. STM Council Minutes, 21 May 1978.

20. Ibid.

21. STM Executive Committee Minutes, 22 September 1978.

22. STM Council Minutes, 24 September 1978.

23. Ibid.

24. Ibid.

25. "Celebrating a Century and a Half," Saint Philomena Parish 150th Anniversary Book, np.

26. Saint Philomena Parish bulletin, 4 October 1981 (hereinafter to be cited as SP bulletin), Saint Philomena Rectory, Pittsburgh, Pennsylvania.

27. The bulletin made absolutely no mention of the demotion at all at the time.

28. Francis X. Murphy, "Priest Who Had Saint Canonized Dies at 91," *National Catholic Reporter,* 10 November 1989, 5. Neumann was the first male saint from America, and in many ways epitomized American Church values. He gained his fame and following primarily as an efficient bishop in Philadelphia, where he increased the number of parochial schools from only two to over two hundred. Litz got his financial backing from the Philadelphia estate of Mother Katherine Drexel, a wealthy Catholic who funded work among American Indians and African Americans, and had her own well-organized (and ultimately successful) movement for sainthood during the same period.

29. Interview with Jane and Dan Quinn, November 15, 1989, Pittsburgh, Pennsylvania.

30. John Rodella, "St. Phil's History," unpublished reflections, 1989. This parishioner's history of the troubled period in Saint Philomena's recent history came into my possession during the parish's recent efforts to write their history for their 150th anniversary.

31. John Soboslay, Jim Gillespie, and Tim Kelly, "St. Philomena Parish: The First One Hundred and Fifty Years, 1839–1989." The authors of this history constituted a committee established to write the parish history for the parish's 150th anniversary. The pastor, Eric Hoog, took the committee's history and eliminated all references to divisive issues in the last thirty years before printing the final history book. Hoog edited out any reference to the division over the liturgical transformation. The division between old and new parishioners persisted until the diocese suppressed the parish in 1994. The division touched even the History Committee, when long-time parishioners expressed concern that the committee consisted of "new" parishioners only. The committee chair had been a parish member for twenty-one years.

32. Rodella, "St. Phil's History." Father Gargani regularly referred to the hallway as the "Corridor of the Saints" in the bulletin, which reflected the nonpejorative meaning that the phrase also had.

33. Soboslay, Gillespie, and Kelly, "St. Philomena Parish," 28; Rodella, "St. Phil's History."

34. Interview with Regina Kelly, October 1989, Pittsburgh, Pennsylvania; interview with Dan and Jane Quinn, November 1989, Pittsburgh, Pennsylvania.

35. Saint Philomena Annual Reports, 1981–83, Redemptorist Archives of the Baltimore Province (RABP). A cursory analysis of attendance figures indicates that the total number of people attending Mass in the parish did not decline until after Gargani's departure.

36. Interview with Dan and Jane Quinn, November 1989, Pittsburgh, Pennsylvania; interview with Regina Kelly, October 1989, Pittsburgh, Pennsylvania; Rodella, "St. Phil's History"; Soboslay, Gillespie, and Kelly, "St. Philomena Parish," 29. The parish bulletins, which Father Gargani wrote, made only brief and innocuous mention of the entire episode, noting in May that two Redemptorists would come to discuss the "needs of our parish community," and then announcing a going-away party for Father O'Rourke in July. SP bulletins, 31 May 1981, 5 July 1981.

37. SP bulletin, 31 January 1982; interview with Dan and Jane Quinn, November 1989, Pittsburgh, Pennsylvania.

38. *Catholic Directory,* 1951, 1965 (New York: P. J. Kennedy and Sons, 1951, 1965). The *Catholic Directory* figures never match those from the parish in any year for which other parish reports survive for any of the parishes in this study. But they always fall near the parish figures, and they always follow the same trends as parish figures over a period of more than a couple of years. The *Directory* reported 591 students at IHM school in 1951, and only 278 in 1969. The enrollment would eventually fall to 117 students by 1980, according to the *Directory,* where it would stay for the next four years. This represents a drop of 80 percent from 1951 and 58 percent from 1969.

39. Board Minutes, 4 February 1969, 2 June 1969, Catholic Interracial Council Collection, Box 1, File Folder 3, Archives of Industrial Society, University of Pittsburgh. The Catholic Interracial Council charged that the parish had already compromised its ethnic integrity by admitting Italian students, but these likely were Catholics.

40. During martial law in Poland in 1982 the parishioners sent crates of food, clothing, and medical supplies for relief. The bulletins regularly updated parishioners on Polish needs, and the parishioners responded generously. Ironically, the same bulletins that requested food aid for Poland reported the distribution times for surplus government cheese and butter. The parishioners themselves sought food relief.

41. Mike Brourman, "Ethnic Poor of City Organize to End Neglect," *Pittsburgh Post-Gazette,* 15 September 1969, in *Pittsburgh,* ed. Roy Lubove (New York: New Viewpoints, 1976), 247–48.

42. A baptistry is a stand that contains a bowl. Parents or godparents hold a baby over the bowl as the priest pours holy water over the baby's head during the baptism ceremony. The tabernacle houses the consecrated hosts not consumed at Mass. It contains Christ's body, therefore.

43. Interview with Jules and Cathy Coelos, 27 February 1990, Bethel Park, Pennsylvania.

44. Interview with Mary Cummins, 13 February 1990, Bethel Park, Pennsylvania.

45. Interview with Jules and Cathy Coelos, 27 February 1990, Bethel Park, Pennsylvania.

46. One parishioner and Father Jendzura insisted, at the conclusion of their weekly benediction, standing along the altar rail, in front of the Sacred Heart and Saint Francis of Assisi statues, that they do things the same way at Immaculate Heart of Mary as they do in every other parish in the diocese. They have completely modernized. Interview with the author, May 1989, Pittsburgh, Pennsylvania.

47. Literature in a special rack at the back of Saint Philomena Church told parishioners, "We should not merely be present as simple spectators. . . . We should put our stamp on the entire act of worship and make it ours." Anthony M. Buiono, *The Mass, Keys to Better Participation* (Ligouri, Mo.: Ligouri Publications, 1987), 4.

Index

Timothy Kelly

is associate professor of history at Saint Vincent College.

www.ingramcontent.com/pod-product-compliance
Lightning Source LLC
Chambersburg PA
CBHW060325100426
42812CB00003B/880